WITHDRAWN

PORTRAITS OF
RUSSIAN PERSONALITIES
BETWEEN REFORM
AND
REVOLUTION

BY THE SAME AUTHOR

Russian Literature from Pushkin to the Present Day (Methuen)
Pioneers of Russian Social Thought (Oxford University Press)

PORTRAITS OF
RUSSIAN PERSONALITIES
BETWEEN REFORM
AND
REVOLUTION

RICHARD HARE

CARL A. RUDISILL LIBRARY
LENOIR RHYNE COLLEGE

LONDON
OXFORD UNIVERSITY PRESS
NEW YORK   TORONTO
1959

Oxford University Press, Amen House, London E.C.4

GLASGOW NEW YORK TORONTO MELBOURNE WELLINGTON
BOMBAY CALCUTTA MADRAS KARACHI KUALA LUMPUR
CAPE TOWN IBADAN NAIROBI ACCRA

© Oxford University Press, 1959

309.47

H22p

First edition 1959
Reprinted 1960

46,811
april, 1964

Printed in Great Britain by
Halstan & Co. Ltd., Amersham, Bucks.

PREFACE

In my last book, *Pioneers of Russian Social Thought*, I drew attention to the neglected work of various original Russian personalities, born in the late eighteenth or early nineteenth centuries, who did a lot to guide and shape the changing outlook of their compatriots, although they were neither professional revolutionaries nor contented adherents of the Russian state and *status quo*. Starting with the politically progressive but morally conservative ex-Guards officer, P. Chaadayev, and ending with the heretical but prophetic K. Leontiev, in turn surgeon, diplomat, journalist, and monk, I tried to convey a picture of the wide mental awakening and vigorous endeavour, which stirred educated Russians who matured during the peaceful quarter of a century following the Napoleonic wars.

To illustrate how independent, robust, and honest minds then reacted to the stream of thought and science flowing from the West, I confined my choice to a few individuals, who never sank to the level of passive camp-followers in the wake of organized political or religious movements. They also showed a surprising measure of agreement in the statement of their aims, although they disputed the most fruitful method of fulfilling them. Intelligent Slavophils and Westernizers alike struggled to the best of their ability against a sterile overgrown bureaucracy, and both favoured a discriminating Europeanization of their country, although Europe's ambiguity puzzled them.

The present volume is in part a chronological sequence, bringing my survey down to the October Revolution (1917). But the two volumes also overlap in time, because in both I have taken single human life-spans as the most natural and intelligible units of comparison, and sought in them illuminating focal points for diverse particles of a whole period in flux. Moreover, the individuals represented here belong to a wider background, for they include outstanding revolutionaries, thoughtful statesmen, internationally famous authors, influential religious thinkers, and obscure but remarkable civil servants or journalists, in so far as they were all drawn willy-nilly into the same maelstrom of contemporary strife.

To write once more, even from a special angle, about men whose major works have since become world-classics, the author should be able to contribute something new in judgement or revealing fact. Even if these literary giants could mean as much to us as they did to a previous generation, our interest in them has grown calmer and much more selective. But numerous newly-discovered or suppressed writings of theirs have been published for the first time in the Soviet Union, and some penetrating freshly-documented studies of them have been written there. The volumes of *Literaturnoe Naslyedstvo*, published annually by the Soviet Academy of Sciences, are a mine of information. B. Eikhenbaum's original book about the young Tolstoy, the study of Dostoyevsky texts and unpublished notebooks by A. Dolinin, P. Sakulin and N. Belchikov, V. Polonsky's materials for a biography of Bakunin, the essays and research of N. Brodsky and M. Kleman on Turgenev—to mention but a few—have not yet been assimilated in foreign estimates of nineteenth-century Russia, nor have they been translated into English, though they are known to specialists.

In taking fresh evidence into account, I have not echoed the interpretations of Soviet critics, and I have left suggestive analogies with present-day experience to the reader's own imagination. Sometimes I have tried to redress the balance, when eminent nineteenth-century people have served as figureheads for religious or political campaigns, or when they have been buried in a grave of stony silence or standardized contempt.

Because the state muzzled frank comment on political or social grievances, public frustration forced Russian imaginative writers to play a part as social teachers, moralists, and occasional prophets. Whether reluctantly, or gladly, no major Russian writer managed to escape this moral pressure, which was not an unmixed blessing, though it made them speak for many inarticulate victims of the Russian state machine. To this factor, and not to their intrinsic talent, both Tolstoy and Dostoyevsky owed their first popular appeal and influence. Turgenev dutifully wove a social theme into the subtler psychological pattern of his novels. Tolstoy derived much more misery than satisfaction from being exalted as a *public figure*, but he implored people to be guided by his writings, rather than by his life. He said that the valuable part of himself, having gone into his work, provided the sole reliable key to his real personality. Since he was world-wide in his impact, many-sided and constantly misunderstood, Tolstoy has received two chapters in this book.

One urgent question haunted the minds of nineteenth-century Russians, whether they were writers, civil servants, revolutionaries, or statesmen. Must their country continue to follow the beaten track hitherto laid down by the West? Was it right that her self-identification with the unfolding of the West should be so whole-hearted and far-reaching, or ought it to grow more cautious and selective? Did 'progress' demand an inevitable Russian movement towards Western constitutional monarchy, republicanism or parliamentary government, comfort and ease of living, plus a Western mode of industrializing her vast untapped material resources?

The almost romantic reverence, which Russians felt for European culture in the late eighteenth century, undoubtedly gave place to mounting scepticism and revulsion, as the nine-teenth century proceeded. They began to debate whether the technical and industrial preponderance achieved by Western countries had not been bought at the price of selling their souls to a commercial devil. But what, if any, alternative course lay open to Eastern countries, rapidly moving in the same direction?

The sweeping administrative, judicial, and educational reforms of the early eighteen-sixties gave the first answer to these burning questions. Asserting a stronger faith in new institutions than in new people, they further *westernized* the Russian Empire along the main functional lines of modern Europe. But historians of every political colour observed that these reforms, radical as they were, failed to achieve their stated purpose. Hence the note of tragic disillusion which sounds through the writings of the eighteen-sixties, and the partial return to autocratic rule in the following decades. The firm bureaucracy of Alexander III also encouraged a rising national *mystique*, leaning on a hazy Byzantine inheritance and orthodoxy, though deriving more modern intellectual support from the racial and national self-worship fostered by Schelling and Hegel.

But the revival of unlimited political power was hardly matched by a corresponding growth of administrative intelligence. The new autocratic government failed to master or control the economic upheaval which the Liberal period had ushered in. After a hopeful beginning it stood condemned, under Nicholas II, not through cruel wickedness or hopeless poverty (for it was humaner than its predecessors and the country was more prosperous), but by fumbling inefficiency and pigheaded ignorance. It became clear that, for better or for worse, the Russian Empire after 1881, guided by Pobyedonostsev, Vitte, and Stolypin, though committed to an industrial society, still followed a harder path, diverging from that of Western Europe and America.

1958

R. H.

CONTENTS

LIST OF ILLUSTRATIONS

ACKNOWLEDGEMENTS

I wish to thank various authors, scholars and librarians, who have helped me with their advice and knowledge. I am indebted to Mr. P. A. Stolypin for having read in manuscript the section devoted to his father, Peter Stolypin. I am grateful to Miss Dorothy Galton for reading the proofs. The following journals have kindly given permission to include in this book material first published in articles which I wrote for them: *The Times Literary Supplement*, *The Russian Review* (U.S.A.), *The Slavonic and East European Review*.

R. H.

A. V. NIKITENKO

from a portrait by Kramskoy

CHAPTER I

A PLEBEIAN CONSERVATIVE OF THE REFORM PERIOD, A. V. NIKITENKO

EVEN staunch advocates of historical determinism concede that its individual victims are free to choose between fixed alternatives. More optimistic historians find wider loopholes of escape from mass-predestination. The observant have discerned that historical events can provoke, in the people who live through them, a chain of unpredictable emotional reactions. These can lead to unexpected alterations in the next phase of action. This type of unevolutionary or inconsecutive pattern of change is noticeable in periods of large-scale public disappointment, such as occurred in Russia immediately after the first flush of mid-nineteenth-century reforms.

After the grim fiasco of the Crimean War and the sudden death of Nicholas I, violent discontent in every class not only forced the new Emperor and his advisers to work out realistic plans for reshaping Russian public affairs from top to bottom, but impelled them to put their conclusions immediately to the test of practice. A warm refreshing breeze of personal endeavour and sensible co-operation seemed to be dispelling the chilly mists which had obscured Nicholas's strenuous promotion of 'orthodoxy, autocracy, and national character'. The abolition of serfdom, the separation of the law-courts from arbitrary administrative rulings, trial by jury, local government bodies, all initiated in the late eighteen-fifties or early eighteen-sixties, were amazingly liberal and far-reaching measures (measured by previous Russian standards). And these sweeping institutional changes coincided with a vigorous upsurge in Russian literature, music, and intellectual life, which continued sporadically for many years, long after the naïve social optimism of the reform period had petered out.

But in every sphere, without exception, practical results fell short of the soaring expectations which they had aroused. Laws and institutions, which had grown slowly and organically in Europe, were transplanted rapidly to an ill-prepared and alien Russian background, in the expectation of prompt and gratifying improvement. The wave of disappointment spread as a natural outcome of exaggerated faith in the magical transforming power of new Western models. It bred in the minds of those who experienced it a blend of bewildered suspicion, anger, and self-reproach, followed by the indignant desire to find a scapegoat.

Why should methods which had demonstrably improved material and scientific standards (if not the inward culture) of many Western countries, fail to secure similar solid benefits for semi-Asiatic Russia? In one important respect the blame for failure was not shifted to the *foreign devil*, but honestly attributed (without loss of national self-respect) to the germanized Russian government and its monstrous bureaucratic system. Almost every thoughtful Russian, regardless of his class and social status, from Slavophil landowners like Koshelyov, down to radical journalists, like Chernyshevsky, agreed that the emancipation laws were half-hearted, muddled, and too rigidly administered, and that the payment of redemption dues for their land imposed a heavy economic burden on the shoulders of resentful peasants.

The puritanical Chernyshevsky and his *narodnik* (populist) followers led that discontented section of the educated class which fell back reluctantly on a peasant rebellion, because they could no longer believe either in the 'good intentions' of the government or in its ability to carry out sound undertakings, forced upon it by threats from below. More penetrating contemporary observers of the Russian scene received less attention than they deserved. Tolstoy, writing in 1862, referred ironically to 'the great unforgettable epoch of the rebirth of the Russian people . . . when from all sides appeared *problems* (as in the year 1856 every concourse of circumstances was called, of which no one could make head or tail)—the problem of the Cadet Schools, of the Universities, the censorship, oral tribunals, the banks, the police, the emancipation, and plenty of others. Everybody tried to solve them; they wrote, read, argued, drew up endless projects; everybody fought to amend, destroy, and alter *everything*, and all Russians, like one man, rose to an indescribable state of enthusiasm. That was a condition which occurred twice in the nineteenth century, in the year 1812, when we thrashed Napoleon I, and again in the year 1856, when Napoleon III thrashed us!'

Between Tolstoy's ironical detachment and Chernyshevsky's austere self-dedication to revolt, there came a less vocal body of middle-class opinion, which exerted a stabilizing influence on the course of events, although it received almost no publicity. A. V. Nikitenko (1804–77), a liberated serf, worthily represented that hardy, honest, and energetic section of the rising middle class, which formed the principal moral backbone of post-reform Russia, and retained chastening instincts from the severe patriarchal environment which had moulded it in childhood. His unspectacular, but industrious and observant life reflects the sounder personal strivings of the period. Born a serf, belonging to the fabulously wealthy Sheremet'yev family, he rose to be a professor of St. Petersburg University, an academician, historian of Russian literature, and a respected member of numerous educational and censorship committees. His father had been trained as a singer for the renowned choir of the art-loving Count Nicholas Sheremet'yev. This nobleman, suffocated by a surfeit of splendid luxury, knowing no other law than his own latest momentary caprice, became as much a burden to himself as he had been to many of his dependants. From childhood Nikitenko witnessed indignantly how his gifted father was frustrated and held in thrall by estate-agents and petty tyrants. The unfortunate man's outbursts of irritable rage were sometimes vented on his son.

During his parents' wanderings Nikitenko spent some years in a fertile Ukrainian village, where the prosperous and kindly state-serfs impressed him deeply. Illiterate, without schools, almost self-contained in their economic needs, they had remained unsoiled by the ominous nineteenth-century industrial civilization which was conquering Russian towns. Thieves, swindlers, and drunkards, he noted with amazement, were almost unknown to them. Even before his father's death in 1819, his mother was obliged to bear the burden of keeping the poverty-stricken family alive. He did all he could to help her, and soon started to earn a little money by acting as tutor to the sons of neighbouring merchants. At the age of sixteen, he bought a pistol, powder, and two bullets. From that moment he felt that he had freed himself from needless fear, and noted that he could die at any moment he decided for himself.

A lucky chance opened the way to his future career. Alexander I, in his support of the Holy Alliance, knew as well as Metternich how to employ religion as an instrument of political control. But he also encouraged the spread of voluntary Bible Societies throughout Russia. In 1822 the town of Ostrogozhsk founded a local branch of that organization and nominated Nikitenko to be its secretary. The post was unpaid, but carried a more than compensating social prestige. The Bible Societies formed a skilful semi-official means of promoting literacy together with a sense of civic duty. Nikitenko's keen efficiency, his lucid speeches, soon brought him to the attention of the societies' president, Prince Alexander Golitsyn, then in charge of a department called the 'Ministry of Spiritual Affairs and Public Instruction'. This powerful, benevolent, and persevering man took the young secretary under his protection in St. Petersburg, and spared himself no pains in persuading Count Sheremet'yev to liberate him. The latter at length agreed to free Nikitenko, though only after long obstruction and with an extremely bad grace.

Soberly rejoicing in his hard-won personal freedom, Nikitenko worked assiduously to justify it. He completed his academic education and quickly rose to high positions in the censorship department and St. Petersburg University. Shortly afterwards he began to keep a diary, unique in its outspoken comment on the whole course of Russian public life, seen from the angle of a man who combined the variegated and disparate functions of a censor, university professor, government official, and journalist.

The morbid suspicions of the censorship department, and vindictive personal persecution of independent thought, conducted (both openly and secretly) by many government officials, struck him as insuperable impediments to Russian culture. They made sure that people, just starting to learn, were uprooted from 'the only soil in which their spiritual powers might have grown'. He expressed faith in Pushkin's educative stimulus, but deplored his debauchery. 'His conduct was unworthy of a man who spoke the language of the gods.' The censorship law of 1837 upset him so profoundly that he tendered his resignation to his chief, Prince Korsakov. The new law obliged every newspaper article to be passed by two separate censors, supervised by a third controlling official who spied on both of them.

In books or articles on ancient history any suggestion that republicans flourished in Greece or Rome had to be cut out. Only fear of malicious reprisals against him, if he resigned, persuaded Nikitenko to remain reluctantly in the service. He aptly summed up the situation thus: 'Then they wanted to teach philosophy, provided that it conformed to a programme prepared by the Ministry of Public Instruction. Teachers of logic had simultaneously to convince their pupils that the laws of reason did not exist, and history teachers had to prove that Greece and Rome were never republics, but absolute monarchies in the Turkish or Mongol style.'

He noted the silent servility which was creeping over Russian minds, and threatened to extinguish the few remaining sparks of personal integrity or self-respect. He saw an ugly consequence taking shape, a cultivated hypocrisy, which became second nature to all officials. They learned how to appear to be what they were not, how to put lies into every welcoming smile, and into all those words which they used in order to *conceal* their thoughts.

Nikitenko, like the vast majority of his compatriots, greeted the accession of Alexander II. He admired the new Emperor and was charmed by his sympathetic personality. After one interview with him, he wrote: 'It is hard to describe how gentle, devoted, and noble he is. I thought how much good he might do, if only he were surrounded by people worthier of him.' At the same time Nikitenko voiced grave misgivings about the current obsession of the Government with radical legislation and reforms. He feared that the measures taken were at once too hasty and too

B

superficial, and likely to collapse for want of firmly prepared
foundations. He distrusted the fashionable democratic mysticism
of the time, and anticipated that his enemies would therefore
revile him as a 'reactionary'. He felt that they could never understand him as he understood himself. 'I sprang from the ranks of
the common people. I am plebeian from top to toe. But I know
that there can exist on earth no universal happiness, culture, or
benevolence. The masses will always lack those qualities which
alone can render power wise, just, and enlightened. They will
either abuse power or they will hand it back to one man, and
hence re-introduce a despot. We have already experienced personal despotism, but God preserve us from the despotism of the
crowd—of a half-savage brutal democracy! That does not mean I
favour aristocracy; the paths to power should be open to every
person.' [1]

Nikitenko came to the conclusion that the various committees
on which he served rarely promoted any useful business. They
all talked too much, either about unrealizable projects or about
trifling regulations. 'We are *diseased* with committees', he pronounced; 'I should like to abandon them all, since they are useless
both for their stated purpose and for me personally.' He saw too
clearly how many high-ranking officials were nonentities or self-
important busybodies, how much greed and vanity underlay the
actions of even the most responsible public men.

But neither could he form a more favourable opinion of the
political opposition. During the feverish press campaigns at the
time of the emancipation he tried in vain to act as intermediary
between the angry radical journals and the government. He
blamed Chernyshevsky and Dobrolyubov for seeking personal
popularity at any price instead of developing enough restraint
and *savoir-faire* to help the government in dealing with a national
crisis. Later he denounced the *narodnik*, Pyotr Lavrov, as another
baleful progressive, obsessed by that craving for popularity
which leads to softening of the brain. Forward movement was
not enough for them; they must have gymnastic leaps and
dramatic poses, followed by loud applause from an excited crowd.

[1] *Moya povest' o samom sebe*, I, p. 590, St. Petersburg, 1905.

In 1861 he firmly opposed the demands made by students to acquire the right to veto some university regulations, and he noted that in consequence ultra-liberal members of the staff became his personal enemies. They started to intrigue against him, and imputed to him words which he had never spoken. What they called the *heroism* of the students seemed to Nikitenko chiefly impudence or youthful irresponsibility. Meanwhile nobody could penetrate to the heart of the matter, because nobody was encouraged to examine it or to say frankly what he thought. Nikitenko observed that the younger generation identified mental growth with a blind hostility to every directing power and every moral sanction. A mild dose of imported learning had been enough to make them dizzy. Hence arose that wanton libertinage of mind, which, instead of being condemned, 'we are now prepared to praise, as a genuinely native characteristic of our broad and generous Russian nature!'

While he conceded to radical journalists due credit for their long-term intentions, he deplored their political ineptitude, their mule-like obstinacy, and their evil influence on youth. Fancying themselves as creators of a new 'public opinion', they had accustomed students to revere the rebel bandits Sten'ka Razin and Pugachov as far-sighted statesmen and legendary heroes. 'Our journals have become extremely insolent, omniscient, and intolerant. . . . Young minds are not necessarily the best minds, and it is easy enough to turn their energy towards destruction. . . . Nothing is easier than to infect young minds with theories— however absurd and unrealizable they may be—with superficial knowledge and contempt for whatever is strict, serious, and fundamental.'[1] Journalists were also persuading the public to despise every level-headed article and balanced judgement, unless it was simultaneously strident and radical in tone. 'It is as if in teaching our people how to drink, we try to hinder them from acquiring a taste for anything which does not make them *drunk* immediately!'[2]

It disgusted Nikitenko that educated Russians, who ought to have known that the French Revolution had signally failed to

[1] ibid., II, p. 118.   [2] ibid., loc. cit.

revive or morally improve the French, should now start to
agitate and argue the need for a similar revolution in Russia. 'A
horrible future they are preparing for Russia, these ultra-pro-
gressives.' They had no patience to reflect and settle down to
work, because they yearned for drastic dramatic scenes, in which
they could play the leading parts. Often they yielded their unstable judgement to some irritable impulse of the crowd. And he
noted the absurd flattery paid to crowd psychology: 'When
people in the mass have no idea whatsoever where to go, but feel
that they must go somewhere quickly, that urge is called the
spirit of the age.'

In 1862 Nikitenko was appointed a member of the Imperial
Commission for reviewing the press laws. Despite the battle
which he fought against clumsy and overbearing censorship, he
believed that freedom from censorship provided no solution,
since even partially emancipated newspapers and journals could
betray their trust and debauch impressionable minds. In casting
about for means to overcome these hitherto bad results, he discussed with the poet Tyutchev and the Minister of the Interior,
Count Bludov, a quixotic-sounding scheme for forming a select
committee, capable of guiding writers and journalists 'with
patriarchal care and love'. But in June and July of the same year
the journals *Contemporary* and *Russian Word* were closed down
by administrative order for eight months, and all schools were
put under strict state supervision. The terrible fires which ravaged
several districts of St. Petersburg had alarmed the government
into grim retaliation. Their origin was never clearly traced, but
suspicion fell on political incendiaries in the service of the
clandestine revolutionary group *Young Russia*. The repressive
measures, thus provoked, put an end to rosy hopes about a
kindlier and more stimulating censorship. That department fell
into even more invidious subservience than before, through being
controlled by the Ministry of Public Instruction, but supervised
by the Ministry of Internal Affairs, in other words by the secret
police.

Nikitenko's position as editor of the official journal *Northern
Post* had become intolerable. He complained that any convict had

a better life than he had. Being held responsible for every printed word, every comma inserted or omitted, not only was he racked by anxiety until each number had appeared, but after publication he had to face reprimands both from the reading public and from the government. While the former expected to be mentally stimulated or instructed, the latter, accustomed to obedient, cautious civil servants, had no idea how to use independent men of letters; the government simply aimed at publishing and advertising the maximum number of official decrees and circulars. In May 1862 Nikitenko resigned his editorial post. He had done his utmost to combine in this journal the more constructive 'official' line with suggestions from the educated public—who were its only readers—but such a fusion had proved to be a hopeless task.

He began to doubt that serious and honest minds, whatever they achieved in individual work, could cure the spreading cancer of social demoralization. Materialist teaching, he said, had won a devastating victory by making its converts more discontented and mentally lazy than they had been before. Neither had its highly rational claims managed to curb the crudest superstitions. He observed that in St. Petersburg spiritualist séances had become the rage—a reaction against the extinction of religious belief. 'Thus by one kind of madness they try to drive out another kind.'

Western reaction to the Polish revolt of 1863 turned his mind from home affairs to what he deemed to be the brazenly impudent interference of European outsiders in a Russian family quarrel. 'The whole of Europe has now begun to scold us,' he complained. Europeans, bursting with righteous indignation, accused barbarous Russians of committing atrocities in Poland, and called every Pole a hero, but they said or knew nothing about the barbarous behaviour of Poles themselves. He pointed to a few examples of it, including an unfortunate Russian who had just been brought to the capital. Polish rebels had captured this man and cut off his nose, ears, and tongue. Other Russians had been flayed or buried alive by Poles. Yet Nikitenko admitted that Russians had still done nothing *collectively* to earn the respect of Poles, who had every reason to fear and oppose their rule.

The shot fired at Alexander II in 1866 by the student Karakozov shocked Nikitenko deeply. He believed that this attempt, although it failed, produced a terrible result. For it caused the Emperor's faith in the Russian people, for whom he had worked so hard, to change into resentment. Although Alexander II remarked philosophically to those who congratulated him on his escape, 'Evidently Russia still needs me', his conduct of affairs from then onwards became more vindictive. While Nikitenko never wavered in his belief that the liberation of the serfs had been a great step forward, he blamed the government severely for leaving the ignorant and doubtful masses without firm leadership from 'benevolent and enlightened people'.

Thus the Emperor had to pay the penalty for his own sins of omission. Stronger measures were imperative before it became too late, for the sole alternative to social chaos lay in creating a revived respect for law, for its compulsory force, and in the *fear* which alone makes law effective. Intensified and haunting fear must therefore dominate everybody. The Emperor must fear revolution, the grandees withdrawal of favour, the official must live in terror of his superiors, the rich man of thieves, the poor man of the rich, the criminal of the law courts, etc. Kindly humane motives had no binding force, except for a few individuals with hypersensitive consciences.

Whereas in the West people still believed in concrete satisfactions, even if these amounted only to making money, working, or enjoying comforts brought by science, Russians no longer seriously believed in anything. They had indulged in such an orgy of misapplied ideas, so grossly abused the little freedom they had won, that in the end they found themselves no better off than under the old despotic power. 'The liberals rage against the absolutism of the government', Nikitenko wrote in 1869, 'and they are right to be angry. But why do they limit their hatred to one chosen kind of despotism, and not extend it to that of their own obstinate opinions?' [1]

At this time Nikitenko regarded Prussia as his country's natural and irreconcilable enemy, 'if only because we saved her twice'. He implied that Russia had saved Germany from conquest

[1] *Moya povest' o samom sebe*, II, p. 384.

by Napoleon, and that nothing can more infuriate national pride than to receive gratuitous favours from another nation. During the Franco-Prussian War he bitterly lamented the ruin of France, while admitting that her own lack of moral backbone was to blame. 'One feels terrified for France; she has socialists, communists, constitutionalists, legitimists, Orleanists—but no Frenchmen.' Yet he refrained from adopting the specious Hegelian argument of a predestined struggle between vigorous young nations and degenerate old ones. The German nation-state, moulded by Prussia, had amply proved her military strength, and it was *new* enough. But Nikitenko identified it with a relapse into savagery. 'It is not the Germans and the French who are fighting each other; it is the past and the future. The ghost of the feudal medieval past has risen from the grave and threatens Europe.' [1] Under the shadow of 'benevolent' Prussian bayonets the world would no doubt quieten down, and all the problems agitating European countries might be calmly decided by the Prussian General Staff. That would be the price of peace, but was it not too much to pay?

Meanwhile the French consoled themselves for their humiliating defeat by making witty sallies about the insolence of German officers. Nikitenko, like many Russians, accepted Bismarck as an instrument sent by fate to punish the French nation for 'their frivolous conceit and for the social disorders which they had provoked throughout the world by their revolutionary propaganda'. That retribution might be well-deserved, he noted ruefully, but the Prussian role of executioner remained a horrible one.

Nikitenko's mounting hatred of a triumphant military Germany provoked an outburst of his own latent national pride—a deep-seated and recurrent mode of reaction in Russo-German contacts. He started to rail against the Germans as slaves of work, mechanical beavers, and compared them unfavourably with good-natured Russians who were none the less 'capable of doing more work in one day than other people in a month'. He accused them of being self-centred to the marrow of their bones,

[1] ibid., II, p. 417.

the reverse of open-hearted Russians. 'A German will never be generous enough to forget an injury. But a Russian, after fighting an enemy, will turn into his brother, give him food and drink, and forget that his face was bloody from the enemy's blows.' Judging by contemporary Germans, he continued, unquestionably the most scientific people in the world, intensive scientific upbringing did not improve the quality of human beings. The crushing weight of learned mediocrity killed imaginative talent and blunted more creative minds.

To do Nikitenko justice, the compensating Russian virtues, which his germanophobia brought home to him, were purely personal qualities, in no way civic, national, or government-inspired. His view about the possible inculcation of the latter remained negative as before. 'We have neither genuine patriotism nor civic loyalty. Those can only emerge from the common people, but our people are a *herd*, without the slightest sense of duty or legality. We have plenty of words and institutions borrowed from Europe, but here those words are merely hollow sounds. Our society is like a huge reservoir filled with boiling acid. Whatever new ingredient you throw into it dissolves at once. Suicide is spreading like an epidemic.'

He feared that one negative strain in Russians might wreck flattering hypotheses about the Russian nation's future supremacy —namely, their lack of consistency, stability, and precision. In order to keep going, they needed to be bound hand and foot. 'And that is why they feel so sure about the need for stern government. It saves them from themselves. It is the only thing they can take seriously.' [1] Any society based on such shaky personal morality would gravitate between enslavement to the free gratification of its vices, the resultant drift to chaos, and the next stage of total self-surrender to yet another despot.

Towards the end of his life, Nikitenko began to take a passionate interest in the *Eastern Question*, and thereby found in England a new spiritual enemy of Russia. Like many of his compatriots, he soothed his disappointment in domestic affairs by dwelling on

[1] *Moya povest' o samom sebe*, II, p. 500.

constructive foreign openings for Russia, notably on her moral mission as a champion of the Balkan Slavs against their Turkish overlords. But England blocked this opening by her support of the declining Ottoman Empire. 'For one reason alone', he wrote in 1877, 'Russia has become indispensable to Europe's welfare; she is now the strongest bulwark against English barbarism, which has taken upon itself the protection of Asiatic Moslems from the civilization of Europe.' At this point the humanely educated and democratic ex-serf finally joined forces with the governmental pan-slavs and nationalist merchants of the late eighteen-seventies, in singling out the British Empire as their country's most deadly enemy and commercial rival, both in South-eastern Europe and Central Asia.

He persuaded himself that in this conflict, Russia, despite her acknowledged faults, embodied the spiritual heritage of European Christianity, while England stood for an unholy alliance with the heathen powers of darkness, for the sake of nothing beyond her own material enrichment. 'In India', he wrote in 1876, 'there are over fifty million Moslems. . . . From this it follows that the English queen is not a Christian sovereign, but a Moslem one.' And since Disraeli had obtained for her the title 'Empress of India', that title obliged her to protect her Indian subjects. England's policy, he deduced, was to turn Turkey into yet another of the Moslem vassal states, whom England forced to buy her manu-factured goods, and simultaneously to threaten Russia in the Bosphorus. 'Russia is now the last irreconcilable and eternal enemy of England, who can never sleep securely in her island, so long as Russia remains powerful.' [1]

But though these dramatic foreign clashes served to distract and stimulate Nikitenko's mind, they did not blind him to the scene at home. Surveyed from the repressive eighteen-seventies, the hopefully turbulent period of reforms since 1856 provoked this sober summing-up. 'In the early years of the present reign, I was enchanted by fine and noble beginnings which promised a better order for Russia, without being forced into violent up-heavals or painful sacrifice. Competent people then felt ashamed

[1] ibid., II, p. 559.

not to co-operate with the government in carrying out its good intentions. And I was then considered to be among the competent . . . but after a time, bitterly disillusioned, I became convinced that in our country good things are fated only to begin, but not to go ahead, or reach a satisfactory goal.' Whoever sincerely loved human ideals and strove for their realization in his country, could not escape experiencing 'profound disgust for the people and society of our time'.[1]

It hardly makes sense to number Nikitenko among the disappointed Russian liberals—because he never had one good word to say about them. He thought they were unprincipled opportunists, unstable but dogmatic. 'Who are our liberals?' he asked. 'Half-educated, without thorough knowledge of any subject, having squeezed out of books a few drops of democracy, socialism, communism, or some other -ism, they throw themselves in a drunken frenzy against whatever does not conform to their opinions, and think that they can lead society like a flock of sheep.'

Meanwhile the majority, through force of inertia or habit, submitted or cringed to whoever held the reins of power. In 1873 he remarked that although the petulant political satire in Turgenev's novel *Smoke* had irritated him at first, he now believed it to be justified. Any collective improvement in Russia could only be the fruit of a much more practical and thorough education over a long period of time. To make that feasible, the government must encourage the maximum initiative in science and the arts, and scrupulously confine its own tightening severity to a narrow administrative sphere.

He therefore cursed the renewed emphasis laid on Greek and Latin in the state educational system, and denounced the authorities' *idiotic* idea that the prolonged study of Greek and Roman literary classics would promote obedient citizens and a respectably conservative mental aristocracy. The same type of education had flourished in France without impeding the eruption of a revolutionary volcano. And society now had to suffer needlessly, because applied science had fallen out of favour. Cholera and

[1] *Moya povest' o samom sebe*, II, p. 481.

smallpox raged throughout Russia, new industrial enterprises kept on going bankrupt, while men who might have learned to be efficient engineers, doctors, or financiers, were forced to waste years of their youth in struggling with the syntax and declensions of useless dead languages.

In 1872, conversing with Ivan Aksakov about censorship, he pronounced it to have become again every bit as savage as it had been in the days of Nicholas I. 'Our mental and moral forces are paralysed, we are going straight back to the days before the Crimean War.' He approved of drastic restrictive action to raise public morality and respect for the administration. But clumsy and stupid escapades, like the suppression of the mild journal *Beseda* (Discussion) and the burning of harmless books, caused the government to forfeit what little respect remained for it, and to make it ridiculous as well as hated. Meanwhile the best-intentioned censors, frightened of their exaggerated responsibilities, trembling for their skins at any deviation from official platitudes, tended to play for safety, and thereby spread discouragement among the vital people who had most to give. That department surpassed itself in 1872 when it objected to a social comedy written by the eminent (and even notoriously conservative) novelist Pisemsky, who, when he ventured to inquire in what manner his writing might find favour, received the unanswerable reply: *'Better not to write at all.'*

At the end of his life Nikitenko stood equally apart from the pompous official orthodoxy, then gaining the upper hand, and from more popular types of Russian 'progressive', who surrendered their unsteady minds to each new wave of intellectual fashion which emerged from Europe. He seems to have been endowed with less worldly cunning and vanity than the latter, but with more honesty, culture, and reasoning power, even though he resembled them in finding some dramatic *bête noire* (preferably a foreign one) an indispensable mental stimulant.

Nevertheless, his pet aversions were no more rigid than his political ideas. His diary shows the astonishing degree to which his beliefs were transformed, not by succumbing to the pressure of other people's obstinate opinions, but by his own revised, independent understanding of events. It also reveals a mental and emotional evolution, far more characteristic of his *milieu* and period than is recognized by many foreigners, who have exaggerated the destructive revolutionary strain in Russian nineteenth-century history.

M. BAKUNIN

from a portrait by an unknown artist

CHAPTER II

AN ARISTOCRATIC ANARCHIST, MICHAEL BAKUNIN

I. ROOTS OF THE RUSSIAN ANARCHIST

ALTHOUGH recurrent revolutionary plots, and attacks against state authority, became a familiar undertone of nineteenth-century Russia, it was not until 1905 that they acquired at home either widespread respectability or conspicuous success. On the contrary, stolid Russian patriots throughout that period tried to persuade themselves that their revolutionaries were abnormal hybrids, aliens to their native land, luckless victims of a virus, imported from degenerate Western Europe.

Ivan Aksakov voiced this attitude when he deplored 'that vindictive spirit of denial and destruction whose *emergence from the West* has captured our defenceless youth'. He denied that the savage phenomena of underground conspiracy, incendiarism, and political murder had any living roots in Russian soil.[1] If this attribution were wholly true, we Europeans should admit a direct paternal responsibility for the various Russian revolutions, and feel a stronger sense of guilt or pride, according to the way we regard the outcome.

Personal responsibility for historical events cannot be pinned down so easily. Although the French Revolution in its early stages, plus striking precepts picked up from French and German writers, helped to form the characters of Russian nihilists and anarchists, the finished product proved to be more startling and explosive than any sum total of ingredients imported from abroad. It made Aksakov's diagnosis look partial and far-fetched. Not only was a *Russian type* of revolutionary emerging in the semi-European environment of nineteenth-century Russia, but this type grew partly from native roots, and had inherited traits from centuries of mixed experience, distinct from the history

[1] Aksakov, *Sochineniya*, vol 2, pp. 695–700, Moscow, 1886.

of the West. The Russian type was complex, *sui generis*, acting mainly on its native land, but also, through its European links, injecting a new and unpredictable current into the modern European revolutionary movement.

The Russian rebel *mood* sprang from a cumulative sense of instability and frustration which afflicted the hierarchy of society from top to bottom. After long smouldering, with sporadic outbursts in the ancient peasant communes, it acquired a conscious shape among the mentally rebellious aristocrats of the nineteenth century. Catherine II had wiped out the most formidable mass revolt (1773–5) led by the Old-Believer Cossack Pugachov. A motley ill-assorted crowd of peasants, roving Cossacks, vagrant labourers, Volga boatmen, resentful Bashkirs, state serfs torn from their village homes and assigned to the Ural mines and metal works, joined to make common cause in that rebellion. But the Russian participants were not coherently united by the nature of their grievances, and the Bashkirs merely continued the time-honoured colonial revolt of Asiatic nomads against the eastward expansion of the Russian Empire.

Nicholas I, a generation later, suppressed with equal ferocity the military *coup d'état* organized by the Decembrist officers (1825). By their lucid plan of action, and humane outlook, the Decembrists evoked among cultured Russians a sympathy as deep as the horror and alarm which the brigand Pugachov and his marauding army had roused in their sterner fathers. Yet both revolts had broken against the same immutable stone wall. Only the bitter protests which inspired them were far from smothered. Failing to find an outlet or release in normal life, they were driven inward with an aggravated force. Sullen serfs continued to murder their masters and supervisors. During twenty years (1835–54) 230 landowners and bailiffs met violent death. And perplexed Russian statesmen continued to rack their brains for some solution not yet tried.

Meanwhile the efforts of the aristocracy, deflected from a broader sphere of action, were afflicted by a brooding speculation. The poet-historian Karamzin voiced this mood when the grim French Revolution ruined the lively hopes of those who had worshipped brilliant eighteenth-century France. 'Where is the fruit of all that science and wisdom? Century of civilization, I no longer recognize you,' he lamented; 'plunged now in blood and flames, surrounded by murder and destruction, I can see you no more. Hearts, numbed by these horrible events, grow used to crime, and start to lose their sensibility' (*Correspondance*, 1795).

But French *enlightenment* had provided Russians in almost equal measure with mental ammunition for the hard-headed and lofty stimulus for the soft-hearted. Herzen said of his father's *hard-headed* generation: 'Voltairian philosophy armed them with all the instruments of dialectic and irony, capable of justifying their own state of slavery in relation to the sovereign and their own state of sovereignty in relation to their serfs.' Only a few emotional serf-owners like Radishchev, moved by Helvetius and Rousseau, felt conscience-stricken about their peasants' poverty, cried out against callous government officials, and appealed for more honest judges and fewer arbitrary laws.

The French Revolution administered the first cold douche to Russian Francophils of every shade. No longer 'bliss was it in that dawn to be alive'. Many like Karamzin, felt bewildered and deceived, but Russians still loved France for all that she had promised and aspired to be. The flame of their enthusiasm might burn lower, but neither the evil Robespierre nor the war-lord, Napoleon, could extinguish their sympathy for French elegance and taste. After driving Napoleon's armies from their ravaged country, the sons of Russian Voltaireans bore little or no malice against France. And they watched with renewed hopefulness the parliamentary novelties which began to modify the restored French monarchy.

The liberal-minded autocrat Alexander I, before he became spellbound by religious charlatans, had given 'Congress Poland' its independent constitution, drawn up in 1815 by Polish patriots, together with a parliament, full internal self-government, independent finances, and an army. He granted these generous concessions despite the fact that 85,000 Poles had been seduced to fight against him in Napoleon's Grand Army. And he talked publicly about extending similar institutions throughout the

Russian Empire. But after 1820 the insidious infiltration of total Russian government control had twisted the Polish constitution out of shape, though leaving it nominally intact.

In its essence the Decembrist conspiracy strove to impose on a new sovereign that rational policy, which the last one, Alexander, had first firmly supported, and then surreptitiously betrayed. It was the culminating outburst of two generations of Russian Francophils, concentrating on a campaign of political action to *curb* state power. But the Decembrists had proved inept in handling political tools. Their failure marked a turning-point, the end of effective French enlightenment in Russia, and the beginning of the philosophic German chapter in Russian mental history.

II

Michael Bakunin (1814–76) stands out as the most ominous and powerful figure dominating the anarchist movement of the nineteenth century. The first Russian intellectual, fired by German learning to become a full-time professional revolutionary, he was also the first Russian to conceive social revolution in cosmic terms and on an international scale. He would admit no clash of aims between European national revolutionaries and Slavs within the Russian Empire ('the prison-house of nation-alities'). His enigmatic personality, self-contradictory, but perpetually dynamic, fascinated or horrified his educated con-temporaries, but it could never be ignored by them. And for the masses, who never met him (especially in the Latin countries), his name became a legend, sanctified by his years of lonely and poverty-stricken struggle against overwhelming odds, by his imprisonment, exile, and spectacular escape from Siberia.

The part played by Bakunin as an adventurer or martyr, and as an object of hero-worship (in an age which strove to believe in human heroes) is more important than his scientific con-tribution to political and social thought. His only first-class biographer, E. H. Carr,[1] aware of that preponderance, treated

[1] E. H. Carr, *Michael Bakunin*, London, 1937.

Bakunin's writings as mental episodes scattered along the course of his tempestuous career. Yet closer acquaintance with these intimate episodes may provide the best surviving clues to parts of the Bakunin mystery.

The more matter-of-fact intelligentsia of today, untouched by his live magnetism, to whom he looks like a cold extinct volcano, can less afford to ignore his written outbursts. Though prolix and shapeless, they reveal sparks of truth and astonishing discernment. A pattern can be found running through their characteristic incoherence, a sense of method in their madness, especially when his thought is closely linked with his erratic life. Often his own piercing vision pricks the bubble of his spurious reputation, and dispels the atmosphere of exhilarating make-believe, with which he endeavoured to surround himself.

A modern mind, approaching Bakunin as a pathological case, may well inquire: how could he be both such an influential figure and such a tremendous fraud? But is not a striking ability to deceive people imposed on ambitious aspirants to public leadership? Are not the most brazen political and religious charlatans often idolized by their contemporaries? To understand Bakunin's duplicity, he must be seen in perspective as a symptom and victim of the Empire organized by Nicholas I.

His father, Alexander Bakunin, after retiring from the Imperial diplomatic service, had devoted himself to the management of his 'nobleman's nest' at Promukhino, and to the education of his eleven children, of whom Michael was the eldest. Though Alexander Bakunin played no part, except as a counsellor of cautious moderation, in the secret societies which generated the Decembrist revolt, he maintained close personal contact with the Decembrist brothers Muravyov, who were blood relations of his wife. Michael was eleven years old in 1825, old enough to remember vividly the event. But he showed no signs of sympathy with the rebels until much later. Neither did he record having been shocked in childhood, as Herzen did, by witnessing the cruelties of serfdom.

Growing up in the gentle melancholy stillness of his country home, surrounded by admiring and submissive sisters, he felt

c

in harmony with his surroundings, and his boyish imagination started to soar freely through the intoxicating realm of German speculative thought. 'We led a lonely life', he wrote, 'among the clouds of philosophic theory.'

Yet even at this early stage Bakunin scorned ideas which did not lead to practical fulfilment. He fancied himself in the role of a man of action, whose aim, after having steeled his character, was to *dominate* people by the force of his ideas. He also discovered that thought is futile unless will-power guides it. 'The will', he wrote in 1833, to a friend of his mentor, Stankevich, 'is the principal essence of man, when it is illumined by the holy rays of thought and feeling.' While still a student at the military cadet school in St. Petersburg he managed to convince himself (with Hegel's help) that the cult of his 'interior being' was more than idle self-indulgence. Following the Hegelian dialectic, it would pass over to its opposite, the negation of the human ego, as 'the true sense of spiritual life'. 'That is why death in its most positive sense accompanies the sublime moments of our existence', he wrote to his sister Varvara. He implied that Hegel's philosophy had supplied him with the secret of spiritual rebirth.

Bakunin's first major trial of strength took place in 1835, when he came into sharp conflict with his family. In a letter from Moscow he explained to his father that he had renounced an official career, since he had resolved to study philosophy, and meanwhile to earn his living as a teacher of mathematics. That decision crowned a fatal sequence of events. After three years of study in the Artillery School, Bakunin had done badly in his final examinations. As a mild disciplinary punishment, the authorities sent him off to serve with a regiment on the Polish-Latvian border. Insufferable boredom and loneliness consumed him there.

It seems that he never tried, or found, the average officer's escape in a round of gambling, drink, or casual love affairs. He wrote (a trifle priggishly) about himself: 'I am quite incapable of finding any charm or satisfaction in the dirty bog of sensual enjoyments, unworthy of a human being.' But it is a fact that no worldly allurement could then distract Bakunin from his obsession with philosophy, though he showed no glimmerings of radical or revolutionary thought. Yet his resignation from the army (1835) and his refusal to take a job in the civil service, marked the first step towards his future as a permanently rebellious nomad. He was starting to burn his boats.

His father resolved to make one more effort to save Michael from himself, and in a letter, written more in sorrow than in anger, he summed up the situation: 'I have received your letter from Moscow, and see that your head is still suffering from the same fever, and that your heart is silent. . . . True philosophy consists not in visionary theories and empty word-spinning, but in carrying out everyday obligations to family and society. You neglect these obligations for the pursuit of chimeras, and chatter about some *internal life* which compensates you for the loss of everything else . . . But meanwhile you do not know how to escape from yourself. The dejection which weighs upon you is the inevitable result of injured self-respect, an idle life, and an uneasy conscience . . . One way is still open for you to prove that your heart is not quite dead . . . Efface the past by your obedience, and rather believe your blind father than your blind —call it what you will!' [1]

This pathetic letter left Bakunin quite unmoved—unless it strengthened his determination to cast off the tyranny of paternal counsel. But his sporadic attempts to earn a living soon subsided (as they always did henceforth). He chose the easier alternative of borrowing money from his generous friends. In 1840 he departed joyfully for Berlin, whose university in the eighteen-thirties had become the Mecca of continental intellectuals.

III

A year and a half of study in Berlin, absorbed in Hegel's categories, had a cathartic effect upon Bakunin's mind. It finally cured him of 'the prevailing philosophic disease' (as he described this craving) but it confirmed him in incurably Hegelian habits. He admitted in one of the sincerer passages of his *Confession*: 'On closer acquaintance with metaphysical writings, I became

[1] op. cit., p. 29.

convinced of the triviality of all metaphysics. I sought life in them, but found merely death and boredom; I sought deeds, but found absolute inaction.' He could no longer open a single philosophic book without experiencing a sense of nausea. Yet he remained contemptuously aloof from political and social problems. His restless active mind had led him to an impasse, facing a cold and horrible void.

Rescue came to him in 1841, through his meeting with Arnold Ruge, editor of the *German Yearbooks*, and chief animator of the Hegelian left-wing movement. Bakunin, feeling resentfully that he had been duped by Hegel, now announced his great discovery, that real philosophy ought to be a negation of philosophy, that cloudy and congested thought must totally dissolve, to take shape in large and exuberant deeds. Yet this discovery proved him to be still a prisoner of Hegelian dialectic. 'I understood at last', he said, 'that life, love, and action can be grasped only through plunging into life, love and action. I finally renounced transcendental science—for all theory is *grey*—and threw myself headlong into practical affairs.' For the first time Bakunin found that true religion lay in 'political action and the social struggle'.

But instead of changing Bakunin's mode of life, this act of faith provoked a fresh excursion into thought—in the shape of his famous article 'Reaction in Germany', published in the *German Yearbooks* (October 1842). By identifying his private *impasse* with the dire needs of European society, the *demon of destruction*, which lurked inside him, received a philosophic justification. 'Are you living people, do you believe in anything?' he asked dramatically. 'Do you know what you want, or can you actively desire it? . . . Has introspection, that epidemic of our time, left a single part of you intact? Are you not penetrated, broken, and maimed by it? . . . The disinherited class, which includes the majority of human beings, is everywhere taking on a menacing attitude. We say to the Positivists—open your spiritual eyes, and let the dead bury their dead. Convince yourselves at last that the spirit, eternally young, eternally reborn, can no longer be found by searching among ruins of the past. We warn advocates of compromise to open their hearts to truth, to free themselves from their poor blind wisdom, from theoretical arrogance and slavish fear which can only paralyse their souls. The air is sultry and heavy with storms. Everyone whose living organs are not numbed can see with trembling expectation the approach of a future which will utter the decisive word. Let us put our trust in the eternal spirit, which destroys and annihilates only because it is the inscrutable creative source of life!'

For a left-wing Hegelian, launching a new thesis on its cycle, that chain of catastrophic reasoning seemed gratifyingly normal. For never did Bakunin prove more enslaved to Hegel than when he formally renounced philosophy, and threw his hated books into the bonfire that was due to start the wider conflagration. His indelibly imprinted mind was groping towards a course of action dictated by Hegelian terms.

At least he had broken that wall of ice which separated his self-centred mental ferment from the whirlpool of mundane affairs. Yet step by step he had condemned himself to be a philosophic outcast. Had he decided earlier to become a man of action, his intellectual gifts and fiery energy, harnessed to some professional career, might have brought him far along the road to glory, as a Governor or Field-Marshal in the service of the Russian Empire. Now it was too late to retrace his fateful steps.

Exiled and penniless, without professional training, the would-be leader had no alternative. He must recruit his own private army and general staff from the crowd of international malcontents and riff-raff, among whom he had cast his lot. Those who preached revolutionary change, he said, could never succeed unless they also shone as active leaders, unless they were possessed by devils. But Bakunin knew that Pestels failed without Pugachovs. The former must enlist the brigand rank and file, and make their pent-up passions flow like molten lava from a volcano in eruption. Neither Pestel nor Pugachov had any use for kindly or objective intellectuals. Lenin was at one with Bakunin when he exclaimed that he would rather employ a professional safe-breaker in the revolution than the philosopher Plekhanov.

IV

Bakunin's departure from Berlin marked the starting-point of his long career as the mendicant monk of a non-existent revolutionary Church, and a reckless conspirator who aspired to lead an international rebel army. After some wandering in Switzerland, he settled in Paris, where he met Karl Marx, whom he immediately disliked, though he admired his erudition. In 1847 he moved on to Brussels, where he started to complain that Marx perverted the minds of honest working men. 'The Germans,' he wrote to Herwegh, 'Bornstedt, Marx, and Engels —especially Marx—are plotting their usual mischief here . . . He is carrying on the same futile activities as of old, corrupting the workmen by making them cerebral. The same crazy theories, the same discontented self-satisfaction. . . . Vanity, malice, squabbles, theoretical conceit and practical cowardice, endless theorizing about life, activity and simplicity, and in fact a total absence of life, action, or simplicity. They have made the single word *bourgeois* a term of abuse, which they repeat *ad nauseam*, though they themselves are ingrained bourgeois from head to foot . . . In such company you cannot breathe freely.' [1]

A worthy German ex-tailor, called Weitling, belonged to a small group of communist artisans who had formed an organiza-tion called *The League of the Just*. But Weitling became friendly with Bakunin, and persistently expressed his revolutionary feelings in a mystically Christian manner. This was anathema to Marx, who eventually hounded the unlucky man out of the Workers' Movement. He escaped further persecution by emigrating to America, one of the first proletarian refugees to flee so far from organized proletarian tyranny.

Repeatedly Bakunin won affection and sustained loyalty from simple artisans of diverse nationalities, who remained uneasy when confronted by the chilly Marx. But the hold which he secured over educated men, though equally due to his exuberant charm, proved more precarious. Their judgements throw a sharp light on his character, for they record a similar blend of quick attraction,

[1] op. cit., p. 146.

followed by disgust. The historian Granovsky said that he felt enthralled by Bakunin's brilliant mind, but found him *unheimlich* (horrifying) on closer acquaintance. Belinsky, who sat at his feet to learn the Hegelian lore, called him 'spiritual father and pastor', but added later: 'He is a wonderful person, an original lion-like character—one cannot deny that—but his pretensions make friendship with him impossible; *he loves ideas, not people.*' Finally, after an unhappy affair of the heart with one of Bakunin's sisters, he declared: 'I tell you frankly, briefly and clearly: *I loathe* Michael, less for himself than on account of his sisters, because he has distorted their divine natures.'

Turgenev's subtle and observant mind hit off Bakunin's duplicity when he compared him to a dromedary, a camel with two humps. He also admitted that in his *Rudin* he had reproduced traits of Bakunin, his brazen facility for sponging on his richer friends and for playing with the feelings of his mesmerized victims, but offset by a redeeming prophecy that 'his words have scattered good seeds in young hearts'.

Probably Herzen was the man who knew him best, through all his ups and downs. The nickname 'Big Liza', which Herzen's young family invented for Bakunin, paid tribute to that naïve enthusiasm which endeared him to children. Herzen liked this strain, but he saw deeper. He was struck by the tragedy of a tremendous talent gone to waste. 'At the bottom of this man's nature', he observed, 'lies the seed of a colossal activity, for which he could find no employment. A *Columbus without an America,* and even without a ship! He bears within himself the potentialities of an agitator, a tribune, an apostle, leader of a party, a heretic priest, a tireless fighter.'

On the whole, with the exception of Herzen, his Russian contemporaries exerted less influence on Bakunin than he did on them. But his fluid mind remained receptive and alert to every fresh impression. In Paris he met Marx's arch-enemy the French anarchist, Proudhon, and pronounced him to be 'one of the most remarkable Frenchmen of our time'. The two had much in common, and it is conceivable that Proudhon's pet idea of federal republics springing up from below, putting an end to war between sovereign states, inspired Bakunin with his project of a vast Slav federation to replace the Austrian and Russian Empires.

But Bakunin did more than restate Proudhon with a Russian accent, for the latter, despite his feud with Marx, distrusted Slavs and favoured Germans. During this period in Paris, Bakunin made personal contact with a number of Polish, Czech, and South Slav exiles, and the intensified pan-Slav colouring of his radical thought dates from then. To begin with, he thought more about forming a Slav federation outside Russia than of any universal Slav mission led by Russia. His nascent pan-Slavism had a vaguely racial but decidedly anti-national bias.

For every sovereign nation was doomed through selling its soul to his *bête noire*, the administrative state. Thus he could deplore Czech national separatism on the same grounds as he condemned the Russian Empire. He described himself as an admirer of the Russian people, but in no way a patriot of the Russian state. He repeated that the modern Russian state was an artificial German superstructure, and therefore the deadliest enemy of Slav aspirations both inside and outside it. At a banquet held for emigré Slavs in 1847 he delivered a stirring speech, offering to the Polish nation, 'in the name of the *real* Russian nation', an alliance against 'its *German* Emperor Nicholas'.

v

The Paris rebellion of 1848 gave Bakunin a heaven-sent opportunity, and the first taste of battle for which he had long been craving. From early morning until late at night he dashed from workmen's meetings to barricades, exhorting, organizing, elaborating plans. Throughout that month of 'spiritual intoxication' he hardly slept. 'Revolution is an instinct rather than a thought', he wrote to his friend Herwegh, and scolded 'the philosophers, literary men, and politicians who rely on their little made-up systems, and therefore lack that instinct'. But some of his own colleagues found Bakunin's volcanic instincts more of a liability than an asset. The newly-appointed republican chief of police is said to have made the classic remark about him: 'What a man! On the first day of a revolution he is a perfect treasure—on the second he ought to be shot.'

Moreover, the Paris revolution shed its glamour for Bakunin the moment it settled down into a routine. And he felt that he owed his first allegiance to spreading revolt among fellow Slavs. French associates were relieved to get rid of him on outwardly friendly terms, and Flocon, a member of the provisional Government, lent him sufficient money for his journey. Bakunin left for Frankfurt, Berlin and Posen. Thence he hastened on to Prague, in order to arrive in time for the opening of the Slav Congress, which met in June under the presidency of the Moravian, František Palacký.

This Congress, abortive as it was, had historical importance, and taught Bakunin useful lessons about disunity of purpose among the Slavs. It went further than a mere provincial airing of grievances among Slav subjects of the Austrian Empire. Though a Czech national temper dominated it, the presence of a vocal Polish delegate, Libelt, and of Bakunin as a Russian delegate, made it a vehicle for discussing prospects of Slav international solidarity. It provided a representative Slav counterblast to the nominally democratic (but in tone downright pan-German) deliberations of the Frankfurt Assembly, with which it synchronized.

Only one agreed document issued from the Congress, a *Manifesto to the Peoples of Europe*. Its avowed object was to draw the attention of other European peoples (ignorant of the facts) to the cruel fate of submerged Slav nationalities in Turkey, Prussia, and in the Austrian and Russian Empires. It demanded for the Slavs nothing more than 'the same state rights as are enjoyed by the Magyar and German nations'. And it forestalled alarm at the prospect of Slav solidarity by claiming that Slavs did not plan, like Germans and Magyars, to revenge themselves, or extend their supremacy over other races.

The President of the Congress, Palacký, was responsible for the published version of this innocuous document, but Bakunin was one of the delegates invited to assist in drafting it, though no trace of his radical attitude emerged. On the other hand, in documents which Bakunin submitted to the Congress, but which were not accepted by it, he voiced his conviction that freedom for the Slav peoples could never be won without the prior destruction of both the Austrian and Russian Empires. Palacký preferred to find a way of federating Slav peoples *within* the Austrian Empire, as the best check both to German preponderance and Russian ambitions. On two points only Bakunin appeared to be in harmony with Palacký, in mounting Germanophobia and in dread of the Russian Empire.

The letter, which Palacký wrote to the Frankfurt Assembly, accused it bluntly of seeking to establish a federated German state in place of the existing federation of princes, in order to guide the German nation towards political unity, and in this manner expand the German *Reich*. But a worse peril threatened the Austrian Empire. 'You know, gentlemen,' Palacký went on, 'what Power it is that holds the entire East of our continent. You know that this Power, grown to vast dimensions, expands, decade by decade, in far greater measure than is possible for countries of the West. . . . You know that every step which it takes along this path, threatens at an ever-accelerated pace to give birth to, and establish, a universal monarchy, an infinite and inexpressible evil, a misfortune without measure or bond, such as I, though heart and soul a Slav, would profoundly regret from the standpoint of humanity, even though that monarchy be proclaimed a Slavonic one.' [1]

Either of these passages might have been written by Bakunin. It was beginning to dawn on thinking people that the pursuit of national aspirations, whether German or Slav, did *not* coincide, as liberals supposed, with the spread of democratic institutions. But Palacký, Slav though he was, cherished none of that hatred against the Habsburgs which Bakunin expressed against the Holstein-Gothorp Romanov Empire. For he accepted the Austrian Empire, as by nature and history the bulwark of Europe against invasion from the East. He feared that the demands of Frankfurt Germans, if fulfilled, would reduce Vienna to the

[1] *Slavonic and East European Review*, vol 26, p. 405, 1947-8.

role of a provincial town, a metropolis without a *hinterland*, and hence without a *raison d'être*. 'I must reject emphatically', he wrote, 'the idea of a republic within the frontiers of the Austrian Empire. Think of it, divided into sundry republics, some considerable in size and others small—what a perfect basis for a universal Russian monarchy!' [1] But the Slovak Palacký's alternative solution, to unite the Slavs under an anti-German Austrian Empire, was suspect to Bakunin, the Great-Russian Slav.

In that same month of June the Congress dispersed, after an insurrection of artisans and students had broken out in Prague. Bakunin's *Appeal to the Slavs* and its preliminary drafts, summarized his radical reaction to these events. It stated that only the peasant and labouring class, and no more the middle class, could now support his revolutionary faith. It urged the destruction of the Austrian Empire. Meanwhile Slavs must expect no help from Russia. But he imagined that an Eastern European Slav federation outside Russia would provide the impetus for widespread revolutionary propaganda and action *inside* Russia.

To start with, Prussian Silesia, a large part of East Prussia, Czechs, Ruthenians, Poles, and Southern Slavs, must break off from Germany and Austria. A revolutionary Hungary would be *obliged* to enter this future Slav Union. The prompt totalitarian sequel which follows on this free anarchic foundation is striking. Bakunin describes it more like a super-state than a loose federation. His so-called Slav Council wields unlimited power. He pours scorn on parliamentary parties, and refutes those who doubt the advantages of the new dictatorship over the old autocracy. The difference he explains, is that monarchical power, in order to make itself indispensable, aims at keeping its subjects in a perpetual state of infancy, while dictatorship is ready to render its own existence superfluous by leading people towards maturity. This specious case for a *transitory* dictatorship, familiarized by Marx ('the withering away of the state'), is noteworthy when stated by Bakunin, because he later contradicted it so vigorously.

Bakunin played an active part in the Dresden insurrection of 1848. He could have escaped while it was petering out, but

[1] op. cit., p. 308.

chivalrously (or quixotically) refused to leave his comrades in the lurch. The Saxon police arrested him, and confined him in the prison of Königstein. Humanely treated, but cut off from the outside world, he sank into a state of apathy, treating with contempt the complicated legal proceedings preparatory to his trial. In January 1850 the competent Saxon court sentenced him to death, but in June they commuted this sentence to imprisonment for life. Meanwhile diplomatic negotiations, of which he remained ignorant, settled his transfer to the Austrian Government, who sent him to the fortress of Olmütz. There the guards kept him permanently in fetters and chained to the wall of his cell. His own printed words and well-known actions provided the strongest evidence against him, and therefore he invented no defence.

His published *Appeal to the Slavs* could fairly be interpreted as one long plea for wiping the Austrian Empire off the map of Europe. The *Political Confession* which he wrote in Olmütz is frank, though he shifts the emphasis on his conspiratorial activity from the Austrian to the Russian scene. 'We may argue about the case for revolution in various countries,' he wrote, 'but in Russia there can be no doubt about it. In that country, whose whole life is organized immorality, revolt must be a moral action.' [1]

After thirteen months in Saxon and eleven in Austrian prisons, Bakunin heard the sentence of the Austrian court. Like its Saxon predecessor, it found him guilty of high treason, condemned him to death, but commuted that penalty to imprisonment for life. On the same night, following a secret agreement between the Austrian and Russian governments, he was taken to the Russian frontier and handed over to the gendarmes there. The Austrian officer in charge insisted on keeping Bakunin's chains as the property of the Austrian government. They were removed on the spot and replaced by Russian ones. ' "Ah, my dear friends," Bakunin exclaimed, "the chains of my country seemed to me lighter, they gladdened me. And I smiled gaily at the

[1] V. Polonsky, *Materialy dlya Biografii M. Bakunina*, vol. 2, p. 6, Moscow-Leningrad, 1923–33.

Russian officer and his men. I said to them: "One returns home to die". The officer replied: "No talking is allowed".'

Taken to Petersburg, Bakunin was shut up in the Peter and Paul Fortress. After waiting for two anxious months in solitary confinement, he began to think that he had been forgotten, when one day the door of his cell opened to admit Count Orlov, the Tsar's aide-de-camp. Nicholas I knew how to vary his methods of interrogation to suit the character of the culprit. Orlov brought to Bakunin a message from the Tsar, telling him to write a full confession of his sins, as if he were a son speaking to his spiritual father, rather than a criminal confronting his judge. Both this approach, and its psychological timing, were admirably chosen.

Bakunin felt touched by the Tsar's magnanimity, and flattered by his personal attention. The prospect of laying bare his soul before his sovereign, the man whom he feared most and could not help respecting, appealed to his dramatic instinct. The outcome, Bakunin's *Confession*,[1] first published in 1921, seventy years after it was written, is an amazing record of his mental Odyssey. Its fulsome flattery to the Tsar, the author's self-castigation, his abject penitence for his misdeeds and mistaken outlook, throw a flood of light on his unstable personality. Its detailed narrative of his European adventures, and their cumulative effect on him, provide a key to his underlying motives.

VI

The *Confession* cannot be explained as a skilfully woven tissue of lies, designed by Bakunin to mollify Nicholas, and thereby win some remission of his punishment. Only a few passages, the personally flattering ones, those in praise of Slavs, and breathing hatred against Germans, may have been written with this end in view. Indeed the Emperor's marginal comments confirm that they succeeded. But other sections were bound to offend Nicholas, especially the stinging criticism of his home and foreign policy, and Bakunin's warmth towards his *noble*

[1] V. Polonsky, *Materialy*, vol. 1, pp. 100–248.

artisan comrades who fought on the Paris barricades. Nor was it in his temperament to sustain hypocrisy.

Had he successfully hoaxed Nicholas, he might have been expected to boast about it to his friends. Yet when he wrote to Herzen from Irkutsk, he described his open-hearted frankness. '*A quelques exceptions près*, I told Nicholas the whole story of my life abroad, all my plans, impressions, and feelings, without sparing him a number of instructive comments about his home and foreign policy. My letter, taking into account my clearly desperate position, and the energetic character of Nicholas, was written firmly and boldly, and for that reason it pleased him. For one thing I am grateful to him—that after he received it, he never once had me cross-examined.' Bakunin still protested that he kept his pride. 'I wanted one thing only, not to give in, not to resign or betray myself, never to sink to the point of seeking consolation in deceit, to preserve to the end the sacred fire of rebellion' (Letter, 1869).

For Alexander II, who released him from prison, he showed far less respect than he had for Nicholas, who brought and kept him there. 'My release was hard to obtain,' he explained in his letter to Herzen. 'The Tsar, obstinate as a ram, stopped several attempts. Once he went to Prince Gorchakov with a letter in his hand (the same one I had written to Nicholas in 1851) and said: "Mais je ne vois pas le moindre repentir dans cette lettre". So the fool expected me to repent!' Though he called his *Confession* a mixture of '*Dichtung and Wahrheit*' (fiction and truth), that description would apply to almost everything Bakunin wrote. He concealed from his friends that he grovelled at the feet of Nicholas, that he had denounced his own behaviour in terms that bear the stamp of heartfelt penitence. The largely self-created Bakunin legend of the dauntless rebel could no longer be maintained by any honest reader of the *Confession*.

A vagabond in an alien Europe, without money, friends or normal occupation, torn from his peculiar Russian circle, unable to throw in his lot with any foreign group, Bakunin had condemned himself to the role of a *déclassé* and rootless intellectual wanderer. He paints a picture of his loneliness and nostalgia, as he awoke to the untenability of his position. 'After so carelessly cutting off every road by which I might have returned to my native land, I found that I could never become either French or German. . . . Yet to Russian life I could find no way back except by revolutionary and criminal means, in which I then hardly believed, and later, to tell the truth, I believed in them only after morbid superhuman efforts to drown the inner voice which constantly whispered to me about the absurdity of my hopes and plans.

'Sometimes my heart felt so heavy that I would stop at night on the bridge which I crossed on my way home, and ask whether I would not do better to throw myself into the Seine, and drown a joyless and superfluous life.' Even in Prague among fellow-Slavs, indulging in heated but friendly disputes with Poles and Czechs, Bakunin felt as much an outcast as he had been in France and Germany.

'What I saw when I returned to Russia, so unlike my fearful expectation, contradicted all that I had thought, spoken, and written about the cruelty of the Russian government. Now I understand that *severity of law does not exclude human consideration*, and also the contrary, that human consideration does not exclude strict fulfilment of the law. I know how great is my crime, and therefore I expect nothing. . . . I swear to you that not one lie, not even a thousandth part of a lie, can flow from my pen, but I implore you, Emperor, do not demand from me to confess other people's sins. Surely in spirit no one reveals sins other than his own.' The perspicacious Nicholas I underlined these words and wrote in the margin: 'By this he destroys all confidence.'

Bakunin then affirmed that he had never joined a single socialist or communist organization. 'I followed the course of the socialist movement, especially of communism, because I regarded it as the inevitable result of economic and political development in Western Europe.' Here he adds a curiously Slavophil footnote: 'I speak *only* of Western Europe, because in the East, and not merely on Slav soil, communism has no place or sense. Throughout Western Europe one finds decrepitude, weakness, unbelief, and vice—the vice which springs from unbelief. Beginning at the very summit

of the social ladder, not a single person, not a single class, genuinely believe in their mission or their rights. They all behave like
charlatans. Privilege, classes, and power are thus precariously held
together by egoism and habit—a weak rampart against the rising
storm!'

Nicholas underlined the last sentence, which evidently impressed him. At this point Bakunin volunteered a wholesome
comment: 'Communism has spread, and continues to spread, as
much from the top as from the bottom. In the masses it lives as
a vague desire, an instinct to rise higher—in the higher classes as
an indefinite and helpless fear, the result of weakness and an im-
pure conscience. That fear and the unceasing outcry *against* communism, have nearly done more to promote its advance than
communist propaganda itself. It seems to me that the vague,
invisible, half-conscious but omnipresent communism is infinitely more dangerous than the system preached by a few societies.'
'*True*', noted Nicholas in the margin.[1]

While Bakunin made no attempt to minimize his exploits in the
Paris revolt or to deny his guilt, he spoke of self-surrender to a
wave of overwhelming sympathy. 'I assure your Majesty, not in
a single class, never and nowhere, did I find so much self-sacrifice,
such touching honesty, refinement of manners, and kindly cheer-
fulness, combined with heroism, as in the simple uneducated
people. . . . If the French workmen could find a worthy leader,
who knew how to understand and love them, he could work
wonders. Not only I, but all around me, were spiritually drunk.'

With similar sincerity, though in part for the benefit of
Nicholas, he enlarged on his unfailingly pro-Slav and anti-
German motives. 'Hatred of Germans', he announced, 'is the first
foundation of Slav unification. . . .' He skilfully found a tactical
excuse for having failed to show his true Slavonic outlook when
he wrote his *Appeal to the Slavs*. At that time, he explained, 'I
needed to get on good terms with German democrats, and was
obliged to steer a middle course between Slavs and Germans, a
course to which I was ill-suited, unaccustomed, and which I did
not like. . . .

[1] op. cit., vol. i, p. 112.

'Judging by what I have seen, living among them, I doubt whether fate will grant the Germans a long political existence. Recently German democrats have begun to feel the need for strong central government, but they can achieve no effective centralization. The fruit of Protestantism, and of all German political history, is anarchy—between the provinces, towns, and villages—together with anarchic conflict inside every German individual, a clash between his thoughts, feelings, and will.'

It may seem odd that the famous anarchist should hit out so angrily against anarchy (and curse with it the nation that he hated most), but these derogatory remarks confirm Bakunin's frankly *strategic* concern with anarchy, not as an edifying ideal, but as a preliminary solvent for working out a new despotic order. In fact he outlined and justified such a plan in his *Confession*.

'I wanted a republic, but what *kind* of a republic? Not a parliamentary one, with representative government, constitutional forms, and so-called division of executive and legislative powers.' On the contrary, 'I believe that in Russia, more than anywhere else, a dictatorial power is indispensable, to raise up and educate the masses—a power free in its own choice of direction, but unimpeded by parliaments, and surrounded by people who have faith in it.'

Nevertheless, he admitted with disarming modesty, '*I hardly knew Russia*. Living abroad, working from my old impressions and partly influenced by rumours, I invented a fantastic Russia, ready for revolution. I wanted to believe in this, and to persuade others to believe.'

But when he starts to compare Russian society with Western Europe, he departs abruptly from Slavophil hyperboles and faces a choice between prosaic evils. In the comparison Russian governmental vices tip the balance against Russia.

'Western Europe only *seems* to be worse, because all its evils rise to the surface, and fewer remain concealed—whereas in Russia illnesses turn inwards and eat away the social organism from within. In Russia, where the chief motive force is fear, every higher official bullies his inferior, who dares not complain, but inflicts his revenge on the man subordinate to him. In the West

D

a public thief is rarely hidden, and anyone can expose him. In Russia, though everyone may know about the thief, all remain silent, because they are afraid, and officialdom, conscious of its sins, is silent too. It is hard for an official *not* to be a thief in Russia. First, all around him steal, habit becomes second nature. . . . If any man tries to remain honest, his colleagues start a campaign against him, begin by calling him a crank, anti-social, a liberal or a dangerous free-thinker, and if that fails to change him, they will not be satisfied till they have crushed him.'

Bakunin cannot be accused of borrowing his ideas about dictatorship from Marx (who hardly formulated them in print before 1875) any more than from Nechaev, whom he first met in 1869. For this worshipper of boundless freedom, already describes in his *Confession* a *tyrannical* plan to organize international revolution. Three separate and independent secret societies would work under different names, and *unacquainted* with one another, the first designed to deal with the professional class, another with young students, a third with the villages. Each group would owe unconditional obedience to its superior in the hierarchy. Membership would be limited to a small number of experienced and energetic men. These, acting in strict obedience to orders from above, would work upon the masses, who must remain *unaware* of that control. A Central Committee with absolute powers provided the sole co-ordinating link between the three societies.

Having dramatically confessed his guilt in plotting so many world-shattering conspiracies, Bakunin embarked on some frank and modest reflections about his shortcomings. 'I had neither those brilliant qualities nor vices which make statesmen or governmental criminals. I would gladly have submitted to another man's will, for I always loved and respected discipline when it is founded on conviction and faith.' But his incorrigible temperament destroyed any discipline he wanted to impose upon himself. He was afflicted, he complained, by 'a love of the fantastic, of extraordinary unheard-of adventures, opening up a boundless horizon, where no one could guess the issue. *Peace drove me to despair.* I ought to have been born in the American backwoods—not in an orderly society of citizens—or among Western colonizers, where life is one endless struggle against savages and untamed nature. If fate had made me a sailor, I might by now have been a respectable man, without any thought of politics, and seeking no other adventures and storms than those natural to the ocean. . . .'

As for his socialism, it all derived from simple moral feelings. 'I felt more sympathy for the common people than for the characterless and dissipated class of Russian nobles. On the former rest our hopes for resurrection . . . I saw in them freshness, a broad spirit, a clear mind (not infected by corruption), and Russian vigour—and I used to think, what would that people become if it were given liberty and property, if it were taught to read and write? I impudently and rebelliously answered this question in my mind and writings thus: the Government will never free the Russian people, because, despite its unlimited power, it is limited by many circumstances, bound by invisible threads to its own pampered administration, to the selfish interests of its officials, and still more because it does not *want* the Russian people to be freed, educated, or uplifted, seeing in them above all a soulless machine to be used for the conquest of Europe . . .

'They may ask me, what do I think now? Tsar, it is hard for me to answer such a question . . . Many things have changed within me, but can I say with a good conscience that there have not remained traces of the old disease? One truth I have thoroughly understood; that the science of Government and political action is so great and difficult that few are able to grasp it with a mind unprepared by education—that much in the life of governments and nations cannot be judged by ordinary criteria, and that much, which seems to us in private life burdensome and cruel, becomes in a higher political sphere quite indispensable.

'I understood, in a word, that my own desires and actions were in the highest degree absurd, senseless, impudent, and criminal—criminal against you, my Tsar, against Russia, my country, against all political, moral, divine, and human laws!' [1]

'I also asked myself: "What does Russia gain by all her conquests? If half the world submits to her, will she be happier, freer,

[1] V. Polonsky, *Materialy*, vol. I, pp. 167-8.

or more prosperous? Will she even be stronger? Will not the
mighty Russian Empire fall asunder if she expands her boundaries
still further? Russia will have to bear on her own shoulders the
crushing burden of that immense, complicated and enforced centralization. She will make herself hated by other Slav peoples, even
as she is already hated by the Poles. In the end, after earning the
hatred of all, she will begin to hate herself, without having found
in her obligatory conquests anything better than torment and
slavery." '

True to the dialectical rhythm which runs through this document, Bakunin followed his spurt of outrageous frankness with
a sharply contrasting passage, to underline the remorse and horror
which he now felt for his 'political madness'. 'Tsar, I have not
tried to soften my expressions . . . I have said enough to show
you the licentious abandon of my thoughts . . . I stand before
you as a prodigal son, wandering and vicious, before his offended
and angry father.'

As he nears the end, he adds a note of humble supplication to
the long strain of penitence: 'Tsar, do not order me to rot away
in lifelong imprisonment. Let the harshest penal servitude be my
lot. I accept it thankfully, as a mercy; the harder the work, the
more easily will I be able to forget myself in it. But in solitary
confinement, thought and memory become an inexpressible torture . . . one goes on living against one's will and one can never
die.' He signed himself 'the repentant sinner, Michael Bakunin'.[1]

VII

Nicholas, after dryly noting that the document was *most instructive*, passed it on to his son, the future Alexander II. He
graciously granted Bakunin permission to see members of his
family in the presence of a witness, but he left him under lock and
key. Even Bakunin's iron constitution started to give way. He
contracted scurvy, and all his teeth fell out. The death of Nicholas
in 1855 spurred him to make one final bid for his release. If he
failed this time, he told his brother, he would commit suicide. In

[1] op. cit., p. 248.

this frame of mind he wrote his *Appeal to Alexander II*, signed 'the imploring criminal', praying to be rescued from the slow death of solitary confinement, to be given one last chance 'to support my family as a useful and active servant of Your Majesty'.[1] This plea sounded far-fetched, since Bakunin had never supported anyone financially, least of all himself. But the entreaties of his mother, aided by her influential Muravyov relations, tilted the scales of punitive justice in his favour. Alexander permitted him to be removed from prison and transferred to a penal settlement in Siberia.

Bakunin's behaviour during his Siberian exile is full of the same spontaneous duplicity, the same bewildering blend of sincerity and fraud, which dominated his *Confession*. Only his pan-Slav mysticism, at which he vaguely hinted in the latter document, takes on a new lease of life during the curious friendship which he developed there with his Empire-building cousin, the Governor-General Muravyov-Amursky.

He also began to write flattering letters to the editor of *The Russian Messenger*, the notorious Katkov, at that time a 'national liberal', not yet ripened into Chauvinist maturity. Bakunin offered to contribute informative articles about the economic potentialities of Siberia and the Amur. The offer came to nothing, but Katkov noted with surprise that Bakunin appeared to be living in Siberia quite comfortably, not in dire poverty, with plenty of time to read French novels, and without doing hard or serious work.[2]

In fact Bakunin won the confidence of a kind-hearted businessman, who generously paid him two years' salary in advance for nebulous services he was to render for the local Gold Mines' administration. He congratulated Katkov on the stand he had taken against the commune in favour of private land-ownership for peasants. The most vehement strain in his letters warns against the threat to Russia which would emerge from any successful Slav federation within the *Austrian* Empire: 'If Austria were to become Slav, what would be left for Russia? Can you imagine that Poland would remain partitioned as she is at present? Impossible. She would re-unite, and under the auspices of a Slav Austria she would

<hr />

[1] op. cit., p. 288.   [2] op. cit., vol. 2, p. 498.

take from us, one after the other, Lithuania, White Russia, and the Ukraine. Do you want two Slav worlds, one Eastern while the other becomes Western? That would be against nature, and the one would sooner or later swallow up the other. Let Russia rather swallow up Austria. It is not even a big piece' (Letter, 1858). Such projects of territorial expansion were unlikely to win favours from the Russian government (which then respected the integrity of the Austrian Empire, including its Slav subjects). Bakunin wrote to Herzen in 1860 that he longed to return to Russia, to find some more devoted men of action like his cousin (Governor-General Muravyov), 'a man whom we are in duty bound to regard as *one of ours*'. He roundly reproached Herzen for having misunderstood and vilified Muravyov in *The Bell*. He claimed that the programme of political action privately adopted by this 'serious and energetic man, one of my best friends', coincided in essentials with his (Bakunin's) own, namely, (1) to liberate the serfs and give them land, (2) institute public law courts with a jury system, to which all state officials, as well as ordinary citizens, must be answerable, (3) extend education through the medium of the state, (4) introduce local self-government by measures of de-centralization within the Empire, but *without* any constitution or parliamentary system, by means of an iron dictatorship for emancipating the Slavs, beginning with Poland, then followed by a fight to the death against Austria and Turkey.

How far the attribution of this programme to Muravyov displayed a flight of Bakunin's wishful imagination, how far it was the outcome of intense but vague political discussions which they conducted together throughout the long Siberian nights, we cannot know for certain. But it is true that Muravyov treated the Decembrist and other political exiles with great respect, and boldly petitioned the Petersburg government to amnesty some and permit their return to European Russia. He even requested as the reward he would most welcome for his own services (in negotiating the important treaty with China, which in 1858 ceded the vast Amur region to Russia) that pardon and a restoration of full civil rights should be granted to Bakunin, Speshnov and Petrashevsky.

In his letter to Herzen (December, 1860), Bakunin dwelt on the sole alternative he could see, apart from the drastic course which he (and Muravyov) advocated, a continuation of the disintegrating liberal régime of Alexander II. (We should remember that this letter was written before the Emancipation Edict.)

'Insipid, jealous, full of hatred,' he conjured up the Russian official environment of 1860, 'the empty numbness of a heart which has stopped beating, together with generous words, re-sounding phrases accompanied by petty actions . . . behind it all shelters a society so mean and horrible that one feels sick; for in Russia words make one want to vomit, the stronger and more brilliant they are, the more nausea they provoke . . . Now journalism is in its heyday. The Panaevs[1] triumph. All who have learned to wield a pen beat their breasts excitedly, while hollow sounds emerge, because they have been emptied of their hearts. Phantoms, lavish in eloquent and sterile words, they gesticulate in noisy delirium. People who live among them lose their own vital strength.

'The only time they come to earth is when their vanity is pricked—the sole remaining passion of these distinguished persons, who possess only the rhetoric of every other passion. . . . In a word, they are fit for nothing except to be handed over to the executioner. We need miracles, prodigies of mind, and will-power, to save Russia. I have faith in the latent force of Russian people, in a "third estate" of liberated serfs, of *petit-bourgeois* priests' sons, those among whom the ingenious and bold initiative of the nation is still preserved.' [2]

Thus Bakunin pronounced judgement on the host of liberal officials and progressive intellectuals so busily engaged in schemes for reforming Russia, although he excluded people like Muravyov from the list of the condemned. Others fan the flames of revolution despite their efforts to extinguish them. 'The Russian Revolution will be terrible,' he concluded, 'for nothing else will have the

---

[1] I. Panaev, assistant editor, with Nekrasov, of the radical journal *The Contemporary*.

[2] M. Bakunin, *Correspondance*, ed. M. Dragomanov, p. 108 et seq., Paris, 1896.

power to rouse us from our fatal lethargy. Action may wear men out, but banality makes them fade and shrivel up.'

In 1858 Bakunin married Antonia Kwiatkowsky, a Polish girl to whom he had given French lessons, daughter of an employee in the Siberian gold-mines. He praised her as a Slav patriot 'free from her country's Catholic ideas', and expressed satisfaction that 'she shares my aspirations with all her heart'. It seems that their marital relations never went beyond this plane of platonic comradeship. But the event stirred Bakunin to one of his sporadic attempts to earn a living. In a humble letter to Prince Dolgoruky, he begged to be allowed to take up work which would enable him to support his family: 'And then I shall try by my deeds to prove how deeply I feel gratitude, how sacredly I intend to keep my honest word and oath.'

Muravyov's friendship and support opened many Siberian doors which might otherwise have remained closed to a political exile, and that may account for the kindness and material help lavished on Bakunin. Muravyov left Siberia and returned to Petersburg in 1861, but Bakunin continued to exploit the social prestige built up through his cousin's patronage. From the new Governor-General Korsakov he obtained a permit enabling him to travel down the Amur river. He readily gave his oath that he would return to Irkutsk as soon as his business was completed.

While thus lulling suspicion, he explained in a letter his ulterior motive: 'I also gave myself another pledge, to escape at any price.' After reaching the mouth of the Amur river, he embarked surreptitiously on a Russian ship which was leaving the port of Nicolaevsk. Next, by skilful bluff and trickery, he managed to transfer himself and his scanty baggage to an American ship bound for Japan. After a journey of five months, crossing the Pacific, the American continent and the Atlantic ocean, he arrived safe and sound on Herzen's doorstep in London.

VIII

Here he started a new phase of journalistic work, an uneasy collaboration with Herzen on his free Russian newspaper *The*

Bell. Having spent seven consecutive years in Austrian and Russian prisons, and four in the isolation of Siberia, Bakunin returned to contemporary turmoil like a ghost from the past. Recognizing the big gaps in his experience, he placed himself, to start with, at Herzen's disposition. 'I acknowledge with a feeling of happiness', he said, 'that your talents and science place you far above me.' But Bakunin's temperament would never let him play second fiddle, even to a superman. While he had acquired no fresh ideas, he returned to his old charge against the Austrian Empire with redoubled vigour.

At this time Austria-Hungary, rather than the Russian Empire, seemed to Bakunin the biggest obstacle blocking the way towards a Slav federation of minor states. 'Out of that will emerge in all its grandeur the free Slav federation, the *only way out.* . . .' Indeed, carried away perhaps by Herzen's counsels, or by the prospects opened after the Emancipation Edict, Bakunin declared his readiness to give the Tsar a final chance to prove his worth. His pamphlet *Romanov Pugachov or Pestel* (1862) stated that a Romanov Emperor might succeed, where rebellious efforts of peasants and noblemen had failed, provided that he fulfilled the people's needs. 'We will gladly follow this Romanov, if he could renounce being the Petersburg Tsar in order to become the people's Tsar.' This sweeping concession to the Romanov dynasty was short-lived. The moment he heard about the inception of a new secret society, *Land and Liberty*, he plunged into it and started to plot monster peasant uprisings throughout Russia.

When the Poles revolted in 1863, he promptly submitted to the Polish leaders a fantastic scheme for fomenting a *jacquerie*, and volunteered to form a Russian legion on Polish soil. The Central Committee in Warsaw, with noteworthy level-headedness, declined these offers. Nothing daunted, Bakunin decided to start a revolt in Finland, rather than be cheated of playing his part. He embarked for Sweden. In Stockholm his genial personality, and overwhelming capacity for bluff, won him an audience with the Crown Prince and a cordial reception at official banquets, where Swedish punch and political speeches flowed copiously.

Bakunin passed himself off as a representative of the Polish

national movement and of the Russian *Land and Liberty* organization. Allowing his imagination to run riot, he pictured this
struggling little underground society as a vast concern with
branches throughout Russia, and on the verge of raising its own
army. He took care to present himself to Swedish notabilities and
journalists in the guise of a national democrat rather than as a
world revolutionary. In an article published in the Stockholm
Aftonbladt (1863), he wrote: 'In fighting for the liberation of the
West I was convinced that in so doing I was fighting for our
national freedom. . . . In this country,' he hastened to add, 'so
happy, so peaceful, where progressive all-round development can
be felt in every direction, ruled by one of the most popular
monarchs in Europe, any man who tried to conduct revolutionary
propaganda would be an absurd fool.'

The failure of the 1863 revolt marked a major débâcle for
Bakunin, through the number of blows it dealt to his prestige.
The Polish insurgents who had embarked with illicit firearms on
the steamship *Ward Jackson* accused him of having turned the
expedition into a farce. The *Land and Liberty* Russians were non-
plussed by bombastic statements which Bakunin made about
them, and by his groundless claims to act on their behalf. The
Swedes, who had welcomed him with open arms, felt resentment
when they found out they had been fooled. From London Herzen
wrote letters, fuming with indignation, withdrew all collaboration, and threatened to disown Bakunin publicly in *The Bell*.

From this turning point Bakunin's mind moved towards that
global anarchy for which his name is best remembered as an advocate. He departed with his wife to Italy, to launch new world conspiracies in a more care-free sunny atmosphere. On a final visit to
London he called on his rival Marx, who asked him to join his
recently founded International Association of Workmen (September 1864). Bakunin had reason to suspect Marx of complicity in
spreading the malicious rumour that he was a Russian Government spy, but he judged it politic to accept his rival's offer, and
promised to lend a hand in fighting the objectionable patriotic
Italian socialism, propagated by Mazzini. Marx coldly and precisely recorded his satisfaction that Bakunin remained one of the

rare people in whom, after sixteen years, he saw evidence of 'progress and not a backward movement'.

In fact Bakunin did not stir a finger to promote Marx's International. On the contrary, he began to be busy with schemes for a world-wide organization of his own, a so-called *International Brotherhood*, divided into *National Families*, but under the control of an *International Family*. He called it *Projet d'une société internationale et révolutionnaire—sans phrases*. None the less he wrote affectionately to Marx from Florence in 1865, addressed him as *carissimo*, and apologized for having failed to answer any of his letters. 'I understand better than ever before how right you were to choose the high road of economic revolution, and to scorn us who wander along the paths of national or political enterprise. . . . My Fatherland will henceforth be the International, of which you are one of the principal founders. You see therefore, dear friend, that I am your pupil, and I am proud of it!' [1] At this point the Slavophil Bakunin appears to join hands with the workmen who 'have no country'. But his cordial outburst was not unmixed with diplomatic strategy. Bakunin explained in a letter to Herzen (1869) that he flattered Marx both from a sense of justice and for tactical reasons.

In 1869 Bakunin wrote a long letter to clarify, rather than to remove, a number of issues which divided him from Herzen. It made no attempt to bridge their differences, re-stated vehemently his own aims, then enumerated a catalogue of Herzen's political errors, and called on him to mend his ways. Failing this recantation, he said he would feel obliged to break with Herzen, 'if not in the goal, at least in the method of attaining it'.

It has often been assumed that Bakunin shared official Slavophil belief in the virtues of the Russian village *commune*, and wanted to preserve that ancient institution. This letter proves that, far from accepting the *mir* as the foundation stone of a new social order, he advocated its complete destruction, and condemned Herzen for having fostered rosy illusions about its future role. 'Tell me,' he asked, 'though proud of your theory, which nobody understands or admits, why did you never seriously answer the

[1] V. Polonsky, *Materialy*, vol. 3, p. 138.

question, how can the Russian *commune* conceal a mysterious virtue and latent force? . . . Your prized *commune* stagnates in its manure, motionless for over a thousand years. Savage suspicion and ignorance, patriarchal vice, an obstinate kingdom of Chinese ceremonial, contempt for human personality, or complete ignorance of it. Cold bestial cruelty, absolute slavery of custom, thought, feeling, and will, that is the spirit of your thousand-year-old, senseless decaying corpse!' [1] He reminds Herzen of the brutal systematic tyranny which the *mir*—always ready to sell rights and justice for ten litres of vodka—exerts over every individual who dares to show the smallest sign of independence. Add to that the tendency of every member, once he has been elected to the rural administration, to turn into a bullying official. '*You* discover two essential virtues in the *mir*—absence of Roman law, and customary instead of legal rights. The latter includes every peasant's right to a piece of land. So far so good. But behind this custom lies the deplorable idea, attributing the ownership of all land to the state and to its chief, the Tsar.' Therefore the Tsar can order the bodily transfer of whole populations from one territory to another, without provoking a murmur. Yet a single peasant may not move from his place without an official permit. The state obliges him to accept bad land, for which he must pay heavily.

'Our rural *commune* has never evolved; it has experienced no interior development. . . . Every peasant who attains some degree of well-being does all he can to get away from the *mir*. . . . Emancipation has only changed the form. Yesterday's serfs, obliged to work for their masters, are today transformed into serfs of the state. Having in many ways replaced the landowner, the rural *commune* has become a blind and docile instrument, manipulated by government officials.'

Society *cannot* evolve peacefully on such a basis, Bakunin concluded. The peasant *must* revolt against his own stagnant communism at the same time as he revolts against the state. For the state had engulfed and corrupted even local semi-autonomous bodies. 'Phenomena, which in other countries are transitory or

---

[1] M. Bakunin, *Lettres à Herzen et Ogaryov*, ed. M. Dragomanov, p. 224, Paris, 1896.

intermittent, acquire with us continuity or immutability, the negation of everything human in the name of the state and its interests. It seems to me that ever since the foundation of the Moscow Empire, after the murder of popular life in Novgorod and Kiev, after the suppression of the Stenka Razin and Pugachov revolts, the only right and effective action in our unhappy shameful country has been *reaction*. And can you expect that systematic reaction, which follows a logical process in Russia, will produce miracles in the psychological world? . . . It is the duty of us refugees outside Russia to insist on the urgency of destroying that detestable Empire' (Letter, July 1866).

Therefore Bakunin could never condone Herzen's ban on political assassination, even when commonsense took Herzen's side. 'I, like you, do not expect that regicide in Russia will be of any help. I am ready to agree that it does harm, by reviving a temporary sympathy for the Tsar. But neither am I surprised that others fail to share this view, and that under the weight of the present intolerable situation, men should arise, less philosophically developed but more energetic than we are, who believe that the Gordian knot can be cut with a single blow—and I sincerely respect them for thinking thus, and for carrying out their intentions. . . . For all the Gods in the world I would not consent to throw a stone at Karakozov. He is *one of us*, outside that crowd of lackeys, cringing at the feet of their masters.' Strangely enough, it was a young peasant who seized the arm of Karakozov and deflected his aim, thus saving the life of Alexander II. There was a moral in this affair, Bakunin said. 'The Trubetskoys, Volkonskys, Petrashevskys, and Karakozov, implacable enemies of Imperialism, all belonged to the *nobility*. The Susanins, Martianovs, and Komissarovs, defenders and saviours of Autocracy, all spring from the common people.' [1] Once more Bakunin affirmed himself as the rightful heir of the noble Decembrist rebels.

But he is no longer prepared, as he was in 1861, to give the Romanovs another chance. 'I simply do not understand your letters to the Tsar,' he wrote to Herzen. 'I see in them the evil that they may foster in immature minds, the thought that it is still

[1] op. cit., p. 237.

possible to expect something good for the people from *any state,* especially from the All-Russian state. . . . You were frightened, and yielded to the venal outcry of the Moscow and Petersburg journalists, supported by the disgusting mass of landowners and the morally bankrupt majority of Belinsky's and Granovsky's pupils (your own disciples, Herzen!), that old humane-aesthetic brotherhood filled with a bookish idealism which, alas!, failed to withstand the onslaught of the filthy Russian governmental reality.

'You showed yourself weak, Herzen, confronted by that betrayal, which your lucid, penetrating, severely logical mind would have recognized, if your sinking heart had not obscured it. I detect in your voice a note of injured irritated grief—you preach to them, appeal to their conscience, exactly as you appeal to the Emperor's, instead of spitting once and for all in the face of that old public, turning your back on it, and addressing yourself to a new young public, the only one able to understand you broadly and open-heartedly, the only one with a will to act. . . . They are national patriots (Katkov, Samarin, Aksakov), you are an honest socialist. Therefore, if you are consistent, you must fight every state hostile to the social interests of all nations. Either that, or you find yourself working for *state socialism,* and you become reconciled with the vilest and most formidable lie which our century has engendered, official democracy and red bureaucracy!'

Bakunin remembered that he owed Herzen an explanation of his apparent *volte-face,* and the tactical one which he offered is plausible enough. 'When I exhorted Alexander II to declare himself Tsar of the people and the *zemstvos,*[1] to abolish classes and decentralize the administration, to give land to the peasants, to free the subject provinces, who did not want to be tied hand and foot to Great Russia, I deliberately called on him to destroy with his own hands the Russian Empire; in other words, I wanted his political suicide. But I knew as well as you do that the Emperor was condemned by the force of events to continue the system of Peter the Great. If I indicated to him the other way, impossible for him to follow, it was because I wanted to rouse in the minds

[1] Local government councils.

of the public a recognition that the Tsar's authority could *never* be reconciled with the happiness of his subjects.'

After all these errors Herzen's fame had crumbled. His *Bell* was ringing in the void. Only one course, which offered a hopeful outlet, remained open to him. 'Seek a new public in the young people, in the half-taught disciples of Chernyshevsky and Dobrolyubov. . . . But do not try to nourish them on half-lights, half-truths, and hints. Stand up again in the open, renounce your false and surely useless tactfulness. . . . Do not curse the young, but rally them, scold them when they are ridiculous, but respect their honest work, their heroism and sacrifice. Formerly you felt strong, and strength is always generous-minded, even towards its enemies. . . . Do not grow old, Herzen, do not turn into a Jean Jacques Rousseau, but remain always our powerful Voltaire.' [1]

Bakunin's exhortations had no effect on Herzen, except to provoke a lively correspondence in which both men stuck to their own guns. When Herzen reluctantly decided in 1869 to stop publishing *The Bell*, Bakunin protested: 'What does it matter even if you sell no more than five hundred copies? They will secure at least three thousand readers. It is not a trifle to be able to speak freely in these times, even to three thousand Russians.' [2] But Herzen was sick of political controversy. The Nihilists of the sixties went out of their way to anger and insult him, and hard as he tried, he could not admire them. He felt that he had nourished vipers in his bosom. In his *Letter to an old Comrade* he explained why he could never follow Bakunin into a holy war of annihilation.

IX

From 1868, Bakunin's struggle with Marx, to win leadership of *The Workers' International Association*, began in earnest. In the previous year Bakunin attended the Congress of Peace and Freedom, organized in Geneva by democratic parties of the major European nations, as a protest against war. The presence of Victor Hugo from France, John Stuart Mill, from England, and Garibaldi from Italy, gave this gathering a distinguished air.

[1] op. cit., p. 272.   [2] op. cit., p. 266.

Its fine speeches attracted the attention of the Press. But after the second meeting of the League in Berne, Bakunin resigned from it, complaining that it was verbose and ineffective, and with some like-minded dissentients he founded his *International Social Democratic Alliance*.

He next applied to Marx to admit this *Alliance* as a corporate unit into the ranks of the *Workers' International*, ostensibly to provide a more efficient general staff for the latter organization. Marx's dark suspicions were immediately aroused. 'Herr Bakunin', he wrote to Engels in 1869, 'is condescending enough to offer to take the workers' movement under Russian patronage.' Marx rejected the application, and Bakunin then agreed to dissolve the *Alliance*, if its local branches could be received into the *International*.

Bakunin told Marx that 40,000 Russian students were impatiently waiting to throw their energies into the revolutionary cause. Engels's comment on this remark unveils the national feuds seething within the Workers' International. If anything could ruin the Western European movement, he protested, 'it would be the importation of these forty thousand ambitious, hungry Russian Nihilists, budding officers without an army—which *we* are to provide for them. A priceless assumption that, in order to unify the European proletariat, it must be commanded by the Russians! . . . Under cover of their international principle they will worm their way in among the workers everywhere, insinuate themselves into leading positions, and bring with them all those intrigues and brawls which are inevitable among Russians!' [1]

Marx and Engels were convinced that a secret society, pulling the strings of action, operated behind every open organization patronized by Bakunin. Marx charged Bakunin with trying to disrupt the International under the pretext of enlarging and improving it. The latter remained equally convinced that Marx's *International* concealed a secret core, in which Marx reigned supreme. But Marx, buoyed up by an overwhelming sense of his superiority, could afford to dispense with subterfuge. He scarcely troubled to conceal his contempt for uneducated people. Ever

[1] E. H. Carr, *Karl Marx*, p. 237, London, 1934.

since he got his own way in drafting the first rules of the *International* ('the thing was not so difficult, because one had only artisans to deal with'), his technique was to drive out people whom he could not dominate. Bakunin, on the other hand, aspired to be a concealed dictator wherever he could not openly play the leading part. He transferred the dark conspiratorial methods of the Russian *underground* into the hitherto more open setting of European class-conflicts.

But Marx, unlike Bakunin, frankly disapproved of encouraging national autonomy within the International Workers' Movement. When English members of the *International* wanted to form a Regional Council for England, Marx pronounced that it would be stupid to treat England as one country among other countries; she should be treated as the *metropolis of capitalism*. Since the General Council stood in the happy position of being able to place its hand on this great lever of proletarian revolution, it would be sheer folly to allow that hold to fall into merely English hands. An important function of the General Council was to promote disruptive foundations such as the *Land and Labour League*, which later, in the public execution of their duties, *appeared* to be spontaneous movements within the English working class.

In his fight against Bakunin Marx used every weapon that could serve his purpose. During the Peace League's Congress in Lausanne, he attacked 'absurd proposals', such as 'equality of classes, abolition of the right of inheritance', as the first step in social revolution. He poured scorn on Bakunin's horror tactics and on his 'habit of abusing the Western bourgeoisie in the tone of Muscovite optimists who attack Western civilization—in order to palliate their own barbarism'. The *Volkstaat* (official organ of the German Social Democratic Party) revived the old slander—started in 1848—that Bakunin and Herzen received subsidies from a pan-Slav committee in Moscow under the auspices of the Petersburg government.

At the 1869 Congress of the *International*, Bakunin dramatically demanded a public refutation of this slander. The court brought in a verdict that the editor, Liebknecht, had behaved

E

'with criminal levity' in spreading the rumour that Bakunin was an agent of the Tsar. Bakunin thereupon folded Liebknecht's retraction into a spill, lit a cigarette with it, and held out his hand to the offender. Thus, despite the efforts of unscrupulous enemies, Bakunin managed to gain ground and win respect. Marx, seeing no alternative except to crush him before he became too strong, began to engineer the expulsion of his rival from the *International*. The Hague Congress of 1872 provided the occasion for this dénouement.

The main charge Marx brought against Bakunin was that, contrary to his obligations as a member of the *International*, he had founded a secret society called the *Alliance*, which contained statutes hostile to those of the *International*. Whether in fact a secret '*Alliance*' continued to exist, after the public '*Alliance*' had been dissolved, could neither be proved nor disproved.

But Marx's trump card against Bakunin at the Hague Conference became a personal one. Bakunin had started to translate Marx's *Kapital* into Russian, taken some payment in advance from the prospective Russian publisher, and then dropped the work—all characteristic actions. Marx, in recommending Bakunin's expulsion from the *International*, tried to prove that he had used fraud and threats to avoid fulfilling his commitments. The supporters of Marx made a majority. Bakunin was expelled, and Marx saved the *International* from falling into the hands of the Bakuninists. But he emasculated it by carrying through a vote to transfer the seat of the General Council from London to New York.

In England the *International* could not be made safe from the English; on the continent of Europe it remained in danger of being engulfed by Bakunin. Marx triumphed over his two rivals, but paid the price of committing political suicide. For the *International*, rooted in European grievances, could barely survive its abrupt transplantation to America. Rumbles of indignation began to be voiced against Marx. His denunciation of Bakunin won him a Pyrrhic victory, but added to his enemies. How strangely edifying that a man, who devoted his life to denouncing bourgeois crimes, should strike down a revolutionary colleague for having taken a few unearned roubles from a bourgeois publisher.

Bakunin showed throughout a strain of generosity to Marx, mingled with hostility, but never swamped by petty spite. 'Let us take this opportunity', he wrote, 'to pay homage to citizens Marx and Engels, famous leaders of the German Communist faction. We feel a deep and genuine respect for them. But though we do justice to the tremendous service which they have rendered to the *International*, we must still oppose at the sword's point their false authoritarian theories and dictatorial presumption. We oppose also their technique, their machinations, underground intrigues, wretched personal quarrels, dirty vituperations, which have always been a hall-mark of German political struggles, and which they unfortunately brought into the *International*.' [1] In a letter to the editor of *La Liberté* (1872) he paid tribute to the organizers of the campaign for his expulsion. 'The Marxians, sure of their majority, organized it in advance with skill and care, without paying much attention to morality, truth, and justice, so often celebrated by them in words, so rarely in deeds. They threw off that mask.'

X

This semi-personal semi-ideological duel compelled Bakunin to think again about the deep differences dividing him from the man whose disciple he had called himself. Two future probabilities perturbed him: the dim prospects for any human culture reorganized under Marxian intellectual drill, and the total slavery which the Marxian state, despite all protests to the contrary, seemed fated to promote. Was it not the height of impudence to assert that a small group of intellectuals could become the brain and soul, directing the whole revolutionary movement—'that is such an outrageous heresy against common sense and historical experience alike, that one involuntarily asks oneself, how could a mind so penetrating as that of Marx arrive at it?' [2]

[1] L. Schwarzschild, *The Red Prussian*, p. 346, London, 1948.
[2] V. Polonsky, *Materialy*, vol. 3, p. 375.

Bakunin declared that all attempts to put science and doctrine at the top of human government, to make a *school of thought* the source and guide of living, would inflict misery on human beings, dry them up, and transform them into a dull and slavish herd. In his pamphlet *The Knouto-German Empire and International Socialism* (1871) he identified the German school of Communists with the worst religious and political despots of the past, those who, starting from the most exacting ideal demands (which quickly evaporate and wear out) lead later to the most horrible material results.

To clinch his argument, he compared the Greek and Roman civilizations of the ancient world. Which of the two was more materialistic and earthy in its starting-point, but more humane and ideal in its result? Surely the Greek, he answered. Which was the more abstract and ideal in its origins, and sacrificed the real human individual to the nominal freedom of the citizen with juridical rights, the inward development of human society to the abstraction of the state? The Roman Empire, he answered.

Similarly today, the civilization of Germany stands for all that is pure, abstract, and categorical. But what are its results? Unattainable ideals are fatally distorted into a disgusting materialism. Bakunin denied any fundamental difference between German idealists and their materialist heirs, between the followers of Hegel and those of Marx. Both involved the bloody sacrifice of tormented human beings on the same altar of futile but merciless abstractions.

Bakunin apologized for dragging theology and metaphysics (which he cordially hated) into political and social matters. But the two spheres had grown entangled. They needed to be dragged apart and understood, in order that the doped minds of citizens could be restored to sanity and health. Bakunin denounced every organized religion as a collective insanity, the more powerful through being traditional, rooted in a remote and savage past. He described 'the Christian absurdity' as 'the boldest and most monstrous of religious hoaxes'. 'There must have been profound dissatisfaction with life, a terrible emotional thirst, but almost complete beggary of mind, in order to accept it.' But contemporary social idealists, who had renounced organized Christianity, showed no signs of having freed themselves from religious bondage to the state.

'Of all despotisms, those maintained by doctrinaires or inspired by organized religion, are the vilest. They are so jealously attached to the glory of their God or doctrine, that no place for freedom or respect remains in their heart, no spark of sympathy for living people. . . . Learned scientists treat human beings like rabbits for their social experiments, are ready to flay them alive in the name of science.' [1] These people, obsessed with working for some abstract goal, pour contempt on transitory mundane matters, unaware that they themselves are just as transitory.

At this point Bakunin came close to Tolstoy. For he preached a similar revolt of life against pseudo-science, or against the rule of scientists. He never discouraged scientific research (which he said would be 'a crime against human betterment') but he wanted science to serve human needs, not scientists' ambitions. He would rather relinquish science altogether than be ruled by learned men. Vague optimistic talk about the future 'intellectual aristocracy' filled him with dismay. 'Learned scientific men', he said, 'are always self-satisfied, in love with themselves, and though they lack vital strength, they want to interfere with everything. Their learned abstract breath would dry up every source of life.' Did Bakunin have Marx in mind when penning these remarks, which resemble what he said about Marx elsewhere?

Bakunin never considered whether a grim Marxian state might not appear to many a lesser evil than happy-go-lucky statelessness. Only a weak state, he grudgingly admitted, could be virtuous, 'and even then its desires are wicked'. While Germans had found their fulfilment within and through the state, for the livelier Slavs the state had been a *tomb*. Therefore Slavs must seek liberation *outside* the state, not only in fighting against the German one (already incorporated in their own odious government), but in an international struggle to destroy every surviving state. Their leaders should be aware that the same *fluid* quality, which

[1] M. Bakunin, *Izbrannye Sochineniya*, ed. V. Cherkezov, vol. 1, pp. 236 et seq., Petrograd, 1922.

in the past had made Slav peoples politically weak—their incapacity to create a Western type of state—now enabled them to stake their claim to useful action. For the Slavs there remained only two alternatives—since no moderate-sized state could exist independently in modern times. Either Slav states would mercifully vanish, or else there would arise a single all-devouring Russian state, lashing its subjects with the knout (*The Knouto-German Empire and International Socialism*, 1871).

'In spite of the immense complexity of modern states, developed to a climax of absurdity, I believe that the days of states are numbered.' Brushing aside its claims to regulate industrial society, Bakunin identified every strong state with a despotic lust, which cannot do otherwise than mutilate its subjects mentally and morally. He saw this exemplified in the powerful post-1871 German Empire. 'The further expansion of this German *highest good* is the main striving of Mr. Marx, who tries to repeat, for his own profit, through the medium of the *International*, the feats and victories of Bismarck. That pan-German reaction, in the art of disguising despotic actions under liberal democratic masks, has outdone its teacher, Napoleon III' (*My Personal Relations with Marx*).[1]

It exasperated Bakunin that people could discuss the advent of international solidarity, while they wanted to preserve the nation-state—'Is not that to dream about the universal state, i.e. universal slavery, the old dream of the great Emperors and Popes. . . . Of course between the politics of Bismarck and those of Marx there is a difference, but between the Marxians and ourselves lies an abyss. . . . I detest Communism because it concentrates the strength of society in the hands of the state, which ruinously squanders that strength in its service, whereas my principle is the abolition of the state, which has perpetually enslaved, exploited, and depraved mankind under the pretext of making it more moral and civilized.'

Bakunin accused the Communists of fraud when they claimed to be internationally representative. For, strictly speaking, their membership was confined to Germans—or to people mesmerized

---

[1] V. Polonsky, *Materialy*, vol. 3, pp. 287 et seq.

by a German intellectual spell—whereas the majority of revolutionaries in Italy, France and Spain, the Swiss Jura, Belgium and Holland, plainly preferred the more impulsive Anarchist school—not to mention the Slav peoples, who demonstrated, whenever they got the chance, that they stuck to their own brand of local autonomy.

Between these two schools of socialism, as much as between the rival nations which adopted them, no reconciliation could take place. Argument, negotiation, compromise, presuppose some bond of common interest, or neutral territory. But neither existed between the Bakuninists and Marxians. If concessions were made by either side, they could only be tactical moves in a constant war, which could not end till one side had unconditionally surrendered to the other. The desperately resolute Bakunin, who wrote *The Knouto-German Empire and International Socialism*, embodied a new phase, as far removed from the mystical Slavophil who confessed his sins to Nicholas I, as from the doctrinaire conspirator, who once proudly called himself a follower of Marx.

Learned economists have recognized the strain of 'ideological Darwinism' in Marx, who frankly admired Darwin, and compared his 'survival of the fittest' in nature with the history of the class-struggle in society. But Bakunin's attitude had grown equally intransigent. He demanded a fight to the finish. Marx had declared war against the Slavs with a vehemence and exactitude which stimulated Bakunin's appetite for drastic retaliation.

XI

Apart from wounding Bakunin and Herzen by spreading the baseless rumour that they were Russian government spies, Marx was blind to any basic difference between pan-Slavs and cultured Slavophils, or between Russian liberals and revolutionaries. He was haunted by Russian state expansion.

'In the studies of some dilettantes of historical science', he wrote, 'has arisen that clumsy anti-historical movement, which aims at the subjugation of the civilized West to the barbaric East, of towns to the country, of industry and commerce to the primitive agricultural knowledge of Slavonic slaves. And beyond this theory lies the terrifying reality of the Russian Empire . . . that Empire which for the last one hundred and fifty years, thanks to all the wars which it began, has never lost but constantly gained territory' (*Daily Tribune*, 25 March 1852).

Marx referred to the gradual Russian conquest of the Caucasus, Central Asia, and Siberia, accompanied by Russian colonization of vast new territories. But unlike Bismarck, he did not interpret this *eastward* expansion as diminishing the threat to Western Europe. Herzen and Bakunin were only partly right when they compared Marx to Bismarck. For Bismarck remained content to push Russia farther into Asia, provided that she renounced major European ambitions. But Marx cherished the blackest forebodings about the Russian state, in whatever direction it moved.

An extreme statement of Marxian Russophobia was made in two almost forgotten articles which Engels wrote for the *New Rhineland Gazette* in 1849.[1] 'We know now where to find the enemies of Revolution. They are in Russia, and the Slav countries of Austria. No affirmation about the democratic future of these countries, can prevent us from considering our enemies as such.' Without mincing words, the article then recommends 'a pitiless fight to the death against Slavs, traitors to revolution, a war of extermination, terror without scruple, not in the interests of Germany, but in the cause of revolution . . . the coming world war will wipe out from the face of the earth not only reactionary classes and dynasties, but reactionary peoples as a whole. That also forms a part of progress.'

To do him justice, Marx was not static in his attitude to Russia. He relaxed his prejudice enough to bestow high praise on Chernyshevsky, and he took a less jaundiced view of Russian possibilities when he started his friendly correspondence with *narodnik* leaders in the eighteen-seventies. He none the less pronounced it to be an irony that the Russians, against whom he had

---

[1] Quoted B. P. Hepner, *Bakunin et le Panslavisme Révolutionnaire*, pp. 280-1, Paris, 1950.

fulminated for so long, were his persistent admirers, and the first foreigners to translate his *Kapital*.

The clash of temperaments between the rivals was more decisive than their conflict of ideas. In his *My Personal Relations with Marx* (1871), Bakunin explained their underlying enmity with precise detachment. He conceded that Marx was immensely learned, devoᵗed to the proletarian cause, and provided the motive force behind the *International*. But every medal has its reverse side. ... Bakunin found that Marx suffered from three major defects:

(1) Like most professional learned men, he was a doctrinaire, who despised the whole world from the height of his science. 'He seriously regards himself as the Pope of socialism.'

(2) Therefore he hated not only the bourgeoisie, but all people, including socialists, who dared to oppose any of his opinions.

(3) He was pathologically vain and jealous. 'Anyone who has the misfortune to injure his morbid vanity will turn Marx into an implacable enemy. ... He is ready to lie, to invent and circulate disgusting slanders. He called me a sentimental idealist—and he was right—I called him a treacherous, cowardly, and vain pan-German—and I was also right.' He observed that Marx loved his own person more than he loved any of his friends or disciples, for no friendship with him had withstood the slightest wound to his vanity. He therefore liked to surround himself with insignificant *yes-men* and flatterers.

'One may rightly say,' he concluded, 'that within the circle of Marx's intimates there is little brotherly frankness, but plenty of intrigue and diplomacy. Everyone stands on his guard for fear of being made a scapegoat. The whole of Mark's *entourage* conducts a plot for securing the best places within it, a silent struggle to find some compromise between the self-loves of the various persons concerned.' [1] Though Marx has a big intellect, he is 'a disgusting character; vain, irritable, envious, treacherous, and a terrific intriguer, like all Jews'.[2]

The last word of Marx, as of the whole social democratic

---

[1] V. Polonsky, *Materialy*, vol. 3, p. 299 et seq., M.L., 1923–33.
[2] ibid., p. 265.

school—was the concealed despotism of a ruling minority, disguised as the organ of a so-called majority will. But this minority, Marxians say, will consist of labouring men. . . . 'Yes, perhaps, but *former* labourers, as soon as they turn into rulers and representatives, cease to be artisans, begin to despise the whole labouring class, no longer represent the common people but merely their own claims to rule it. Whoever doubts this, cannot know human nature.'

The *élite* will be a set of *scientific socialists*. That phrase constantly recurs in the writings of Marx and Lassalle. But Marxians, knowing that the rule of learned men must turn into the most oppressive, humiliating, and contemptible government in the world, despite its democratic forms, console us with the thought that this dictatorship will be temporary and brief. 'We answer, no dictatorship can have any other goal than to perpetuate itself. . . . A state must continually devour, in order not to be devoured, conquer in order not to be conquered. There is no cruelty, sacrilege, deceit, robbery, or dirty treachery, which it will not commit in its own interest. It sucks people's blood like a vampire.'

The polarity between Bakunin and Marx acquired a fresh intensity during the Franco-Prussian War (1870). Marx, falling into the role of a German patriot, called the German invasion of France a defensive war on Germany's part, and argued that through a Prussian victory German state power would grow more concentrated, 'which will be useful for the centralization of the German working class'. Bakunin, on the contrary, lamented the misfortune which had overtaken 'that attractive, fine, and noble national character, that lucid French mind. . . .'

In the consolidation of Germany, hailed with patriotic enthusiasm by Prussian junkers and labourers alike, he saw the devastating march of military government. It heralded the triumph of German officers, nothing more civilized than formalities, and 'that special kind of officers' arrogance, showing servility to whatever stands higher in their hierarchy, and impudent contempt to whatever, in their view, stands lower—above all to ordinary people, and to anyone who does *not* wear a uniform. . . . Look at this civilized beast, this lackey by conviction, and executioner by training ... —a modest blond youth, but proud and senti-mental. He knows Schiller and Goethe by heart—the whole great humanist literature of this century has passed through his head, without depositing a single human thought or feeling in his soul.' [1]

After the Franco-Prussian War, during the rebellion at Lyons, which started a short-lived local commune, Bakunin rushed to throw in his lot with the insurgents. But he wrote from there in 1871: 'I begin to think that France is finished. She will turn into a German province ... she will succumb to the doctrinaire socialism of the Germans, who can say only as much as German bayonets will permit.' After the collapse of the Paris com-mune, he observed with alarm the resigned indifference of French workmen, the way in which they shrugged their shoulders in acquiescence to the dictates of the Third Republic. He could only prescribe a stronger dose of his old medicine; the French needed to be shaken by more shattering calamities, restored to life by formidable traumatic shocks. Bakunin was reluctant to face the truth that people less restless than himself had grown sick of revolutionary turmoil, and were more likely to be stunned than stimulated by continuing to live on a volcano. He urged that the anarchist advance-guard must work and expand, 'in order to be ready when the demon awakes'.

In 1869 the notorious Nechaev had escaped from Russia to Switzerland, where he met Bakunin, whose own talent for make-believe he almost surpassed. Bakunin became enthusiastic about his energetic young recruit, whom he affectionately nicknamed 'Boy'. Nechaev, who styled himself the plenipotentiary of a Russian revolutionary committee (which did not exist at all), received from Bakunin authority to act in Russia as a representa-tive of the latter's equally non-existent European Revolutionary Alliance. Bakunin is believed to have been the joint author of Nechaev's *Revolutionary Catechism*, composed during their friendly association in 1869. It defined the model revolutionary type in no uncertain terms: 'For him every action is moral,

[1] V. Cherkezov, *Izbrannye Sochineniya*, vol. 1, pp. 160 et seq., Petrograd, 1919.

provided it promotes the revolution . . . all soft enervating feelings of personal relationship, love, gratitude, or honour, must be conquered in him by a cold passion for the revolutionary cause.'

Not till Nechaev fled from Switzerland, after stealing a number of personal papers belonging to Bakunin, Natalie Herzen, and Ogaryov (in case he might want to blackmail their owners), did Bakunin awake to the fact that his friend frankly practised what he preached. Shortly after his return to Russia (November 1869) Nechaev murdered a student, called Ivanov, whom he suspected of disloyalty to the 'cause'. The lesson taught him by this sinister young man seems for the first time to have shattered Bakunin's more ambiguous beliefs. In a letter to his friend Tallandier, he honestly summed up his revised estimate of Nechaev, in whom he now saw a disastrous embodiment of his own teaching.

'He is a devoted but dangerous fanatic, an alliance with whom must be fatal for everybody. To start with, he worked for a secret society. Now this society exists no more, for all its members have been arrested. Nechaev alone incorporates the society, tries to create a wider organization abroad, and the way in which he sets about it is detestable. Obsessed by the catastrophe which overtook his Russian organization, he convinced himself that in order to build up an *indestructible* society, he must imitate the policy of Machiavelli and incorporate the system of the Jesuits— for the body unlimited violence, for the soul a network of lies.' [1] Among other projects he wanted to direct a gang of thieves and brigands in Switzerland, to seize money for financing his cause. 'He will read your correspondence, steal a compromising letter in order to blackmail you. . . . He will seduce a young girl, and get her with child, solely in order to cut her adrift from conventional morality.'

Bakunin had hardly championed 'conventional morality' when he advocated burning to the ground town-halls and castles, destroying title deeds to property, suppressing 'stupid journals', and all manifestations of 'chattering anarchy'; but he was less sure about murder or political assassination, and he drew the line at

[1] M. Bakunin, *Correspondance*, ed. M. Dragomanov, p. 326, Paris, 1896.

fraud and blackmail. He condemned attempts being made in Russia to stir up peasant revolts by issuing forged manifestos from the Tsar. And the cynical criminal he had discovered in his young hero, Nechaev, shocked him to the core. 'We must understand at last,' he ended his letter, 'that on Jesuit lies nothing solid or lively can be built, that revolutionary action can never thrive or find support on vile and base passions.' [1]

If Bakunin's entanglement with Nechaev reveals him as a poor judge of character, its sequel does credit to him in facing the consequences of his amazing gullibility. His attitude both to fellow revolutionaries and rivals became much calmer. When Marx, after planning his expulsion from the *International*, followed this up by a malicious pamphlet, featuring a lurid version of the Nechaev episode, Bakunin decided that the time had come for him to make a statement revising his conclusions up to date. 'All this business', he announced, in September 1873, 'has disgusted me profoundly with public affairs. After fighting all my life, I am tired out. I am over sixty, and a heart disease makes my lot still harder. I no longer feel within myself the strength, and perhaps the necessary faith, to go on. . . . I am therefore retiring from the field of battle, and now ask from my dear contemporaries only one boon, oblivion. Henceforth I shall trouble no man's peace, and all I ask in my turn is to be left in peace. . . .' [2]

A letter, which he wrote in the same year to the *Fédération Jurassienne*, contained the following words: 'The last nine years have seen the development within the *International* of more ideas than are necessary for the salvation of the world, if indeed the world can be saved by ideas, and I defy anybody to invent a new one. . . . It is no longer a time for ideas, but a time for deeds and facts.' [3] Meanwhile Bakunin had retired to a villa near Lugano, and no longer worried about shaping world affairs.

Nevertheless Bakuninist 'cells' were spreading within Russia, and outstanding *narodniks*, like Axelrod and Vera Zasulich, claimed to be his followers. They had obeyed his earlier call: 'Leave your universities and academies. Go to the people.

[1] op. cit., p. 379.
[2] V. Polonsky, *Materialy*, vol. 3, p. 434.   [3] ibid., p. 437.

Remember, friends, that educated youth cannot presume to act as teachers, benefactors, or dictatorial guides, but merely as agents to release the people's own energy and efforts.' Yet he was not much exhilarated by his belated success in Russia. Three years before his death he wrote: 'Russians have always distinguished themselves by their herd-like behaviour. At present they are all anarchists. But the fashion for anarchy is passing, and after a few years there will not be a single anarchist left among them.' [1] Time has proved him to be more right than wrong in this prediction.

Die-hards still urged that the true anarchist should pluck stimulus from defeat, be spurred towards untried methods of achieving an anti-authoritarian society—but was it not demanding the impossible from disciples, when even the master had abandoned the vain struggle? For though Bakunin's efforts formed the minds of many Russian revolutionaries, all his attempts to stir up revolts had ignominiously petered out. He recognized this situation when he wrote from Switzerland to his friend Elysée Reclus: 'To my despair I have discovered, and discover every day anew, that the masses have absolutely no revolutionary idea, or hope or passion; and where these are absent, you can work as hard as you like, but obtain no result whatsoever.' [2]

Bakunin also recognized how his hold over European labour organizations had been handicapped by foisting on them underground practices peculiar to their Russian counterparts. Such loyalty as he retained from workmen, sprang from a personal sympathy, which had little to do with his stormy doctrines. The astonishing devotion of the Italian workmen who came to visit him at his villa near Lugano, and worked for him without a wage, testified to the spell which he still cast over simple people.[3] He died there in June 1876.

Bakunin's old national feud with Marx flared up in an unexpected form after the October Revolution (1917), when German Marxians began to accuse the Bolsheviks of desecrating the honour of their worthy compatriot, Marx, by having dragged him

[1] M. Bakunin, *Sbornik Statyei*, p. 220, Moscow, 1920.
[2] Quoted, E. H. Carr, *Michael Bakunin*, p. 478.
[3] A. Bauler, *Bakunin, Byloe*, June 1907.

in as their patron saint. 'Defend our dead friend against such an insult to his memory . . . This world revolution would have found from its very beginning no more determined opponent than Marx. His political goal was always a democracy, and never an Asiatic despotism, whereas the Bolsheviks, supporters of the Soviet system, are in reality followers of the anarchist Bakunin.' [1]

[1] W. Blos, *Marx oder Bakunin? Demokratie oder Diktatur?*, Stuttgart, 1920.

CHAPTER III

IVAN TURGENEV

I

IN an age of discriminating literary taste and stricter morals, Ivan Turgenev (1818–83) began to touch the hearts of West European readers as a master of sensitive limpid language, an exquisite and thoughtful story-teller, the most urbanely international and highly civilized, the least uncouthly *Russian*, of the somewhat bear-like literary Titans, who sprang to life in nineteenth-century Russia. Partly through this reassuring capacity for being at home in good society everywhere, and because he showed himself to be an artist with a strong social conscience, he charmed educated Europeans of the late nineteenth and early twentieth centuries, who felt a closer kinship with him than with the sternly exacting, monumental Tolstoy, and who recoiled from the feverish pathological strain permeating Dostoyevsky.

Nevertheless, despite his warm reception as a writer of international import and his own sense of belonging to the Western world, Turgenev was dominated by deeply personal traits, by a single overpowering love, by a nostalgia for the Russian countryside, and by a constant self-effacement which submitted to the moral despotism exerted by his home environment, although he loathed his country's politics.

His acutely responsive temperament neither shaped nor strove to alter human minds, but drew the substance that he wanted to embody from the fleeting impressions and controversies of his day. Yet he managed to transform this personal weakness and self-surrender into a rare measure of imaginative strength and truthfulness, which have made his literary work survive the test of time.

Most of his novels, and a number of his stories, incorporate with an alert sense of duty the social problems uppermost in his

I. S. TURGENEV

from a photograph

country when he was writing.[1] Some of his literary notes refer to his characters as carefully chosen specimens of contemporary types. His concern, to catch and record in flight the rapidly changing pattern of Russian society, has been quite correctly emphasized in recent Soviet comment on Turgenev. Soviet critics, having awarded him the commendable label of 'critical realist', have jumped to the conclusion that he found grave fault with his surroundings (what honest writer in any age does *not*?), and tend to interpret his sympathy with active idealists of his day as a proof that he supported the aims, if not the methods, of later political revolutionaries.

Luckily, great redeeming virtues saved Turgenev from sinking to the banal level of the controversial publicist in fiction— above all, his disturbingly lucid mind, his fastidious sense of beauty and harmonious proportion, and the fact that he drew his literary characters from models he had met in life, and never created heroic puppets voicing ready-made ideas. No doubt his contemporary Chernyshevsky hated serfdom in theory as profoundly as Turgenev did from personal experience, but since he knew neither serfs nor their masters intimately, a taste of sterile bitterness remains after his eloquent indignation has evaporated. Chernyshevsky's vituperative articles could never conquer the lasting impression conveyed by *A Sportsman's Sketches*, which distilled the poignant mixed emotions of Turgenev's childhood and youth, spent on his mother's estate at Spasskoe.

His acute intelligence forced him to be honest and always to see beyond the agitated moment of which he formed a part. Then his unerring sense of measure made him the heir of Pushkin in demonstrating that the art of writing must master the auxiliary art of abbreviation, of turning long-drawn-out, shapeless, or irrelevant experience into sharp and vivid verbal patterns.

Harassed by the parade of pretentious gossip, dry pedantry, or deceitful self-justification, which discouragingly accompanied the spread of literacy in his time, pained by the spiteful and venomous personal disputes which topical literature engendered, he

---

[1] See I. S. Turgenev, *Polnoe Sobranie Sochineniy*, St. Petersburg, 1898; *Sobranie Sochineniy*, Moscow, 1949.

F

constantly asked himself Faust's leading question: '*Was ist der langen Rede kurzer Sinn?*' ('What is the short sense of that lengthy speech?') He pursued evocative brevity with so much zeal and skill, that his best novels and stories are packed with a tenser concentration than similar works by his contemporaries, who, with all their talent, rarely rid themselves of rambling long-windedness. Chekhov alone surpassed him later in that mastery, but Chekhov had also learned a lot from him.

II

Turgenev's father, a handsome, charming, and impecunious cavalry officer, had married for money an ugly but energetic heiress six years older than himself. Neither the capricious and abnormally vindictive mother, nor her elegant, aloof husband, who habitually talked to their own children in French, knew how to educate them, still less how to win their hearts. The young Ivan, who lived in terror of his mother, might have loved his father, had the latter not kept him subtly at a distance. But he found the warm companionship and affection, for which he craved, among his mother's house-serfs, victims of the same arbitrary punishments and outbursts of savage temper, which darkened his own childhood.

In 1838 he left Russia for the first time, determined to gather useful knowledge from abroad. He went to study philosophy at Berlin University, although, he wrote later, 'neither Belinsky, nor I, were really philosophers at all, and we were unable to think in that abstract German manner—in any case we were trying to find in philosophy everything in the world except pure thought'. He observed that the yearnings of his puzzled contemporaries, to find guidance and help from foreign countries, curiously resembled the search made long ago by ancient Slavs, to select better rulers for themselves from among foreign Varangian Vikings. Like their remote ancestors, the more sensitive young men of his day recognized with humiliation that their country, although 'great and abundant' remained unhappily 'devoid of order'. 'So I flung myself head foremost into that German ocean, required to purify and revive me, and when at last I emerged from its waves, I found myself a *Westernizer*, and so I have always remained' (*Literary Recollections*, 1868).

When Turgenev returned from Germany to Russia in 1842, he took a post in the Ministry for Internal Affairs, where he composed a thoughtful memorandum, entitled *Some Remarks on the Russian Economy and the Russian Peasant*, which, however, attracted no attention. He soon lost patience with the humdrum civil service, and resigned from it, without rising higher in the hierarchy than the lowest rank of Collegiate Assessor. The university professorship in Petersburg, which he had hoped vaguely to obtain, failed to materialize. So he turned into an unattached man of letters, enjoying long philosophic conversations with his friend, Belinsky, and paying court to the magnificent singer, Pauline Garcia Viardot, whose compelling art and personality together had enthralled him on her first visit to Petersburg in 1843.

The beginning of this life-long infatuation, added to his impetuous retirement from the civil service, roused the anger of his mother, who took her revenge by abruptly cutting off his monetary allowance. For the first time Turgenev experienced acute poverty, and was obliged to borrow money from his friends. He none the less managed to follow the Viardot family when they returned to France, and stayed with them at their country home in Courtavenel. When the 1848 revolution broke out, he hurried to Paris. But in his *Recollections* he revealed with a blend of calm adult judgement and firm revulsion how far these stormy events belied his expectations. The course of recent history had proved to him that men did not yet deserve that fuller civic freedom for which they vainly craved. He was more impressed by the nonchalant vendors of chocolate and tobacco, who did brisk business with the excited crowds, while armed artisans mounted barricades in the streets of Paris.

Though enslaved by his love for Madame Viardot, which she coolly permitted, without reciprocating it, Turgenev felt another motive impelling him to go abroad in 1847. He had begun to hate the air he breathed in Russia, and had to put a wider distance between himself and his mortal enemy, serfdom, in order to attack that enemy, and thereby fulfil his solemn 'Hannibal's oath'. Even as Gogol took refuge in Rome before he could compose *Dead Souls*, so Turgenev, as he declared, might never have collected the mental force required to write *A Sportsman's Sketches*, had he remained in Russia.

His mother died in 1850, an unrepentant tyrant to the last, grimly unreconciled with both her sons, whom she nearly disinherited. Lying on her deathbed, she ordered her serf orchestra to play the gayest minuets and polkas in an adjoining room, and instructed her bailiff to sell every scrap of her property at any price, to burn down the whole house, if necessary. Nevertheless, Turgenev, and his surviving brother, were lucky enough to inherit a substantial fortune. It conferred on him the inestimable advantage of being able henceforth to write at leisure, on serious themes of his own choosing, which he could work out with sincerity and devoted care, regardless of popularity or financial profit, although both later came his way—the more gratifyingly through being unsolicited.

A Sportsman's Sketches (1851) conjured up in the most vivid and delicately suggestive prose the strangely original characters and intimate atmosphere of the country districts which he knew and loved from childhood. The book made him famous overnight, chiefly because it revealed attractive human qualities in serfs, at a moment when many intelligent Russians felt apprehensive and conscience-stricken about serfdom, and when heartfelt sympathy was joining with plain economic self-interest to work in favour of their liberation. The book is said to have convinced the impressionable Alexander II (then Crown Prince) that his first duty must be to emancipate the serfs.

Undeniably the serf characters, even when hopelessly degraded, emerge as nobler human beings than any of their masters, though always through limpid narrative pictures, undisturbed by any attempt to assault the reader's mind with sentimental sermons. Yet these extraordinary personalities are far from average specimens of their class, and some show an ominous premonition that the peasant, the moment he has ceased to be a serf, may rapidly succumb to the worst temptations which beset a freeman. Certainly the forester ex-serf Biryuk treats the erring peasants with more sadistic savagery and contempt than the most ruthless landlord's bailiff.

Khor, the prosperous self-made yeoman in the story *Khor and Kalinich*, an industrious tiller of the soil and tradesman, had skilfully won independence from the commune, and cut off his obligations to his master—yet he remained by his own wish juridically a serf, because he shrewdly preferred to deal with one landlord, whom he knew, than to be at the mercy of a crowd of anonymous officials, whom he could never know.

The prominence which Turgenev assigns to Khor may partly serve to set him up as an exemplary *success story*, for properly aspiring peasants to emulate. Yet he is a hard, calculating, almost cynical man, less attractive than his poor friend, Kalinich, who charms by his happy unselfish nature and gentle face, 'clear as the evening sky'. The serfs who are least absorbed in promoting their material advancement remain the most lovable and striking characters, even when their uncritical loyalty and devotion appear wasted on unworthy masters. We are touched by the modest Yermolai who, without hesitation and although he could not swim, threw himself into the water the moment his master ran the risk of being drowned.

But when he followed up his scrupulous desire to do full justice to long-suffering serfs, Turgenev sometimes overshot the mark. He drew a veil over squalid scenes of violence in the villages, when a wild brute would take possession of the steadiest peasant. With discreet *Victorian* reticence he soft-pedalled the final drunken orgy in his fine story *The Singers*. And he never finished his projected sketch *The Eater of Earth*, which told how revengeful serfs seized their greedy master, and devised an appropriate death for him by forcing down his throat eight pounds of good black earth (a story plausible enough, and based on fact).

His sketches of provincial landlords serve chiefly as a sombre background for bizarre, picturesque and rare peasant characters. How far these petty serf-owners had departed from the majestic and lavish *grands seigneurs* who set the tone in Catherine's day! Even if they had grown slightly less uncouth and coarse than Gogol's Nozdryov or Sobachkin, they still failed to acquire either disciplined character or distinction of mind. Whether they were male or female, citizens of the world or country bumpkins, most of them remained singular specimens of moody and arbitrary egoism. Mr. Penochkin is true to type when he gives orders for his *valet-de-chambre* to be flogged in the stables, merely because the master's bottle of wine had not been warmed to the correct temperature.

Since the Napoleonic Wars, numerous Russian landlords had travelled in France and Germany, studied in foreign universities, and served conscientiously in the government departments of St. Petersburg. But though they had learned to be more amiable, argumentative, and well-informed, they rarely knew how to manage, let alone to improve, their neglected agricultural estates. The Slavophil Lyubozvonov, who had just returned from Germany, advertised his rediscovery of native patriotic virtue by growing a long beard and walking about in a coachman's boots, *kaftan*, and red high-necked shirt. His puzzled peasants watched him with silent amazement when he called them together and invited them to join him in singing a good old Russian song. Meanwhile the bailiff took advantage of his eccentric employer to fleece the serfs more thoroughly than before. Although they grumbled, they endured their hardships with fortitude, and they still preferred a severe, business-like master to a milder one, whom they immediately suspected and despised, as being weak or foolish.

Despite his westernizing zeal, Turgenev came closer to those purely moral Slavophils, who linked the desperate poverty of the peasants with their master's vain desire to keep abreast of Western fashions. Extravagant and snobbish tastes in dress, entertainment, and ostentatious luxury, imported from abroad, estranged the Russian gentleman still further from the simple people for whose welfare he remained responsible. And when they gave full rein to their expensive European whims, the richest landlords could ruin their large estates.

Several fantastic contrasts occurring in this upper layer of

Russian Europe emerged in the novel *A Nobleman's Nest* (1858).
Lavretsky's father, a confirmed Anglomaniac, forced his only son
to eat raw meat, perform Spartan physical exercises every morning, and to run about bare-legged, wearing a Scotch cap adorned
with a cock's feather. Though he referred to his son proudly as
'the child of nature created by me', the boy was the chief victim of
the harsh divergence between his father's generous all-embracing
theories and the pettifogging tyranny which he practised in his
home. The head of the inexperienced young Spartan was easily
turned by the first seductive whiff of Western Europe which
he encountered. For his vampirish Russian wife turned out to
be an exquisitely polished adventuress, an embodiment from
top to toe of the latest morale imported from the glittering Paris
boulevards. Even the correct and up-to-date Russian civil servant
Panshin is unmasked as a conceited, heartless, and superficially
Frenchified snob.

Only the more naïve Germanophils of the early eighteen-
thirties escape the trenchant satire which Turgenev lavished on
Russian Francophils and Anglomaniacs. The old German musician, Lemm, is a lonely, gifted figure and a loyal friend, and
equally good is that pathetic admirer of the German philosopher
Schelling, the father of Berseniev (in the novel *On the Eve*), who
devoted his whole life to writing a single intricate philosophical
book, of which nobody could understand a word, but on his
deathbed told his only son: 'I hand over the torch to you; hold
it, my friend, until the end comes!'

Here again, Turgenev's Slavophil strain betrayed no trace of
chauvinist antiquarianism or self-centred patriotic arrogance, but
firmly pleaded for a wiser, more discriminating mode of selecting
and learning from the West. Why pick out all the poisonous
rubbish when nourishing food remained in plenty? In any case it
was now too late for Russians to retreat from exciting temptations
offered by the outside world. On that crucial point even the
Slavophil Lavretsky agreed with his Western opponent Panshin:
'We have fallen ill because we are still no more than half Europeans; we can cure ourselves only by taking a stronger dose of
what has harmed us!'

III

The metaphysical riddles and bewilderment which afflicted Turgenev's youth had quite calmed down when, at the age of thirty-five, in the rural tranquillity of Spasskoe, he composed his first novel, *Rudin* (1855). This over-educated rootless hero shares some of his author's personal characteristics, notably his fastidious taste and high-pitched tenor voice, but he is chiefly drawn from the ups and downs of Turgenev's Berlin friendship with Bakunin, a man in whom abnormal emotional instability was fatally combined with a passion to dominate other people's minds.[1] Rudin, like Bakunin, had mastered the born orator's gift of rousing a transient glow of enthusiasm in his hearers' hearts, but he shared the orator's notorious incapacity to grasp and pursue consequences which should have followed from his alluring words. He could inspire a virtuous young lady to run away with him, but was then horrified to go one step further with her. Any fascinated listener of Rudin's might fail to perceive what his glorious eloquence was driving at, and yet the heart expanded and 'something radiant would blaze up in front of him'.

Rudin stirred people from their apathy and mechanical routine, lifted them for a moment out of themselves, but he lacked substantial character or pertinacity. Therefore his disillusioned admirers later turned against him, and cursed him as a hypocrite or charlatan, who had tricked them. In fact, he could not follow any prolonged course of action, simply because 'he had no vital faith, no fire in the blood'. Yet his friend Lejnyov did more justice to him; when seeking for the hidden best, he generously passed over ingrained defects, and pointed to one redeeming quality in Rudin: 'He has enthusiasm, and believe me, that is the most precious quality in our time. We have all become so insufferably reasonable, indifferent, and sluggish; we are asleep and chilled; and we should thank anyone who stirs us up and warms us, even for one moment. . . . Who has the right to say that he has not been of use, that his words have not scattered good seeds

[1] See I. S. Turgenev, *Materialy i Issledovaniya*, ed. N. Brodsky, p. 118, Orel, 1940.

in young hearts, to whom nature has not denied, as she did to him, the ability to fulfil their good intentions?'

In 1856, after having lived apart from Madame Viardot for six years, Turgenev returned to make his home with the Viardot family in France. He appears to have found there again the short-lived happiness which he had experienced during his visits to Courtavenel in 1847 and 1850. But later in the same year he departed for Rome, where he conceived and partly wrote *A Nobleman's Nest*.

Lavretsky, the hero of this novel, is a more fully rounded, sympathetic, and adult character than the insubstantial Rudin. Even when he had renounced the empty search for personal happiness, he did not dwindle into an elegant idler or a thwarted, nomadic rhetorician, but returned from educative travels to settle down and till his native soil. Although he felt attached to the vegetation, sounds and scents of the Russian land, rather than to its human inhabitants, he could claim to be a more honest and useful citizen than the showy official Panshin, whose trite Western catchwords sounded hollow when he argued with the quiet Lavretsky.

No other novel of Turgenev's draws a sharper contrast between his two favourite and recurrent types of Russian woman. The gentle, self-effacing but strong-minded Liza (a successor to Pushkin's Tatyana), confronted with the polished and seductive Varvara Petrovna, Lavretsky's wife, can hardly conceal her inward horror. Varvara introduced herself to Liza with the mincing mannerisms of a Paris courtesan, and impudently asked her to be 'kind'. 'The expression of her face as she pronounced this word, her sly smile, her cold but caressing look, the movement of her hand and shoulders, her dress, her pale mauve gloves, her whole being—roused such a feeling of repulsion in Liza, that she could not answer a single word.'

Turgenev's mastery of pregnant reticence, of an art whereby the unwritten words and moods evoked by what is written, convey a fourth dimension of meaning to the reader, approaches perfection in this novel. No wonder that he recoiled from the

pages of psychological excavation indulged in by his contemporary Dostoyevsky. ('My God, what sour stuff, the stench of a
sickroom, needless mutterings!', he wrote about the *Raw Youth*
in 1875.) For his own characters revealed themselves sufficiently
either by their deeds, or by the marked contrast between promising words and commonplace behaviour. Since for him another
person's soul must always remain 'a dark forest', he shrank from
any superfluous attempt to probe with cold scientific fingers the
inmost depths of human personality. It seemed to him senseless
and disgusting to drag into the broad light of day, and dissect
under a microscope, what no microscope could possibly discern.
Inscrutable feelings would be no less powerful when they were
only pointed to and passed by, like those of Liza buried alive in
that convent, when she saw Lavretsky standing at the service in
the aisle.

In his next novel, *On the Eve* (1860), Turgenev responded
to agitated discussions of the eighteen-fifties, which challenged
public-spirited writers to create at last a forceful and salutary picture of idealists in action. Whether in literature or life, the critics
repeatedly complained, a surfeit had been reached of sensitive but
ineffective characters, beating in the void their luminous wings
in vain. And the majority of these critics, who had fallen under
Chernyshevsky's spell, urged self-respecting authors to find
some resolute literary heroes, whose worthy aspirations need
not rob them of healthy common sense and will-power.

The dedicated young Russian lady, Elena, and her Bulgarian
patriot, Insarov, provide Turgenev's answer. But although the
novel is permeated by that intense spiritual atmosphere peculiar
to Turgenev, its major characters, far from revealing a labour of
love, appear to have been created from a sombre sense of duty,
and suffer from defects attendant on the author's concealed
struggle to fulfil uncongenial obligations. 'Here they are, the
heroes you want so badly,' he seems to say, a trifle wearily;
'admire them if you can!'

Tolstoy shrewdly observed that in this novel Turgenev showed
no sign of being carried away by his own major characters, as he
had been in *A Nobleman's Nest*, and that he succeeded better

with the minor and negative ones, with whom he felt at home. 'There are in this book excellent *negative* types,' Tolstoy noted, 'especially the artist and the father . . . but the girl is hopelessly bad. Turgenev shows no humanity, or sympathy with his creations; he exhibits monsters whom he scolds, but does not pity. This jars painfully on the tone and intention of liberalism, which he aims at in every other way' (Letter, 1861).

The modern reader may dislike Elena as heartily as Tolstoy did, and yet he must admit that she shows a keen spirit and lively mind, despite her morbidly *exalté* temperament. Even if her craving to render service borders on the pathological, that abnormality was not without a cause. Emotionally frustrated, haunted by obscure desires, she had idolized her parents each in turn, and afterwards cooled down towards them both, when she saw how far they fell below her expectations. She next befriended beggars and sick people, took under her protection hungry dogs, unwanted kittens, sparrows which had fallen out of their nests. She would rush to rescue flies caught in a spider's web. Her father laughed at her and teased her. She made no more intimate friends, except a beggar girl, who soon died of fever. But the same thought continued to torment her: 'How can one go on living without love, but who is there to love?'

Neither her conventional parents, nor her young admirers, the self-indulgent artist Shubin, and the good-natured but dreary student Berseniev, could arouse in her that boundless devotion, which she felt capable of giving. She could never love such people in the way she needed, nor could she accept inferior substitutes.

In the preface to the first collected edition of his works, Turgenev explained the factual genesis of this novel.[1] A country neighbour of his, a shy and eccentric young man called Karateyev, had brought to him a manuscript before leaving to take part in the Crimean War. He modestly begged Turgenev to read what he had written, and then to honour him by using it any way he wanted.

In Karateyev's story a Russian girl falls in love with a fervent

[1] *Polnoe Sobranie*, vol. 3, p. v, St. Petersburg, 1880.

Bulgarian nationalist, and later travels back with him to his own country. Reading this, Turgenev suddenly exclaimed: 'Here at last is the hero I have been looking for.' He needed only to shape a theme which had fallen ready-made into his hands. That unexpected Bulgarian solved his problem, of finding a Slav personality, endowed to overflowing with exemplary civic virtues, strength of will and single-mindedness, preached so indefatigably by leading critics.

Insarov became credible in the shape of a *Bulgarian*, simply because such high-minded political fanatics were not yet flourishing on Russian soil. But did they, on closer scrutiny, seem quite desirable anywhere? Turgenev delineated Insarov with more painstaking veracity than enthusiasm. When critics reproached him for making his hero an artificial wooden creature, he defended him by explaining tersely that he had probably given to Insarov as much reality as he deserved.

Cadaverous, angular, with a hollow chest and thin hard lips, he would never conquer hearts by a handsome physique or cheerful strength. Insarov embodied a new type of *intellectual hero*, a man of action (if we must use the hackneyed term), but ruled by a single *idée fixe*, to liberate his country from its Turkish overlords. He is equally devoid of charm, of flexibility in reasoning, or spontaneous feeling, and his only serious conflict consisted in how to reconcile that ready-made patriotic goal with his unexpected love for a foreign girl. That very problem Elena conveniently solved for him, by accepting him completely, together with his Bulgarian monomania.

It was enough that he provided her with a heaven-sent outlet for boundless love and work. She had refused the successful government official whom her parents wanted her to marry, and disliked him as a stubborn, empty-headed though honest 'man of iron'. She found in Insarov another man of iron, but one who immediately attracted her. Indeed he rose to importance, not on his own, but through the exhilarating, electrifying effect which he produced upon Elena. Like the superb singer whom she later heard with him in Venice, she could confidently throw away every superfluous tie, and *find herself* through her absorption in

Insarov. 'She suddenly crossed that boundary, which can never be defined, but beyond which beauty lies.'

Elena's last letter written to her parents after Insarov's death, proved that his power of moulding her destiny remained as strong as it had been during his lifetime. He still controlled her future from the grave. 'You will never see me again,' she wrote; 'yesterday Dmitri died. But I have no other country now except his country. There his people are preparing for war. I shall go to them as a nurse and look after the sick and wounded. I have learned Bulgarian and Serbian. . . . Fate has not united us in vain. Perhaps I was responsible for his death, and now it is his turn to draw me back to him. I sought happiness, and I shall find, perhaps, death. But as for returning to Russia, why should I? What is there that I can do in Russia?'

As often happens in Turgenev's stories, the minor trivial characters survive and flourish, while the stronger, more passionate ones, die young. Shubin became a successful mediocre sculptor, living comfortably in Rome, where rich American and English tourists provided him with easy conventional commissions. Berseniev, the young scholar, received a stipend to study in Heidelberg University, where he started to write historical articles with involved titles, such as *About the Significance of the Urban Principle in the Problem of Civilization.* He wrote in a heavy pedantic jargon, thickly interspersed with foreign words and abstruse quotations, for that was the scholarly idiom encouraged by the universities.

Life had treated neither of them harshly, yet they were hardly recognizable as the two innocent young students who lay on the grass and meditated, in the opening chapter of the novel. They had devoted that expansive summer afternoon to trying to find a few magnetic words which might draw people into closer harmony, instead of aggravating the latent discord which distracted them. After Berseniev had suggested art, patriotism, science, freedom, justice, Shubin inquired lightly: 'What about love?' Berseniev admitted that love might also be a uniting word, 'but not the kind for which you thirst, not love as enjoyment, but love as sacrifice'. The more frivolous Shubin disagreed with his earnest friend, but to avoid acrimony, they changed the awkward subject, and started to talk about their eccentric Bulgarian acquaintance, Insarov. The story then began appropriately to unfold Elena's sacrificial love for him, revealing the sense of what the mild Berseniev could only hint at, for such a feat was quite beyond his range.

Turgenev's next novel, *Fathers and Children* (1861), owes its enduring fame to the enigmatic figure of Bazarov, and to the impassioned controversy which he aroused among the rival critics. It is a high tribute to Turgenev's detached artistic power that while the radical circles attacked him for descending to such a wicked caricature of 'progressive youth', Russian conservatives indignantly complained that Bazarov embodied a dangerously sympathetic portrait of their deadly enemy, the revolutionary Nihilist.

Turgenev explained later that he had based his Bazarov on a young provincial doctor, whom he met in a railway carriage, and who made an indelible impression on him. For this man suggested a *new type* of person coming to the fore, arresting and rather sinister, a sombre creature, only half emerged from barbarism, energetic and sincere, but evil, and condemned to die prematurely, because he could never go beyond the threshold of the future.

The radical critics could not grasp the fact that a good writer is bound to portray the truth remorselessly in the manner *he* has seen it, even when that truth conflicts sharply with his personal sympathies. Turgenev had made Bazarov wholly insensitive to art, not because he (the author) felt such philistine coarseness in himself, but on account of what he had candidly observed in the young doctor's temperament. Bazarov's rough disdain for Chopin and Pushkin, for the pure music and literature cherished by 'the fathers', his harsh unceremonious manners, his passion for dissecting frogs, strike Turgenev as symptoms of a nascent scientific barbarism. Yet even Bazarov had the saving grace to feel disgusted at a later stage by his own meanly technical attitude to human progress.

Though convinced on principle that any kind of love, beyond

the elementary needs of physiology, betrayed a contemptible backsliding, he none the less fell hopelessly in love with the cold and serene Madame Odintsova, and then began to hate himself for yielding to a stupid, out-of-date, 'romantic' state of mind.

Prince Kropotkin remarked acutely that although Turgenev may have admired Bazarov, even with a tinge of envy, he certainly did *not* love him. For Turgenev's involuntary fascination ought not to be confused with love. He said himself that he bore no grudge against Bazarov, and had felt drawn towards his personality, despite its harsh and ugly features. Bazarov was not a guttersnipe, and even if a pliable aristocrat may be attracted by the gutter, he need not sink into its mud. Least of all should he expect the gutter to reciprocate his tender feelings. 'How can Bazarov fail to excel the man with the perfumed moustache?' Turgenev asked. 'If I put my hand upon my heart, I feel no guilt before him, and I could not honestly provide him with useless graces. . . . It would have been easy to represent him as a mere ideal, but it was impossible to brand him as a wolf, and then to make excuses for him.'

He told his friend Lopatin later that what disturbed him most in *Fathers and Children* was that pure art no longer existed for people like Bazarov. Must one conclude that a craving to satisfy material appetites could never be reconciled with any love for beauty? The original Don Quixote, mad as he was, had at least preserved an invincible belief in the beauty of his Dulcinea, but 'the Don Quixotes of our day see plainly that their Dulcinea is a thoroughly ugly creature, and yet they continue to run after her' (Letter, 1856).

In the end Bazarov proved to be an energetic specimen of our old friend, the familiar 'superfluous man'. On his death-bed it dawns on him that revolutionaries, such as he, are of no practical use to anybody. His last desire is to see again the woman he had loved (and hated himself for loving). He begs her to kiss him, which she has never done before, and confides in her the lesson of his life: 'I also thought that I would never die until I had achieved a lot, because the task in front of me was worthy of a giant, and now the whole task of this giant consists in dying decently . . . My father will tell you how much Russia lost in me. Of course that is all rubbish, but still, don't disillusion the old man . . . So Russia needed me . . . no, clearly I was not needed. But who then remains a necessary person? The shoemaker is needed, the tailor, the butcher . . . sells meat . . .'

The critics of the eighteen-sixties and seventies complained with mounting irritation that Turgenev had lost sympathetic contact with his native land, that he failed to respond, or adapt his literary work, to the pressing needs of the rapidly changing times. Putting it more bluntly, Turgenev's sensitive writings failed to reflect the critics' monotonous social sermons. He should by then have been inured to their campaign, but it still roused him to fury when pompous busybodies pronounced in public, and with feigned regret, that their great writer had ceased to represent the living Russia.

Though Turgenev made his permanent home in Baden after 1864, and migrated to Paris after the Franco-Prussian War, he returned to visit Russia almost every year. He also met hundreds of Russians travelling abroad, including choice specimens of the younger generation, who flocked to European universities. Though he paid scant attention to the rising commercial middle class, confining himself to a few satirical sketches of them, he probably knew a wider cross-section of Russian society than most of his critics did.

Turgenev adored the gentle and orderly rhythm of life which still prevailed in small German principalities. He found the best Germans efficient, clean, modest, and attracted by ideals. So he was wont to consider that Germany, rather than France, foreshadowed the wiser, more internationally tolerant and balanced civilization of the future. His letters show that he wholeheartedly sided with the Germans at the beginning of the Franco-Prussian War.[1] But the Prussian defeat of France in 1871, followed by the overbearing behaviour of Prussians intoxicated by their victory, caused him to change his mind. The hitherto unfamiliar strain of

[1] K. Wiegand, *I. S. Turgenev's Einstellung zum Deutschtum*, p. 15, Leipzig, 1939.

German arrogance shocked him, and he deplored their annexation of Alsace-Lorraine, although he welcomed the downfall of
Louis Napoleon's flashy Second Empire.

After he had transferred his home from Germany to France
(principally on account of Madame Viardot), Turgenev began
to frequent the literary circles of Paris, where he made numerous
acquaintances, though the shy Flaubert seems to have been the
only French writer who became a close personal friend. He
remarked that the French, despite their ancient culture, remained
the most shamelessly self-centred people in the world, unmoved
by anything that happened outside the charmed circle of their
small domestic life. And the salacious anecdotes, which his
French friends repeated with such gusto, astonished him by their
cynical contempt for women. When they congratulated him on
the merits and success of his own novels, even in French trans-
lations, he was inclined to shrug his shoulders about their polished
insincerity. 'My lovers are neither gay nor voluptuous,' he remarked—'they make the reader think. But the most trivial
novel of Octave Feuillet really pleases the French more than all
mine put together!'

While Turgenev valued and acknowledged the intellectual
stimulus which he derived from Paris, French literary circles
admitted more grudgingly that they had much to learn from
him. They treated him often with a touch of patronizing con-
descension. An entry in the famous Goncourt diary remarks
how 'the sweet giant, the amiable barbarian, charmed us during
supper with his blend of naïveté and *finesse*'. Though Turgenev's
natural modesty saved him from harbouring personal resentment,
he regretfully concluded that the French had no desire to delve
deeply into the truth about important matters, let alone about the
peculiarities of Russia.

He already referred to the Paris intellectual milieu in 1856,
as 'a lifeless bustle, pretentious, vulgar, and impotent'. He failed
to find in it even sincere criticism, only 'a wretched acquiescence
with everything and everybody'. Yet he did more for a few
outstanding French writers than they ever did for him. He helped
Flaubert both materially and morally, and he went out of his

G

way to get Zola's novels and Maupassant's stories published in Russian periodicals.

IV

Smoke (1867), the most topical, but artistically the weakest and most dated of Turgenev's novels, is important as a bold gesture of revenge against the incorrigible vices of his compatriots. It satirized with equally unsparing candour the conceited bureaucratic officials, the muddled liberal and conservative nobility (which still tried to cultivate his favour) and the harsh left-wing intellectuals (who detested him for his independent standpoint). Despairing of Russia as a political entity, which went from bad to worse, Turgenev ventured to suggest that his unhappy country might vanish from the face of the earth, without provoking a sigh of regret from any quarter—that even the savage natives of the Sandwich Islands had shown more originality than natives of the Russian Empire, because they had at least invented their own canoes, whereas such national Russian products as the *knout* and the *samovar* had been derived from foreign countries. Of course these anti-national tirades unleashed furious counter-attacks against their author from numerous outraged patriotic Russians. Dostoyevsky, stirred to a characteristic frenzy, demanded that all copies of *Smoke* should be seized and burned in Russia by the public hangman.

Apart from the uniting thread of a pure love story, the novel is centred round disputes about the social state of Russia and her immediate future. The verbally indefatigable participants turn over every aspect of this hackneyed problem, until it begins to resemble a long-masticated piece of chewing gum, which has lost all juice and flavour. Among this crowd of self-indulgent talkers appears Litvinov, a quiet young landowner, who has systematically studied agriculture abroad in order to practise it at home, and deeply shocks his 'public-spirited' compatriots, by confessing to them that he has retained no *political* convictions whatsoever.

Like Turgenev himself, Litvinov found it hard to settle down to work in a country where he could never speak his mind effectively, and where police terror and revolutionary despair kept on goading each other into spasmodic outbursts. But like Lavretsky, though with more scientific knowledge, he none the less returned to till his native soil. In Baden he found the Russian generals, who held the reins of power, as negative as the revolutionary talkers had become grotesque. Both were steeped in hazy patriotic sentiment, but that was all they had in common.

While General Ratmirov showed off his graces in an elegant décor and round of fashionable duties and entertainments, the socialist Gubaryov revelled in his shallow bookish learning and trite denunciations; neither tried to find some deeper sense in the complex European culture which surrounded them. Card-games, roulette, spiritualistic séances, including serious attempts to mesmerize a crayfish, such were the pastimes of Petersburg high officials, the most edifying distractions they could find to fill their abundant leisure in a German watering-place.

Like Levin and Kitty in Tolstoy's *Anna Karenina*, Litvinov and his fiancée Tatyana impart the only enduring strain to a bored and degenerate society, where futile or destructive personalities would otherwise be overwhelming. Irina, General Ratmirov's wife, had been Litvinov's friend when she was still an obscure young girl, living in Moscow with her impoverished aristocratic parents, and he a student at the university. When he met her again in Baden, both her seductive charm, and the inward revulsion which she began to feel against the *milieu* which was slowly crushing her, combined to make Litvinov lose his head. He broke off his engagement to Tatyana, and offered to elope with Irina. Only her calculating hesitation, her reluctance to abandon the luxury and ease to which she had grown accustomed, came to his rescue in the nick of time.

He returned alone to Russia, racked of course with pangs of self-reproach, which he sought to allay by plunging into the cares of managing an estate, thoroughly neglected in his absence. He handed over a lot more land to his disgruntled peasants (although he knew that they would farm it worse than he did), started a local factory, and organized a small farm of his own, employing a few hired labourers. Eventually Tatyana pardoned him. They married and settled down. One of Turgenev's rare 'happy endings', it conjured up a small oasis of quiet industrious country life, protected from the widening wilderness created by a horde of corrupt careerists and female vampires who preyed upon them.

Tolstoy drew similar contrasting pictures between the decent, inconspicuous provincial nobility and the glittering urban vices of official St. Petersburg. Irina and Anna Karenina are both brilliant women, married, without love, to prosperous officials. The smooth comfort of Irina's life barely conceals her secret sadness. But if for a time she retained a slumbering conscience, it never grew so acute as Anna's, and her slighter capacity for love was easily exhausted. Turgenev aptly summed her up as 'that pure golden vessel already filled to the brim with poison and with mud'. In her splendid Petersburg apartment, the heavy velvet curtains, fine carpets, and subdued lighting, seemed skilfully designed to soften every strident sound or crude sensation, which might seek to enter from outside. Her drawing-room turned into a temple of muted respectability, and the conversation at her tea-parties, touching on patriotic or religious topics of the day, rarely rose above a gentle murmur. Yet people used to shake their heads and say about her: *'C'est une âme égarée.'* And her numerous admirers, whether young or old, often felt afraid of her, and of the sharp judgements which would fall unexpectedly from her lovely perfumed lips.

Potugin is in part Turgenev's mouthpiece, and the speeches where he condemns his country are devastating in their force and clarity. Nor did the patriotic storm which Turgenev aroused against himself cause him to relent one jot. More timid souls might be content to say: 'I blush for my country, and remain silent.' Turgenev, despite his habitual moderation and reserve, here spoke out boldly and without a blush. He even defended Potugin against his angry critics. 'I find that Potugin does not really speak enough, judging by the general fury which this character has aroused against me' (Letter, May 1867). Pisarev, one of the few critics who commended the biting social satire which permeated *Smoke*, reproached him for failing to move forward, for omitting any sequel to his energetic Bazarov. 'What on earth have you done with him?' he complained. 'Did the last Bazarov die in 1855, because he cut his finger?'

Turgenev knew that it had become *de rigueur* to impregnate imaginative literature with social controversies, so that deeper human strains beyond those topical concerns were likely to be pounced upon by critics as unimportant or old-fashioned. But although he had been brazenly political and topical in *Smoke*, the form it took annoyed the critics. They still hankered for a new Bazarov, while Turgenev had already left him far behind.

He explained with mounting conviction in the eighteen-seventies why the Bazarovs were no longer needed. The mountain of human history in labour had temporarily brought forth a revolutionary mouse. Not only strong, colourful, revolutionary characters, but all outstanding, sharply individual talent or intelligence, were at a discount in the period of humdrum social service which appeared to lie ahead. 'We need to know how to sacrifice ourselves without an atom of glamour or excitement, how to accept petty and obscure work without abhorrence. . . . We need nothing beyond the sense of duty. . . . Our people now need helpers rather than leaders, and only when that period is over, will powerful original personalities come into their own again. . . . The reign of mediocrity has started—we shall not see its end. . . . It is high time for us in Russia to abandon the thought of moving mountains from their places, with tremendous shattering results' (Letter, 1874).

v

Turgenev's acute controversy with Herzen in 1862–3 revealed the divergent paths which they had taken, and the sheer impossibility of their being reconciled again. Neither could now fairly be described as *liberals* in the old easy-going European sense.[1]

[1] See H. Hirshkowitz, *Democratic Ideas in Turgenev's Work*, New York, 1932.

But whereas Herzen was moving towards a mystic faith in hidden peasant virtues, Turgenev steadfastly upheld a minority of the educated class in Russia as irreplaceable champions of any civilization worth preserving. When Herzen started to idolize the peasant, it merely demonstrated to Turgenev the ecstasy of a sceptic, grown sick of his own scepticism, who now turned away his eyes and stopped his ears. Since all his earlier idols had crumbled one by one, he set up a new altar to the *sheepskin cloak*—'that *unknown God*, of whom we know next to nothing, but who simply enables us again to pray, believe, and wait'. Yet the peasants before whom Herzen bowed 'remain conservative to the core and carry within themselves all the makings of a bourgeoisie, with their stuffy, dirty huts and their reluctance to share any civic responsibility'.

'I begin to think', Turgenev wrote to Herzen, 'that in your constantly repeated contrast between the West, outwardly glittering, but ugly in soul, and the East, plain to look at, but beautiful within, there is a falsity. Russia is no Venus of Milo, chained up and maltreated by her European stepmother; she is a young girl similar to her elder sisters. . . . Even if her hips are rather wider and she is no longer . . . she will make her way in the world like the others. We Russians belong to the European family of nations by our language and our nature. Therefore, following immutable laws of physiology, we must pursue the same evolution as they have. I have never yet heard of a duck belonging to the duck species, which started to grow fins like a fish!' (Letter, November 1862).

When Herzen diagnosed the sickness of contemporary society, he tried to make Russia a unique exception to the rule elsewhere. 'You are like a doctor,' Turgenev observed, 'who after finding every symptom of a chronic illness, announces triumphantly that the patient will be cured, because he is a Frenchman! . . . The dust-storm of which you speak is not only blowing in the West; it envelops us also; but since you have lived nearly a quarter of a century outside your country, you have rebuilt another Russia in your head. . . . In my opinion, Russia is neither so young nor Europe so old as you conceive them. We are all in the same boat, and there is no romantic prospect for us Russians to pronounce unique new words. . . .

'I am no Nihilist myself because, so far as I can judge, I discern tragic features in the fate of the whole European family of nations, including Russia. None the less I remain a European, and love the banner under which I have stood ever since my youth. You, however, break it with one hand, and with the other, grope for a new banner, invisible to us.'

Though Turgenev admitted that he was by nature anything but a politician, he claimed to be ahead of Herzen in political wisdom. He had always sympathized with gradualist liberals of the old school, in the English dynastic style, yet men who expected salutary reforms to be conferred on people *from above*. He told Herzen frankly, he would rather remain wholly aloof from politics than accept a political monstrosity of the Bakunin or Ogaryov variety.

But Katkov, editor of the nationalist *Russian Messenger*, and other organs of the right-wing press, attacked him savagely for consorting with dangerous émigrés, and thereby encouraging enemies of the Russian state. In 1863 matters went so far that he received through the Russian Embassy in Paris a formal order to return to St. Petersburg, to answer serious accusations —an order reinforced by the threat that all his property would be confiscated by the Government in the event of his disobedience. He promptly wrote a personal letter to Alexander II (and sent a copy of it to Herzen) explaining that he had always pursued the disinterested career of a man of letters, had never acted as a political agent, and that he in no way shared the present extreme convictions adopted by his former friends.

He none the less returned to Russia in 1864, pleaded his case in person before the Senate, and encountered no difficulty in convincing them of his sincerity. The simple fact that he met so-called *revolutionaries* abroad from time to time, had been magnified into that kind of ominous political plot, with which zealous informers, anxious to earn their keep, liked perpetually to alarm the Russian Government. Bakunin, as usual, owed him money, and his old-womanish chatter spread the most spiteful slanders about Turgenev. Neither was Herzen mollified by Turgenev's frank letter to the Tsar. He immediately published in *The Bell* his sardonic comments on 'a grey-haired Magdalena of the male sex, whose teeth and hair have fallen out from remorse, tortured by the thought that his sovereign was unaware of the abject repentance which has made him break off relations with the friends of his youth'.

Turgenev's break with Herzen was inevitable, since he had abandoned even his liberal hopes that Russia would grow into a viable political organism, at the very time when Herzen was reverting to his mystic cult. The desperate acts of the younger revolutionaries horrified Turgenev. After Karakozov's abortive attempt to murder Alexander II in 1866, he attended a solemn thanksgiving service in Baden, and wrote to his friend Annenkov that he trembled at the thought of what might have happened to Russia, 'if that crime had succeeded'.

Yet his growing scepticism about Russia's political future in no way damped his admiration for practical idealists whom he discovered in the younger generation. In 1873, the Tsar, alarmed by the usual wildly exaggerated reports of plots hatched in foreign countries, issued a peremptory order for all the Russian female students, then studying in Swiss universities, to return home. That exodus led directly to the impulse which started educated young men and women 'going to the people'—a movement in its beginning so full of unselfish service, so little tainted with violence or sinister conspiracy against any government, that it was bound to attract Turgenev's support.

Well-bred young ladies went to work as midwives in remote villages, students of law or medicine started to live in peasant huts and learned to be woodcutters, shoemakers, or blacksmiths, at the same time as they conducted missionary educative propaganda. The future regicide, Sofia Perovskaya, daughter of a former governor of St. Petersburg, worked and dressed like an ordinary artisan's wife. The new *Elenas* no longer needed to run away with Bulgarian fanatics, or to ask hopelessly, what can we do in Russia? They found brave young compatriots to share their work, but of course they soon transgressed the law, and both sexes began to fill the Russian prisons.

When Turgenev compared Russian youth of the eighteen-seventies with the preceding generation, he found the former, especially the young girls, incomparably superior. 'They are so simple and fresh, and they know what they want,' he said. They had shed the slovenly mannerisms and loose Bohemian behaviour which had cheapened the earlier 'emancipated' generation, unforgettably caricatured by Turgenev in the figures of Madame Kukshina and Sitnikov (*Fathers and Children*). Turgenev cultivated the socialist exile Lavrov, in Paris, subscribed to his journal *Forward*, and through him met and studied many young Russian exiles. In 1879 his friend, A. Filosofov, sent him a whole collection of diaries, letters, and verses, written by young *narodniks* in Russia. Curiously enough, these human documents made less impression on Turgenev than did his encounters with live human specimens in Paris. He wrote back to Filosofov: 'I could name to you young people with opinions much firmer and more clear-cut, and to whom I, as an old man, take off my hat, because I feel in them a real vigour of talent and mind' (Letter, 1879).

VI

Hostile critics, like Mikhailovsky, grossly exaggerated the degree of Turgenev's ignorance about active *narodnik* personalities. It had become the fashion to poke fun at him as an animated museum piece, an amiable but out-of-date old gentleman, who chose to live in voluntary exile, sheltered from the uncomfortable turmoil of events at home. Yet many of the younger revolutionaries, who knew that Turgenev retained personal ideals at variance with their own, still felt drawn to him as a supreme artist, able to portray rare human beings who quietly sacrifice their lives to an unknown God, without a thought of personal gain. Turgenev liked to think that the admiration which he aroused in these young people, showed not that he had yielded to their more prosaic outlook, but that they had come half-way to meet him.[1]

Kropotkin, who warmly approved the anarchist strain running through the *narodnik* movement, might easily have been dismayed by Turgenev's bleak and negative judgement of its outcome in *Virgin Soil* (1877). Yet he viewed this novel as a sound interpretation. 'Turgenev,' he remarked, 'with his usual amazing insight, brought out the salient features of that movement, the incomprehensibility of the agitators to the peasants, or rather the typical inability of most agrarian socialists to understand the peasant, on account of their artificial approach to him through history and sociology.'

Another staunch supporter, the exiled Lavrov, who reviewed *Virgin Soil* in the English journal, *The Athenaeum* (February 1877), observed that the artist had rightly been struck by the far-reaching *effect* of this movement on the souls of Russian youth. Lavrov did Turgenev justice by refusing to criticize, as if they were omissions, aspects of village life which he had never undertaken to describe. For Turgenev refrained from attempting a comprehensive picture of inchoate, disturbed peasants with their rankling grievances. He focussed on the salient psychology of that small section, which he knew best, the young *narodnik* agitators, provincial landlords and officials.

The basic character of Nejdanov he derived from a young exile, A. Onegin, who after escaping from Russia had started to live listlessly in Paris, where Turgenev met and encouraged him. Clearly conceived as a *roman à thèse*, *Virgin Soil* takes shape as a record of historical events, the story of a well-intentioned group, which failed to rouse the peasants to revolt against their landlords and officials. Fully aware that he might lack convincing substance, observed in detail on the spot, he travelled to Russia in 1874 for the avowed purpose of studying the mind and face of *narodnik* activity in country districts.

Nejdanov, son of an aristocrat and a peasant woman, was appropriately designed to serve as an intermediary reconciling these

[1] See M. Kleman, *Turgenev v Vospominaniyakh revolyutsionerov semidesyatnikov*, Moscow-Leningrad, 1930.

two classes. But he found, to his dismay, that he had ceased to believe in the course to which he was committed, and no longer loved the woman who had abandoned all her other ties for him. Step by step he forfeited her esteem and abandoned his own self-respect. The peasants, to whom he preached his flimsy gospel of revolt, began to despise and laugh at him. He finally lost face, when they made him drink to excess in a public house and carried him home in a drunken stupor.

Though convinced that his 'cause' was futile, he clung to his comrades through a sense of loyalty. But his conscience made him urge his fiancée, Marianna, to renounce him, in order to marry a worthier man, the factory-manager, Solomin. To shoot himself, though hardly the happiest solution, demonstrated some courage and devotion. It was better than a slow decay, and it saved Marianna from continuing to sacrifice herself for him, which she would otherwise have done. Though Nejdanov wanted to be a hard materialist and adopted a brazenly cynical pose, his actions belied his words, and proved him to be unselfish when the crisis came.

Nejdanov's suicide, the ironic fate of Markelov, the landlord who, after stirring up his peasants, was then betrayed by them and handed over to the police, far from implying that Turgenev harboured a personal bias against revolutionaries, recorded truthful symptoms of what happened to the *narodniks* when they went beyond peaceful educational work and started agrarian agitation. Yet Turgenev felt irresistibly attracted by impetuous people, and the ideal strain, dominating these Russian *Don Quixotes* in their clumsy exploits, still fascinated him.

The censorship officials detected his undertone of sympathy in *Virgin Soil*, despite the abysmal failure which it depicted, and therefore tried to stop its publication. They pointed out, with some degree of justice, that 'the destructive principle of the movement towards the people is presented in a favourable light'. They were disturbed by the firm energetic characters of Solomin and Marianna, and scented treasonable designs in the irony with which Turgenev unmasked liberals like the Sipyagin family. In Sipyagin the scheming careerist and state functionary had extinguished the last spark of personal integrity. Though Turgenev never formally changed his political outlook, he clearly began to deplore the faint-heartedness and hypocrisy shown by many so-called liberals; he said that 'we good and generous liberals' dared not risk the smallest part of our own security, because we entirely lack temperament and civic courage.

The figure of Solomin provided Turgenev's first imaginative attempt to round off his scattered comments on the rising need for patient citizens, who would carry out humble unspectacular work without fuss or impudent pretensions. It was high time, he said, for a serious novelist to demonstrate that an intelligent man need not always be a sick or useless man! Chernyshevsky's efforts to portray such figures had produced chilly moral prigs or quite incredible altruists. But Solomin is a plausible personality, calm, balanced, and clear-headed, without being inhumanly repulsive. His years of scientific apprenticeship in nineteenth-century England had taught him to be a cautious opportunist. His solid common sense is a refreshing antidote to a surfeit of muddle-headed or feckless individuals. A streak of rugged vigour and shrewdness saves him from being abstract or uniformly grey.

After he marries Marianna, they found together a model factory in the Urals, an undertaking which enables them to prove by their example that constructive people, capable of necessary work, have at last emerged from the hitherto fruitless ferment of the *narodnik* movement. The author summed up, a trifle too pointedly: 'one must work virgin soil, not with the harrow, which slides over the surface, but with the plough, which penetrates it deeply. That plough cannot be revolution, but only enlightenment and culture.' [1]

Turgenev was still fighting a battle on two fronts, against the rigid state bureaucracy, and also against the aberrations of misguided revolutionary youth, whose good intentions he respected. But fear of censorship compelled him to veil or tone down his strongest thoughts. These ardent people had been falsely represented either as a gang of criminals or as romantic heroes.

[1] See H. Granjard, *Ivan Tourguénev*, p. 421, Paris, 1954.

He saw them simply as brave and honest individuals, for the most part, but doomed because they fought for a cause so full of pitfalls, and so far beyond the range of real fulfilment, that it could only lead them to a miserable fiasco.

There lurks however, in the background, a mysterious man of action, who gives peremptory orders. This harsh, Europeanized Asiatic, Vassili Nikolaevich, 'dark, thick-set, with the high cheek-bones of a Tartar, a coarse face and lively eyes' (so Nejdanov describes him), is a portent of the not so distant future, which Turgenev discreetly hints at, without trying to delineate what was bound to be obscure to him. This man stands apart from his *narodnik* helpers, whom he employs to serve his ends. His cool business-like cunning is equally remote from practical idealists, like Marianna, and from luckless martyrs, like Nejdanov, who threw themselves into the struggle chiefly in order to escape from their own haunting doubt.

The storm of virulent and angry comment provoked by *Virgin Soil* made Turgenev take a solemn vow to stop writing novels altogether. The chief critics vied with each other in condemning him. He humbly admitted that he had perhaps undertaken a task beyond his powers, though he had felt compelled to work out this fascinating subject of Russian social transformation, which he had been observing at close quarters and turning over in his mind for many years.

His motive had been disinterested, to seize in flight the salient features of a transient but vital movement, to record the underlying truth. He had never sought public applause or financial gain. 'I recognized', he wrote, 'that life was moving in a definite direction. I traced a sketch, and pointed towards the right road to follow. Of course that is not enough. Now it only remains for a serious artist to quit the scene, and leave the way clear for other people to act and work' (Letter, March 1877). He had fulfilled a preparatory public service, so far as that kind of service lay within an artist's power.

But he had hoped for a few more signs of human sympathy than he received. He confided his deep disappointment to his friend, Polonsky: 'Again I sit at my desk alone, while downstairs my poor friend sings something in her broken voice. . . . The grave, it seems, hurries to engulf me, the day passes like a flash, empty, aimless, and grey. I have lost any right or wish to go on living, for there is nothing more for me to do, expect, or even to desire' (Letter, April 1877). Yet despite the critics' fury, he knew that he had been truthful within the limits he had set himself.

He only regretted that he had not aimed higher, by embodying in *Virgin Soil* hitherto unrecorded features of the uniquely Russian socialist, not only 'a knight of the dagger and of dynamite', but a stoically desperate idealist, poles apart from the calculating self-centred socialists of Western Europe, who fought so obstinately for higher wages, but rarely saw further than the ends of their own noses. For Russian terrorists preferred heroic suicide to any tepid compromise, and Turgenev pointed to the rapid spread of suicide among educated Russians as the gravest social problem of the period.[1] He told the *narodnik* writer Zlatovratsky: 'With what satisfaction I would portray the *nameless man*, together with that reckless sacrifice of oneself, and of everything which other people value and have always valued. Surely only a Russian could either imagine or be capable of such a feat!'

His story *The Desperate Man* (1881) reverts to an earlier period in order to sketch this recurrent Russian type. A decent and polite young landowner, with a sound brain and iron constitution, suddenly runs wild, for no apparent reason, sells his estate for a song to a cunning speculator, and dashes off to Moscow, where he spends his remaining cash on drunken revels among the gypsies. Always good-natured, kind, and considerate, even when intoxicated, he ended as a ragged beggar on the roads. Had he been born a decade later, such a man might easily have become a leading terrorist. Then as now, Turgenev observed, we find the same inexplicable craving to destroy oneself, the same innate melancholy and boundless yearning.

While he tenderly condoned errors of judgement, crazy escapades, and downright crimes, so long as they sprang from

[1] op. cit., p. 449, Paris, 1954.

sympathy or a sense of duty, Turgenev recognized that these fine young men and women remained total strangers to the dark suspicious people whom they tried to help. The keen university students who went to cobble or till the soil, in remote villages, proved even less capable of fusing with the average peasant, than the landowners who had the advantage of growing up with him from childhood in their rural noblemen's nests. For his urban admirers the peasant remained a sphinx, without an Oedipus to guess his riddle. Even when they shared his life and started to wear a peasant's shirt and hat, his enigmatic personality still eluded them.

More unexpectedly the modern peasants, since they had ceased to be downtrodden serfs, began to shed the glowing personal qualities which had formerly ennobled them in Turgenev's eyes. The charming and strangely original figures which enliven *A Sportsman's Sketches* are not matched by a single attractive portrait of an emancipated peasant in his later works. In *Fathers and Children* the touch became lightly ironical. Nicholas Kirsanov's servant, 'a man of the new improved generation', his hair plastered down with grease, was proud that he now wore patent leather shoes, and towards the end of his life 'grew quite rigid with stupidity and self-importance'. And the peasants in Bazarov's village, instead of singing nostalgic ancient folk-songs, began to bawl vulgar street ditties, talked to their master in a soothing sing-song voice, but among themselves joked about him contemptuously as a buffoon.

In *Virgin Soil* the picture of the average peasant grew still more sombre. Slovenly, dirty, chiefly in love with drink, often treacherous and sinister, he can no longer be treated with impunity as a simple good-natured oaf, who will respond kindly to a helping hand. Some cruel, harsh, and cynically material trait had wormed itself into the hearts of peasants, whose rare unworldly virtues enchanted him in the pre-Emancipation *Sportsman's Sketches*. Such undeniable deterioration of character, coinciding with the course of political events in Russia since 1861, led Turgenev reluctantly to conclude that his country had failed to benefit from liberal Westernizing measures, reforms undertaken from above, which were the most drastic modernizations he had ever favoured.

VII

His frank correspondence with Herzen revealed this cumulative disappointment more directly than his novels and short stories. Finally, tired of demonstrating the impotence of even the best ideas to serve as a spur to social progress, he shook off the cramping fetters of civic obligation, and ventured into the inviolate sphere of human contacts with supernatural powers. He also found an exhilarating moral compensation in practising his consummate mastery of the Russian language. 'Strange', he noted, 'that these four qualities, honesty, simplicity, freedom, and strength, exist in the Russian language, but do not exist in the Russian people. Yet they will be realized among the Russian people,' [1] he added, with an invincible desire to make that act of faith.

His *Song of Triumphant Love* (1881) and *Klara Milich* (1883) bring out a new vein in Turgenev's talent. They vibrate with an irresistible but trance-like mood, through which sensitive people fall under the spell of stronger magnetic personalities, or gladly surrender themselves to be ruled by unseen impersonal forces. It would be wrong to call these stories mystical, still less religious, in any normal sense. In both of them the mutual love between man and woman accumulated some uncanny force, stronger than any physical tie, and forged an unbreakable chain, which bound the weaker person like a helpless slave to the stronger one, who triumphed like a conqueror over him. The love that grew stronger than death, which overcame the fear of death, far from being a state of bliss, ruled over its victims like a remorseless taskmaster, admitting neither equality of status, freedom of choice, nor harmonious union between separate souls.

All the old topical preoccupations of Turgenev are abandoned in his *Poems in Prose*, which rise to an effortless mastery of clear evocative language, despite occasional fumbling on a rarified

[1] op. cit., p. 457.

philosophic plane. Their prevalent mood recalls a letter which he had written many years earlier to Madame Viardot: 'The only live soul is the one within ourselves, and perhaps a little given to us by our surroundings—but that is a faint glow which ancient night tries constantly to extinguish' (June 1849). Turgenev's last printed words dwell on this isolated, fragile human citadel, attacked from every side by brutal or blindly mechanical forces, and where the bleak a-morality of nature abets the treachery of humans to their greatest benefactors.

The critics found fresh fault with him for writing so poignantly about a neutral nature, unconcerned with human welfare, and about individuals, however gifted they might be, doomed to be misunderstood or ignored by the majority, and then annihilated, even if they rose to reign briefly over them, like 'Caliphs for an hour'. They were indignant that he made no further effort to provide that dose of moral uplift, which was expected to gild the bitter pill of every 'public-spirited' writer. They accused him of turning into a pessimist and cynic, perhaps because they felt ashamed that he honestly saw through many fetishes and bogus consolations which made up the precarious social optimism of their day. Only later, when the more artificial props of collective optimism had been bodily removed, did Turgenev's sceptical attitude to social and scientific panaceas appear less shocking, and perhaps more ultimately beneficial, than it had seemed to his contemporaries.

Several of the *Poems in Prose* show Turgenev all the more attached to such delights as he could still discover in the passing scene, because he knew that they could never be repeated. The satisfaction was no less intense through being transitory and rare (*The Azure Kingdom, How Beautiful and Fresh the Roses were*). Other poems reveal a total absence of his gentle lyrical strain, but compensate by being packed with a mature and trenchant worldly wisdom. His *Rule of Life* sums up the motive of mutual recrimination with a sharp contemporary sting: 'If you want to annoy and injure your opponent,' said a sly old fox to me, 'accuse him of the very same fault or vice which you know to be in yourself. . . . In the first place, that will make other people

H

CARL A. RUDISILL LIBRARY
LENOIR RHYNE COLLEGE

believe you are yourself without that vice. Secondly, your indignation may sound perfectly sincere, for you can turn to advantage the stings of your own conscience. . . . If you are yourself a lackey at heart, reproach your opponent with being a lackey, whether of civilization, of Europe, or of socialism!'

One poem, *The Threshold*, differed from all the others, both in its mode of presenting abrupt alternatives, and through its resolute forecast of the future in terms of personal choice. A Russian girl stands on the threshold of a huge dark building. A voice calls out to her: 'And you, who want to cross that threshold, do you know what awaits you?'

'I know,' the girl replies.

'Cold, hunger, hatred, mockery, contempt, prison, sickness, and death itself?'

'I know.'

'Complete estrangment, loneliness?

'I know, I am prepared. I will endure all the ordeals and blows.'

'Not only from enemies, but from close relatives and friends.'

'Yes . . . from them also.'

'Good. You are ready for the sacrifice.'

'Yes.'

'A nameless sacrifice? For you will perish—and nobody will ever know whose memory they should honour.'

'I need neither gratitude nor pity. I need no fame.'

'Are you prepared to commit a crime?'

The girl bowed her head . . . 'I am ready for that also.'

The voice did not renew its questions for a while.

'Do you know,' it said at last, 'that you may cease to believe what you believe in now. You may understand that you deceived yourself, and ruined your young life in vain.'

'I know that also, and none the less, I want to go in.'

'Go in.'

The girl crossed the threshold, and the heavy curtain fell back behind her.

'Fool', a mocking voice called out: 'Saint', came the answer from another side.'

The censorship authorities, who feared only that this poem

would serve to sanctify attacks against the government, refused to pass it. It was illegally printed by the *Narodnaya Volya* in 1883, but not openly published until 1905. People then suggested, but without convincing evidence, that Turgenev had the regicide, Sophia Perovskaya, in mind when he composed it. However that may be, the feeling which it conveys can hardly be monopolized by social revolutionaries, though some of them might be glad to share it.

Turgenev needed all his stoical detachment to face the more private ordeals which clouded his last years. His only daughter had married a Frenchman, who first squandered her money and then took to drink. In 1882 she was obliged to leave him, together with her two children, and her father had to sell land and personal possessions to provide for her. In the same year he fell ill with cancer of the spine, which the French doctors diagnosed as *angina pectoris*, and treated wrongly. Continual acute pain began to affect his reason. He asked to be given poison, and refused to see his closest friends. Shortly before his death in 1883, he failed to recognize Madame Viardot, when she entered his room, and cried out that she was worse than Lady Macbeth. In intervals of composure he recalled his social duty, wrote his last poems in prose, implored Tolstoy to resume literary work, and dictated a farewell letter to his peasants at Spasskoe, urging them to drink less alcohol, and to encourage their children in regular school attendance.

CHAPTER IV

F. M. DOSTOYEVSKY

I

F. M. Dostoyevsky (1821–81) is perhaps the only major Russian writer whose Western reputation stands on a higher level than the position assigned to him, both now and in the past, by harsher judgements passed upon him in his native land. Even though he has not been taken quite seriously in the Western world, outside intensely intellectual circles (despite the legion of contemporary writers who have a nodding acquaintance with his work), he seems from the start to have cast an enthralling spell over diverse Western minds of international breadth and stature. For hardly a single eminent literary critic of the late nineteenth and early twentieth centuries, from the Danish Brandes, the German Meier-Graefe, to the French André Gide and the English Maurice Baring, has omitted to write at length about him, often in terms of glowing admiration, though mingled with bewilderment and alarm, but rarely contradicted by dissentient minds voicing downright disgust or boredom, as a number have done today.

Most of these earlier writers fastened on Dostoyevsky as more strikingly original, psychologically *clairvoyant* and prophetic, if not more gifted as an artist, at least more unmistakably and uniquely *Russian* than either Pushkin, Turgenev or Tolstoy. No other novelist in the world had yet managed to combine the acute nervous thrills and tension demanded by a full-length detective story, with an equally dramatic clash of philosophic and moral conflicts, charged with such force and fury, that they could transmute elemental human passions into frantic mental lusts. This 'Shakespeare of the lunatic asylum', wonderfully arrayed at times as a pure Christian mystic, this 'Russian *Marquis de Sade*' (as Turgenev called him), the voluptuously *cruel talent*, who revealed a newly-discovered delight, both in plumbing the lowest depths of moral degradation and in torturing his own literary characters on

F. M. DOSTOYEVSKY

from a portrait by Perov

[Radio Times *Hulton Picture Library*]

the rack, this preacher of a national holy mission to consecrate the efforts of the hitherto despised and humiliated Russian *Chosen People,* managed to fill the most influential European men of letters with a blend of wonder, curiosity, and fascinated horror.

During the last two decades, however, signs have multiplied to show that the previous generation's almost ecstatic attitude to Dostoyevsky is well on the wane, where it has not disappeared and given place to violent critical antipathy. Through having partly initiated, and partly been absorbed by, the psycho-analytic entanglements peculiar to much twentieth-century fiction, his far-reaching influence on Western novelists is of course admitted, but no longer with that sympathetic thrill which formerly caused sensitive souls to swoon over the tormented and tortuous characters inhabiting his novels. He has turned instead into an ominous warning symbol of modern human pathology (deprived of his old diabolical or magnetic charm) nearer to the blend indicated by some of his portraits, where the proud and benevolently rational forehead of a Greek philosopher clashes with the sullen suffering eyes of an unwilling Christian martyr, and with the cruel mouth of a potential debauchee. One of his more discriminating Russian admirers, Prince D. S. Mirsky, frankly labelled him 'a potent poison', which should not be recommended except to people who are either strong enough to overcome it, or innocent enough to remain uncontaminated by it.

We can appreciate that his more sinister traits first gave a forbidden thrill to late Victorian English novel-readers, who were growing tired of Trollope's cathedral towns with the soothing clatter of teacups and polite conversation on a vicarage lawn. For Dostoyevsky brought to the surface a disquieting current of suppressed and morbid cravings, which more civilized people had hitherto preferred to thrust firmly back into the respectable darkness of their subconscious minds. But when, on closer scrutiny, his explosive characters turned out to be more abnormal than himself only in degree, but by no means different in kind, the educated European, having duly unearthed his darker self, been sharply warned about the kind of monster he might easily become, no longer felt drawn by its dramatic novelty, or desired to go on looking at his own image in such a distorting and unflattering mirror.

The recent decline in Dostoyevsky's reputation and potency as a writer has been widespread, since we have become too painfully familiar with the psychological strains which his intellectual men and hysterical women exemplify, and we no longer need their torments to wake us from our long-since troubled slumbers. A genuine but discriminating appreciation of his powerful artistic work continues.[1] It is sometimes mingled, and unfortunately confused, with admiration for his moral courage in a life-long struggle to overcome his own disease and to cope with crippling financial debts. Even those who hate his work can hardly fail to be impressed by his cat-like vitality, and by his survival of ordeals which would have broken or stunned a multitude of less resilient men.

Dostoyevsky's own outspoken and petulant dislike of almost everything which he encountered in Western Europe, including his blunt assertion that to live there is worse than deportation to Siberia, in no way impeded his initial popularity with European readers, who were inclined to ignore his angry patriotic outbursts, although these were less ambiguous than his involved philosophic and religious arguments, which persistently attracted them. But while his temperamental hostility to modern Europe resembled that of a revolutionary fanatic towards a hated old régime, his feelings for his own country rose to a frenzy of religious and national conservatism, beside which the old motto of Nicholas I (*Orthodoxy, Autocracy and National Character*) sounded apologetically mild and tolerant.

For that very reason his Soviet compatriots, while sincerely praising his 'diseased talent' have flatly contradicted many Western critics, by denying either that he revealed deep-rooted and characteristically *Russian* vices, or that he foresaw the grimmer national-socialist symptoms which would make the future Russian state an object of alarm to milder states. Noting the rarity of good-natured simpletons, and the almost total absence of spiritually

[1] See F. M. Dostoyevsky, *Polnoe Sobranie*, Moscow-Leningrad, 1926–30; *Sobranie Sochineniy*, Moscow, 1956 (most recent Soviet edition).

balanced individuals, from Dostoyevsky's vast portrait gallery, they even accused him, as V. Yermilov did, of having wantonly blackened or ignored 'true and important features' of real Russian people. Others have compared this native Russian disgust with Dostoyevsky to the rage of Caliban, seeing his own features too accurately reflected in a mirror. Yet Soviet critics like A. S. Dolinin and V. Yermilov, emphatically denied that Dostoyevsky portrayed *representative* or *Russian* types, either as they were in fact or might conceivably become. The critics skilfully found a foreign alibi by setting him apart as the super-pathologist of a small disintegrating *Westernized* section of Russian society, of its sickly, deformed, and transitory aspects, and in his forecasts a precursor of the German Fascists, but bereft of spiritual links with the noble Bolsheviks who later saved his native land.

Yet they frankly admit a danger of upsetting the mental balance of the Russian masses, if Dostoyevsky's work could be read and judged by every citizen. They demand that an *élite* of leading Soviet intellectuals should study his work thoroughly, solely in order to overcome and contradict every *reactionary* position which his mental attitude supported, and could still support.[1]

His famous satirical novel, *The Devils*, his cordial personal relations with the Procurator Pobyedonostsev and the court entourage of Alexander II, have thus been deplored as a shameful example of the manner in which Dostoyevsky debased himself, by coarse pamphleteering against the revolutionaries and by writing servile letters to the Tsar's family and friends.[2] But he is praised as a perfect specimen of his breed. And even when he sank to the level of '*mental lackeys of the triumphant bourgeoisie*', his Soviet critics assert proudly that he remained a mighty Russian writer, who stood out among these lackeys like a giant among Lilliputians, and that the chief international fighters against the spread of socialism throughout the world have all been his conscious or unconscious pupils.

[1] See Introduction by A. S. Dolinin to *F. M. Dostoyevsky, Pis'ma*, Moscow-Leningrad, 1928.
[2] See L. Grossman, *Dostoyevsky*, etc., *Literaturnoe Naslyedstvo*, Moscow, 1934.

The skilled dialectician must therefore learn to defeat protagonists of Dostoyevsky *on their own ground.* He must explain (but to Dostoyevsky's discredit) the astonishing fact that the rebel, who had been sentenced to Siberia for dabbling in Fourier's Utopian socialist dreams, returned to kiss the hand that punished him, and to promote a grim theocracy, where Church and State could scarcely be distinguished, a modern industrial version of Byzantine Orthodoxy, against which neither Catholic Rome nor the Protestant followers of Luther would be able to compete.

To conquer and eliminate the mind of Dostoyevsky after knowing all its intricacy and twisted passion, has therefore been prescribed by the Soviet *élite* as an important spiritual exercise for hardening Party initiates. It should help them to eradicate the last remnants of sloppy philanthropy, with which bourgeois society might infect them. It must dispel the dangerous suspicion that the Soviet Union might have incorporated more of Dostoyevsky's forecasts than it contradicted, and that he himself was the prophetic advocate of a revolution, which he opposed in political form, but hardly in national pride or governmental *mystique.*

That official Soviet utilization of Dostoyevsky, as an instructive historical phenomenon, a vital stage in training up-to-date leaders (who can never afford to neglect the study of their enemies' minds) had already taken shape during the early nineteen-twenties. Judging by recent utterances provoked by the seventy-fifth anniversary of his death, that approach, though more outspoken and class-conscious, has remained substantially unchanged.[1]

II

Dostoyevsky's father, a military surgeon of moderate ability and morose temperament, had become in 1821 resident doctor at the Hospital for Poor People in the heart of Moscow, where, appropriately enough, his son Fyodor was born and passed his childhood. The family lived modestly but not in abject poverty. Dostoyevsky's father married the daughter of a merchant. This sensible and devoted soul brought a dowry to her avaricious

[1] See *International Literature*, No. 2, Moscow, 1956, and *Ogonyok*, 6 Feb. 1956.

husband, who, in addition to his salary, earned money from taking private patients.

In 1831 he bought in the Tula province near Moscow a property, which included two small villages and about a hundred male serfs. The little Fyodor soon felt drawn towards the struggling peasants by the same compassion which had brought him close to the wretched patients in his father's hospital. He and his brothers were brought up strictly, with few distractions and no luxuries, but his parents believed in spiritual discipline and imbued the children with an early respect for art and letters. In the long winter evenings the family used to read aloud Karamzin's edifying *History of Russia*, or the poems of Pushkin and Derzhavin. In 1837 Dostoyevsky's long-suffering mother died of consumption.

The father then decided to send his two elder sons to the School of Military Engineering in Petersburg. From the start Dostoyevsky hated this school for its deadening routine, and he shunned the majority of his school-fellows, of whom he complained that, already at the age of sixteen, they could think of nothing more exalted than acquiring safe jobs at the earliest opportunity and indulging in vicious pleasures. Yet he worked strenuously, though with a sense of martyrdom, to master the uncongenial curriculum of geometry, algebra, and drawing plans for military fortifications. He began to write desperate letters to his father, imploring him to send a little more money, enough to buy such elementary necessities as tea, sugar, or a pair of boots. But the old military doctor, crazy with avarice and boredom, slowly drinking himself to death in his tumbledown country-house, vented his evil temper on his own sons as much as on his serfs. And Fyodor began to hate his father for such perverse egoism and meanness. In 1839, however, the old man was brutally murdered by some of the serfs whose lives he had made unbearable.

While it is idle to indulge in calculations as to how intensely Dostoyevsky had *desired* or even plotted his father's death, we know that the sudden and horrible end shocked him, and his novels reveal how he could rarely banish from his mind a lurking sense of personal guilt. Freud was later provoked to write a long abstruse article on the subject of Dostoyevsky's *Oedipus Complex* (July 1929). Nor can we deny that in *The Brothers Karamazov*, where parricide is the dominant theme, the half-witted lout Smerdyakov, who murdered the old Karamazov, is accounted less guilty and responsible than the intelligent Ivan, who merely *wanted* his father to be murdered, and planted the idea of it in Smerdyakov's brutish head.

After graduating from the School of Engineering, Dostoyevsky was granted the rank of lieutenant. But in 1844 he objected to taking up an appointment far from Petersburg, and seized his chance of resigning from a service for which he had always felt temperamentally unsuited. Throughout his life, he remained ill-equipped, either to earn money, to preserve what little he had got, or to spend it sensibly.

Finding himself already in debt, he started to translate French novels, and composed his own first novel, *Poor People* (1845), written in the old-fashioned form of an exchange of letters. Though its hero portrayed a down-trodden petty official, of the type brought into fashion by Gogol's *The Overcoat*, he was not such a dim and squashed nonentity as Gogol's Akaky Akakiovich. For under the ragged uniform, with missing buttons, of Dostoyevsky's simple drudge, there still beat a generous and pathetic heart.

This novel lacks all the mental complications and nervous tension permeating his later work, but its sincere though tearful sentiment won for it loud applause from the critic Belinsky. Hailed as the rising humanitarian author, on whom the sacred mantle of Gogol had fallen, Dostoyevsky found himself unexpectedly hoisted into popularity. He confessed that he felt intoxicated by his sudden fame, and had allowed himself to grow so dissolute that 'I simply cannot live decently any more' (Letter, November 1845). He also admitted that he was unpardonably ambitious and conceited, and that when fortune smiled on him, 'I ruin everything by my damnable character.'

Belinsky, however, carried away by his impetuous prophecies, expressed bitter disappointment in Dostoyevsky's subsequent stories, *The Double* (1846) and *The Hostess* (1847). Their strain of lonely phantasy and neurotic mental conflict puzzled him, and struck him as a dismal anticlimax after the early promise shown by *Poor People*. He wrote to Annenkov, 'We have all been taken in by our gifted Dostoyevsky,' and he quarrelled with his former protégé, who started to hate Belinsky for having let him down, and accused him of being so fickle and pliable that on literary matters alone he changed his mind five times a week. In fact, Dostoyevsky was beginning to display signs of the intermittent persecution mania which afflicted him.

He noted with harsh irritation that rising new writers, like Herzen and Goncharov, threatened to become his rivals. Although no longer an obscure beginner, he was still far from being an established author. He sank into fits of apathy, alternating with feverish expectation, but all the time he saw himself tottering on the brink either of disaster or of resounding fame—for a merely lukewarm success seemed just as galling to him as starving in a garret.

III

Living thus, he first met the eccentric landowner Petrashevsky, and in 1847 he began to attend the latter's conspiratorial meetings, principally in order to distract his thoughts and gratify his avid curiosity. He found these secret discussions a more stimulating pastime than the endless card-games or local gossip of social gatherings in St. Petersburg. Some of these young men, like Speshnyov, were sternly training themselves to become apostles and martyrs (if need be) of some movement designed to renovate society from top to bottom. But A. P. Milyukov, writing rather cautiously, long after the event (*Literary Encounters*, 1890),[1] noted that although Dostoyevsky used to read voraciously the French socialist writers, Saint-Simon and Fourier, he remained sceptical, and had remarked that life in a *commune* or a *phalanstery* would really be more horrible than life in a Siberian prison, and that level-headed Russians would find no practical sense in these

---

[1] See N. Belchikov, *Dostoyevsky v Protsessye Petrashevtsev*, p. 41, Moscow-Leningrad, 1936.

sincere but stupid theories. Fourierism, he explained later at his trial, might be a peaceful system, without hatred, and charm the soul with its graceful form, 'But it is undoubtedly harmful in effect, through the mere fact of being an intellectual system, and because, however attractive it may sound, it remains an unrealizable Utopia. Yet the harm done by these Utopias, if I may so express myself, is more laughable than terrifying.' [1]

It seems that even in the eighteen-forties Dostoyevsky could not justly be named either a revolutionary socialist or a republican, but at most an impassioned political dreamer and diligent freethinker, yearning to get rid of serfdom and the bonds of censorship—though hardly more so than many of his educated compatriots. Even later Soviet commentators on the Petrashevsky plot have not claimed that Dostoyevsky belonged to the extremists—rather the reverse.[2] As it happened, the numerous reforms of the eighteen-sixties implemented many of the Petrashevsky plans.

The young men belonging to the group were enthusiasts or brilliant dilettantes, deprived of normal outlets for their mental energy, but with even less aptitude for hatching plots than their ill-fated predecessors, the Decembrist officers. Among other things, they compiled a politically tendentious dictionary of foreign terms incorporated in the Russian language, which, by giving topical twists to well-known words, reversed their established meaning. Thus it defined *optimism* as 'an unsuccessful attempt to defend theism against the crushing attacks of practical atheism, which are inspired by the facts of life itself', and *Christianity* as 'aiming at the establishment of liberty and the abolition of private property'.[3]

Dostoyevsky had read to a meeting of the Petrashevsky group Belinsky's famous letter of reproach to Gogol (banned by the censorship). He made no attempt to deny this crime at his trial, but protested that it was wrong to accuse him of being a socialist, merely because he liked to study serious books about current social problems. A graver offence was that he had been friendly

[1] op. cit., p. 91.   [2] ibid., p. 58.
[3] E. H. Carr, *Dostoyevsky*, p. 50, London, 1931.

with Speshnyov, the most reckless and ambitious member of the group, from whom he had also borrowed money; and they had talked about setting up a secret printing press to publish forbidden literature.

All the so-called conspirators, including Dostoyevsky, were arrested in April 1849. Yet after five months of investigation the Commission of Inquiry still found them innocent. It could not produce a sound legal case for punishing men, guilty of nothing worse than discussing vague revolutionary intentions, which had never been consummated by criminal acts. The Russian Government, however, smarting from the pricks of the 1848 revolutions in Europe, and goaded into a vindictive frame of mind, smelt conspiracy and espionage everywhere, even in the harmless chatter of young idealists. It therefore transferred the Petrashevsky case to a military tribunal, where it was finally judged by martial law, and not as a civil case. That tribunal condemned Dostoyevsky to four years' penal servitude, followed by compulsory service as an infantry soldier, on the ground that he had 'nourished criminal projects' and illegally publicized the forbidden letter of Belinsky.

But the prisoners were left in ignorance of their fate. They were taken, without a word of explanation, to the Semyenovsky Square, and suddenly heard the death sentence abruptly read out to them by a stammering official, standing on a platform surrounded by soldiers armed with rifles. Dostoyevsky frequently described his reaction to this shock, but never more vividly and objectively than over twenty years later in his *Diary of a Writer* (1873): 'We Petrashevtsists, standing on the scaffold, heard our death sentence without the slightest feeling of repentance. Of course I cannot say that with certainty about them all. But I think that most of us would have deemed it dishonourable to renounce our thoughts and strivings. . . . In those last moments some of us, I am sure, instinctively examined ourselves and took our young lives into account. Perhaps we repented of other misdeeds (of those which in every one of us secretly lie heavy on the conscience). But that action for which we were condemned, those conceptions which dominated our souls, seemed to us not merely to need no repentance, but rather to purify us through martyrdom, and for that much else might be forgiven.'

Perhaps he had inwardly been craving for some spectacular catastrophe to save him from his dim and wretched hand-to-mouth existence. His arrest and punishment, unmerited though they seem, came almost as a godsend, for they irrevocably lifted him out of the commonplace rank and file, and opened his way to a grander though more painful future. Later he used to remark that he had been condemned justly, not for any political crime, but because he *needed* to endure penal servitude in order to learn lessons vital for his salvation.

When therefore 'the infinite clemency of His Majesty the Emperor' a few minutes later, commuted the death sentence to a four-year term of convict labour, Dostoyevsky could honestly describe that drastic day as the happiest one he had ever known. Some of his colleagues, however, instead of exulting, as he always did, in shattering emotional crises, felt nervously exhausted and sickened by the official farce that had been played at their expense, and almost regretted that they had not been shot outright.

Nicholas I had deliberately employed these blunt methods with a view to terrifying the young scatterbrains into repentance, followed by heartfelt gratitude to a gracious government for granting their last-minute reprieve. But the clumsy experiment failed (even with the hypersensitive Dostoyevsky) because no penitence could be wrung from any man without some prior sense of guilt. And Dostoyevsky, despite his haunting private guilt-obsessions, knew himself to be a blameless citizen. He felt grateful to the Government for punishing him, only because he had already fallen hopelessly in love with pain and suffering, as the sole stimulus on which his peculiar nature flourished.

Dostoyevsky's private letters, mostly sent by messenger and uncensored, provide authentic insight into his prison life at Omsk, whereas his later book, *Memoirs from a House of the Dead* (1862), was mellowed down both by the lapse of time and by fear of censorship. The letters frankly describe the non-political convicts, among whom he lived, as rough, vindictive, and self-willed men, whose hatred for their social superiors was boundless. 'When you were masters,' they used to jeer at him, 'you always injured the common people. But now that you have fallen on evil days, you try to be our brothers.' 'They would have devoured us if they could,' he noted. 'A hundred and fifty foes never wearied of devising different ways to persecute us; it was their joy and principal diversion. Our sole shield was our indifference and moral superiority, for they remained always conscious that we stood above them. All around me reigned endless ill-will, turbulence, and quarrels, added to perpetual espionage and the impossibility of being left alone for a single moment. Now I have come to fear only men and tyranny. I dread simple men even more than complex ones' (Letter, February 1854).

As soon as he had been transferred from prison to military service, he implored his brother, Michael, to send him books, of which he had been starved; he specified a German dictionary, a translation of the *Koran*, Kant's *Critique of Pure Reason*, and Hegel's *History of Philosophy*. His choice indicates how educated Russians of that time were soaked in German thought, through which they sought an answer to their own pressing moral and religious problems. Nor had he any need to mask or falsify his feelings in writing to his brother. 'For nearly five years,' he confessed, 'I have been living under constant surveillance. . . . To be alone is a natural need, like eating and drinking; but through that concentrated communal existence one begins to turn into a wholehearted hater of mankind. The perpetual companionship of other people works like poison or the plague. It makes one grow unjust, evil and malignant' (Letter, March 1854).

While confessing how penal servitude had warped his mind, Dostoyevsky accepted it as the heavy cross his conduct had deserved. Living among thieves and proud unrepentant murderers, who openly despised him, he none the less relieved his uneasy conscience by abasing himself in front of his tormentors, and started his strange idolization of the Russian common people. He said that in this hell on earth he had sometimes known the joy of finding a noble impulse in the soul of a criminal, and that a few such moments compensated for a multitude of horrors.

While he was serving as a common soldier in Semipalatinsk,

a young official, Baron Wrangel, befriended him, lightened his drudgery, and helped to promote him to the rank of sub-lieutenant (1856). In the course of his struggle for permission to return to European Russia, he composed a respectful ode to Nicholas I, and a coronation poem in praise of Alexander II, which he sent with a letter to Wrangel in Petersburg. Indeed he left no stone unturned to win the favourable attention of the powers that be. It would be hard to find a more abject letter than the one he wrote to General Totleben, voicing heart-rending appeals to be forgiven: 'I was guilty of the intention (but only of the intention) of acting against the Government. I was lawfully and quite justly condemned. . . . I know that I was condemned for dreams and theories, but surely these are modified in course of time, and so is a man himself. Why therefore should I suffer now for old errors of which I recognize the folly? . . . I want to be a useful citizen, to leave the army and resume civil employment' (Letter, 1856).

In the end General Totleben intervened on his behalf, and in 1859 an Imperial rescript gave him permission to leave the army and return to live in European Russia. Dostoyevsky had just married Maria Issayeva, the consumptive widow of a civil servant who had drunk himself to death. The prospect of his pardon sent him into raptures of civic gratitude. 'Your Majesty is like the sun,' he wrote, 'which shines on good and bad people alike. You have already made millions of your subjects happy. Be again merciful providence to a poor orphan, to his mother, and to an unhappy sick man who is ready to give his life for the Emperor,' etc. (Letter, 1859).

IV

Dostoyevsky's zeal to serve his sovereign and country, to expiate, to prove himself worthy of the gracious pardon which he had received, marked with equal sincerity the project upon which he now set his heart, the foundation of a monthly journal, edited by him and his devoted brother, Michael. After the usual cumbersome delays, he received the censor's approval in 1858, and the journal, *Vremya*, started to appear in 1860. Unlike his contemporaries, Tolstoy and Turgenev, Dostoyevsky felt in his element as a journalist (of the kind which believed it had a vital and edifying message to communicate). *Vremya* marks the beginning of his influential career as a columnist and social critic, a career which he always cherished, and actively resumed in the last years of his life.

The first editor's foreword stated plainly that *Vremya* was to be no ordinary journal, since it aspired to promote the understanding of Russian national character in all its latest social manifestations. 'Formerly we reproached ourselves', he pointed out, 'for our failure to be European *enough*. But now we think quite differently, for we know that we can *never be Europeans*. We are convinced that we are a nation apart, in the highest degree original. . . . It is not in vain that we speak all languages, that we sympathize with the interests of every other European people, that we understand the sense of happenings totally foreign to our own interests. Nor is it in vain that we have shown so much vigour in judging ourselves severely, to the amazement of foreigners, who have called us creatures devoid of self-respect, and without a country, merely because they fail to see that our capacity to move away for a moment from our own soil, in order to judge ourselves without prejudice, is in itself a sign of strong character—while our ability to survey foreigners with indulgence is a great and noble gift of nature, and one of which few nations are capable' (*Vremya*, 1861).

Dostoyevsky's entry into journalism after his return from Siberia marked a vigorous awakening of conservative thought among a section of Russians hitherto disinclined to think at all, or accustomed to regard such activity as the monopoly of a few suspect intellectual acrobats, like the old scholastic theologians or the new radical reformers. But the latter had already won the mental battle waged in the eighteen-fifties—chiefly because they controlled the major non-governmental journals, talked louder, and knew how to exploit the magic name 'progressive'.

Dostoyevsky appeared on the scene at a crucial moment, and began to lead a counter-attack against the radicals, whose

I

blighting sterility he found nakedly revealed in Chernyshevsky's best-selling novel *What to do?* (1863). He felt impelled to refute Chernyshevsky's priggish rationality, his call to unnatural feats of coldly calculated self-sacrifice, and the smug contentment of his well-fed co-operative Utopias. Dostoyevsky's tawdry vicious little egoist in *Notes from Underground* (1864) lacks the hearty bite and ferocity of the old *apache* underworld, but he is unpleasantly contemporary. Sick and spiteful, he may seem a feeble counter-blast against the orderly industrious Puritans of Chernyshevsky's novel, but he betrays perverse, irrational undercurrents, peculiar to the urban human animal, which Chernyshevsky had blissfully ignored or brushed aside. A man yearns to break away from the mathematical tyranny of reason.

Nor did Dostoyevsky start his long fight in a mere fit of pique. He now opposed the radicals (and plainly said so) because he detected in them an arrogant contempt for honest and decent Russians, whom they treated as expendable guinea-pigs for testing their pet theories. He distrusted their pedestrian minds, which failed to discriminate between obvious vices of the Russian people and healthy instincts, which remained pledges of its future growth and renovation.

Although he knew that many of his compatriots now recoiled from the icy grip of plausible Western doctrinaires, he never relied on their support, but foresaw that his opponents would revile him as a man-hating reactionary, simply because he tried to see further and deeper than their shallow optimism would permit. He spoilt his own case, however, when he accused the radicals of having *first* implanted in Russia germs of revengeful class-warfare, derived from Europe. That accusation was absurd, if only because the Russian Empire had been disturbed for centuries past by sporadic peasant risings.

And though Dostoyevsky must have known that his country remained a morbidly class-conscious hierarchy of official ranks, his head was so much turned by the statutory Emancipation of the Serfs (1861) that he could write effusively in the same year: 'We Russians have no class interests, because, strictly speaking, we have no classes; we experienced no Gauls or Frankish conquerors, no privileges marking by external signs what every man is worth; because for us nothing but education, and the moral qualities of every person, determine that person's value. Our new Russia has understood that there is only one cement, one bond, which unites and reconciles us all, and that is a spiritual union, based on our culture. . . . Our country knows that she is only just beginning,' he urged, 'but that is vitally important, because our whole future depends on the first step we take' (*Vremya*, January 1861). Russian society had not yet grown conservative, merely because it had so little to conserve; but let Russians once acquire achievements worth upholding, then they would turn quickly into staunch Conservatives.

We should recall that Dostoyevsky returned to the capital from his living grave, at a time when the energetic strivings of the Reform Period could still infect him. He found that an outburst of mystic national sentiment was pushing more writers and journalists towards the hitherto unfashionable Slavophil cast of mind, although the average level of their taste and judgement remained abysmally low. People were becoming so obsessed with displaying their 'social usefulness', that a crowd of talkative busybodies, sitting on unnecessary committees, began to complain that they could find no time for reading books—as if serious reading was a pastime for the leisured few—or soothed their uneasy minds by reading only the most blatantly topical newspapers or textbooks.

As a whole-time journalist, obliged to struggle for a living, Dostoyevsky knew that the commercial outlook for his journal was far from brilliant. But public response encouraged him, for after starting with a mere 2,000 subscribers in 1861, *Vremya* acquired over 4,000 in the course of a single year. A similar flair for responding to latent unsatisfied desires in educated people is evident in many of Dostoyevsky's novels. He proved that journalistic talent, feeding on topics of the day, need not kill serious imaginative writing, if it remained content to reach only a small cross-section of an independent-minded thinking public.

V

In 1862 Dostoyevsky undertook his first journey to Western Europe. Judging by his letters, he seems to have been the world's most irritable and least inquisitive traveller, dashing hectically from one town to another, with neither the time nor the desire to study foreign habits and absorb instructive new impressions. He arrived in Paris without knowing a single soul there, lodged in a cheap hotel, found the city 'terribly sad' and 'nearly died of boredom'. London, where he spent eight days, he admitted to be slightly less intolerable, mainly because he was lavishly entertained there by the brilliant Russian exile, Herzen. He mixed with the grey crowds, watched pretty prostitutes drinking gin by gaslight with their clients in haunts along the Haymarket, while missionaries walked about distributing religious tracts. Nowhere does he seem to have noticed, or been attracted by, refreshing landscapes, magnificent buildings, or fine works of art. Even when he stayed in Florence, he wrote about little except the stifling heat and the perpetual noise which made sleep impossible. In Dresden he felt repelled by the flock of busy tourists, moving with guidebooks through the picture gallery, and gazing with a numb sense of duty at Raphael's serene Madonna.

In *Winter Notes on Summer Impressions* (1863), Dostoyevsky sketched his hasty loathing of France and England, both godless countries, worshipping the golden calf, choked by a wealth of material devices which their citizens proudly mistook for civilized advance. He felt no urge to probe into the mental life of Europeans beneath the superficial phenomena conveyed in squalid crowd scenes and newspaper headlines. Taking it for granted that genuine artists must have become extinct in a nineteenth-century Europe dominated by technicians, mighty banks and men of business, he virtually ignored the existence of other gifted spiritual rebels, reformers, writers or musicians.

In 1863, as previously in 1848, an incident in international politics uprooted Dostoyevsky's life. The Russian Government's suppression of the Polish revolt had aroused a fever of excited comment in Petersburg journals. The critic Strakhov wrote about it for *Vremya* an insufficiently guarded article, which was completely misread and misconstrued by nervous censorship officials. The Ministry of the Interior promptly ordered the journal to be suspended for a year, so that Dostoyevsky's whole future was at stake. When at last he cleared up the official misunderstanding (not before he had incurred crippling financial losses), he struggled to continue the journal under a new name, *The Epoch* (*Epokha*). Then his brother Michael died suddenly in 1864. He bravely shouldered responsibility for his brother's debts as well as for his destitute children, and passed a desperate year haggling with moneylenders, and shady lawyers, devising dodges to evade the more insistent creditors, and trying to placate the police. But by the spring of 1865 *The Epoch* was still running at a loss. He then decided to abandon it, and escape abroad, hoping at last to find a minimum of peace, enough to embark on more substantial literary projects which now filled his mind.

VI

Staying in Wiesbaden, he yielded to his favourite temptation and gambled away his last remaining funds in the Casino. He cursed all Germans when the hotel manager refused to serve him a single meal until he had paid his bills. Half starving, and imprisoned in his bedroom, he nevertheless started to write *Crime and Punishment* (1865).

It has become an accepted practice to approach Dostoyevsky's complex novels as if they were composed of various separate layers, corresponding to higher or lower levels of his own consciousness. The acute states of mental tension, in which he reigned supreme, are often said to emanate from the highest level, and deemed superior to less entangled but equally vigorous strains, in which he came closer to the leading Slavophils and psychological writers of his day. While this distinction may help to explain Dostoyevsky, it leads people astray when it denies that his semi-religious Slavophil emotion lent its own lurid colour even to the highly enigmatic conflicts in his novels. In *Crime and Punishment* that Slavophil strain is less prominent than in later novels, but the private mental states of Raskolnikov are already interwoven with dramatic social themes.

Here is a familiar modern tragedy, starting from the eternal greed for money, or for the power which money confers on men, since they are made to feel like helpless worms without it. The novel mercilessly unfolds the physical and moral ruin which over-takes gifted young people, who starve in rags and squalor, while money accumulates in the hands of loathsome parasites and barren adventurers. The desperately poor student Raskolnikov lacks no external inducement to become a rabid social rebel, even as Dos-toyevsky himself had abundant reasons to sympathize with Raskolnikov's temptations to murder and to steal.

For Dostoyevsky's own aunt, from whom he had managed to borrow a mere 10,000 roubles, was a miserly rich old woman, who gave away large sums for decorating churches and for prayers to save her worthless soul, but never stirred a finger to help her struggling relatives. Raskolnikov's clear thought: 'Murder the old woman and take her money; will not thousands of good deeds atone for one paltry crime?' could hardly fail to have invaded Dostoyevsky's mind during his long bankruptcy. Raskolnikov calls his victim a vile 'blood-sucking louse'.

But the real crisis hinged on the mental attitude of the murderer towards his crime, before and after. For Raskolnikov, despite his destitution, could not kill the old moneylender in a fit of uncon-querable impulse, nor through a calm conclusion that he could thereby save himself and his dear ones from beggary and sickness. He could only screw up courage to murder her, in order to con-firm an ambitious theory that he had superhuman powers, and hence the right to spurn normal moral rules, binding for lesser men. He must, at any cost, prove himself equal to Napoleon. 'A real master, to whom everything is permissible, bombards Toulon, organizes a massacre in Paris, expends half a million men in a campaign against Russia. And statues are put up to that man after his death. . . . Anyone who is greatly daring proves himself right in other men's eyes!'

Yet do not Raskolnikov's Napoleonic cravings resemble those of the legendary frog, who puffed himself out until he burst? For he turned out barely resolute enough to commit the murder, and far too weak to benefit by its results. He could not even force himself to use the old woman's money. The diabolically skilful state prosecutor knew how to play with him like a cat with a mouse, to keep him in a constant state of apprehension and alarm, until emotional pressure broke his nerve and drove him to confess his guilt. It was then that the ignorant, tortured Sonya showed herself to be a saint for him, the only person able to sustain the shattered young man, whom she voluntarily accompanied to Siberia.

Intellectual arrogance and smug self-satisfaction remained for Dostoyevsky the most deadly sins. Therefore a criminal led astray by passion deserved more esteem than a just man who was never tempted. And an *unwilling* generous prostitute, like Sonya or Nastasya Filipovna, could tower above a formally pure but insignificant young woman, like Aglaya in *The Idiot*.

It is revealing that Raskolnikov in penal servitude, though impelled by a burning sense of shame, by anger against his despicable weakness, feels not an atom of repentance for his crime. Why had he stopped half-way? he asked himself. Of course he had broken the letter of the law and shed human blood, yet his motives had been good. Former benefactors of mankind, who rose to power by crime, might also have been punished and deflected at an early stage, yet they had gone ahead, while he had failed. Later the reader receives a hint that Raskolnikov is starting a new life with Sonya in Siberia. 'The heart of one contained infinite sources of life for the heart of the other.' The story ends with this moral gesture, tentative and vague, confirming what critics like Shestov and Mirsky have observed, that Dostoyevsky's harmonies and solutions remain always on a lower or shallower level than his conflicts and irreducible tragedies.

While he was ready to defend a man who broke the law in a fit of righteous indignation, he showed horror for the intellectual criminal, who sought to justify an evil action by pleading a good objective. For him, a man who commits murder for some principle resembles a society which resorts to revolution for the sake of a calculated public benefit. Cold-blooded murder for gain in private life turns imperceptibly into planned revolution for still more elusive gain in public life. Thus the pathetic Raskolnikov and his dilemma form a natural prelude to the sinister monsters, Stavrogin and Peter Verkhovensky, prominent in *The Devils*.

Indeed Raskolnikov's catastrophic nightmare during his illness brought him close to the main theme running through *The Devils*. He dreamed about a terrible unheard-of world-disease, emerging from the depths of Asia, and spreading westwards into Europe; new trichinae, microscopic parasites, would take possession of men's bodies. 'But the same creatures turned out also to be living spirits, endowed with mind and will. People who absorbed them became at once *possessed* and mad.' Yet never had all these people been so invincible in their judgements and scientific certainty, so filled with pride and missionary zeal. Seeing nothing beyond an absolute truth which resided in themselves alone, they would perish in a war of all against all, provoked by their self-centred moral blindness.

VII

In February 1867 Dostoyevsky married Anna Snitkina, his amazingly efficient and devoted typist, who managed to stabilize his domestic life, and by degrees to regulate his erratic monetary affairs.

Staying in Geneva, which he described as 'a dull, stupid and gloomy Protestant town, with a frightful climate', he coincided with a Socialist *Peace Congress* graced by the presence of the Italian Garibaldi. 'This rabble', Dostoyevsky wrote contemptuously, 'is stirring up the whole unfortunate artisan class. In order to attain final peace on earth, they want to uproot the Christian faith, annihilate the Great Powers, by cutting them up into a lot of small countries, abolish monetary capital, then declare that private property is held in common by everybody—and all that without a single convincing proof of any kind!' (Letter, August 1867).

Travelling from one continental lodging house to another, Dostoyevsky indulged in his luxury of hatred against modern

Europe. It hardly entered his head that a handful of living Europeans saw ugly and destructive aspects of the new epoch as clearly as he did himself. He preferred to condemn Europe, and let her go to hell, to see her as an impressive graveyard of superb ancient monuments, where no fresh spiritual creation could possibly take place. He could thus relieve his petulant hostility by occasionally laying wreaths on lovely tombstones marking Europe's past, while he strenuously preserved himself from catching the disease carried by her latest plague-stricken descendants.

With something akin to the love of a boa-constrictor for his smothered prey, or of a bear for the animal which it hugs to death, Dostoyevsky revelled in ambiguous sentiments about the strong emotional ties which still bound Russia to the West. 'For the contemporary Russian,' he declared, 'Europe and the fate of the great European race are as dear as Russia herself and the fate of his own country . . . the peoples of Europe do not know how dear they are to us. We Russians have two fatherlands, Russia and Europe, even when we are Slavophils.' Under the international strain distinguishing Dostoyevsky's patriotism, there lurked an angry menace, torn from the heart of a lover who had suffered unforgivable disappointment. 'It is for us to devour Europe, if we do not want to be devoured by her,' he affirmed. Was that the impulse which guided the historic mission imposed on *Holy Russia*, and were her 'brotherly feelings' comparable to the emotions of a spider which *loves* the captured fly that feebly struggles in its web?

During his hasty visits to European art-galleries, Dostoyevsky was impressed by lurid German paintings of crucified Christs with deep stigmata and bodies covered with bloody sweat, by pictures of martyred saints displaying their mutilated limbs and wounds. He assigned a reproduction of Holbein's *Dead Christ* to one of Rogozhin's rooms in *The Idiot*. Yet he remarked that such terrifying images of Christ might cause some people to lose their faith entirely. Calm benevolent Christs, glowing with physical health, of the type created by Titian and Correggio, seem to have gratified his uneasy longing to find elsewhere the compensating harmony which he lacked within.

Though the gruesome medieval torture-chamber may have been closer to Dostoyevsky's heart, the serene and sunny figures of the Man-God emerging from the Renaissance, awoke in him nostalgia for that remoter pagan world, which Pushkin had in part revealed to him. In later life Dostoyevsky hung a reproduction of Raphael's Sistine Madonna in his bedroom, so that his eyes would fall on it when he woke each morning. He needed more than ever a gentle, calm religious picture, to save his mind from being clouded over by the murky recesses and convulsions of the erupting Russian underworld.

During his European travels, an enthralling new project started to ripen in his mind, how he could represent 'a positively good and noble man' embodied in a tragic novel of contemporary life. 'Nothing can be more difficult than such an attempt,' he wrote, 'especially today, for the morally beautiful remains a pure ideal, and all ideals, both ours and those of civilized Europe, are far from having been worked out. . . . Cervantes' *Don Quixote* remains the most perfect figure in the whole of Christian literature, but he rises to nobility through being at the same time a comic character. One feels compassion for the ridiculed comic man, who does not know his own worth as a good man' (Letter, January 1868).

Prince Myshkin, the principal character of *The Idiot*, takes shape as a Russian *Don Quixote*, even more out of place in his modern environment than Cervantes' prototype was in ancient Spain. His chaste hypersensitive nature, ruled by altruistic impulse, becomes more credible through making him a victim of epilepsy, in which he becomes a projection of the author's self. Yet, far from fulfilling Dostoyevsky's plan to create a perfect man in fiction, this Christ-like innocent, equally attentive and kind to everybody, without an atom of self-assertion, is exasperatingly incompetent in handling his coarser-grained contemporaries.

His meek character, his sure intuition, colour him with a rare moral beauty, but they bring no practical help to a single person whom he meets, let alone himself. He belongs to a wonderful but visionary world. The most that he can do is to emanate a fleeting charm, to soothe overwrought minds by his fervent words, while hastening a tragic dénouement.

The inexperienced and rather prim Aglaya needed a robust male protector, if not a master, but could never be managed by such an overgrown child as Myshkin. The outraged Nastasya Filipovna needed an energetic friend to save her from the craving to humiliate herself and sink deeper in the mire. Myshkin's mute sympathy only intensified her hysteria and sense of unworthiness, and how could she accept his sincere but not very insistent offer of marriage? Myshkin, though aware of her predicament, remained powerless to persuade her. 'Her pride will never forgive me for my love,' he patiently observed; 'She ran away from me to prove that she is a street-woman.' His inhuman self-denial finally drove Nastasya under Rogozhin's knife, and threw Aglaya into the embrace of the first Polish emigrant who wooed her.

Though Myshkin is *clairvoyant* enough to foresee the series of catastrophes that are bound to happen on account of him, he cannot avoid a single one of them. A slave of his own presentiments, he advances like a sleepwalker towards the abyss, which will engulf him in final mental darkness. A sick man himself, he infected everyone he met, and hoped in vain that active human vices would melt in front of his pure virtue, like wax before a fire. 'The Prince has made us all ill,' Nastasya exclaimed to the perplexed Rogojin in a moment of horrified lucidity. If Dostoyevsky intended Myshkin to represent a modern Christ set down in 'Holy Russia', his fate leaves no doubt that a returned Christ is quite unwanted, and would be crucified or driven mad if ever he appeared on earth again. Perhaps his worldly failure was due to be redeemed by some more valuable spiritual task, but this remains concealed to normal mortals. If Myshkin acquires tangible importance for Christian Orthodoxy, it is only by serving as a mouthpiece for Dostoyevsky's artificial tirades against the Catholic Church.

The prince, who has returned from a sanatorium in Switzerland, tells his compatriots that the Roman Catholic Church in Europe has become a menace worse than open atheism, because it had allowed itself to turn into a disguised continuation of the old military Roman Empire. After swindling so many true believers with its cold hypocrisy, it had provoked atheistic socialism as a final protest. Every socialist movement in Europe, he explained, had begun simply as an emotional reaction against the deceptive Catholic reality. Like atheism itself, these movements had been born from desperate disappointment, from a longing to quench the spiritual thirst of human beings, which treacherous or impotent religious organizations (Protestant and Catholic alike) had proved by their barren worldliness that they could never satisfy.

This grandiose politico-religious theme, that Europe's manifest spiritual bankruptcy provided Russia's golden opportunity, haunted Dostoyevsky with the power of an obsession. He returned to it in *The Brothers Karamazov* with the picturesque Legend of the Grand Inquisitor, and it burst out again at frequent intervals in his *Writer's Diary*. He began to conceive the whole protracted struggle between the rival nations and races of nineteenth-century Europe, not as a prosaic modern form of national competition to win commercial markets and wield more industrial power, but as a fateful prolongation of the old fanatical religious wars. And he looked forward with relish to a final death-struggle between the rival branches and perversions of the Christian faith, fixed in their latest and largest national moulds, a struggle which would end in an extermination of the weakest.

For a time, he thought, the united German Protestants might prevail over the monstrous combine made by the Catholic Church, which now courted mass support through allying itself with Western socialists. But ultimately purer Eastern Orthodoxy would triumph over both these rivals, because the march of history must bring forward a people which had been so long condemned to silence, and was less pampered and corrupted by material greed and easy living. If Orthodox Russians had not existed, they would have had to be created, in order to convert cynical Western races to that sense of brotherly kinship which they had lost. Odd as it may seem, that is how Dostoyevsky pleaded the cause of militant pan-Slav Orthodoxy. He gave his blessing to compulsory international fraternity, provided it could be achieved by devout Russians.

Though Dostoyevsky expressed diffidence about the literary craftsmanship of *The Idiot* (written under extreme pressure for the monthly *Russian Messenger*), he firmly defended the fertile originality and importance of the conflicts which he formulated in it. It seemed to him that a vast part of the Russian mode of living had passed totally unobserved by any sensitive historian. Even the moon had been more closely studied by scientific observers than the real underlying Russia.

When the shocked realists protested that he indulged in nightmarish fantasy, they betrayed that they themselves had got stuck in lifeless records of trivial everyday events. He claimed to be a more genuine *realist* than they were, because he had caught and recorded half-submerged realities, invisible to the naked eye, disturbing eruptions which other writers had either failed to notice or had squeamishly passed over. All those mental torments, criminal cravings, outbursts of despair and suicides, far from being figments of his feverish brain, were constant and daily happenings throughout Russian life. 'Is not my fantastic *Idiot* really the most everyday truth?' he wrote to his friend Strakhov (Letter, March 1869). Apart from that, *The Idiot* remains a masterpiece of literary art, for its chaos is shot through with an epic grandeur and clarity which can never be grasped by a hasty or superficial reader.

VIII

The longer Dostoyevsky stayed abroad, the less he liked the European scene, and the more absorbed he grew in following the course of events in Russia. He avidly devoured Russian newspapers and periodicals, trying to feel less painfully cut off from the native background which still gave substance and vitality to all his work.

Collecting every detail about the gruesome murder of the student Ivanov by the young revolutionary, Nechaev, he decided to base a whole new novel on that ominous affair. The work fired his imagination with the thought that he might thereby save the younger generation in the nick of time, before its soul was

strangled in the trap of crazy logic, which false prophets had prepared for it. If only he could make people understand what was
boiling in his heart, he felt that he could render great service to
his country's future.

Profoundly disturbed by Nechaev's cold criminality, he sought
a consoling parallel in the familiar bible story about the devils
who passed out of a sick man in order to enter a herd of swine
and make them mad. He accepted this murder as a sign from
heaven that similar devils, which had recently possessed and
nearly tortured to death the Russian social body, were now beginning to leave it, and to pass over into individual human
monsters, like Nechaev and Serno-Solovevich. These *possessed*
creatures, like the biblical herd of swine, would finally rush over
the edge of a cliff and kill themselves, and then afflicted Russia
would return to health and sanity.

This ambitious theme fascinated Dostoyevsky, though he felt
terrible misgivings that he might spoil it by inadequate and over-
hasty writing. 'It is almost too burning a theme,' he wrote to
his friend, Maykov. 'Yet never have I worked with so much ease
and satisfaction. . . . I must express certain thoughts, for I am
carried away by all that has accumulated in my heart and mind;
even if it results in no more than a tendentious pamphlet, I *must*
speak out' (Letter, October 1870).

The Devils (1871), now accepted as a politically prophetic
novel, was regarded at the time as a brilliant but wildly vindictive
caricature of various revolutionary and other public figures. The
more vocal conservatives praised it as a bold revelation of the
unsavoury truth about these scoundrels and degenerates; while
radicals attacked it as a treacherous slander, fabricated by a
revengeful renegade.

In fact it contained a prescience which neither party recognized,
for no living rebels, not even Nechaev, still less Bakunin,
could have been so completely diabolical as the imaginary
Stavrogin and Peter Verkhovensky. In creating these characters
Dostoyevsky anticipated the ultimate 'petty devil' of the novelist,
Sologub,[1] and the cynical intellectual gangster, who came into his

[1] T. Sologub, *Sobranie Sochineniy*, St. Petersburg, 1909-12.

own in the twentieth century. But he also demonstrated that
devils of this type could never dominate for long their human
victims, unless they resorted to the *shock treatment* or large-scale
fraud, inherent in Shigalev's projected social system.

'To begin with, the whole level of education and talents must
be lowered, for a high standard in science or art is accessible only
to superior minds—for which we have no use. . . . Tear out
Cicero's tongue, blind the eyes of Copernicus, stone Shakespeare
—that is Shigalevism.' People must be made ashamed to hold
their own opinions, terrified to differ from their neighbours. By
depriving individuals of any right to choose between alternatives,
personal morality would vanish altogether. 'Every member of
society will watch his neighbour and inform on him, for every
person belongs to the whole community. All are slaves, and all
become equal in slavery' (*The Devils*).

The new slaves would be kept docile and afraid by masters
more cunning than the world had known before. For if the
masters allowed the overriding claims of family, personal love
and aspiration, to re-assert themselves, then the desire to own
private property would revive as well. 'We shall kill that desire,'
Verkhovensky proclaimed. 'We shall authorize a wild debauch
and stifle every genius in the cradle.' And so the lust for unrestricted individual liberty would forge the new chains of a grim
tyranny—a retribution that might paralyse human feelings for
ever in the habits of a mechanized ant-heap.

By a stroke of genius Dostoyevsky made even the consummate cynic, Peter Verkhovensky, fail in his striving to become a
law unto himself, and secretly adore the man who most despised
him, when in a crisis he started to grovel before Stavrogin and
followed him like a dog. 'When night has descended over Russia,'
he told his hero, 'the earth will start to weep for the old Gods
. . . then to whom shall we turn for rescue?' In an amorous
whisper Verkhovensky then outlined his crazy plan. He counted
on Stavrogin to act the part of Ivan Tsarevich, the Crown Prince
in hiding, who would suddenly appear in public and announce a
righteous rule of law to be maintained by him. The disillusioned
people would be ready to believe in him, because he was

handsome, proud and energetic as a God, and sought no corrupt advantage for himself. Then the cunning revolutionaries would weave their false legend round him, in order to seduce and hold the crowds.

The inhuman, weirdly empty aristocrat, Stavrogin, is an even more arresting figure than the adventurer and schemer Peter Verkhovensky, who embodies a sharp reaction against his verbose and lazy, but very human, father (a caricature of the historian, Granovsky). To critics who had been crying out for energetic literary heroes, Stavrogin provided a concrete answer. Here was a man of immense physical and mental strength, yet unable to find an outlet which gave him inward satisfaction.

So he turned into a debauchee and desperado, driven to hunt persistently for any sensation which might momentarily dispel his gnawing boredom, but no longer capable of being moved by natural joys, or even hurt by natural pain. On receiving a violent blow in the face from his former disciple, Shatov, instead of hitting back, he silently controlled himself, in order to test how it felt to endure in silence the bitter extremes of anger and humiliation. He fought reckless duels, had a small girl whipped for a theft which she had never committed, afterwards violated her, and then allowed her to hang herself.

To strain to the utmost that self-imposed atonement (which he also sought) he married deliberately a hideous and deformed half-witted woman. When every escapade and self-inflicted anguish failed to bring him peace of mind, he found a stimulating novel sport in working with the underground revolutionaries, although he felt indifferent to their aims.

While this robust and masterly young nobleman turned step by step into a moral cripple, his handsome features froze into an immobile mask. His formerly zealous disciples, Shatov and Peter Verkhovensky, slowly lost faith in his magnetic strength, and suspected his integrity. Then he began to despise himself, to recognize in dismay that he lacked even the saving grace of ending as a tragic figure. He saw his own image in the sober light of day, as no more than 'a dirty scrofulous little demon, with a cold in the head—not even a successful demon'.

Though Shatov had sought release in his own Messianic Russian faith, he was another distracted victim of Stavrogin's diabolical charm. His chief, Verkhovensky, decided to murder him, solely in order to *forestall* his betrayal of the revolutionary group to which they both belonged. That is exactly what happened to the student Ivanov in the historical *cause célèbre*. At first attracted by their alluring words, Shatov had later grown to hate his sinister confederates. His sense of civic duty now compelled him to denounce them, but fear of reprisals made him hesitate to take the final step. Thus he unconsciously gave the cunning Verkhovensky time enough to organize his murder as a collective act, which would bind the remaining members of the group together through the blood which they had jointly shed.

Dostoyevsky made the most of Shatov by turning him into a mouthpiece for one of his pet beliefs, derived from Hegel, that several nations can never sincerely share a single God. When Gods are thus degraded into communal property, personal faith in them must die, and their nations, to whom they are no longer sacred privately, begin to crumble and decay. Every strong self-respecting nation must therefore worship its own exclusive God, and fight to the death against all rival Gods. To put it bluntly, God becomes a handy instrument for endowing devalued national character with a new set of mystic charms, and hence for justifying further exploits which national vanity may dictate. Though Shatov quibbles over such a bald conclusion, he admits as much when Stavrogin asks him outright whether he believes in God or not. For he stammers in reply: 'I believe in Russia, in her Orthodox Church,' and adds (only under pressure and as an afterthought): 'I—I shall believe in God.'

Impassioned theological disputes, unmasked and brought down to a coarse political plane, virulent personal abuse, face-slapping, enigmatic hints at sexual vice, perverse mental thrills derived from torture, all crowded together in a chaotic nightmare, combine to make *The Devils* the most repulsive of Dostoyevsky's novels, though it is socially illuminating. While he successfully infects the reader with a horror of his major characters, Dostoyevsky brings them to life with such intimate relish

K

that he seems to have fallen under the spell of their diseased obsessions. Largely because of its topical theme, and its attacks on living celebrities, like Nechaev and Turgenev, *The Devils* received more controversial publicity, and hence popular success, than any of Dostoyevsky's previous novels, which were artistically superior.

IX

In 1872 Prince Meshchersky offered Dostoyevsky the editorship of *Gra*z*hdanin* (*The Citi*z*en*), a mystically nationalist and harshly anti-European journal. He started to publish there his *Writer's Diary*,[1] a strikingly modern type of journalistic commentary, in which he conversed informally with his readers, forestalling their objections to his thought, analysing and answering their pet preoccupations—a diary *full of tricks for the public*—as he described it—but designed to guide their minds through the tortuous turmoil of contemporary problems. Despite its fragmentary and anecdotal character, an inner consistency runs through the *Writer's Diary*. It throws light on numerous underlying factors affecting both Russia's tense domestic situation and her long-term foreign policy, and it suggests how she could use her power to shape beneficially the future of the world.

Though Dostoyevsky found fault with Slavophils for hankering after pre-Petrine Russia, he re-stated as his own belief the Messianic national ambition voiced by Shatov in *The Devils*. He condemned Westernized liberals and socialists alike for their harmful attempts to accelerate by jumps the slow organic stages of national growth. Two centuries ago, he said, Peter tried to give Russian history a terrific push towards the West, so that the whole country got stuck in a slough of despond. Impenetrable public apathy, the result of too many shattered expectations, had now become a chronic Russian handicap.

Not only did the Western state apparatus, grown more un-

---

[1] F. M. Dostoyevsky, *Polnoe Sobranie*, vols. 11 and 12, Moscow-Leningrad, 1926–30. (Complete English translation by Boris Brassol, *Diary of a Writer*, New York, 1949.)

wieldy in despotic Russian hands, crush people whom it tried to discipline, but imported humanitarian codes were fostering a sickly, and even cowardly, attitude to crime. Speaking with the undeniable authority of an ex-convict, Dostoyevsky urged that stern sentences of imprisonment or penal servitude would be far *healthier* for society than over-merciful acquittals and light sentences, which were becoming prevalent in the law-courts. He cited some recent instances; a wife who murdered her husband, a man who stole cash, had been acquitted without any penalty, because bad environment and extenuating circumstances were pleaded in their favour. A sadistic peasant, who beat his wife until she hanged herself, was found guilty but 'deserving clemency'. People who delighted in such feeble softness towards criminals could feel no strong compassion for their innocent victims. They merely planted incurable cynicism in the souls of scoundrels, who might have benefited had they been made to suffer severely for their crimes.

Dostoyevsky seized this opportunity to explain his withering contempt for Russian liberal reformers. He accused them of being debauched, like revolutionaries, by egalitarian doctrines, differing from them, not in their grossly materialist beliefs and aims, but chiefly in their caution, hypocrisy and laziness. Liberalism having been in vogue since 1861, careerists knew how to use it to their maximum advantage. Men of this kind, Dostoyevsky claimed, are the first to embrace the idea of importing into Russia ready-made cures from abroad. Their motto is 'Let there be any change whatsoever, so long as it entails no extra work for us'.

Neither liberals nor revolutionaries had one scrap of disinterested sympathy for the common people, still less for their morally conservative spirit. They set themselves up as a higher stratum, segregated from the herd, whom they secretly despised, but wished to dominate. Nor did they make any serious effort to protect simple people from being degraded to their own worship of money, self-indulgence and easy gain. If they had their way, they would gradually transform healthy Russian raw material into a faceless impersonal rabble, no better than the vulgar pleasure-loving crowd which was multiplying in the Western world. They forgot that responsible work remained the surest medium for converting stunted souls into serene and honest ones.

Dostoyevsky had found the tough but sentimental German *Bürger* no better than his counterparts in France and England. Through the mouth of Versilov in *The Raw Youth* (1875) he condemned the Franco-Prussian War, and judged its degrading aftermath to be the beginning of the end of European ascendancy throughout the world. 'At that time I heard most distinctly the funeral bell tolling over Europe. The French had just burned down the Tuileries. They succumbed again to the fatal illusion that men can reconstruct their country's welfare by the sole light of reason.' Wherever consistent logic had prevailed, personal slander and national conceit began to reign supreme. 'The Frenchman became *nothing but a Frenchman,* and the German grew more intensely *German* than at any previous period of his history. Therefore both of them did deeper injury to their own countries than they had ever done before. In the whole of Europe there was not left a single genuine European.' At the Peace of Frankfurt he heard guttural German voices, boastfully demanding vast monetary reparations, fine cigars, plenty of champagne, and hostages.

Despite his personal dislike of Germans, the rapid growth of German power in Europe after 1870 roused Dostoyevsky's admiration. The ruthless character and governmental genius of Bismarck fascinated him. As a sworn enemy, alike of the Catholic Church and of all socialist organizations, and hitherto markedly successful in his fight against them both, the Prussian Bismarck was putting into practice some of Dostoyevsky's favourite precepts. He even began to praise German maid-servants, post-office officials, etc., and to contrast their prompt efficiency with the unreliability of their equivalents in his country.

In his last years Dostoyevsky spoke out decisively in favour of a long-term Russo-German alliance based on rational power-politics. He said in his *Diary of a Writer,* 'Germany *needs us* more than we imagine, not for some temporary advantage, but forever.' He found fault with the Emperor Alexander I for having sacrificed Napoleon to the national ambitions of minor European countries, instead of partitioning the world between the established French and Russian military Empires. 'In 1812, after driving out Napoleon, instead of making peace with him, we moved into Europe and tried to make her happy. But then all those nations, which we had liberated, began to regard us with the utmost ill-will and suspicion. Did Russia not help to consolidate the new German states, but what did she gain by serving Europe in this way? Turks and Semites have become spiritually closer to Western Europeans than we are, for Europe is *terrified* of our ideas.'

He urged that it would be fatal to repeat the same mistake by opposing Bismarck at this vital juncture. Germany, now Russia's natural ally, should be allowed to dominate the West, so long as Russia was left in charge of the Eastern side. Carried away by the dazzling prospect of their joint victory over less important European nations, he wrote with mounting relish of a Europe due to be hacked to pieces, tortured and re-shaped by the Attila horde of German armies, until 'after rivers of blood and a hundred million deaths', the true Eastern form of Christianity would prevail, triumphing alike over German Protestants and French Catholics, who would by then have conveniently annihilated one another.

Though he condemned the military feats of Prussia ('the most learned and enlightened of nations fell upon another equally learned and enlightened one, and devoured it like a wild beast') he did not shrink from exalting the still more blood-curdling historical phase which he described as 'the free universal Slav unification of Europe'. Evidently the same action, in which he saw a German crime, could turn into a blessing, when performed by virtuous Russians!

Like most mystic nationalists, Dostoyevsky drew a sharp but prejudiced distinction between just and unjust wars. The latter, undertaken by inferior foreign countries, and serving sordid stock exchange interests, merely debauched and ruined their unlucky nations; the former, waged by his own country, fought for a universal and disinterested cause, chased away personal cowardice and idleness, both launched and clarified those ideal aims which only a great nation with a soul is obliged to put into effect. On balance it seems that Dostoyevsky's temperament preferred the drastic stimulus of war to all the calmer arts of peace.

'In what manner', he asked, 'is the present kind of peace prevailing between civilized nations superior to open war? Lasting peace, rather than war, tends to harden and bestialize human beings, to generate cruelty and cowardice, fat egoism, and most of all intellectual stagnation. Owners of wealth grow coarser in feeling; the healthy sense of elegance becomes perverted into a thirst for whimsical excesses and abnormalities. Art, meaning genuine art, develops during periods of protracted peace, only because it rises in opposition to that ponderous and vicious slumber of the soul' (*Diary of a Writer*, 1877).

He had no use for the comforting Slavophil belief that Russia might serve as a uniting link between East and West, a sympathetic intermediary to reconcile conflicting blocs of European and Asiatic races. For apart from the prudent alliance with Germany, which he advocated, he favoured a complete rupture between Russia and the West, an escape from that spiritual bondage to which Russian Westernizers had for too long condemned their country.

For Dostoyevsky felt a closer affinity with Asiatic countries than with the modern West. In that he anticipated the Soviet alignment. He proclaimed that Russia would fulfil her civilizing mission (which he here identified with her colonial policy) by turning eastwards into the vast mainland of Asia. When General Skobolev finally crushed Turcoman resistance to Russian arms in Central Asia, Dostoyevsky wrote in tones of exuberant enthusiasm: 'Another fierce and proud people has bowed before the white Tsar. May this victory resound all over Asia. . . . For it holds out far greater promise to us than Europe, and is perhaps our principal future outlet. When we turn to Asia with our new vision of her, there may occur something similar to what happened in Europe when her Renaissance explorers first discovered America. . . . In Europe we were only hangers-on or slaves, whereas we shall go to Asia as masters and civilizers. . . . Build

at least two railroads, one to Siberia and one to Central Asia. . . .
But most of all our civilizing mission will lift up our own spirit,
will give us dignity and sense of purpose, will provide an outlet
to many a restless mind, to the anguished, the lazy, and to those
tired of doing nothing' (*Diary of a Writer*, 1881).

'Oh, if instead of us,' Dostoyevsky petulantly interjected,
'Englishmen or Americans had inhabited Russia, they would
surely have discovered *our America*, lands still less explored than
the interior of Africa. Can we even know what riches may lie
concealed in the bosom of these boundless lands? But *they*
would get at everything, metals, minerals, and innumerable
coalfields.'

While eastward colonial expansion would still provide Russia
with ample *Lebensraum*, it pleased Dostoyevsky to think that
overcrowded urban Europe would sink into a humiliating communism (which she would soon begin to loathe), would be forced
to send her children to dismal barrack-like institutions, while
families forsook their private homes and started to live in standardized collective settlements. Only Russia would be spared this
degradation, for 'we shall have wide expanses, meadows and
forests, and our children will continue to grow up in their parents'
homes, among pleasant gardens, cultivated fields, and not in stony
barracks' (*Diary of a Writer*, 1881).

X

Dostoyevsky wrote with equal pride, but more coolly, about
Russian domination of Eastern Europe, and her eventual conquest
of Constantinople. At that time the *Eastern question* consisted in
the struggle undertaken by Balkan peoples to free themselves
from Turkish overlords. 'We are inflexible in our desire to help
the Slavs,' wrote Dostoyevsky, 'we thereby continue to consolidate the Slav faith in Russia and her power; we accustom them
more and more to look on Russia as their sun, the centre of
Slavdom and even of the entire East.'

Western Europe, frightened of this outcome, was trying by
every means to take the southern Slavs under her tutelage, to

steal them from Russia, 'to set them forever *against* her. Those liberated Slavs will proudly announce to the entire world that they have grown into enlightened nations, whereas Russia remains crudely barbaric. They will indulge in parliaments, orators, and public speeches. Their vanity will be immensely flattered when they read telegraphic despatches about themselves printed in Paris and London newspapers. . . . It is England's intention that the eastern Christians should start to hate us as strongly as she hates us already. . . . But England's interest is not a world interest.' And he concluded that the southern Slavs will recognize, when some great calamity occurs, if not before, that Europe is and must remain the natural enemy of their unification. That the southern Slavs might feel no desire to be politically unified, least of all under Russian rule, did not occur to Dostoyevsky.

At a time when, despite occasional wars, expanding European prosperity remained the wonder of the world, Dostoyevsky declared that the major European nations were being steadily undermined from within. He thought that the Jews alone might manage to survive the downfall of those nations whose banks and financial plans they partially controlled, for they would contrive to make any disaster that occurred redound to their own advantage. Nobody can blame Jews for disliking Dostoyevsky, but when they bluntly call him anti-Semitic, they are apt to forget that he sympathized with poor Jews, and frankly advocated the extension of full civic rights to oppressed Jews in Russia, 'in so far as the Jewish people can prove their ability to accept and use those rights without detriment to the native population' (*Diary of a Writer*, 1877).

But he accused the average wealthy Jew of thriving on the ignorance of people among whom he settled, never stirring a finger to raise the level of their education or economic status, though extracting for himself the maximum advantage from all Gentiles. Jews, he said, had recently triumphed in Western countries, because their own craving for wealth without responsibility had become a characteristic of the age. Yet he clearly anticipated the horrors of rival 'national socialisms', as a bad alternative.

Dostoyevsky was not a bit impressed when Western Europeans boasted about their individual liberty and equality before the law. He retorted that they conceived liberty solely in terms of financial security for themselves—and laws guaranteeing it—while in fact the greed of property-owners and the insatiable envy of those who owned less but wanted more, remained the stark underlying motives. But curiously enough he attacked monetary capital, not on the usual moral grounds, but because, in order to maintain its mobility and expansion, it demanded the maximum international peace, without which it would scurry into hiding or remain unproductive. Private capital had thus a vested interest in maintaining perpetual international peace. For peace-lovers that might be a signal merit, but not for Dostoyevsky. One section alone of European society, the proletarian fourth estate, bore a grudge against capital, and even that was not on principle, but merely because it resented owning too little of its own. For the proletariat yearned to seize capital from those who had it. And Dostoyevsky spoke for a vast 'insulted and injured' Russian fourth estate, angry with the richer outside world.

Therefore his ardent national conservatism, thirsting to acquire more Russian wealth, in no way prevented him from being a rabid revolutionary, where Europe was concerned. While taking the poorest view of revolutions at home, he revelled in the maximum damage they could do abroad, and welcomed every sign of moral anarchy and degeneration which could hasten Europe's ruin. Believing that industrial class-warfare in the West was Russia's best ally, that a Europe weakened by internal strife would help a transfer of power to Asiatic countries, he looked forward to the ultimate submission of an exhausted West to the more primitive and numerous peoples of the Eastern world.

He urged the contemporary Russian man, drawn by two worlds at once, and still wavering between them, to abandon modern European loyalties and emotional ties, while reaping all the benefits of European technique. The Russian must conquer his old hereditary contempt for Tartars, and turn himself into an independent Asiatic, championing fellow-Asiatics against the West. For dazzling opportunities to lead the Eastern world now lay within his grasp, provided he revealed himself to be the relentless political and economic enemy of her Western rivals. On the moral plane, *The Dream of a Ridiculous Man,* a topical parable which Dostoyevsky published in his *Diary,* pointed to the Russian *progressive,* hypnotized by European socialists, as the arch-villain of the piece, for he alone had debauched the hitherto happy and innocent inhabitants of a golden age. Only after they had lost their former natural contentment, did they start to be seduced by his artificial plans for universal happiness; only after turning into criminals through his bad example, did they begin to talk about *abstract* brotherhood and *theoretical* humanity, invent a code of justice, and draw up legal penalties to enforce it by violent means. Dostoyevsky deplored that young Russian women, instead of becoming devoted wives and mothers, were being perverted by the same 'progressives', who persuaded them to abandon their families and undertake more 'useful' work. 'Science can manage very well without you,' he used to say to ardent young blue-stockings, who pestered him for his advice; 'but the family, children, and kitchen, they can never get along without women'.

XI

The final composite Russian man, elaborated by Dostoyevsky in *The Brothers Karamazov,* showed strong Asiatic traits, both in the stormy and impulsive Mitya and in the meek, mystic, self-effacing Alyosha—though profoundly modified by the icy Western reasoning power of Ivan—if it is legitimate to see these three brothers as separate aspects of one man, who might embody all three of them at once.

By contrast Dostoyevsky turns respectable members of the middle class, the decent magistrate and jury, into dim colourless creatures, the more so because they come closer to modern Europeans than any of the Karamazovs. He sardonically caricatured the clumsy and superfluous court proceedings, and when the jury found the innocent Dmitry guilty, and he is condemned to penal servitude, the author implicitly condemns the smug obtuseness of the judge and the dry legal fetish which he serves. All three Karamazov brothers, far as they deviate from every conventional norm, are vital despite their abnormality. Even when they talk to excess about whether God exists or not, and whether all things are permissible, they remain sincere and striking characters. But though they excite and compel attention, they somehow fail to charm. Perhaps they too plainly incorporate rampant social maladies which have gained the upper hand, and such a picture of triumphant sickness can only fascinate an infected mind. Dmitry is morally sick, and therefore emotionally unstable. Ivan is mentally sick, paralysed by doubt. For moral sickness the only cure was to accept punishment, specifically undeserved, but deserved as a retribution for a misspent life. For congenital mental illness no cure was possible, but it might teach healthier people to resist infection. Dostoyevsky tried to build up the spiritually healthy Alyosha as a pointer towards a finer human solution. Alyosha's austerity verges on priggish superiority, and hardly achieves that serene balance which his author had in mind. But the young monk leaves his monastery, and returns to work in the wicked world, while remaining pure in heart. He embodies, however inadequately, a primitive Christian ideal and a powerful Buddhist legend. He helps people who morally need him most, while never imposing himself upon them.

The uncontrollable erotic mania of the evil old father resembles, as an obsessive lust, that political madness which runs through revolutionary characters in *The Devils*. Mitya yields to the same impulse, and to the same prostitute, as his father, however strenuously he reproves and hates himself for doing so. None of the brothers would indulge in all those pages of impassioned intellectual dispute, unless they were racked by guilty impulses and hesitation. They argue more in order to convince themselves than to persuade other people, and for the modern reader they waste too many words over burning issues which now seem tepid or irrelevant.

Since Ivan is by far the most rational and self-conscious of all three, he is more verbose and can be mentally vivisected. Dostoyevsky defined Ivan's rebellious attitude as 'a synthesis of contemporary Russian anarchism', except that he deceived himself less grossly than the average anarchist, because his penetrating mind saw further.

In a letter to the editor of *The Russian Messenger*, Dostoyevsky unfolded this part of his plan for *The Brothers Karamazov*. 'Our stupid but terrible Russian socialism (because youth is carried away by it), takes a definite direction, and so it seems, energetically. Bread, the Tower of Babel, i.e. the approaching socialist Empire and the complete enslavement of human conscience—that is where the atheist and desperate denier now arrives. Our Russian socialists differ from others in being more conscious Jesuits and liars, who will not admit that their ideal is that of raping human conscience and reducing mankind to the level of a herd of cattle. But my socialist (Ivan Karamazov) is at any rate an honest man, who frankly agrees with the Grand Inquisitor's views about the human race, and admits that the Christian faith, apparently, has placed human beings on a much higher level than they deserve to be.' [1]

The *Legend of the Grand Inquisitor* has been commented on *ad nauseam*, and it can safely be left to theologians to decide whether Dostoyevsky was himself a devil's advocate or a devout Christian. His privilege as an artist allowed him to be emphatically both in turn. But the central fact, round which all discussion hinges, is that the Grand Inquisitor condemns and imprisons the returned Christ as a politically dangerous heretic. It is also undeniable that Dostoyevsky makes his Inquisitor, the Catholic statesman, and Ivan, the frankest of Russian revolutionaries, fully agree, both in their diagnosis of human weakness, and in their prescription how to cure its modern malady.

Both claim that human beings, although they crave for wider freedom, and obstinately cling to what they have, are none the less spoiled by it, and bungle their opportunities of choice. Who can blame ordinary people if they cannot shoulder the burden of

[1] L. Grossman, *Dostoyevsky i Pravitel'stvenye Krugi 70kh Godov, Literaturnoe Naslyedstvo*, p. 98, Moscow, 1934.

responsibility, which can with difficulty be borne by the strongest and most cultured ones? Better to grant them the quiet obedient content of simple creatures, such as they are by nature, to demand less effort from them, and direct them as before, by miracle, mystery, and authority, the best powers on earth to conquer, charm, and discipline such puny rebels. In short, the Grand Inquisitor is clearly not a Christian. His contempt for human beings, his plans to enslave them, make him approach the social system designed by Shigalev and Peter Verkhovensky.

XII

In the last numbers of his *Diary of a Writer*, which occupied Dostoyevsky until his death, he delved more deeply into the psychological starting-point which he held responsible for breeding revolutionaries. Believing that material abundance led to more crimes than poverty did, he found the root cause, not in hunger, but in a mounting revolt against the tyranny of boredom, monotony and mechanical convention, and in the emotional instability which inflamed ignorant people with specious novel theories to *justify* their criminal instincts. He confessed to having been a helpless victim of this state of mind at the time he became a member of the Petrashevsky group in the eighteen-forties. But he had learned his lesson. 'Those among us, contaminated in those days, but who later emphatically renounced this chimerical frenzy, all this gloom and horror which is being prepared for mankind under the disguise of regeneration and resurrection—we were then wholly ignorant of the true cause of our malady, and therefore unable to struggle against it' (*Diary of a Writer*).

Meanwhile honest and helpful mental strife was starting to lighten oppressive mental darkness, even though that effort came from poor obscure people, the only ones who never twisted thought to justify or veil their selfish aims. But in course of time that seed of honest thought would germinate in the minds of millions, who would then no longer be content to live like brutes, and would refuse to be consoled 'by fish pies, gay debauch, or basking in the admiration of their official inferiors'. For ideas will gradually infect even people who never think at all. Until then, when people ceased entirely to believe, either in priests, in liberals or in socialists, they would long to kill themselves, apparently without reason, but in fact because of anguish. For that same exasperation, which bred revolutionaries, was clearly reflected in the rising suicide rate.

Dostoyevsky cited the example of the seventeen-year-old daughter of the chastened rebel, Herzen. She had soaked a piece of cotton-wool in chloroform, tied it round her face, and left a note in which she wrote: 'I am undertaking a long journey ... should I not succeed, I would like people to gather together and celebrate my return with a bottle of *Cliquot*.' Did she specify champagne, Dostoyevsky asked, 'because she could not conceive a filthier or more abominable picture than this drinking bout to mark her resurrection from the dead?' What an indescribable disgust for life must have invaded the mind of this young girl.

Mistakes and perplexities of the mind might be resolved by logical analysis and later by the logic of events. But errors of the heart were fatal, and harder to eradicate. Failure to solve them led not only to individual suicide, but could infect whole nations and induce a degree of blindness impenetrable to truth, no matter how persistently it was pointed out. Often that deliberate blindness re-modelled the outside world to fit its own darkened vision, and an entire nation might perish and prefer to die, obstinately clinging to its blindness, rather than consent to be cured of it by facing unfamiliar and disturbing facts.

The upper classes understood that leaders of the proletariat were tempting their followers with rich bribes and greed for plunder. To go on pleading moral or spiritual aims had become obvious hypocrisy and waste of time. The proletarians themselves, without admitting it, had abandoned moral effort, though they still pretended to seek nothing for their own benefit but everything for *the public*, for *humanity*, etc., while in fact they got ready to fight for bigger shares of other people's property. The unrepentant *bourgeois* rejoined that human beings can only be reduced to total acquiescence by terror, espionage, and the ceaseless control of despotic government. 'Both sides are terribly wrong,' Dostoyevsky pronounced, 'and both will perish in their crimes.'

He still preferred, however, to call mutual class-hatred an alien European *impasse*, which had only started to show its ugly face in Russia. Unfortunately Russia's democratic intellectuals had shown themselves to be, not understanding friends, but concealed enemies of their own people, going among them, nominally to do them good, yet scorning the people's traditional customs and ideals. Nor had they improved when they forsook their intellectual pride, started to indulge in Tolstoyan eccentricities, took hold of wheelbarrows and announced: 'I am not a nobleman, I want to work as a peasant.' For their previous education would certainly prevent them from turning into satisfactory agricultural labourers. Rather than put on a badly fitting smock of assumed simplicity, they would do better to understand and lighten the peasants' heavy burden.

His speech at the unveiling of the Pushkin memorial in Moscow (April 1880) aroused a tumultuous sensation. Young students in the audience swooned from excitement, enthusiasts showered him with bouquets, and even his enemy, Turgenev, blew him a kiss. He reconciled Slavophils with Westernizers, by pointing to new responsibilities which every educated Russian of today must shoulder. He must translate into action that response to the character and genius of *past ages* and of *foreign nations*, that creative sense of international kinship, first demonstrated by Pushkin, who, alone among world-poets, had the power to re-incarnate within himself the finest qualities of alien nations, without abandoning his own.

Pushkin presaged the future destiny of Russia in his guiding idea of her universality, derived from her response to other countries, and in his reliance on the moral strength of her common people. His work on foreign themes had proved how only a Russian could creep inside a foreigner's skin and yet remain himself, unlike Shakespeare's Italian characters, who always spoke and behaved like stolid Englishmen dressed in theatrical costumes. Though Pushkin had lived many years ahead of average Russian consciousness, later Russians, thanks to being educated through his works, could master the purest aspirations of older European culture, and feel a brotherly kinship to French, Germans, and other nationalities, despite the fact that these older nations never reciprocated their friendly advances, but made up their minds to dislike and despise Russians as dangerous upstarts and competitors.

Hence arose what Dostoyevsky grandiloquently called 'our urge to render universal service to mankind, sometimes even to the detriment of our own momentous and immediate interests . . . Every national individuality lives for itself alone. We, on the other hand, now that the hour has come, will begin by becoming servants of all nations, for the sake of their mutual reconciliation.' But he voiced a pained surprise and anger that 'the mighty of this world, those who till now have triumphed in it, always look upon these Russian expectations with utter derision and disdain, being unable to imagine that anyone can believe seriously in the brotherhood of men. . . . In this respect Europe completely fails to understand our national ideals—or rather applies them to her gauge—and therefore attributes to us her own thirst for plunder, violence and exploitation of weaker countries.'

But even Dostoyevsky hardly expected that foreigners would believe him. And he was thinking, less of his country's state policy, than of its victims, the hard-pressed Russian people. At least they did not pretend, as many foreigners did, that their vices ought to be considered virtues. 'Judge the Russian people,' he repeated, 'not by the degrading crimes which it commits so often, but by the great and holy things to which, in the midst of its degradation, it constantly aspires.' Judge them, in other words, not by what they do, but by what they sometimes want to be, not by any hell which they may manage to create, but by the sublime intentions with which they pave it lavishly. That was asking a lot from those who felt crushed or smothered by the Russian state.

Though the concluding political tune, which Dostoyevsky sang so loudly a few months before his death, may sound stridently melodramatic to European ears, it remained sincere for him, and by no means an isolated outcry, for a substantial

Russian chorus echoed it. Neither was it altogether new, for it throbbed with the same pangs of unrequited love, expressed by Lermontov's *A Hero of our Times*, magnified in Dostoyevsky's case to national dimensions, and twisted into a longing to inflict revenge. Dostoyevsky, with his thwarted international sympathies, might well have repeated in company with Pechorin: 'I was ready to love the whole world, but no one understood me, so I learned to hate. For fear of being mocked, I buried my best feelings in the depths of my heart, where they died. When I spoke the truth, no one believed me, so I began to master the arts of deception.'

When Dostoyevsky attributed his own frustrated strivings to the future mission of his country, he plunged into Utopian spheres and mingled wild conjectures with alluring possibilities and stubborn facts. But he knew how to stir the hearts of patriotic readers when he crowned with laurel wreaths the lice-covered heads of poor emancipated peasants, praised the drunkard with a heart of gold, and repeatedly forgave the repentant sinner, however flagrantly he went on sinning.

Even if a later generation could accept, as an act of faith, Dostoyevsky's claim that broad generosity and warm brotherly instincts are peculiar to the Russian people, how can this be reconciled with his ghastly picture of the Russian *underground man*, with his own hatred of modern Europe, and his vindictive outbursts against other races, especially against Poles, Jews, and Turks? And by what sheer conjuring trick could he transfer to the Russian political apparatus qualities which, on his own evidence, were confined to individuals or to imaginative art? A dramatic clash of total opposites remained the very air he breathed, and dominated Dostoyevsky's mind until the end.

L

CHAPTER V

THE YOUNG LEO TOLSTOY

I

OF various ways in which an inconvenient legacy of genius can be ignored by later generations, the simplest is for the creator to remain unrecorded or anonymous, but the more frequent is to be so smothered in a spate of superfluous records, gossip, and detailed documentation, that the eminent victim is first put upon a pedestal, and then laid aside on library shelves as a graded historical specimen, accessible to zealous students who revere the past, but artificially remote from contact with average modern citizens.

Considering the sheer quantity of literature which has piled up round L. N. Tolstoy (1828–1910), in addition to his voluminous but severely biased frankness about himself, people may justly wonder whether anything worth saying about his life and work could by now remain unsaid, and yet feel less than ever able to decide how he can help them, if at all, and which of the strongly conflicting interpretations of him comes nearest to the truth.

A similar predicament never seems to have deterred the tireless commentators on Shakespeare, who continue unabated. Tolstoy's less numerous but more variegated admirers, back-to-the-landers, evangelical revivalists, sectarians, ideal anarchists, spiritual epicureans, and even some sober literary historians, who each conducted controversies about him, have often done more to blur than to clarify the picture of his complex personality, and have overlaid it with a thick varnish of catchwords and partisan platitudes.

It may seem strange that, despite his world-wide fame, and the volumes of comment which he provoked, Tolstoy has neither been explained away nor naturally understood. If the reading public of today ignores him, it is due more to this confused remoteness, than because people have already assimilated all he had

L. N. TOLSTOY

from a portrait by Kramskoy

to give and passed him by. Such inward movement of historical judgement as still survives, untouched by mercenary advertisement, admits that his relevance has grown with time, despite the practical absurdity of actions which he recommended in his sour old age. While the personal aspirations which he took so much to heart may seem far-fetched, quixotic, or strangely out of date to matter-of-fact twentieth-century minds, the fiercely destructive human conflicts, to which he drew attention, have assumed a more ominous shape and inescapable urgency, only dimly sensed by his contemporaries. For many of the ugly and catastrophic crises in the world of politics, social relations, and creative art, which he foretold, have now visibly occurred on a much larger scale.

His contemporaries, with a few rare exceptions, never saw Tolstoy steadily or saw him whole, perhaps because he came too close to them, and made so many bitter enemies or meek disciples. His frank but explosive temperament could never tolerate a lasting compromise in combat, even when he reluctantly submitted to a temporary truce. And his critics could neither like nor understand a man, who not only towered above them in mental vigour, but thunderously attacked most of the social and intellectual fashions of his day, even when he knew that they had gained the upper hand.

Tolstoy's own version of himself, though more precise, and differing from those provided by his disciples, his critics, or his enemies, is not always more reliable. With our wider knowledge of the total facts about him, we cannot accept at its face value his habitual self-reproach and self-indictment, least of all the naïve black and white picture of two separate Tolstoys, an ambitious, vain, and lustful man before 'conversion', and a purified penitent afterwards, though with backslidings which were dutifully deplored.

His best biographers, from Aylmer Maude to Ernest Simmons, have provided an unbiased narrative of his life. They have also mapped out the intimate interaction linking the pressure of events upon him with the pattern of his imaginative work, down to the tragic *impasse* between his settled patriarchal habits and the unrealizable rigours of his last ethical obsessions.

But his disciples have probably done more damage to a proper understanding of their master than any hostile critics. For they singled out his dubious senile phase, that of an agrarian evangelist, as the goal and sum total of his achievement. Long impassioned arguments, pursued on elevated planes of theology and morals, which now seem artificial or obsolete, formed part of the mental climate peculiar to the educated class of late nineteenth-century Europe. Therefore Tolstoy's laborious restatement of Christian and Buddhist teaching (adapted, as he imagined, to serve real modern needs) attracted *then* far more attention than we may now think that it deserved, and it gave a false, one-sided impression of his dynamic personality. Yet we should be thankful that the revivalist ferment of that period accidentally brought the real Tolstoy into the orbit of many thousands, to whom he might otherwise have remained unknown.

There is now no need to linger over that exhaustively discussed religious phase, still less over the naked details of his private life, which his biographers and his own remorseless diaries have more than sufficiently revealed. But Tolstoy claimed that a genuine artist takes out of his life the valuable part, and transfers that to his work. All background relics of raw material, a maze of physical and mental anecdotes, often sordid or contradictory, should fade away before the towering shape which he imposed on them. Tchaikovsky came to a similar conclusion when he noted, after his disappointing personal contact with famous writers and composers, how he learned that their *works*, musical or literary, are by far the most interesting part of them.

Tolstoy remained a powerful literary artist long after he had logically condemned the cult of pseudo-art. Hence his revived social judgements owe their vitality, less to the threadbare penitence of a puritan iconoclast, than to the struggle for survival of an inborn creative conscience, growing in depth and scope. Waves of subconscious feeling, imperative moral instinct and reverence for the intrinsic laws of art, governed Tolstoy's mind throughout his life, and, equally before and after his 'conversion', they set the standard by which he tested bare convictions, the utility of social institutions, and the likely *human* value of many scientific discoveries which were then beginning to transform the world.

Therefore the mental and emotional upheaval which he described in his *Confession* needs no religious explanation, if it can be grasped as a natural crisis, forced upon him, when he saw the ominous interaction between degrading forms of art and the inward life of human beings exposed to its ravages, and also when he knew that he had reached saturation point in his own creative work, and could go no further in the same direction. Once he recognized that he could never surpass his former masterpieces, *War and Peace* and *Anna Karenina*, and refused to write easy but inferior imitations of them, like a cynical best-seller lured by gain, he began to feel the imperative urge to move into a new, untried sphere, and switch from the tense nervous drama of Europeanized Russian society into the more limited but refined simplicity of his later peasant tales and parables.

Official Soviet commentaries on Tolstoy have not encouraged fresh interpretation of his work.[1] The Academy of Sciences commendably undertook to publish a monumental edition, designed to collect every scrap and variant of his writings which can be found.[2] Prime importance is still attached to Lenin's statement, which rather surprisingly summed up Tolstoy as 'the mirror of the Russian Revolution'. (Lenin, who wrote that sentence in 1908, referred of course to the revolution of 1905.) That political approach has not prevented Tolstoy from becoming, in selected editions of his work, a more respected and widely-read author in his native land today than any contemporary Soviet novelist.

Lenin called Tolstoy a comic prophet, discovering new recipes for salvation. He contended that Tolstoy did not understand the Russian revolutionary movement; if he had, he would never have opposed it so vehemently. But Tolstoy claimed that he understood the revolutionaries better than they understood themselves, and that was why he fought against them. Lenin admitted that people

[1] A massive volume, *L. N. Tolstoy v Russkoy Kritike* (Moscow, 1952), collects the views of numerous leading critics of Tolstoy, but begins by recommending any Soviet writer on the subject to master Lenin's method of analysis.
[2] L. N. Tolstoy, *Polnoe Sobranie*, Moscow-Leningrad, 1928, etc.

might logically ask, was it not misleading to call Tolstoy the 'mirror' of a movement which he misunderstood, and therefore reflected inaccurately? But he answered, no, it was *not* misleading, because Tolstoy's own self-contradictions reflected the ambiguous, puzzled attitude of Russian peasants towards the revolution. 'They wept and prayed, reasoned and dreamed, wrote petitions and sent deputations, wholly in the spirit of Leo Tolstoy,' who thereby mirrored the weakness and inadequacy of the peasants' inchoate revolt against the established order.[1]

This judgement reveals the fragmentary interest which a single-minded politician may feel for a many-sided artist. But in one respect it is correct. Tolstoy *did* come close to the peasants in his wary hostility to encroachments by the Russian Government, and Lenin showed sound sense in foreseeing, as early as 1908, that many peasants would oppose the Bolsheviks as strenuously as Tolstoy had opposed the earlier social revolutionaries—a prediction amply confirmed by the votes cast for the political parties which formed the short-lived Constituent Assembly of January 1918 (dissolved by Lenin after a single session), and later by the desperate peasant revolt against collectivization of farming by the Soviet state.

II

Tolstoy lived perpetually under the spell of his childhood memories, for his earliest pure impressions moulded his whole future life. 'Happy irrecoverable time,' he wrote, 'will that freshness, freedom from care, longing for love, and strong faith, which belonged to childhood, will they ever return? What time can be better than when these two prime benefactors, innocent gaiety and the longing for love, provided the sole motives in our life?' Yet already in the semi-autobiographical story *Childhood*, the sensitive pagan and the reproachful moralist within him were fighting for the upper hand: already, as in the later Tolstoy, passionate impulse and minute analysis clash and yet contribute to one another's intensity. Only then the conflicts, which later

[1] L. N. Tolstoy, *Sobranie*, vol. I, p. 5, Moscow, 1948.

grew so harsh, involved, and overwhelming, were confined to ominous storms in a teacup, charming trifles which rose to importance in the harmless play of a lively child's imagination, and gave a brief delight, before they were obliterated by that adult stage, 'when the soul is stifled by all those lies which kill the life within us'.

One of the earliest scenes in *Childhood* gives a revealing glimpse of Tolstoy's innate capacity for simultaneous dual feelings. When Karl Ivanich clumsily woke him in the morning, and he opened his eyes, he felt at first a violent hatred for the whole person of the German tutor, including his repulsive dressing-gown and ugly cap and tassel. But that impulse was quickly followed by a guilty sense of shame, pity and affection for the good old man, so devoted to him and his little sister. The sharply conflicting emotions brought tears to his eyes, and a sudden desire to laugh.

Tolstoy's mother died when he was two years old. Through the mists of memory he could form no exact picture of her features, but he constantly recalled the beautiful smile which lit up and transformed the expression of her face. In the story *Childhood* the motherless child's unsatisfied craving for love found a warm response in the serf housekeeper, Natalya Savishna, who, he said, 'exerted such a powerful and good influence over the whole development of my emotions'. Tolstoy's patient and chivalrous attitude to the often exasperating emancipated peasants of his later life remained coloured by his indelible impressions of devoted house-serfs, whose whole life consisted in loyal unquestioning service to their masters. He records how Natalya Savishna refused indignantly to accept the legal freedom offered to her by her mistress, whom she loved and served happily until her death: it never entered her head to change or improve her social status.

Tolstoy's father, who died when he was nine years old, had served in the Russian army during the Napoleonic wars, but he retired in 1819 with the rank of Lieutenant-Colonel. Although he was too well-bred to display a rebel mood, he found the state service irksome and irritating, and spent the remainder of his life administering his wife's estates, which involved him in many lawsuits. He kept aloof, both from official circles and from the commercial classes which were starting to flourish in the towns. When he died, devoted female relatives took charge of the orphan children. Thus the young Leo grew up in quiet rural surroundings, among cultured, independent, but by no means wealthy landowners, all closely linked to agricultural pursuits, and to a majestic nature of wide fields and ancient forests.

The study of law and oriental languages at Kazan University failed to arouse any particle of his immense latent intellectual curiosity. But one of his professors inspired him to write an incisive comparison between Montesquieu's essay *L'Esprit des Lois* and the *Nakaz* (instructions for a code of laws) written by Catherine the Great. Here he characteristically found fault with Catherine's 'petty vanity', and forecast his later hostility to a coercive state by remarking that any positive legal code, in order to benefit people, must be derived from the moral law within us; law must coincide with conscience.

In 1847, when a division of the family property between him and his brothers took place, he decided to leave the university without taking a degree. He received as his share the estate of Yasnaya Polyana near Tula, together with 350 male serfs and their families. He began to feel an awakening sense of responsibility for those dependant human beings now entrusted to his care, and he decided to settle down at once to agricultural work in Yasnaya Polyana.

The inner story of his first attempt to embark on social and agricultural improvements on his own estate is told in *A Landowner's Morning* (1852), the prelude to a larger work *The Russian Landowner*, which he planned but never carried out. In this story the young landowner writes to his aunt in Petersburg: 'Is it not my sacred and plain duty to promote the happiness of these seven hundred people for whom I am now answerable to God? Is it not a crime, for the sake of my personal ambition or enjoyment, to abandon them to the treatment of coarse village elders or bailiffs? And why should I seek in any other sphere opportunities to be useful and to do good, when I have already open to me such a noble and satisfying obligation? I feel that I am capable of being a good landowner, and for that I need neither diplomas nor an office.' The aunt's reply is impregnated with a more mature worldly wisdom than Tolstoy had yet acquired from trial and error. She observed that in order to be an efficient landlord one should possess a cold, stern character—which her nephew lacked—that it is easier to make happiness for oneself than for other people, and that his pet wish to show off as a local benefactor came dangerously close to self-indulgent vanity.

The young man persevered against his aunt's advice. He organized a free medical service in the village, and built stone cottages to rehouse the poorest peasants. But they obstinately refused to move out of their tumbledown wooden hovels. Passive resistance, lack of confidence in him, defeated all his efforts to improve their lot. Instead of gaining gratitude or some co-operation from his peasants, he had to fight their attachment to routine, subterfuge, silent suspicion, and exasperating helplessness. In the end he admitted that he would have been wiser to follow his aunt's advice.

In 1848 Tolstoy left Yasnaya Polana for Moscow, and a little later he moved on to Petersburg. In both cities he plunged into a round of social engagements, dissipation, and gambling. He announced, however, that he had now determined to become a man of the world, to make a career, and give up building castles in the air. And he strenuously cultivated all the urban conventions and pleasures which he later condemned so heartily through knowing them too well.

Yet in his diary, already determined to over-correct any impudent propensity to boast, he laid bare his endless deviations from the *rules of conduct* which he had started to set himself.[1] While he had treated with kindly indulgence his father's amorous escapades and passion for gambling, his tone hardened the moment he found and described similar vices in himself. Sensuality, and his repeated failures to resist it, tortured him more than any other vice. His brother Sergei called him at this time a thoroughly empty-headed fellow. He also began to feel disgusted with his mode of life, and in the spring of 1851 he abruptly abandoned it by departing for the Caucasus, to serve there as a volunteer in the Russian army.

---

[1] 'I fall into despair because my left moustache is higher than my right, and for two hours I straighten it out before the looking-glass' (*Diary*, 1851).

III

The exhilarating change of scene, the daily round of garrison duties, punctuated by military raids against the native Caucasian tribes, took Tolstoy's mind away from his habitual introspection. With keen enjoyment of his own bravado he took part in fierce fighting against the Chechenians, whose villages the Russians sacked and burned. But soon he registered misgivings about the double-faced activity of the Russian Government in its steady, relentless colonization of the Caucasus and Central Asia. His well-known hatred of modern war started to take root, for his sympathy was stirred by the primitive, turbulent but warm-hearted Asiatic tribesmen, who fought so desperately to preserve their precarious independence against the overwhelming force of Russian arms and the spread of Russian state administration.

The Caucasian stories of this early period contain all the elements of the tragic *Hadji Murat* (1904), written with singular freshness during his declining years. Here he began to forge that inexorable chain of reasoning, which in the end compelled him to deny that the sovereign rulers of the Russian Empire, in transforming heterogeneous Eastern Europe and northern Asia into a single centralized state, had served the advance of civilization, in that spiritual sense which he attached to it. Even before he fought in the Crimean War, Tolstoy harped on the evil and senseless brutality displayed in war, started to probe into its psychological causes, and tried to discover how otherwise normal men, the moment they blindly submitted to their governments' commands, could be persuaded to mutilate and murder one another, without feeling any qualms of conscience.

His story *The Raid* (1853) asked some dangerously leading questions about the inmost nature of so-called warlike virtues. 'Can a horse be called brave,' he wrote, 'which, because it is terrified of the whip, hurls itself down a steep precipice where it will be smashed to pieces, or a man who, to assert his vanity, resolves to kill a fellow-creature, and thereby exposes himself to the danger of being killed? In every danger there lies a choice. Does it not depend on whether that choice is prompted by a noble motive or

a base one, whether it should be called courage or cowardice?'
Significantly, this identical passage, struck out of Tolstoy editions
by the Tsarist censorship prior to 1905, has been deleted with
equal care from popular Soviet editions of Tolstoy's stories.[1]

Observing the jokes and light-hearted talk habitual to officers
and soldiers before they start a battle, he marvelled that they
showed no trace of that nervous anxiety which he experienced.
At the same time he asked probingly: 'What did their stoical attitude, their *sang-froid* really prove? Was it firmness of mind, indifference to danger, or did it betray carelessness, indifference to life
itself?' And then followed another tormenting question. 'War,
what an incomprehensible phenomenon it is; when one's reason
asks, is it just, is it necessary?—an inner voice always answers, no.
Only the persistence of this unnatural strife makes it seem
natural, and nothing but the instinct for self-preservation makes
it seem just.'

In his next story, *The Wood-Felling* (1853), he took advantage
of his recent military experience to analyse the soldiers who
composed the Russian army, and divide them into three major
psychological types, which he called *submissive, commanding*, and
desperate. In his opinion the first type, although by far the commonest, was also the most admirable, because of its great humility,
patient endurance of hardship and acceptance of the will of God.
The commanding type he divided into two sub-varieties, the
severe and the *political*. The former, often brave and imaginative
leaders, he admired almost as much as the long-suffering submissive rank and file. On the other hand he already loathed the
politically-minded commanding type. These, he said, were always
literate men, clever in speech, but treacherous in action; they gave
themselves superior airs in the presence of the common soldier
and refused to smoke the same tobacco as he did. Tolstoy regretted that such men were visibly increasing both in numbers
and in influence, although they rarely made such efficient soldiers
as their less talkative *severe* counterparts. As for the *desperate*
types, they were brave enough, and often fascinating personalities,
but wholly unreliable.

[1] See L. N. Tolstoy, *Sobranie*, etc., vol. I, *Biblioteka Ogonyok*, Moscow, 1948.

We know from Tolstoy's diaries at this time that he shunned the noisy gatherings of his brother officers, whose diversions seldom went beyond games of chance, drinking parties, and repeating endless anecdotes about the Caucasian campaigns. He found relief in reading books, shooting snipe, mixing with the local Cossacks, and keeping a diary, which gave him useful practice in his probing self-analysis, and in discovering other characters almost as paradoxical as his own. He outlined his own worst faults as 'laziness, lies, over-eating, indecision, the desire to show off, sensuality, too little pride'. At the same time he suffered from a vague frustration. 'I am so ambitious,' he noted in 1854, 'and that craving has been so little satisfied, that often, I fear, I would prefer fame to good works, if I had to choose between them.' Meanwhile in one of his worst lapses into gambling, he lost so heavily that he was obliged to sell the big house in Yasnaya Polyana in order to pay his debts of honour.

Tolstoy had ample opportunity to observe the stupid, casual manner in which a promising young officer could abuse his golden opportunities in order to promote his self-destruction. He summed up this theme in his short story, *Records of a Marker* (1855). Here, before the young man shoots himself, he leaves an explanatory letter, which in its searching mental honesty and evocation of remorse is eminently Tolstoyan. 'God gave me everything that a man could want, wealth, a good name, intelligence and noble strivings. But since I had determined to enjoy myself, I covered with filth all that was good within me. . . . I am not dishonoured, not even unhappy; I committed no crime against the law, but I did worse than that; I murdered my feelings, my own mind, my freshness. . . . And now I am constantly falling lower. I know that I am falling, yet I cannot stop myself. . . . But what in fact has ruined me? Was there any strong passion that could explain or justify my fall? No, there was none. Cards, champagne, billiard balls, rainbow-coloured bank-notes, cigarettes, women for sale, those are my memories. Horror overwhelmed me when I suddenly became aware what an immeasurable gulf now separated me from all that I had tried to be!'

IV

Towards the end of 1854 Tolstoy petitioned to be allowed to join the regular Russian army, already fighting in the Crimean War, 'most of all on account of patriotism, of which at that time, I must confess, I had a bad attack', as he described it in a letter. His first Sevastopol story is written in the same expansive mood. It delighted the Emperor so much that he later gave orders for it to be translated into French. As Tolstoy's personal impression of the staunch defenders on the bastions of Sevastopol, it rings true, and shows no trace of patriotic platitude or tritely nationalist bravado. His instinctive pang of horror at the first sight of wounded and mutilated men was redeemed by a stronger exhilaration; 'Wanting to say too much to express my sympathy and amazement, I can find no words, or I feel how inadequate are the words which come into my mind, and I bow silently before that mute unconscious greatness and strength of spirit, that shyness in front of its own merits.' He compared unfavourably the quiet efficient courage of common soldiers ('heroes unaware of their own heroism') with his own excitable ambition and longing to win high military distinctions. But here he touched lightly on that theme, and only started to harp on the humiliating contrast in his next sketch *Sevastopol in May*.

This second story submits the serving Russian officers to the same merciless psychological dissection which he had practised on himself. He concentrated on their defects, queried any redeeming virtues, and laid their sordid underlying motives bare. At the same time his deep-seated doubts about the need and justification for war took a more uncompromising shape. 'All the problems left undecided by diplomats are even less decided by gunpowder and blood.' To put it bluntly, the resort to war renounces a solution, for it proves that civilized nations have surrendered reason to insanity. And men on the edge of the grave, in the thick of slaughter, still dream about military decorations and promotion in rank. 'Personal vanity is the most distinctive feature and sickness peculiar to our century.'

Why, Tolstoy asked, could Homer and Shakespeare write so

stirringly about love, honour, or patient suffering, while the literature of our age had faded into an endless chronicle of 'snobs and petty vanity'? And as the stature of the individual shrinks in scale, both real heroes and downright villains vanish from the scene, obliterated by the sole remaining hero, naked *truth*, who then turns out to be a chilly substitute for even the most unsatisfactory human beings. But having resolved to unveil the worst, at any price, to *debunk* the false romantic glamour which still clung to war and war-like courage, Tolstoy was content to blacken the character of his brother officers and condemn his own. Absorbed in this negative over-correction, he remained strangely silent about the moral failings of any soldier below commissioned rank, as if the higher officers had acquired a monopoly of vice, while their subordinates all shone as paragons of virtue.

But Tolstoy felt uneasy in his judgement. 'Perhaps what I have said belongs to those evil truths which, unconsciously hidden in the soul, ought not to be disclosed, like dregs of wine which spoil it, if they are poured out.' In the third Sevastopol story (*Sevastopol in August*, 1855) he tried to restore the balance by introducing better officers. Yet it turned out the most colourless and laboured of all three stories—as if the Crimean campaign had ceased to touch his heart. It elaborated the familiar cooling down of patriotic ardour under the clumsy impact of administrative machinery. The young lieutenant Kozeltsov might have become a proper hero if, in the first flush of enthusiasm, he had gone straight from his country home to the bastions of Sevastopol. But only several months after he had volunteered did he at last receive a formal inquiry as to whether he belonged to any masonic lodge. And then he had to wait three months longer before his first military appointment. Tolstoy put in a good word for the frustrated young man, who would have to undergo a lot more moral suffering, before he became 'quiet and patient in work and danger, as we are accustomed to see the Russian officer'. And that was the most that anyone could expect of him, for his original enthusiasm could never be revived.

The story ends with the surrender of Sevastopol after its stubborn defence for eleven months against a numerically superior enemy. Tolstoy memorably recorded how Russian soldiers received the sudden order to retreat. First came a stunned surprise and bewildered disappointment; then arose sharper, more poignant feelings, a mixture of remorse, shame and anger. Almost every soldier, he concluded, 'looking back on the west side from abandoned Sevastopol, with an inexpressible bitterness weighing on his heart, sighed and inwardly cursed the enemy'.

The three stories, taken consecutively, as they ought to be, leave an overwhelming impression of genuine human sacrifices made in vain. Their journalistic actuality and detail bring out sharply the cumulative sense of official muddle and futile national effort, created by the Crimean War on the mind of a young officer who took an active part in it. Because an armchair pacifist on principle, who had never smelt gunpowder, could not possibly have written them, their innate pacifist feeling is all the more compelling. The first sketch is hardly an exception, for its breath of patriotic fervour springs from a fleeting mood, which, when it turns into sober narrative, contrasts the feats of silent courage, shown mostly by obedient soldiers, with the vulgar military appeal of flying banners, martial music, and decorations for valour. The naked ugliness of modern war is visible even here, its helpless victims tortured for no apparent purpose. If the stories stop short of fixing responsibility on the brutal stupidity of national governments, they already hint at the limits of human endurance and the mounting thirst for vengeance.

Tolstoy made the utmost of his war service, not as a professional career, in which he sought promotion (although he was in fact recommended for a military medal, the George Cross), but simply as a means of observing the behaviour of his fellow-creatures in dangerous and extraordinary situations. While he showed no less bravery than many others, he never troubled to please his superior officers, and sometimes annoyed them by dashing about like a war correspondent in search of the fullest and most exciting story. He had not studied the technique of currying favour. In November 1855 a military order transferred him to St. Petersburg.

V

The twenty-seven-year-old artillery officer, fresh from the battle front, now plunged for the first time into the intellectual circles of the capital, where he was already known to readers of the monthly periodical, *The Contemporary*, as a rising literary star. For Nekrasov, Dobrolyubov, Chernyshevsky, and other members of the editorial staff, who had studied each other's vagaries inside out, perpetually argued and patched up their irritating verbal disagreements, it came as an exhilarating shock to face this talented *enfant terrible* from the outside world of action, a serving officer and hereditary landowner, hitherto untouched by literary cliques and journalistic diplomacy.

Nekrasov wrote enthusiastically about him: 'What a dear energetic noble young man—a hawk, perhaps an eagle—he is even better than his writings, and you know how good they are!' [1] This eager competition among the Petersburg journalists to make a fuss of Tolstoy and win him for themselves, soon showed a less attractive side. It became a question, who would first succeed in taming this gifted savage, in securing him as a regular contributor to a single journal, and thereby as a potent advertisement for their own school of thought, contributing, incidentally, to their financial profits and prestige.

Though Nekrasov made strenuous efforts to win Tolstoy's friendship and esteem, he soon began to be disturbed by what he called his pupil's lack of 'social sensibility'. For Tolstoy, on closer personal acquaintance with them, instinctively recoiled from identifying himself with *The Contemporary* editors, in what seemed to him their indiscriminate capitulation to fashionable clichés, and their over-excitement about urbanization and democratic institutions, then being hastily introduced to Russia from Western Europe. He was shocked by the conceited contempt which these radicals displayed for ancient Russian customs, and by the harsh, irritable and angry tone, which Nekrasov and Chernyshevsky had made prevalent.

The commercial attractions of professional anger were just be-

[1] B. Eikhenbaum, *L. Tolstoy*, vol. 1, p. 208, Leningrad, 1928.

ginning to be realized. Young writers were paid to howl and yelp with righteous rage. 'Whether in criticism or in fiction,' Tolstoy observed, 'the opinion has now been formed that to be indignant, bad-tempered, and splenetic is a good thing. But *I* find it a thoroughly bad thing. For a splenetic angry man cannot be in a healthy state of mind. Only a loving person is in a normal state to do good and see things clearly.' Chernyshevsky in his turn tried hard, but vainly, to *convert* Tolstoy. Even the flattering patronage and help, then given to him by Turgenev, irritated Tolstoy. Although they shared some tastes, he laughed at Turgenev's ostentatious parade of democratic convictions, at his over-pliable tolerance and nervous impressionability. He suspected him of spiritual flabbiness, of being ready to make concessions in a sphere where compromise became a sin against the Holy Ghost.

In any case the precarious alliance between the cultured noblemen and the newly-educated *raznochintsy* (men of mixed ranks) was falling apart beyond repair, though this was hardly a conflict between rival economic classes, still less between the older generation and its young successor. It was rather the inevitable clash of strong personalities, growing to maturity, while opposed in temperament and desires. In fact Chernyshevsky and Tolstoy not only belonged to the same generation, they were born in the same year (1828). The publication of Chernyshevsky's stodgy treatise, *The Aesthetic Relation of Art to Reality* (1855), crammed with superfluous abstract hair-splitting, was taken in deadly earnest by both sides. It first turned the concealed literary civil war into an open battle, and it provided the radicals with a ready-made set of useful battle cries.

Tolstoy now found common ground with Turgenev in resisting what they both dreaded, the insidious encroachment of trite journalism into the sacred sphere of art. They faced the threat that pompous civic sermons and sour malice would gradually eliminate all purer forms of literature. The normally over-tolerant Turgenev repented of his liberal self-indulgence, and was provoked to write with exceptional emphasis to Drujinin: 'I frequently had the misfortune to take sides against you with *him who smells of lice*—henceforth I shall call him nothing else. Please accept my regrets

M

and my oath to pursue, despise and annihilate him with all permitted and impermissible means. I have read his disgusting book, that accursed dead thing, which *The Contemporary* was not ashamed to take seriously.' But later he wrote: 'I deplore his dryness and coarse taste, yet I admit there is in him some living vein . . . and that is not merely the result of an upset liver, as our dear Grigorovich once said.' [1]

If topicality, burning social grievances, became the supreme or sole concern of art, then spiteful disputes, coarse satires, or cold factual surveys, would usurp the place of beautiful, wise, and timelessly truthful stories. The novel, in Chernyshevsky's hands, turned into a statistical survey of fleeting human types, an argumentative puppet show, exemplifying current points of view. He already squeezed literary art into the background, condescendingly confined it to the expression of ephemeral sensations, a few nervous lights and shades, the unimportant human moods which still escaped the ever enlarging network of scientific analysis. 'Farewell ecstasy, farewell gentle lyrics!' To make people's blood boil coldly with rational indignation, to preach reforms pointed to by incriminating documents, to satirize and condemn, would henceforth cover the range of emotional needs worthy of being catered for by a *useful* literature. That, in brief, was the *Chernyshevsky line*, which devoutly radical writers in the late eighteen-fifties were beginning to pursue with the notorious zeal of recent converts.

When Tolstoy felt impelled to take up arms against this sinister intellectual campaign, he tried to find useful allies among the existing rivals and enemies of *The Contemporary* group. He courted some of the Slavophils, but soon found them too eccentric or dryly antiquarian to serve his purpose.

He then started to cultivate the amiable tea-merchant Botkin, a discriminating patron of the arts, who generously helped the more independent writers, Annenkov and Drujinin. For a time he collaborated with Drujinin's periodical *Biblioteka dlya Chtenya*,[2] and tried to make it a militant organ to combat Cherny-

---

[1] B. Eikhenbaum, *L. Tolstoy*, vol. 1, p. 200, Leningrad, 1928.
[2] Reading Library.

shevsky's jaundiced version of the Gogol tradition, its obsession with squalid incidents and repulsive human deformities. But Drujinin's circle likewise began to indulge in personal invective, called Chernyshevsky *bilious*, a man with little talent but tremendous malice, and dismissed all *angry* writers as pamphleteers, or pettifogging schoolmasters.

Though Drujinin's attack on the enemy camp started vigorously, he presented an alternative, which turned out to be distressingly insipid. For he indulged in a show of moderate epicurean sentiments, a cheerful but rather conceited ease of manner, and addressed an audience (largely imaginary) of respectable, enlightened Russian squires, and well-bred young ladies, who sighed over French novels while they reclined on velvet-upholstered sofas in secluded country houses.

So Chernyshevsky gained ample opportunity to retaliate by accusing Drujinin's circle of being pampered dilettantes (whatever else they might pretend to be) devoid of social responsibility, and content to kill their time conversing airily round a well-spread dinner table.

Tolstoy began to hate these spiteful controversies, and to see that they led nowhere, beyond sterile mutual irritation. The anti-radical literary triumvirate, which he had courted, also disappointed him, and he complained about its members, Drujinin, Goncharov and Annenkov: 'They have all become repugnant to me, because what I really want from them is love and friendship, and they are incapable of giving it to me.' [1] Not that Tolstoy's own behaviour made their task easier, for he offended nearly everyone he met by his tactless sallies and hasty temper.

It provided small consolation to learn that Nekrasov was already being hoist with his own petard of topical literature, loaded with uplifting messages. The latest avalanche of books, booklets, and new journals, crammed with social invective, speculating on the public's love of scandalous gossip, filled him with dismay. Nekrasov frankly told Turgenev that all these newly discovered talents, about which people talked so solemnly, were inflated ephemeral bubbles, that even Saltykov-Shchedrin, in whom

[1] B. Eikhenbaum, op. cit., vol. 1, p. 233.

the public had been taught to revere a genius higher than Gogol, was no better 'than a thick-headed coarse creature, who gives himself ludicrous airs'. He was at his wits' end how to keep up the former standards of *The Contemporary*, and implored Turgenev to remedy a desperate situation by becoming a more regular contributor. He made similar appeals to Tolstoy and to the novelist Grigorovich. 'I realize', he wrote, 'that if I cram *The Contemporary* with stories about official bribery, it is likely to get polluted in the eyes of its present reading public, but unfortunately no other kind of fiction is being written at the present time.' [1]

Both Tolstoy and Turgenev might have patched up their quarrels with the pliable and business-like Nekrasov, if the latter had not given a free hand to the intransigent Chernyshevsky and Dobrolyubov. For they had rapidly transformed the literary section of *The Contemporary* into a harshly monotonous pamphleteering campaign. This factor, more than any other, made Tolstoy and Turgenev break with *The Contemporary*, on grounds which went deeper than temperamental incompatibility with the editors.

Tolstoy ended his contributions to this journal with the story *Albert*. Starting from 1859, his work, as well as that of Turgenev, began to appear in *The Russian Messenger*, edited by Katkov. The change involved a migration from Petersburg to Moscow, but also a transfer of allegiance from what had become a radical *opposition* journal to what was then a liberal organ of *belles-lettres*, before it assumed the militant imperialistic line of Katkov's later *pan-Slav Islam*.

For Tolstoy this strenuous period of close but uneasy dealings with urban men of letters had vital formative importance. It awoke in him the will to fight for his faith in pure literary art. He thanked God that he had never listened seriously to Turgenev, who wanted to convince him that a literary man should think entirely about writing and publishing. While any gifted and honest writer must feel dedicated to his work, how could he reconcile this with being tied down as a professional scribbler in the modern fashion?

An obligation to turn out a stream of articles and stories for

[1] op cit., p. 320.

the sake of earning money, always on topical questions, and in a denunciatory tone approved by leading radical editors, seemed to him no better than degrading mental prostitution. A writer who believed that he had something important to say, that he must say it in his own manner and as the spirit moved him—if he sold his soul to that extent—would surely die of shame.

Tolstoy felt too strongly about the grandeur of his literary vocation to consider abandoning it in a fit of pique, as Turgenev did from time to time. He had confessed almost Napoleonic ambitions to his aunt, Alexandra Tolstoy. 'Whatever I do,' he wrote to her, 'I remain convinced that *du haut de ces Pyramides quarante siècles me contemplent*, and that the whole world will perish if I stop.' If he could never be a military general, he used to say, he would become a general in literature. In 1858 Tolstoy proposed to start a new journal with some like-minded friends, and thereby fight against the tightening stranglehold of commercial and radical vested interests.

He thus outlined his scheme in a letter to Botkin (1858): 'What would you say nowadays when the dirty political stream tries literally to embrace everything within itself, and if not to exterminate, at least to pollute art—what would you say, if some people who believe in the independence and eternity of art, gathered together both in deed (art itself) and in word (criticism) to demonstrate this truth, to save the eternal and independent from the ephemeral cramping distortion, introduced by politics? Can *we* not be such people, Turgenev, you, Fet and I, and all who share our convictions? Everything, whether Russian or foreign, which has artistic quality, would be drawn upon. The aim of the journal would be simple, to provide artistic joy, to make people laugh or cry. The journal would neither argue nor try to prove anything; its sole criterion would be cultured taste. It would neither curry favour with the public, nor go down to the level of public concerns, but it would boldly teach the public in matters of taste, and in nothing else.'

But the level-headed Botkin saw no use for Tolstoy's scheme. Knowing what a heavy routine burden any journal imposes on its editorial staff, he shrewdly recognized that Tolstoy's gifts were not of the kind to make him a successful editor. He also pointed to the unpalatable fact that the Russian public failed to show enough desire for fine literature, to justify the commercial risk of launching such a superior journal.

While Tolstoy reluctantly accepted these practical objections, he remained sure that writers immersed in public controversy and social agitation could never penetrate deeply into human problems, or touch their readers' hearts. For the questions which they discussed never sprang from their own souls, but were superficially drawn from common gossip, nervous irritation, and hastily written newspaper articles.

By some *advanced* people this identification of useful writing with radical journalism was bleakly accepted as a *fait accompli*. Saltykov-Shchedrin had said plainly that the day of imaginative literature was over, because the 'new people' did not need it, and that throughout Europe nobody would want to read Homer or Goethe any more. 'Of course all that is ludicrous,' Tolstoy burst out; 'yet one can hardly avoid bewilderment if the whole world suddenly assures you that the sky is black, when you see it blue. ... What a pitiful time,' he concluded, 'from which all opportunities for creative art will vanish. I wonder whether he means that to be a compliment to our age or a jibe against it. ... I remember how in the eighteen-forties the followers of Herwegh and tendentious poetry shouted about their victory over Goethe and pure art. But what has remained now of their shouts or of the poems of Herwegh? Every political moment in national life demands from literature reactions, which correspond to it and advertise it—but the only enduring works are those which rise above that moment—all the rest turn into social manure' (Letter to Botkin, 1857).

It proved to be a blessing in disguise, for Tolstoy's literary progress and his mental balance, that he still had agriculture and Yasnaya Polyana to fall back upon. To resume the responsibilities of an active landowner became for him a heaven-sent moral support, and an outlet for his tireless energy. Even if his peasants preferred dirt and primitive tools to the cleanliness and scientific equipment, which he tried to press upon them, his prime responsibility for agricultural improvements could still not be shifted to outsiders. When Alexander II announced in March 1856 that he intended to liberate the serfs, he gave the landowners a lot to think about.

Compared with many of his contemporaries, who had become career officers, directors of banks, established civil servants, etc., Tolstoy could hardly be called a worldly success. At the age of thirty he remained an ex-lieutenant, a somewhat disgruntled short story writer, without any dazzling prospects. The young Emperor's remarks about Emancipation awoke in him a revived sense of his local duties, as a descendant of the humane Europeanized landowners of the eighteenth century. The very next month saw him back on his estate urgently working out his *own* plan to liberate his peasants. As in many similar cases, they suspected that their master wanted to bind them in advance by a cunning contract, which would handicap their future. For the rumour had spread that after the Tsar's coronation they would all be freed, and that the Tsar would then legally endow them with far more land than the landowners were ready to give on their own initiative. Tolstoy's more outspoken peasants even suggested that they had a right to *all* his land, and when he told them that he would then be left without a shirt on his back, they laughed at him.

Yet he bore no grudge against his serfs. How could they be blamed for refusing to pay for land, which they imagined, rightly or wrongly, that the Tsar would soon give to them for nothing. Also he recognized the gravity of the situation. 'If within six months from now, the peasants are not liberated,' he wrote in 1856, 'there will be a wholesale conflagration. Everything is ready for it, and if any criminal hand puts a spark to the latent revolt, the entire country will be ablaze.' It seemed absurd to get entangled in discussions of historical justice, or to wrangle about the advantages of one class over another, when it was a plain choice between ruinous civil war or renouncing part of the landowner's land.

Tolstoy admitted from his experience that despotic landowners often bred despotic peasants. Russians needed no Karl Marx to instruct them in the alphabet of class hatred. But he found equal fault with leading liberals of the period, so proud of their humane recommendation that the peasants should be liberated *with land*, that they failed to face attendant problems without which no lasting settlement could ever be achieved. Who was going to answer the pressing question, how much land, which part of the landowner's land, how to compensate the landowner, and who would pay him compensation? Tolstoy knew that none of these inescapable questions would be decided promptly or satisfactorily.

Excitement about the impending Emancipation also accentuated his distrust of the central government and its administrative machinery. He blamed them for forcing even the best landowners into the false and undeserved position of middlemen, alleged to stand between the peasants and favours to be conferred upon them from on high. 'Our chief misfortune', he wrote, 'is not so much the nobles, who are accustomed to talk about the Emancipation in French behind closed doors, but the secretiveness of the government, which encourages ignorant people to expect Emancipation on conditions which they have invented for themselves. . . . The question is of vital concern to everybody, but especially to us small landowners, living in the country, born there, and loving our own neighbourhood. Without my Yasnaya Polyana, I could with difficulty conceive Russia and my whole relationship to her' (Letter, 1858).

As a keen professional manager of his estates, Tolstoy differed profoundly from the average landowner who entered government service, and only visited the country in order to collect his rents, or spend a summer holiday there. Like his father, he aimed at being independent of favours from the Government, and he was not attracted by the commercial class. The peasant (despite his economic backwardness) and everyone else employed in agriculture, remained the country's backbone, and represented for him that vital equilibrium, which was being wantonly upset by the feverish one-sided pursuit of urban development. If the future social health of Russia depended on a regeneration of stagnant Russian country life, it was imperative to find a new mode of rural education. Fired by this undertaking, Tolstoy decided to travel and study in Western Europe, in order to learn on the spot from its educational experiments and mistakes.

In 1857 he spent five months touring France and Switzerland, and in 1860-1 he made another journey to France, Germany and England, with the purpose of studying West European education, especially in elementary schools. In Paris he was struck by a sense of social freedom 'of which we have not the remotest conception in Russia', and he modestly deplored his own 'appalling ignorance'. He met a number of eminent and clever foreigners, including the French anarchist Proudhon, and the author Matthew Arnold, who, in his capacity as Inspector of Schools, introduced him to the English school system.[1] But the self-satisfied belief in the growth of human perfectibility, which he encountered among most intellectuals, filled him with sceptical amazement. Not only did he deplore the short-sightedness which identified mere national enrichment with the spiritual welfare of individual citizens, but he observed that a contrary process of personal deterioration was already taking place. What he saw convinced him that no inward improvement of human character could possibly occur through constant advance in their material standard of living and legal status.

His travels also proved to him that, whether for good or evil, the moral effect on human beings of *unconscious* emotional education, through reading stories and novels, hearing music or absorbing other forms of popular art, infinitely outweighed, especially in childhood, the effect of compulsory education administered by modern schools.

For instance, he noted in Marseilles that the same schoolboy who told him blankly, in answer to a question, that the French King Henry IV had been murdered by Julius Caesar, could talk with animation and amazing accuracy about the characters in Dumas's novels *The Three Musketeers* or *The Count of Monte Cristo*. That case, for Tolstoy, typified the alarming difference in effect between the meaningless, dead, factual history drilled into the boy at school, and the legendary history which he had freely absorbed from lively stories. Similarly he found that the average French workman in Marseilles drew most of his ideas, not from

[1] A letter to this effect signed by Matthew Arnold is preserved in the Tolstoy Museum in Moscow.

newspapers, but from songs and recitations he had heard in the *cafés chantants* of the town.

The sight of a criminal executed under the guillotine drove Tolstoy away from Paris in April 1857. That shattering experience caused him to focus into a single image all that he found repulsive in the so-called progress of European society. The refined tranquillity and comfort of this public 'assassination' seemed to him more sickening and horrible than any scene of carnage which he had witnessed in the thick of the Crimean War. 'What an impudent desire to dispense God's justice,' he exclaimed, 'a justice which is different in the mouth of every lawyer. And in the crowd a father explains to his little girl how neatly and conveniently the machine operates.'

The cold exactitude of the scene, the complacent onlookers watching this spectacle of legal justice, provoked Tolstoy to a characteristic outburst in a letter to his friend Botkin. 'The modern state is nothing but a conspiracy to exploit, but most of all to demoralize, its citizens. . . . I understand moral and religious laws, not compulsory for anyone, but leading forward and promising a more harmonious future; I feel the laws of art, which always bring happiness. But political laws seem to me such prodigious lies, that I fail to see how one among them can be better or worse than any of the others. . . . Henceforth I shall never serve any Government anywhere' (Letter, April 1857).

Even Tolstoy's hatred of militarism betrayed a more ferocious strain than simple love of peace. The sight of old disabled soldiers quietly pottering about the *Invalides* in Paris provoked in him the pitiless remark: 'After all, they are only animals trained to bite. Now they have lost their legs, and it is just as well.' Napoleon's splendid tomb disgusted him. 'This apotheosis of a criminal is horrible.' [1]

The next country visited by Tolstoy was Switzerland, whose mountain scenery pleased him moderately, while he disliked its jovial shopkeeper citizens. It provoked him to write the story *Lucerne* (1857), which registered an emphatic protest against the callous and arrogant conduct of Europe's more

[1] F. Porché, *Portrait Psychologique de L. Tolstoy*, p. 113, Paris, 1949.

prosperous tourists. In this story a ragged vagabond minstrel, who sang like a nightingale, brought all the foreign guests in the hotel flocking to hear him from their balconies and windows. Yet no sooner did the little singer stop, hold out his hand, and murmur shyly, 'Ladies and gentlemen, if you think that I earn anything . . .' than the well-fed and smartly-dressed audience promptly started to disperse, talking and laughing among themselves. Not a single one threw down so much as a copper coin to the poor man, whose songs they had none the less listened to and enjoyed.

Prince Neklyudov (in other words Tolstoy himself), outraged by the manners of this crowd, ran after the little musician and brought him back to sup in the hotel. But it amazed him to discover that the man was too good-natured even to share his indignation. He thought his voice must have been tired, or that his simple folk-songs were not good enough to please the aristocratic guests. 'There it is,' Tolstoy exclaimed, 'the strange fate of talent. People are moved by it and search for it everywhere. Yet nobody understands its power, admits it to be the highest good on earth, or shows a spark of gratitude to real artists who bestow it freely. . . . Why is such an inhuman fact (impossible in any small German, French or Italian village) possible here, where civilization, freedom and equality have reached their highest point, where the most cultured travellers of all nations gather together? And how can these humane people, who in their parliaments, meetings and societies, hotly discuss the welfare of unmarried Chinese in India, the spread of Christianity and civilization throughout Africa, who establish all kinds of societies to improve mankind, how can they fail to find in their own hearts the simple elemental sympathy of one human being towards another?' (*Lucerne*).

In *Lucerne* (1857) and again in *Albert* (1858) Tolstoy voiced that range of vehement social queries which led him over twenty years later to publish *What is Art? Lucerne*, based on a real incident, marks also the beginning of his moral tracts. It virtually identifies aesthetic with moral feeling, although its clumsy overwrought argument spoils the purity of that intention. In *Albert* a similar moral is pointed, but left implicit. A poor violinist, a superb musical genius, but a child in practical affairs, goes towards his ruin unnoticed and unappreciated by a blasé pleasure-loving society. His weak body cannot stand the strain of all that he gives out in his music, and his failings help to drag him down, for he drinks to excess and borrows money without any intention of repaying it. Yet when he lies drunk and half-frozen in the gutter, he hears in his imagination the voice of a friend, stoutly defending him from the slur of public reproach: 'Of course, you may despise, torture and humiliate him, but in spite of that, he was, is, and will always be, infinitely higher than all of you. He is happy and pure; he serves what has been revealed to him by God, he loves only beauty, the sole undoubted good on earth. . . . He seems to you pitiful, but though you despise him, he remains the best and happiest of men.'

Both *Lucerne* and *Albert* were passed over by the literary critics with scanty or trivial comment, for they struck a note too far removed from topical preoccupations. But Tolstoy refused to be discouraged, and his self-confidence increased. 'My reputation has fallen . . . I was at first upset,' he noted, 'but I am quieter now, for I know that I have something worth saying, and the power to say it well. Only I must work conscientiously, exert all my strength—and then let them spit upon the altar!' (Diary, October 1857).

VI

When Tolstoy returned to Russia from his Western travels, its bleak and desperate poverty, the brutality of arrogant officials, shocked him more sharply than before. It had been easy to find fault with what he saw in Europe, but he confessed soon after his return: 'Russia is disgusting. I simply cannot like it. I feel how this coarse lying life begins to encircle me on every side. What a blessing that one can still find salvation in the moral world, the world of art, imagination and devotion!' (Letter to Alexandra Tolstoy, 1857). This did not mean that he had changed his mind about the duties of a double life. He remained true to his earlier decision to treat agriculture as his main bread-winning occupation, and never to mix any commercial motive with his art. But he felt more certain that the healthy agricultural development of Russia demanded a new approach to peasant education. His European tour had shown him that the urban schools of Europe, which Russia was blindly imitating, followed a course contrary to Russian needs and interests. Pursuing this matter with logical thoroughness, as one of vital concern to him, he started his own village school at Yasnaya Polyana in 1859.

In Tolstoy's view the standard Russian school establishments, based principally on German models, suffered from one fundamental defect. They artificially tore peasant youth from their rural background, made them dissatisfied with it; instead of trying to restore them with enhanced ability and powers to the *land*, the medium from which they sprang, and in which they must continue to live and work. A village teacher, Tolstoy urged, instead of trying to implement some pedagogic system and ram it down his pupils' throats, should simply help the peasant child to develop into a better and more efficient adult peasant. To try to 'improve' him by making him want to be a clerk, a factory-worker, or a civil servant, was criminal folly on the part of conceited townsmen. Such attempts to mould their pupils into preconceived new patterns were 'sterile, illegitimate, and impossible'.

Tolstoy found that many of the university-educated teachers sent to the Russian provinces were products of the radical-utilitarian school of thought, without respect or understanding for the long-term needs of Russian rural life. Strange as it may seem, several new teachers, who came to the Tula district after the Emancipation Edict, carrying 'forbidden' literature in their luggage, later changed their minds and became ardent disciples of Tolstoy. Without attempting to convert them, he infected them with his enthusiasm and faith, because he felt no doubt that the theoretical rubbish, with which their heads were stuffed, would melt away from contact with real peasants like wax melts before a fire.

Yet the final outcome hinged more on Tolstoy personally

than on the children or the school itself. For the moment his interest began to flag, the other teachers, deprived of his magnetic guidance, could make no headway. While Tolstoy felt satisfied that the result confirmed his hypothesis, he hardly knew how much of its success was due to his unique gift for inspiring otherwise insipid people.

He claimed that in the course of two years, despite the total absence of compulsory discipline, not one of his pupils ever needed to be punished, that they learned far quicker than children in conventional schools, loved their lessons, and never indulged in coarse language or stupid jokes. A triumph of personal improvisation, perhaps, but not a convincing proof that such erratic educational methods could be made workable by more commonplace teachers.

His experiments showed him, among other things, that a number of subjects normally taught in schools, notably grammar, history, and geography, remained meaningless to children, unless they were related to some tangible imaginative experience of their own. He doubted whether these subjects should be taught at all, except at the university stage. He saw that his young pupils grasped the sense of history in the shape of stirring legends and folk-tales, while history as sober factual instruction left them blank and inattentive. Geographical instruction made still less impression on them. Tolstoy agreed wholeheartedly with the apt remark made by Mitrofanushka's mother in Fonvizin's comedy *The Minor*, when they were trying to coax her son into learning geography. 'What is the good of teaching him the names of all the countries?' she exclaimed. 'The coachman will drive him wherever he may want to go.' It illustrated Tolstoy's rooted objection to stuffing children's heads with names and details, which could acquire meaning only when combined with travel.

Though his main pedagogic principles have annoyed professional educationists by their bald overstatement and lack of system, some of them made their mark in experimental schools throughout the world. His visual method of teaching children how to read, through pictures linked with words, his insistence on manual skill as a counter-balance to intellectual dexterity, are now far from being deprecated as the whims of an eccentric aristocrat. But his wild suggestion that children should learn only what they like, has been more widely followed, and by pandering to idleness has encouraged juvenile crime.

In his article *Progress and the definition of Education* (1862) Tolstoy faced wider implications. He pointed to the dangerous and widening discrepancy between ordinary people's spiritual needs and the slick literature which their educated 'superiors' were craftily producing for their consumption. The spread of literacy to the masses brought with it an immense growth in the circulation of newspapers, journals, and books, and correspondingly high profits for popular writers, editors, and publishers. But the latter, Tolstoy complained, in order to increase their sales, cynically exploited every available means to enlarge the number of their readers. They already resorted to scandalous anecdotes, salacious gossip, monetary inducements to excite the lowest gambling instincts of the public, and to win senseless and degrading prizes.

Not content with this non-stop orgy of self-advertisement, cheap journalism had invaded periodicals and more substantial forms of writing. Serious novelists were being undermined, and persuaded to fight for ephemeral party programmes, while critics, paid by the line, subordinated honest judgement to serve the vested interests of public dispute. The highest peak of popular education, which had been reached in France, made Tolstoy forecast the rapidly approaching day, when every single inhabitant of that enlightened country, having been taught to read and write, would then start to pour out a flood of worthless books and articles, which would finally destroy all taste for reading.

The outcome proved to him that 'the pettiness and insignificance of literature increase in direct proportion to the volume of its organs'. The marked success of literature in providing profits and fame for those who produced and published it, bore no discernible relation to its success in bringing enlightenment to the larger reading public. For it made no attempt to study or satisfy their deeper needs. Consequently the spread of literacy, served by prevailing Western methods, instead of improving the quality of common people, steadily degraded and debauched their minds.

The sacred halo which contemporary liberals attached to education, as a social panacea, had simultaneously encouraged a crazy belief in the march of history, as a law unto itself, which engulfed every individual in some inexorable forward social movement. 'But the law of progress, or improvement,' Tolstoy protested vigorously, 'is written in the soul of every single human being, and can only by grave error be transferred to the history of nations. So long as it remains personal, this law is fruitful and accessible to everyone, but directly it is transferred to *history*, it turns into vain and empty chatter, likely to justify every kind of madness and fatalism.' Therefore personal well-being, far from emerging automatically (as people had been persuaded to believe) from the undeniable advance of technical civilization, was fighting for sheer survival to free itself from the embraces of that thriving monster.

Commenting on Buckle's *History of Civilization* (a widely-read book in the eighteen-sixties), Tolstoy expressed his firm belief that the present forward movement of Western civilization contained one of 'the greatest and most violent evils to which a part of mankind is now subjected, but I do not consider its development to be inevitable'. There was still too little evidence to prove that Russia and other eastern countries *must* be subjected to the same laws of movement as Western European peoples, or that one type of technical advance had shown itself undeniably helpful in countries where it had already taken place. 'If I said that I was living for the sake of progress,' Tolstoy wrote, 'I repeated the words of a man in a boat carried away by the wind and waves, who, to the one important question for him, where are we steering? could only answer, we are being carried away somewhere.' Could not Russians be left to decide their next step for themselves? They were still free to choose between distinct alternatives and need not surrender to a creeping paralysis of collective historical fatalism.

After he returned from his second journey to Europe in 1861,

Tolstoy unexpectedly agreed to function in his district as an arbitrator, a post created by the government to deal with the many quarrels and legal disputes which were then arising between peasants and landlords in the application of the complicated Emancipation Edicts. The local landlords distrusted him, since despite his efforts to be fair, he nearly always sided with the peasants. He had also turned some of his own farming work into co-operative concerns. But the landlords complained so bitterly about the partiality of his decisions against them, that in the following year he was forced to resign. Exhausted from the strain of these dissensions, he departed for a rest-cure in the Samara steppes, there to relax and drink *kumis* (fermented mares' milk) among the nomad Bashkir tribes.

The cure revived him, but it was harshly interrupted by the news that his house at Yasnaya Polyana had been ransacked by the police, in order to obtain evidence of his political disloyalty. His fury and indignation at this outrage knew no bounds. He wrote to Alexandra Tolstoy, a lady-in-waiting at the court: 'So that is how your government makes friends for itself! If you recall my political attitude, you must surely know that always, and especially since my love for the school, I have been entirely *indifferent* to the government, and even more indifferent to the present liberals, whom I scorn with all my soul. But now I can no longer say this. For I feel bitterness and revulsion, if not hatred, against that *dear government*' (Letter, 1861). All his activities in the last two years, his work as arbitrator, his own 'free school', his educational journal, had been spontaneous efforts, with no ulterior motives of which he could feel ashamed. After his return to Yasnaya, he swore that he would leave Russia for ever, and kept a pair of loaded pistols in his room to shoot the police—if ever they returned. His wounded pride and honour made him suffer terribly.

VII

Tolstoy's marriage to Sophia Bers (1862) provided a fresh outlet through which he passed into the happiest and most

N

creative period of his life. For the next fifteen years he moved with solid ground under his feet, with a sense of stability which supported him for the first time as the kind of writer he had for long aspired to be, equally free from rigid social obligations and from the irksome bondage of self-centred literary cliques.

After *The Cossacks* first appeared in print (1863), *The Contemporary*, still an arbiter of progressive taste, pronounced that Tolstoy's career as an artistic writer was obviously finished. It mockingly compared the story with those out-of-date Byronic moods, in which the unhappy civilized hero hunts for soothing oblivion and repose in some far-off primitive country 'where cliffs rise to the clouds and people are as free as eagles'. But what seemed so attractive and appropriate in the romantic eighteen-twenties merely reeked of aristocratic anachronism in the sober public-spirited eighteen-sixties. It derided Count Tolstoy for having lagged so far behind the times.

Tolstoy, however, was not content to let himself be buried alive so easily. He knew that he could refute in two different ways the spiteful verdict passed on him by *The Contemporary*, either by writing a highly controversial topical novel—showing that his attitude to the present was more enlightened and progressive than that of the radicals themselves (a course which both Turgenev and Pisemsky pursued with marked success)—or else by creating a *tour de force* of historical fiction, which abandoned the sordid turmoil of the present day, and found in the past a virgin sphere for striking characters and serious events which stirred the mind.

Tolstoy readily conceded to the impetus of history and inescapable heredity a certain formative direction, which the radicals claimed so noisily to have discovered. But his new historical work of art would also prove implicitly that the radical historians had jumped to unwarranted and preposterous conclusions, which, if they passed unchallenged, would distort and stunt the mental growth of human society everywhere.

He deplored the rapid output in the eighteen-sixties of half-baked novels and stories, hastily flavoured with some piquant popular cause, on the strength of which the authors thought they were absolved from the work of hammering out live characters, or a compact and consecutive literary shape. Bearing these sketchy contemporary pot-boilers in mind, he deliberately chose to write a historical novel, as a far more ambitious and original venture. And he cast it in the period of the Napoleonic Wars, because that time came nearest to his heart and understanding, to his own recent family history, and because in wealth of emotion, psychological vigour and dramatic beauty, he knew that he could make it eclipse the more confused and petty wrangles of the present age.

Not that he felt attracted by the comfortable escapist lure of that type of historical novel then being popularized by Sir Walter Scott. On the contrary, he revolted against knights in shining armour, hackneyed poetic sentiments, and the whole paraphernalia of medieval picturesqueness. He shunned the German romantic vogue for stilted language and its long-winded glorification of sublime mountains and winding rivers. He preferred to call a spade a spade, even when it was a historical specimen.

The past period, which he chose, unlike the Middle Ages, was close *enough* to the present to be still alive, and resembled it in being also racked by wars, political upheavals and institutional reforms. But he wanted to show that even these spectacular events, which professional historians had singled out for such elaborate study, were trivial, or merely destructively important, compared with the normal home and personal life of individuals who managed to survive, and even to subdue, this irritating outward turmoil, but about whom history remained unjustifiably silent.

In this way *War and Peace*, although historical in setting, registered a formal protest against that prevalent view of history which isolated showy fragments of the past, and treated them as if they formed an intelligible and significant whole. Tolstoy accused the 'chroniclers of historical glory', whether in war or politics, of seeing nothing beyond the ugly eruptions in human affairs, and mistaking these eruptions for the flow of life itself. How could men ever feel the normal pulse of history, if they tested it only when it was beating in a feverish state?

We know that Tolstoy had already decided to compose a

novel about the Napoleonic period in Russia, when he wrote to his sister-in-law, Elizabeth Bers, in September 1863, and asked her to look up for him any revealing chronicles, diaries or contemporary records which she could find in Moscow. She wrote back confirming his apprehension that scanty written records covered the Russian *domestic* background of that time, since the attention of almost every educated person was then focused on the Napoleonic Wars. Tolstoy's early draft sketches of the novel reveal his deep concern to remedy these omissions, to discover undercurrents of the historical stream, intimate springs of human conduct, which blunter historians had hitherto ignored. This motive also forced him to revise the accepted judgement of some famous historical personalities, who occupied the centre of the early nineteenth-century stage.

'Were there not thousands of officers', he wrote, 'killed in Alexander's wars, incomparably braver, more honest and virtuous than the voluptuous, cunning and false Field-Marshal Kutuzov? Could the union or non-union of the Papal states with Napoleon's French Empire in any way alter, increase or diminish, the love for beauty felt by an artist who had just come to study art in Rome? When an officer fell on the field of Borodino with a bullet through his chest, and knew that he was dying, do not imagine that he rejoiced about saving his fatherland or the honour of Russian arms, or about the humiliation of Napoleon. On the contrary, he thought about his mother, the women he had loved, the joys and smallness of life; he reviewed his intimate beliefs and convictions. And Napoleon, Kutuzov, the Grand Army, the martial valour of Russians, all seemed to him pitiful and insignificant by comparison. . . . Neither Kutuzov nor the Emperor Alexander, nor Talleyrand, will be my heroes. I intend to write the history of people less restricted than Government servants, independent people, living in conditions more propitious to the human struggle between good and evil, absolved from poverty and crass ignorance, but equally free from the shackles of power, and without those outstanding vices which seem indispensable in order to win a place in historical chronicles.' [1]

[1] B. Eikhenbaum, *L. Tolstoy*, vol. 2, p. 245, Leningrad, 1928.

Thus one motive, pervading *War and Peace*, tried to reveal (without underestimating fugitive but inchoate mass emotions) the vital part played by obscure individuals, whose private deeds and thoughts, although unrecorded, deserved to be remembered with more respect than many perfunctory *public* activities of grotesquely overrated statesmen and generals. So Tolstoy removed from his pedestal the national hero Field-Marshal Kutuzov, though in the final version of *War and Peace* he relented, admitted in him a generous strain, and even transmuted his slow passivity and cunning into a subtle, oriental wisdom. To counterbalance this *debunking* of public figures, Tolstoy discovered unsuspected qualities in the currently despised or hated serf-owning landowners of the same period.

He went out of his way to picture the veneration and esteem which his own peasants felt for the old Prince Bolkonsky. They liked his severity, tempered with a sense of justice. They even felt glad and grateful to him, that he, the master whom they served, was 'a prince, a general, a person entirely *different* to themselves, and never descending to their level'.[1] 'Much as I deplore upsetting the reader,' Tolstoy wrote, 'by something so contrary to most accepted versions of that time, I must warn him that Prince Bolkonsky was in no way a villain, flogged nobody, did not habitually gorge himself, or keep harems, never walled up his wives, and far from being devoted to nothing but whipping his serfs, hunting and dissipation, could not abide that sort of thing, and was a wise, decent and cultured human being, of whom nobody would feel ashamed, if he were introduced into a drawing-room today.'[2]

But Tolstoy omitted this special pleading for Prince Bolkonsky in the final version of the novel, where a strong will and uneven temper showed him even more convincingly as a character, through being cast in a less heroic mould. He went further when he elevated Kutuzov's easy-going lazy temperament into a

[1] op. cit., vol. 2, p. 247, Leningrad, 1928.
[2] ibid.

wise passivity. Yet none of these modifications ran counter to
Tolstoy's guiding motive. They tended to humanize the major
figures by making them naturally inconsistent, thus bringing the
grandiose historical epic more into line with the private family
chronicle.

When radical critics fumed against Tolstoy for falsely idealizing the epoch described in *War and Peace,* he had a ready answer:
'I know very well what characteristics of that epoch are *absent*
from my novel—the cruelties of serfdom, the seclusion of women,
the knout, etc. But after studying various documents of the time,
I could not conclude that all these horrors occurred then more
frequently than similar horrors do today, or did in any other
age. There existed then the same intellectual and moral life as
now, more refined perhaps, especially in the upper classes. If we
imagine that age to have been exceptionally cruel and brutal as
a whole, it is due to certain stories, letters and memoirs of that
time, which have gone out of their way to dwell on striking
examples of brutality and savagery.' [1]

Tolstoy's determination to defend personal aims, beyond the
public sphere, from being distorted by the treacherous pathos
imposed by progressive and patriotic clichés, caused him at first
to give the intimate chronicle pride of place over the epic. In
doing this, he had to be on guard against emerging as the champion of self-centred or paltry personalities whom he disliked as
much as he did successful politicians, and never wished to
justify. Indeed, a pitiless severity governs his attitude to empty-
headed frivolous women like Prince Andrew's wife, to the
luxurious prostitute Hélène, and to the insipid though conven-
tionally virtuous Sonya.

For he maintained that the only characters who could
qualify for his esteem are those still close enough to nature to be
inwardly moved by it, but not in a sentimentally Rousseauesque
or animal sense. Though the wild animal was always close to
Tolstoy's heart, he recognized the gulf separating it from a
human soul. And in the handsome philistine, Anatole Kuragin, he
showed the same brute strength and passion which might have

[1] L. Shestov, *Les Révélations de la Mort,* p. 156, Paris, 1923.

been beautiful and legitimate in a wild beast, become wholly base and disgusting when they dominated a man.

As Tolstoy amplified his characters, the contrast (though it remained) between overrated public figures and undervalued or neglected private people, diminished in importance. Its place was taken by a broader contrast between intuitive yet civilized people like Natasha and Karatayev (or even Pierre under Karatayev's spell) and self-conscious careerists like Napoleon and Speransky. In the most complex characters, Pierre Bezoukhov and Prince Andrew, inscrutable moral instincts and rational sensual desires fight a perpetual civil war for mastery over the same person, whom they inhabit jointly.

Constant modifications of emphasis and shades of character conform to the plan of this vast novel, which changed its projected shape throughout its execution. Yet it remained a firm expression of Tolstoy's thoroughly anti-historical attitude to history. He showed disrespect to so-called *great leaders* of the past because he believed that, far from having *directed* the course of human affairs, they were often self-seeking adventurers or unconscious puppets, pulled hither and thither by forces outside their control. 'To us it is incomprehensible, Tolstoy observed, 'that millions of Christian men killed and tortured one another, merely because Napoleon was ambitious, the Emperor Alexander firm, English policy astute, or the Duke of Oldenburg offended.' Inevitably a sense that fate decides the course of history, that no man can escape his destiny, invades the mind, once it begins to seek for wider explanations, let alone for first causes, or final aims.

Tolstoy was vehemently attacked by critics for dragging into his novel so many indigestible chunks of what they termed *irrelevant* philosophy. In fact the reader can easily skip these chunks, if he is bored by them. Tolstoy, like many thinking people, could not prevent himself from asking fundamental questions, which he knew to be unanswerable. But he felt it was better frankly to admit his ignorance than to answer the same questions with glib certainty, and thereby swindle ignorant people, as he thought his radical opponents were doing with ruinous success.

The historical passages of *War and Peace*, unwieldy though they are, try to enlarge personal consciousness of history; they distinguish between passive surrender to the rushing current of events and that wiser mode of fatalism, which discovers and then obeys inescapable laws of nature governing human actions. Kutuzov did not save Russia from conquest by Napoleon merely by sitting still and doing nothing. He used events to his advantage by calculating that he need not make his army fight the French, so long as frost and hunger remained his most active allies. Though Tolstoy's version of Kutuzov's character and actions cannot be fully substantiated from facts, his falsifications were far from arbitrary, but served to build up a consistent picture.

He contrived to show that statesmen or military leaders, who blindly challenge fate, fare worse than those who seek to disentangle and understand its forces. Without being swayed by patriotic prejudice, Tolstoy saw both the Corsican Napoleon and the Russian Speransky as shallow and presumptuous upstarts, drunk with administrative power over a multitude of human victims.

'Napoleon, presented to us as a leader of that whole movement (as savages imagine the figurehead on a ship's prow to be the power which steers its course), was like a child who, holding on to the cords of a carriage, thinks that he is the driver.' Tolstoy's picture of Napoleon as a vain and pompous busybody cannot be lightly dismissed as a caricature, though it deviates from known historical fact more flagrantly than his portrait of Kutuzov. But it came close to French republican writers, who were doing their best to deflate the Napoleonic myth.

It suited Tolstoy's purpose to make Napoleon's defects outweigh his substantial qualities. He ignored the negative evidence of Napoleon's own memoirs written in St. Helena, which showed him to be less of a megalomaniac, and even akin to Tolstoy mentally, when he made this historical judgement about himself: 'Because I was not master of my actions, because I never succumbed to the madness of thinking that I could force events to fit my own pattern, but on the contrary left my system flexible

... that made me appear treacherous and inconsistent, and caused men to condemn me.'

While Tolstoy deliberately *departed* from historical accuracy in order to create characters closer to his conception of *human drama*, in describing the Russian campaign against Napoleon he often laid on the Russian patriotic colours more thickly than the facts could justify, conveniently forgetting all he had said elsewhere to warn his readers against the snares of military glory and national conceit. Like Pushkin before him, he pictured that mounting wave of enthusiasm, alleged to have drawn all classes of the population together to resist the French invader. But many Russian officers felt more at home in French than when they spoke their native tongue, and could never force themselves to hate a whole civilized country closer in culture to them than their own. The hastily conscripted peasants had only the haziest idea of why the war was being fought at all. Most of them were not even armed, except with pikes. In fact the authorities often deemed it safer *not* to arm them, and sometimes peasants seized the chance to help the French invaders, in order to get rid of their own oppressive native landlords and officials. Also they resisted handing over food and provisions to Russian partisans, who were left behind to harass territory occupied by the French. Tolstoy refers to this, but lightly.

Neither does the warm-hearted treatment of French prisoners by the peasants, described in *War and Peace*, correspond to the testimony of contemporary records, which show that peasants often enjoyed killing Frenchmen, and were callous to the point of sadism. Furthermore, Tolstoy is so keen to demonstrate Kutuzov's masterly inactivity, that he remains silent about the Field-Marshal's well-known military blunders, never mentioning that Kutuzov simply forgot to use three hundred available Russian guns, which might have shortened the Battle of Borodino and saved many Russian lives.[1]

The conservative critic, Konstantin Leontiev, praised *War and Peace* for the great political service which it rendered, through leaving a deep patriotic imprint on the soul of every reader. He

[1] Victor Shklovsky, *Material i Stil*, p. 70, Moscow, 1928.

welcomed it as a sorely needed corrective to the familiar Russian craze for tortured self-depreciation and brooding over their incorrigible vices, as a genial victory over the morbid, defeatist self-analysis, arising out of the Gogol tradition. Glaring historical lapses did not disturb him in the least so long as they promoted healthy and useful emotions, superior to any pedantic worship of factual accuracy. *War and Peace* also showed that tragedy could be *healthy* in kind, and need *not* be deformed and diseased as it was in some contemporary Russian writers, nor, as in Dostoyevsky, the tragedy of doss-houses, brothels and dismal hospitals. The tragedy of *War and Peace* is very *helpful*, Leontiev urged, because it 'disposes the mind to war-like heroism in the service of our country, whereas the tragedies of Dostoyevsky could only tantalise the self-indulgence of psychopathic individuals living in squalid lodging houses'.[1]

The non-Russian reader, who may be shocked by Leontiev's emphatic approval, will admit that the exalted patriotic tone, which dominated the war scenes of the novel, temporarily overshadowed Tolstoy's otherwise pervading pacifist strain. This grand-scale rendering of self-surrender and militant loyalty to the state has endeared *War and Peace*, above all his other works, to Soviet educationists, and it led to the printing of a huge popular edition of that novel at the height of the last world war against Germany.

Yet, if one looks closer, even this patriotic zeal spurns state-worship, and is devoid of democratic sentimentality. For it springs fully armed from Tolstoy's vision of a brave, sympathetic and handsome Emperor, surrounded by loyal and energetic aristocrats, who aroused admiration simply through being what they were. Leontiev severely qualified his own brand of patriotism when he said that he failed to understand the French, who could love *any* France and were ready to serve any kind of French government. He added: 'I want my country to be worthy of my respect.' Tolstoy, for identical reasons, reverted to the period of the Napoleonic Wars, because he discerned in it a constellation of generous individuals, who, by the natural magnetism which they

[1] K. Leontiev, *O Romanakh L. N. Tolstovo*, Moscow, 1911.

exerted, raised the Russia of that time to a position worthier of his respect, than she had become in her ambiguous mid-nineteenth century phase.

Not only the distinctly personal *genre* of national feeling, but the war scenes themselves are largely unexpected and unconventional. Events occur through flashes of perception, which turn the sequence of military operations into a chaotic but alluring mirage. This method helps Tolstoy to minimize the part played by generals, by revealing how little the course of battle corresponded to their commands and planning. Thus the obscure Captain Tushin saved the situation, *not* by obeying his superior officers, but by keeping his battery firing in defiance of orders to evacuate his position.

In many officers acute fear of death fights with an equal fear of showing cowardice, and both forms of fear combine to smother less private feelings. Napoleon's conversation with captured Russian officers is one of the few passages which smacks of classically correct military attitudes. When Napoleon announced: 'Your regiment did its duty honourably', and Prince Repnin replies: 'The praise of a great commander is a soldier's best reward', the reader may wonder whether Tolstoy's tongue is in his cheek, or whether he is making one of his rare concessions to the old chivalrous code of military honour.

That concession, if made at all, is vehemently revoked by Prince Andrew's reflections as he lay wounded and immobile on the field of Austerlitz. Napoleon, though formerly his hero, seemed to him now so pitifully unimportant, such a puny figure, absorbed in his shallow ambition and pride in victory, compared with the exalted, just and benevolent sky, with its free flying clouds, which he saw above him. Though the mighty Napoleon now stood at his side and spoke to him, the Emperor's words conveyed no more sense to Prince Andrew than the empty buzzing of a fly.

Even the fulsome glorification of the Tsar, both descriptively by Tolstoy, and through the medium of young Nicholas Rostov, exudes a purely personal devotion to the person of Alexander I, remote from any stereotyped reverence for the crowned symbol of the Russian Empire. As the Emperor rode over to inspect his regiment, Rostov felt 'as happy as a lover awaiting the approach of his beloved. . . . That sun drew nearer to him, spreading its rays of modest and majestic light, and already he felt himself enveloped in them; he heard Alexander's voice, that affectionate, calm, majestic and yet simple voice.' And at the evening mess Rostov rose to drink to the health, not of His Majesty the Emperor, as they say at official dinner parties, but of the Emperor, 'that good, great and enchanting human being.' A few pages further on Tolstoy described the Tsar objectively in equally lyrical terms: 'A charming combination of dignity and humility shone in his beautiful grey eyes, and his sensitive lips showed the same capacity for varied expression, dominated by pure and benevolent youthfulness.'

Despite Tolstoy's profound and constant hatred of autocracy manifested in the modern nation-state, he must have felt a personal fascination for Alexander I, amounting to a sense of spiritual kinship. The verdict which he pronounced later on Imperial founders of modern Russia, 'the maniac Ivan the Terrible, the drunken Peter I, the degenerate Paul, the parricide Alexander I'—though it made no attempt to distinguish their private vices from their civic virtues—still left him with a reverence for Alexander, which he showed later in his strange story *The Posthumous Writings of the Hermit Fyodor Kuzmich* (1890–1905), reviving the popular legend that Alexander had not died a *natural* death at Taganrog in 1825, but had secretly disappeared in order to spend his last years doing exemplary penance as a wandering monk. Tolstoy saw Alexander as something like a nineteenth-century Buddha, a wise prince who, chastened by knowledge of the ghastly crimes committed in his name, decided of his own accord to renounce kingship, and start to lead an obscure saintly life.

If Tolstoy proved anything implicitly in *War and Peace*, it was the absurdity of turning history into a branch of natural science, capable of leading either to exact conclusions, or of predicting the shape of the future from our fragmentary knowledge of the past. He showed again that history as an art of creating legends exerted a stronger influence on the mind than it did as a rudimentary narrative of scattered facts. As a counterblast directed against the grim topical school of Nekrasov and Pomyalovsky, *War and Peace*, with all its admitted and intentional inaccuracies, brought a whole vanished epoch back to life with more compelling charm, clarity and power of language, than any literary document of current manners had managed to achieve for the modern age.

War and Peace endured the test of time, not because it reflected precisely either the age in which it was written, or the earlier age it wrote about, but because it freely interpreted them both. By making the inner flow and importance of personal and private concerns prevail over the ugly and confused pattern of political and military upheavals, by pouring cold water on the feverish modern preoccupation with institutional changes, by denying that these could intelligibly be called either progressive or reactionary, Tolstoy endeavoured, as he did elsewhere, to demolish the whole misleading radical fixation on discernible laws of history and social change.

The supreme success of his novel in achieving, and going far beyond, all that he had set out to do, far from converting his intellectual opponents to some perception of his talent, roused both radical and conservative circles to a new pitch of vindictive fury. He found himself cursed as a reactionary by the former group, and condemned as a Nihilist by the latter. The contemptuous verdict passed on him by the influential critic, Shelgunov, strange as it may sound today, was typical of the prevalent left-wing attitude to Tolstoy. 'It is lucky', he wrote, 'that Count Tolstoy does not possess a powerful talent. . . . If he *did* possess the genius either of Shakespeare or Byron, no curse would suffice to condemn him.' [1] Shelgunov hated Tolstoy for having dared to draw inspiration from the Russian past, even from the lives of aristocratic families, rather than from the present, instead of singing a dreary modern hymn to social progress or shedding crocodile tears over the lot of poverty-stricken peasants.

Tolstoy fared little better at the hands of the conservative

[1] A. Nazarov, *Tolstoy*, p. 189, London, 1930.

nationalist camp. *They* accused him of showing unpatriotic and cynical disrespect for the Russian war-heroes of 1812, for captiously finding fault with eminent Russian generals and statesmen. Even the critic Strakhov, one of the few who intelligently admired Tolstoy's art, pointed out that parts of *War and Peace* served to unmask the defects, rather than to glorify the virtues of high society in the Alexander period. Some scenes in which the Rostov family figured, brought out the aimless, lazy, over-eaten life of Moscow landowners; and a few passages about the behaviour of the peasants (apart from the isolated and purely folklore figure of Karatayev) suggested sinister bestiality latent in the common people.

The journal *Voice* (1868) condemned him for devoting too much space to historical scenes, and thus ruining the artistic harmony of his novel. The *St. Petersburg News* (1868) pronounced that he had 'forgotten the basic alphabet of art'. *The Russian Archive* (1869) found that his deliberate interweaving of history and fiction had damaged both, and that the novel was overburdened with superfluous detail and irrelevant historical theories. The radical *Deed* attacked the novel violently as a 'disorderly heap of piled-up material' and called its chief characters 'elegant bushmen, mentally fossilised and morally repulsive'. The author of this exceptionally spiteful article, Bervi-Flerovsky, had been a poor fellow-student with Tolstoy at Kazan University, and clearly relished this opportunity of venting his bitter inferiority complex. He also published in 1868 a discursive work entitled *The Position of the Working Class in Russia*, which won much louder applause from Russian critics in the eighteen-sixties than did Tolstoy's masterpiece.

As a rare exception the novelist Leskov wrote a long criticism of *War and Peace* in the *Stock Exchange News* (1869), where he observed that 'Tolstoy's new novel raises for decision many practical and current questions which from time to time repeat themselves with fatal inexorability—much that enables us better to understand the present through deeper knowledge of the past, and even to guess at the future', but concluded regretfully that Tolstoy's work 'will certainly *not* find talented appreciation in our time, because those who call themselves our critics will weigh him exclusively in the scale of their own prevailing tendencies'. Leskov and Strakhov were the only contemporary Russian critics who forecast that understanding of Tolstoy, as a boldly imaginative historical thinker, which grew up later among civilized people throughout the world, though always obscured by the fashionable approach to him as a moral crank and puritan evangelist.

CHAPTER VI

TOLSTOY AFTER *WAR AND PEACE*

I

FOR a whole year after he had completed *War and Peace*, Tolstoy refused to read a single book or journal, and told his friends how mentally refreshed he felt from that abstention. He wrote to his neighbour, the poet Fet: 'I work, cut wood, dig, reap, and never think, thank God, about disgusting literature and men of letters.'[1] When in 1871 the editor of *Grazhdanin* invited him to contribute an article, he replied rather ungraciously: 'If from human weakness I yield again to the passion for writing and publishing, then it would take the form of a book. In truth I hate newspapers and journals, and believe that they do much harm by unproductively exhausting mental and imaginative ground.'

Meanwhile his pedagogic passion had revived, perhaps because he now had children of his own to teach. For a short time he agreed to act as Inspector of Schools in his district, and in 1869 he started to compile a collection of fairy tales and folk-tales for use by schoolchildren. He also enlarged his agricultural responsibilities by buying a new estate in the Samara district, virgin land hitherto untouched by the plough, but reputed to be capable of growing the best wheat in Russia.

In 1872 a bull at Yasnaya Polyana gored one of Tolstoy's shepherds to death, and he was summoned to appear before the local courts on the charge of 'careless maintenance of cattle'. This incident provoked him to such fury and indignation that he again swore he must leave Russia, 'to get away from that horrible sea of self-satisfied vulgarity, vicious idleness and lies, which from every side bursts over that tiny island of quiet industrious life which I have made for myself.' He explained to his aunt, Alexandra Tolstoy: 'If I do not die of anger and depression in prison (where I am sure they will send me) I have decided to

[1] *Literaturnoe Naslyedstvo*, vol. 35, p. 234, Moscow, 1939.

move to England forever, first to settle near London, and then to pick out a house with some land in a healthy place near the sea. To make life in England more agreeable, I must get to know some good aristocratic families' (Letter 1872). Tolstoy's lasting horror of any government which meddled in private matters, his hatred of the police and law-courts in particular, although it verged on pathology, was based on personal experience, and it steadily increased as he grew older. When it flared up in incidents like this, he refused to face the intolerable fact that even he might be a violator of man-made laws. For in his heart he could admit no laws save those dictated or approved by his own conscience.

Conveniently forgetting his former anger against the heartless English guests who were staying in the Lucerne hotel, he now grasped impulsively at the idea of migrating to England, 'because', he wrote, 'only there is personal freedom still secured, admittedly for the benefit of every deformity, but also for an independent quiet life'. This plan to escape from Russia was significant but short-lived. His manifold responsibilities at home could not be shaken off so easily.

A sequence of disastrous harvests afflicted the estate he had bought in the Samara district, and left him with heavy financial losses. He began to think that God was testing his strength of character, as he had formerly tested the patience of Job in the bible. *War and Peace* (according to influential critics), his various farming enterprises, his latest pedagogic publication (*The Alphabet of Social Sciences*, 1871) were all alike in being considered failures. He was experiencing the collapse of his most strenuous efforts and hopes, a moral Battle of Waterloo. He felt again the qualms of doubt which had assailed him, even at the beginning of his married life: 'It is terribly precarious and foolish to tie up one's happiness to things material—a wife, children, health or wealth. No, the wandering monk is right.'

But his persistent vitality held firm, and made him long for a showdown with the pedagogues who had denounced his *Alphabet*. The friendly critic, Strakhov, warned him against wasting his valuable time in fighting single-handed against vested interests,

o

supported by the entire radical press. But he paid no heed, and went to Moscow in order to defend before an Educational Committee his visual method of teaching children how to read. The result was inconclusive, but it had the incidental merit of attracting wider attention to Tolstoy's views, and led to some relaxation of the grip of German routine over the Russian school curriculum. An article by the famous publicist Mikhailovsky entitled *Storm in a Teacup of Pedagogic Water* (1875) ended by cautiously defending the views of the heretical count.

Tolstoy wanted to abandon literary work at intervals, first in St. Petersburg after the Crimean War and his disillusionment with *The Contemporary*, then in the country after *War and Peace*, and again after writing his *Confession*. Yet every interruption turned out to be only a period of lying fallow, the prelude to another creative outburst. For him it verged on sacrilege to regard writing as a regular means of earning money, or as a routine occupation. He set down his views on this subject unequivocally, and rarely deviated from them. 'I think it is necessary to write only when the thought which you wish to express is so persistent that you cannot get rid of it without writing it down. All other incentives to write, personal vanity, and still more repulsive, money-making, can only harm the sincerity and quality of what is written. Another vicious motive, of which contemporary writers are most guilty (all the decadents are)—is the craze to be out-of-the-ordinary, startling, to *épater* and shock the reader. As for hasty and obscure writing, it is harmful, and betrays the absence of any genuine need to express thought. For a genuine need will spare no labour or time to achieve the utmost clarity.'

Even the colossal work of *War and Peace* had not liberated Tolstoy from his craving to find a deeper sense in Russian history. Impelled to explore it further back, he told his friend Fet in 1872 that he was immersed in reading books about Peter the Great and his period. But the longer he studied, the less he felt that he could penetrate into the souls of people whom he found so alien to his sympathies. Whereas Russian history books nearly all glorified Peter as a national hero, Tolstoy found him both devoid of originality and a repulsive character. He concluded that most of Peter's famous legal and institutional reforms were copied energetically from ready-made German models. Because he feared the local power and independence of the nobility, Peter turned them into intimidated civil servants, but this reform, in Tolstoy's view, brought dubious long-term benefits to Russia. As for Peter's private life, his debauchery and crude practical jokes, his liking for upstart adventurers like Lefort and Menshikov, his virtual murder of his own son, Alexei, all these filled Tolstoy with dismay. In the end, after working for a year and sketching a few chapters, he abandoned his project to write another historical novel, by convincing himself that recorded Russian history, outside the eighteenth and early nineteenth centuries, was discouraging and uninspiring.

II

The suicide of a young woman who threw herself under a railway train at a station not far from Yasnaya Polyana is said to have suggested to Tolstoy the theme of *Anna Karenina*. Shortly afterwards, re-reading *Belkin's Tales*, he was struck by Pushkin's direct manner of plunging into the heart of action on his opening page. The coincidence inspired him to start his first major novel of contemporary life. Since, hard as he tried, he could derive no stimulus from Russian history outside the Napoleonic period, he turned away from the assimilated past, and started to interpret the perplexing present age. Thus, both historically and logically, *Anna Karenina* became a natural sequel to *War and Peace*. It pursued the same personal chronicle of interrelated Russian upper-class families, observed over half a century later in the more agitated and complex *milieu* of the Russian eighteen-seventies. But the clearly stated social and moral intentions of the author in composing the two novels stand in sharp and striking contrast.

In *War and Peace* the leading characters remain throughout morally robust and sane enough, both to master their inward conflicts and withstand the hard buffetings of fate. They can forget private concerns, rise to big occasions, and make the utmost of the national crisis through which they live, without being forced into behaving like a rabble. In *Anna Karenina*, on the contrary, inward conflicts grow uncontrollably complicated and confused, cause two attempts at suicide, and the thought of suicide in Levin. Almost all the characters, except Anna and Kitty at times, are weighed down by a burden of intricate social convention, rarely relieved by that impulse and thoughtful initiative which burst out so frequently in *War and Peace*.

Moreover, the impact of mighty happenings from the outside world, which braces the morale of characters in *War and Peace*, is either conspicuously absent from *Anna Karenina*, or, when it occurs, assumes an ambiguous or bogus shape. It is true that the struggle of the Serbian Christians against their Turkish overlords had provoked a mounting sense of Slav solidarity in Russia. But within this mood, the healthier strains of normal sympathy for maltreated racial brothers were drowned by morbid outbursts of religious and patriotic hysteria, cunningly exploited for political motives by the nationalist press.

In *Anna Karenina* the stricken Count Vronsky leaves for the Balkan battle front, in charge of a trainload of volunteers, equipped and maintained at his own expense. But when the sentimental publicist, Koznyshov, congratulated him on the fine example he was setting to the *cause*, Vronsky quietly replied that he could claim no nobler motive than to find some ready means of sacrificing a life, which had grown useless and repugnant to him.

In every individual case, excitement about Slav brotherhood is shown up in all its hollow artificiality, either as a pretext for idle but ambitious men and women to preen themselves in the limelight of nation-wide publicity, or as an opportunity for frustrated misfits to recover their wounded self-respect. Here we have a motley crowd of 'commanders without armies, journalists without a journal', administrators with nothing to administer, or plainly desperate men who have found a respectable manner of committing suicide. Levin struck the basic Tolstoyan note a little later, when he remarked that all this public clamour about helping the united Slav race to open a new phase of world history, seemed to him futile and senseless, compared with real changes which were going on inside his soul. In this irreconcilable clash between outward and inner life *Anna Karenina* differs most markedly from *War and Peace*. For the latest incursion of political and public obligations into the private sphere, far from providing human beings with wider scope (as it did in *War and Peace*), stealthily degraded them by treacherous demands. Katkov, the militant editor of *The Russian Messenger*, was so indignant about Tolstoy's ironical treatment of national enthusiasm for Slav solidarity, that he refused to publish the chapters dealing with it, and they were omitted from the novel.

While *Anna Karenina* lacks the charm of fresh ideal figures, with generous impulses, like Natasha and Nicholas Rostov, and the naïve sense of national unity, permeating *War and Peace*, it surpasses the latter in its exact use of psychological detail, compactness of construction, and in the depth and contemporary complexity put into its major characters. In place of the lyrical vein, which has dried up in Tolstoy, a pitiless truth prevails, a hard relentless light exposes every secret of the overburdened but still living heart. The contemporary novel is far sadder, more inescapably selfish and sordid in the human environment which it conveys, where worldly greed, lust and ambition combine to smother purer emotions which struggle to survive. But, as Tolstoy frequently observed, when questioned about the purpose of his literary work, the subject-matter must be subordinate to the current of feeling with which the author can infect his reader. If the subject of *Anna Karenina* is less exalted and uplifting than the national epic of *War and Peace*, then the period itself, rather than the author, is to blame. Yet the impression conveyed is of more penetrating and concentrated artistic power, though haunted by a sense of impending doom, as if the limits of human endurance had been stretched to breaking point.

When Tolstoy decided to write a large-scale novel about contemporary Russian society, he intended to paint a picture even more forceful in implicit condemnation than his picture of the 1812 period had been in its imaginative charm. According to his intimate friend and biographer, P. Biryukov, he chose the biblical epigraph, 'Vengeance is mine, I will repay', to sound the *leitmotif* of the whole novel, namely the immutability of the highest moral law. Whoever breaks that law must pay a terrible penalty, though it is wrong for mere mortal beings to pass their fallible judgement on the victim and transgressor. But in writing the novel, Tolstoy went far beyond his original intention, and in some ways flatly contradicted it.

It is clear from *Anna Karenina* that Tolstoy's conception of moral law is less Christian than it is Buddhistic, even when he supports it with quotations from the bible. Acting entirely through the medium of personal conscience, it becomes a law in the strict scientific sense of a natural law, from which no one can escape, any more than falling bodies can escape from the laws of gravity. It cannot therefore be modified by outbursts of sympathy, or spasms of transient repentance, by redemption at the expense of other people, or by transferring personal responsibility to anonymous public institutions. For it remains a morality of exact personal feeling, firmly bound at every step to corresponding action. In this way it closely resembles the Indian *karma*.

In a formal sense Anna breaks the moral law, and pays the penalty, despair and a self-inflicted death. But who can fail to ask, is she to blame, and how far is she the innocent victim of forces outside her control? Married off, in compliance with convention and without love, to a dull but successful civil servant twenty years older than herself, she later falls in love with another man. Because her passion carries her away more deeply than a frivolous flirtation, society persecutes her. After a long and painful struggle with herself, Anna leaves her husband and goes to live with Vronsky.

The more cynical society of today might take the sequence of events for granted, and still miss the point. But the most savagely puritanical judge would hardly decide that Anna's action deserved the death penalty. And if this talk about breaking the highest moral law amounts to more than a trite copy-book maxim, why should the worst transgressors escape their penalty, and flourish on their vices like the proverbial green bay-tree? The frivolous Princess Betsy enjoys her various lovers with impunity. And because she knows how to appear to be what she is not, she keeps her position in society, while Anna is made to feel an outcast, because she cannot be a hypocrite.

Anna suppressed for many years her natural longing for love, trying to content herself with the role of a dutiful obedient wife and devoted mother. When her feelings broke through at last, they went against her will. When Vronsky first saw her in the railway carriage, he noticed a vitality held in reserve, but which played over her face and fluttered between her shining eyes and scarcely perceptible smile. 'A kind of superabundance filled her being.' Yet Anna experienced horror and foreboding while she fought against her love for Vronsky, a feeling remote from the bright happiness which united Kitty and Levin in their oasis. Needlessly cruel laws and hypocritical conventions combined to deform Anna's love. But when at last she surrendered herself physically to Vronsky, she experienced a burning sense of guilt and shame, as if they had murdered their real love, made it a lifeless corpse.

Her emotion betrayed her at the races when Vronsky fell from his horse. With challenging effrontery Anna told Karenin that she was already Vronsky's mistress. And her husband coldly commanded her in writing to continue to observe the outward decencies—which were all that he knew or cared about. He thereby forced Anna to tell more lies, to meet Vronsky in secret, and play a constant comedy in society. Her frank and generous nature grew twisted and deformed. Even the insensitive Vronsky noticed a deterioration in her. Before she had been unhappy, but proud and serene, while now she had grown strained, irritable and insecure.

Not only her fear of losing her son, and cherished position in high society, but Vronsky's own uncertain manner, prevented her from breaking with Karenin. She made a *rendezvous* with Vronsky to show him her husband's formal letter. If, on learning the news he told her decisively, 'leave everything and come with me', she had decided to leave her home and go away with him. But she saw, as he read the letter, and lifted his eyes to her, that there was no firmness in his look. Only his words spoke far too calmly about the need for a divorce. And then she knew that her last hope was dashed.

Thus Anna continued to live in her husband's house, to endure his sermons and polite insults, while she carried Vronsky's child. Vronsky in his turn began to look at her as a man may look at a fading flower 'in which he could scarcely recognize that beauty which first made him pluck and spoil it'. She gave birth to a daughter. Then followed the painful, almost hysterical, meeting and reconciliation between Karenin and Vronsky in her bedroom, when she was on the verge of death. But she recovered, broke with her husband, and left with Vronsky for Italy. For the first time in her life she felt happy, but with an *unforgivable happiness*. Her husband's momentary generosity had intensified her lurking sense of guilt.

The stricken Karenin meanwhile abjectly surrendered the control of his affairs to the arch-hypocrite Countess Lydia Ivanovna. When Anna returned to St. Petersburg, the Countess, in the name of Christian principles, forbade Anna to see her son and thus soil the pure memory of his mother. She was obliged to steal like a thief into her own home, and bribe the servants to admit her to Seryozha's bedroom. When she attended a performance at the Opera, people in the neighbouring box walked out, and she was made to feel public exposure as a *fallen woman*!

Staying at Vronsky's luxurious country house, Anna's friend Dolly observed an abundance of what people normally want to make them contented—material ease, good health, a child, and plenty of activity to occupy the mind. Vronsky farmed, improved his estate and built a hospital; Anna studied and made herself an expert on whatever he was doing. But although Anna talked vaguely about being happy, she nervously avoided broaching any intimate subject. Anna could not explain to Dolly why she refused to press Karenin for a divorce, but she burst out at last: 'You cannot understand, it is too terrible. I try not to look into it. You tell me I should marry Aleksei, and that I think too little of it . . . Yet there is hardly an hour or a minute when I do not think about it and reproach myself for thinking—because such thoughts can drive me mad. When I think, I can't sleep without taking morphine.'

For Anna had some presentiment, obscure to Vronsky, and beyond Dolly's comprehension, that it was too late for a divorce or re-marriage to be of any help. Since she now held Vronsky solely by her physical charm, a legal marriage would only tear away the veils and show the ruin of their precarious love. Already they had begun to feel like enemies bound together by a common chain. Alongside the love which had united them, grew up an evil spirit of strife, which she could neither overcome in him nor expel from her own heart. And the thought of suicide crept into her mind, not impulsively, but with calm remorseless logic. 'Death, as the only means of reviving his love for her, of punishing him, and of winning the victory in that fight, which the evil spirit implanted in her waged against him, firmly and vividly arose in her mind.'

Leaving for the railway journey where she would meet her end, while she looked at familiar objects with a sudden clairvoyance, an overwhelming thought flashed through her mind: 'If I could be anything except his mistress, passionately loving his caresses; but I cannot, and no longer want to be anything more. And that desire awakes repulsion in him and anger in me, yet it cannot be otherwise. . . . Let me imagine that I get a divorce and become Vronsky's wife, what new feeling could I invent to bring us close together again? If happiness is too much to ask, at least could I escape from torture? No, no, that is impossible. We are moving further away from one another. I make his unhappiness, and now it is vain to try to alter him or me.'

If Princess Betsy had been in Anna's place, she would have lived with Vronsky so long as she enjoyed his company, and then coolly thrown him over for another lover. But Anna's environment had not corrupted her to that extent. Only by violating her honest nature, did she provoke the vengeance which later overtook her. Albeit in a semi-trance, she put the noose round her own neck, and pulled it tight enough to strangle her. If she did not throw herself deliberately down, she half-consciously allowed herself to fall.

Dostoyevsky, in his well-known article about the novel, rejoiced that it confirmed his pet belief in the basic depravity of human beings, and that it proved how abnormality and crime spring from the depths of human nature, and are rooted far deeper 'than our socialist doctors can ever diagnose'. He saw Tolstoy in his own strong distorting mirror, and had no desire to see him otherwise.

For Tolstoy's novel illustrated rather the reverse of Dostoyevsky's dictum. The vengeance which overtook Anna did not *need* to be explained by any mysterious overpowering evil, if it followed from a law to which her own previous actions had condemned her to submit. She could not escape from consequences which she herself had set in motion. When she defied the conventions of a spiritually blunt society, her defiance was a virtue, not a crime. She could with impunity have snapped her fingers in the face of social vengeance, had she remained true to her inner self. But once she started to stifle her own conscience, she was doomed, as in the Russian proverb: 'If a claw is caught, the bird is lost.'

In *War and Peace* the atmosphere created by the main characters remained bright, pure and invigorating. Though tragedy occurred, it was healthier in kind, because it sprang from disruption brought by the hand of fate, tempered by people's wise fortitude in facing calamities. In *Anna Karenina*, where war and material adversity play a minor part, the tragedy is worse, through being inward and psychological, while the atmosphere is tenser and charged with threatening storms. Under the outwardly harmonious rhythm of living, under the splendid luxury, energy, and still robust health of the Russian upper class, Tolstoy's penetrating eye saw rifts, convulsions, and a relapse into savage chaos. Compulsory mechanical institutions of a new industrial society, rapidly imposed on patriarchal mental habits, had started to paralyse the souls entangled in them.

Anna's brilliant personality glowed against the sombre background of vulgar, crude careerists or commonplace nonentities who surrounded her. Yet *she* became superfluous to the new society, while they did not. Her rare beauty, devotion, and honesty, her lively intelligence, are not needed or appreciated;

they proved to be a handicap and a disaster to her, for she was trampled underfoot on their account. The rustic Kitty and Levin idyll is clearly worked out by Tolstoy to provide a soothing counterpart to the drama of Anna and Vronsky. It repeatedly provides an interlude for relaxation, following scenes charged with acute nervous strain. Although the tamer Levin story seems an anti-climax, it remains a welcome antidote. Kitty, so unlike Anna, is level-headed, feminine, and yet refreshingly efficient, even though the sophisticated reader may be bored by her model domestic virtues and by her 'truthful eyes'— a phrase repeated too frequently by Tolstoy.

Levin also provides an admirable mouthpiece for Tolstoy's own misgivings about the lop-sided concentration of wealth and energy then pouring into Russian heavy industry, coupled with wanton neglect of similar investment in backward agriculture. Levin's solemn self-analysis and fumbling make him an amiable bore. He kept on falling into specious philosophic traps, and then struggling to escape from them; but he did not stagnate. And Levin's questionings gave Tolstoy a chance to demonstrate his distrust of far-fetched reasoning, and his belief that to rely on any comprehensive set of principles betrayed an absence of spontaneity and understanding at deeper levels.

Levin, who lived and worked among his peasants, neither liked nor disliked them collectively. He simply felt himself to be their natural working partner, at times their helper. But his intellectual half-brother, Koznyshev, who only visited the country to spend a summer holiday, and scarcely knew the peasants personally, revelled in high-flown theories about the unique character and tastes distinguishing the Russian common people from all others. In this he resembled Karenin, who habitually expressed categorical opinions about music and art (to which he was totally insensitive) while in his own sphere of political administration he remained shrewdly sceptical and tentative.

Towards the end of the novel, Levin underwent some spiritual transformation, after he had heard a peasant talk about 'living for God'. As a *conversion* this episode is weakly contrived, absurd in its abruptness, and taxes the normal reader's sense of probability.

In practice it has vague results, leads to some mild negative resolutions, which Levin conscientiously enumerates, but which will probably never be fulfilled. He resolved not to quarrel any more with Kitty, not to scold the coachman, to be more kind and considerate to his guests.

Levin's *conversion* remained mercifully incomplete, and he still achieved his happiest moments when he forgot himself in agricultural work and ceased to indulge in mental speculations. 'Formerly, when he struggled to do something beneficial for everybody for mankind as a whole, he noticed that while such thoughts gave him pleasure, the activity which followed from them was inept and futile. But now that he concentrated on his personal affairs, he felt sure that what he did was necessary.' And through being reduced to working for his own satisfaction, he found that he had to live for some force beyond himself. But Levin's haunting doubts, his involuntary thoughts of suicide, his craving to merge emotionally with the peasants, are significant preludes to that desperate state of mind, which led Tolstoy a little later to the position analysed in his *Confession* (1882).

III

Despite its undeniable sincerity, Tolstoy's *Confession* has dangerously misled many people. For the new Tolstoyan disciples it became the Holy Writ of moral liberation; it revealed the essential Tolstoy. But for his wife and more discriminating friends it was a petulant outburst of self-indulgent eccentricity, if not a symptom of senile decay. It distressed Countess Tolstoy, as much as it did Turgenev, to see her husband buried in bibles and religious commentaries, neglecting his family and estate affairs, and allowing his unique artistic gifts to rust. It pained her that he wasted his mental forces on cutting firewood, lighting the *samovar*, cleaning his own room, or making boots.

In any case Tolstoy's efforts to change his way of life failed pitifully to fulfil the part expected of a great religious reformer. He could never become either a saintly hermit or a humble Francis of Assisi, however hard he kicked against the pricks of his unruly nature. His so-called *conversion* was far removed from any standard religious type. Instead of drawing him back into the bosom of the Orthodox Church, or towards any other Church, it intensified his hostility to all organized Christianity. It convinced him that the most conspicuous adherents of all Christian Churches remained blunt, crafty but self-important hypocrites, while alert intelligence, honesty of mind, and virtuous conduct, flourished more frequently among people who admitted that they were unbelievers or free-thinkers.

As for the Russian peasants, he remarked how absurd it was to call them *religious*, simply because they were riddled with superstitions, and enjoyed religious festivals and holidays. For they showed indifference to Church teachings, and heartily despised their priests. Even the sectarians, despite a fanatical streak of their own, hated the Orthodox Church as an organ of Anti-Christ, but they were few in numbers.

Meanwhile, Tolstoy observed, ambitious men of letters and learning tried to set themselves up as an alternative priesthood. For they had recently invented a theory to dazzle the public with the supreme importance of their professional work. They claimed that human life continually evolved, and that in its latest phase they, men of learning, writers etc., were due to play a vital educative part. Without probing into awkward questions about the aims and value of a good writer, they conveniently described him as an artist who *taught* people unconsciously. 'Now', concluded Tolstoy, 'I was considered a superb artist. I wrote and taught without knowing why. For that I was paid plenty of money, enjoyed excellent food, living conditions and society, and thereby I acquired fame. It followed that what I taught must be extremely good. And it proved most pleasant and profitable to be a priest of art.'

But how could this new intellectual *priesthood* prove itself superior to the old religious caste? Tolstoy remarked how its members perpetually squabbled, contradicted and slandered one another. And the new 'priests'—particularly writers—though boastful about their 'public service', were often spiteful and petty in their behaviour, and absurdly vain. 'Terribly strange,' Tolstoy commented; 'our only heartfelt desire was to earn as much money and fame as quickly as possible, but without reflecting either about the means employed, or the goal to be achieved.'

After his marriage, he had been shamelessly content for fifteen years to make himself and his family comfortable. Only now, having accomplished that, did he begin to see his life in a wider but more sombre light. He compared himself to the forlorn traveller described in an Eastern fable. This man found himself suspended over a deep well, and clung to the branch of a tree which mice were gnawing. A dragon lay in wait to devour him at the bottom of the well. The traveller had found some honey on the branch and licked it. 'I saw the dragon clearly, and the honey was no longer sweet to me. I saw only the inescapable dragon and the gnawing mice, and could not tear my gaze away from them.'

Since normal life had lost its former charms for him, he could no longer attract people by the 'beautiful lie' of his art. Yet rational knowledge provided no answer to the questions which tormented him. The wisest men of the past, Socrates, Solomon, Schopenhauer, and the Buddha, seemed to have reached the same tenuous conclusion, that human beings instinctively strove to escape from the bondage of evil and physical destruction.

The young and happy Indian prince, Sakyamuni, as soon as he left his enchanted palace, and encountered sickness, senile decay, and death, hitherto unknown to him, resolved to consecrate his full mental powers on finding a course of action which would deliver him, and his fellow-creatures, from the incurable cancer of physical life.

It might be consoling to discover that many eminent philosophers and teachers of the past had reached the same predicament. Nevertheless, said Tolstoy, 'my position tortured me. I knew that I could find nothing more along the path of rational knowledge, except denial of life, and that I had hitherto found in faith denial of knowledge, even more untenable for me than denial of life.' Could he be right to work out a fresh approach, to reach beyond the centuries of human effort to which he owed his own existence and present state of mind?

So he studied Buddhist and Mahometan sacred books as well as the Christian scriptures. He sought out Russian believers, wandering monks, sectarians and pious peasants. The circle of highly-educated people, to which he belonged by birth, became increasingly repugnant to him. But this activity followed a long maturing process, without sudden upheavals or startling new discovery; and the strength which eventually returned to him sprang from the same natural buoyancy which had filled him in early childhood. Only now he knew that he could no longer survive without it. 'I had been through fifty-five years in the world, and except for those first fourteen or fifteen years of childhood, I lived thirty-five years as a Nihilist, in the literal sense of that word, i.e. not as a socialist or a revolutionary, but a plain Nihilist . . .' (*Confession*).[1]

Tolstoy's *Confession*, despite its habitual exaggerations and harsh one-sidedness, remains a burning human document, *momentarily* sincere and brilliantly expressed. His *Criticism of Dogmatic Theology* (1885), which followed shortly afterwards, managed to make all theology sound absurd. His *Criticism, Analysis and Codification of the Four Gospels* harped on the theme that adaptors and translators of the gospels had obscured the vital truth that Christ never claimed to be more than a mortal man. Tolstoy's theological writings are rarely read today, and they are unreadable for many modern minds. But at the time his shattering attack left little of the historical fabric of organized Christianity standing on its foundations. He salvaged from Christian ethics hardly more than a pitifully vague command to love other human beings, and to resist evil by every means short of physical violence. He left no paradise, no miracles, no redemption, no rising from the dead, no personal immortality. Yet his more constructive moral thought continued to follow Buddhist lines.

Those who expected solid benefits and rewards from their attachment to established churches, indignantly resisted Tolstoy. And his formal excommunication by the Orthodox Church in

---

[1] Even then he was a deist. 'What is God, imagined so clearly that one can ask him to communicate with us? If I imagine him thus, he loses all grandeur for me. He is God, because I cannot grasp his being' (*Diary*, 1860).

1901 confirmed officially that the ecclesiastical civil service had long hated him as their arch-enemy. He received numerous friendly letters on this occasion, together with some threats and insults. One angry correspondent told him that, if he had not yet seen the devil, he need only look into a mirror. A talkative cabman, who drove his French visitor, Paul Boyer, round Moscow at the time, expressed the following choice opinion: 'It seems that this Count Tolstoy worked for the Holy Synod, but they were not satisfied with his service, so they kicked him out. That is a pity.' [1] Others, like Turgenev, who had no use for patched-up relics of theology, deplored the valuable energy that Tolstoy wasted on flogging a dead horse. His brother Sergei said: 'Our dear Leo has licked all the caviare off the bread, and now he offers us the dry crust which remains.'

Tolstoy reached a similar *impasse* in his imaginative work, for directly any of his characters *plan* to sacrifice their lives to serving others, they sink into a grey monotony. So it is with Levin in *Anna Karenina*, with Olenin in *The Cossacks*, with Prince Neklyudov in *Resurrection*; they were in any case unstable people, incapable of leading consistent or saintly lives. Even the few characters who rise to some degree of saintliness are mentally dessicated or warped.

Varenka, an exemplary young lady, tends sick people, is busy from morning till night, and hardly thinks about herself. But we learn that the man she loved had married another girl, since when she had withered away, like a bud which never opened. We are led to suspect that her forced self-denial provided a refuge from the hidden envy which she felt for other people's happiness. Sonya, another *virtuous* character, who meekly renounced her claim to marry Nicholas Rostov, devoted herself to the capricious old Countess Rostov. But her absence of egoism made her dimly negative and insipid, like a barren scentless flower. In a later moral tale Tolstoy presents us with a young man called Pamfiliy, a model of Christian virtues, yet deadly dry, priggish and self-absorbed. We face the paradox that this great master of modern psychological fiction, whenever he preached self-sacrifice and

---

[1] Paul Boyer, *Chez Tolstoi*, Paris, 1950.

altruistic love, proved incapable of creating good characters, in whom the conscious cultivation of these virtues retained a spark of life. The only religious characters who carried conviction were arch-hypocrites, like Countess Lydia in *Anna Karenina*. But in one of his letters he referred to a story which he would have liked to write, and never wrote, summing up the drastic manner in which he set unfulfilled striving above the maximum achievement. 'We have for so long imbibed with our mother's milk an attitude which helps to make us feel secure and self-satisfied, that the more *natural* state of the human soul, in which it aspires from what we know to be bad towards something better, i.e. the painful discrepancy between life as it is and our innate awareness of what it ought to be—has now come to be regarded as a quite peculiar phenomenon. I often imagine the hero of a story which I should like to write, a man, educated, let us say, in socialist circles, first a revolutionary, then in turn a *narodnik*, an Orthodox Christian, a monk on Mount Athos, afterwards an atheist, next a family man, and finally a Dukhobor sectarian. He begins and tries many things, but abandons everything without finishing it. People laugh at him. He achieved nothing tangible, and died obscurely in some hospital. And while he is dying, he thinks how he wasted his life to no purpose. Yet I tell you—that man was a true saint!' (Letter, September 1889).

IV

Though he never fully practised what he preached, Tolstoy took several steps in that direction. He reduced his personal needs to a bare minimum, became a moderately proficient cobbler and a good agricultural labourer. His efforts to be milder and gentler were punctuated by outbursts of suppressed anger. He made friends with N. F. Fyodorov, librarian of the Rumyantsev library in Moscow, in whom he saw an incarnation of pure Christianity, despite his half-crazy belief in bodily resurrection. He became infatuated with the peasant, Suyutaev, who together with his family, cultivated a small commune, in which no one owned property individually. But he still lived

P

comfortably in his country house surrounded by a devoted family and attendants.

He tried to relieve the burden on his conscience by legally transferring to his wife and children all his 'evil' property, together with the heavy responsibility and cares of looking after it. But this 'selfless' Christianity towards strangers, his decision to renounce royalties on his published work after 1881, seemed to his wife a capricious folly, and a terrible selfishness towards her and their numerous children. She asserted, not without reason, that her husband's renunciation of royalties would benefit nobody but the rich publishers. But she herself began to show abnormal symptoms of jealousy and persecution mania.

'Tolstoyan' disciples started to multiply, at first lonely eccentrics, the artist Nicholas Gay, the elderly female school-teacher, Maria Schmidt, his own daughter, Masha, the dissipated ex-Guards officer, Chertkov, now penitent but business-like and domineering, planning to build himself up as the Metropolitan of a new Tolstoyan religion. Countess Tolstoy complained bitterly: 'There is not a single normal person among them; as for the women, they are mostly hysterical.' Such was her unreasoning hatred of anyone who took Tolstoy's attention away from her, that she even accused her husband of homosexual relations with Chertkov. Open quarrels became more frequent, but they did little to relieve the constant tension, and life at Yasnaya Polyana became a hell for both of them.

All kinds of cranks, parasites, and busybodies flocked to hear the new Socrates. Tolstoy's estate not only became the Mecca of Tolstoyans, but its privacy was invaded by inquisitive pilgrims from every corner of the globe. Worse still, Tolstoy began to recognize that he had condemned himself to play a *public* part, which his inmost nature was hardly fitted to sustain. Though few of his visitors had real sympathy with his teaching or his artistic work, they all demanded moral and practical help from him, and he felt obliged not to disappoint their expectations. Because his mode of life failed to reflect his latest teaching, he knew that his words could not burn the hearts of men. Therefore he yearned to suffer imprisonment or banishment, to undergo any martyrdom which might raise him in public esteem, make his ethical ideas irresistible, and at last force worthier people to respect them. He already viewed many of his odd disciples with a scarcely veiled aversion.

He struggled to conquer his mounting irritation, when he had to answer hundreds of impertinent begging letters, and he dutifully perused piles of worthless manuscripts, sent to him by would-be authors. His world-wide fame imposed on him an unexpected burden, and brought him painful perplexity, but little satisfaction.

Among his innumerable visitors, Gorky was one of the few who *saw through* Tolstoy, by observing that, at close quarters, he was totally unlike the image of himself which he had recently projected on the outside world. He noticed, from the tone underlying Tolstoy's ready flow of words, that he preferred to remain silent about many things, that he talked about his favourite Buddhism sentimentally, and about Christ 'coldly and wearily', without a spark of feeling in his voice. Tolstoy confessed to him in an unguarded moment, that too many people had distracted him from the essential. 'I never lived enough for myself,' he said; 'I had to live for show, to gratify other people.' [1]

Tolstoyan colonies, tilling the land in communal ownership, sprang up in surprising numbers, first in Russia, and afterwards throughout Europe and America. But sooner or later they all broke down, either through mutual recrimination among their ill-assorted members, or through sheer agricultural inefficiency. The only agriculturally competent *Tolstoyans* were tough sectarian peasants, like the Dukhobors, who existed long before Tolstoy's teaching, although they were later affected by it through their leader, Verigin, who sought advice from him. But even they, though hard-working and well-behaved among themselves, proved grotesquely superstitious and intractable, whenever they had to deal with people or affairs outside their sect.[2] Gorky nearly started an agricultural colony himself, and asked Tolstoy

[1] M. Gorky, *Reminiscences of Tolstoy, Chekhov and Andreyev* (English translation), London, 1934.
[2] See Aylmer Maude, *A Peculiar People*, London, 1905.

to present him with a piece of his uncultivated land. But later he poured contempt on Tolstoyan converts, comparing them to Russian pilgrims who carry about dogs' bones which they assure everyone are holy relics, and sell to peasants the Holy Virgin's tears corked up in a bottle.

Outside the sectarian groups, the normal peasant's reaction to Tolstoy, in his evangelical phase, is soberly revealing. Men from his own estate were not much impressed by his play, *The Power of Darkness*, least of all by its moral crisis, when the peasant Nikita starts to confess his sins in public. Tolstoy gathered forty of them together in the drawing-room at Yasnaya Polana, where they listened to a reading of the play in embarrassed silence. When the reading was over, he asked his favourite pupil what he thought about it. The man is said to have answered: 'At first Nikita managed his affairs skilfully, but in the end he proved to be a fool— by repenting.' [1] Yet the educated public, whom Tolstoy did not *want* to please, found the play entrancing. Alexander III called it wonderful, and proposed that the censorship ban on its public performance be removed immediately. But later he allowed his judgement to be overruled by Pobyedonostsev.

It appears that even literate peasants rarely read the moral tales which Tolstoy scrupulously designed to suit their mental level. His French visitor, Paul Boyer, recorded his conversation with a local peasant, whom he questioned about his master's literary work. This man, although he had been a pupil in Tolstoy's village school, admitted that he had never read any of his writings; neither had the other members of his family, although they were all literate except his daughter-in-law.[2]

Another visitor left a graphic account, derived from an old local peasant who had known Tolstoy since boyhood. 'They say the Count was a writer,' the old man remarked. 'Well, that may be dangerous. You get plunged in books, and always forced to invent something new. You may manage for a time, but later something happens to the brain. Though nobody knows what it is, one sees the results. Suddenly the Count began to dress like

[1] A. Nazarov, *Tolstoy*, p. 271, London, 1930.
[2] Paul Boyer, *Chez Tolstoi*, Paris, 1950.

a peasant, and sometimes he would walk barefoot. Of course there is nothing wrong in doing physical work for good health. But when you see a nobleman, a master, cleaning the stable, or pushing a barrow of manure, then you feel that a screw must be loose somewhere. I even heard that he invented a religion of his own—imagine that!

'I knew him when he was young. So gay and charming the Count used to be. In winter he would take village girls to drive in a troika, give them vodka to drink, and kiss them each in turn. Who would ever think that he would one day come to all this?' [1]

During the widespread famine of 1891 Tolstoy's energetic work earned him a new kind of esteem. Helped only by a few friends and converts, like the peasant Semyonov, his rapidly improvised food kitchens managed to feed ten thousand persons every day. His article, *The Terrible Question*, about land hunger and land ownership, stirred *personal* opinion in many countries. He was close enough to the peasants to be aware that many of them lived worse than animals, and would so continue until they owned land of their own. Only a few sectarians, who took their religion to heart, rose morally and materially above the common herd.

In 1894 Tolstoy took up the cause of the Dukhobors, one of the rugged peasant sects, which flourished since the eighteenth century, intermittently persecuted by the Russian Government. Not a word about their exemplary industry, good conduct, sobriety, refusal to undertake military service (in spite of being repeatedly flogged and deported to penal servitude), had ever transpired in the Russian press. After collecting full information about them, he sent a burning description of the whole affair to London, where it was published in *The Times* in 1895, under the title 'The Persecution of Christians in Russia in 1895'. For three years Tolstoy waged a stubborn war of words against the Russian Government, until it capitulated under pressure of popular feeling which he had aroused, chiefly abroad, and gave permission for seven thousand Dukhobors to emigrate to Canada, which had meanwhile offered them permanent asylum.

[1] *Le Monde Slave*, vol. II, p. 215, Paris, 1936.

Though he had renounced all royalties on his literary works published since 1881, he wanted to raise on his own the money needed to transport these Dukhobors from the Caucasus to the shores of Canada. He therefore devoted his new novel *Resurrection* (1899) to this purpose, sold its serial rights to the popular Russian journal *Niva*, and its foreign rights to various journals abroad. The immediate and international popularity of *Resurrection* owed less to its author's name and talent, than to world-wide publicity derived from the semi-religious, semi-humanitarian cause which he now ostensibly wrote to serve.

He admitted that he had sacrificed the finer nuances to an indictment of the government, the Law Courts and the Church, and had lacked time to re-write and polish many sketchy sequences. He knew that he had turned the hero Neklyudov into a moral deformity, whose sententious talk and abrupt transformation failed to emerge as a natural part of his inner growth. But he consoled himself that he had to pay this price to help deserving people, and he urged that the fictional form should now be a popular means of advertising his sterner message. . . . 'As in front of a ticket-booth at a country fair,' he wrote, 'a buffoon grimaces in order to lure the public inside the tent where the real play is being performed, so my imaginative work must play a similar role; it serves to attract the attention of the public to my philosophic teaching' (Letter, 1900).

v

The publication of *What is Art?* (1897) marked the mental culmination of a lengthy phase in Tolstoy's life. It immediately provoked a storm of fury, verging on hysteria, among professional art-critics of the day. For they seized and enlarged on a single minor item, which they chose to interpret as an insult to themselves, the suggestion that a peasant with unperverted taste might be a better judge of the kind of art, which *he* needed, than any urban intellectual. Aesthetic critics pronounced the mighty Tolstoy to be a semi-lunatic, an evangelical crank, whose opinions no longer deserved to be taken seriously. Yet they conveniently ignored more cogent statements which he made, showing that art, whether for good or evil, exerts a stronger formative effect on human minds than any number of prosaic facts.

It looked as if the writers who abused Tolstoy most loudly had never read *What is Art?* except those sentences of it which wounded their self-esteem. The book aroused a hornets' nest in Paris intellectual circles. The English philosopher, Bosanquet, in his so-called standard work on modern aesthetics, did not condescend to mention it, and the famous novelist, George Moore, referred to it only in terms of condescending contempt.

Tolstoy had been for long aware that his revulsion against shoddy products of contemporary art was less simple and complete than he had made it sound in his *Confession* (1882). Naturally, if life held no further charms for him, he would be wise to abstain from writing novels, because in such a dreary state of mind whatever he wrote would sound stale or flat. But it was one thing to stop writing for fear of writing badly, another to cast all imaginative stories on the bonfire, unless they served as vehicles for some *defined* religious teaching.

Luckily Tolstoy's creative instinct asserted strongly what his reason remained reluctant to admit, that to formulate an ethical case condemning art was just as futile as finding a logical criterion to justify it. Therefore he talked philosophic nonsense when he fell into the old snare of trying to construct a 'theory of art', but restored sanity to a tortured subject when he plainly described the part played by works of art in training or perverting human feelings.

While his arguments, and their illustrations, are tedious and at times preposterous, his descriptive passages are often precise and full of wisdom. Absurd over-statements in Tolstoy's essay, magnified by bitter professional jealousy of him, have blinded people to the valuable, topical but neglected truth which it contains. When he visited Marseilles on his continental tour in 1860, Tolstoy observed that the *cafés chantants* of the town (the popular equivalent of the cinema at that time) left a deeper imprint on its citizens' minds than any educational establishment through which they passed. Similarly today, the spasms of *rock 'n' roll* have swayed the minds of Western youth, unmoved by more methodical schoolmasters. He concluded from his own experiments that systematic attempts to stimulate imaginative feeling in children tended to kill it, and that the very pupils, who were most imaginatively gifted, showed the strongest aversion to being moulded by their teacher's preconceived ideas.

He felt sure that the need to enjoy some form of art is instinctive in every human being, regardless of race or class, that such a need is healthy, ought to be satisfied by less haphazard means, and saved from the criminally frivolous indifference prevailing at the present time. Taking that as an axiom, he went on: 'I say that if the enjoyment of art by everybody becomes inconvenient and inconsistent, then the reason lies in the character and direction which art has taken recently, a state of affairs for which we *educated* people are responsible. We must therefore be on our guard against foisting a pack of lies on the younger generation.'

Here lies the contemporary key to *What is Art?* At the time Tolstoy wrote, millions of roubles were being spent every year in Russia on the maintenance of academies, museums, conservatories of music, theatres, etc., for what was officially termed the *support* of art. Hundreds of thousands of skilled workmen were forced to spend their lives and energy in gratifying these demands. Since *officially encouraged* art had become so firmly entrenched in national life, and exacted such strenuous financial effort and human labour, one might assume that its purpose must be fully understood, at least by those in charge of its promotion. Yet, incredible though it seemed, hardly a single expert could agree, either about desirable forms and functions of the arts, or still less about what effect they had on human minds.

On the contrary, artists and critics, representing rival schools, instead of working, spent much of their time in bitter personal quarrels and mutual denunciation. In literature so-called realists ridiculed romantics; the latter eloquently attacked and pulled to pieces symbolists and decadents, while the most 'advanced' decadents revelled in their vices, called themselves the heirs of all the ages, and abused their rivals as hopelessly out of date. A similar chaos of petty controversy prevailed in the spheres of drama, the visual arts and music.

Consequently art, while drawing on this vast expenditure of energy and public money, presented no united front, and led to such bewildering dissension, that hardly a single person could say plainly what kind of art was so undeniably good or useful that it justified the sacrifices made on its behalf. The practice of art in modern European society, Tolstoy believed, had grown so monstrously distorted that the *worst* art had come to be considered good, and even the initial perception of its real aims had been clouded over. Thence arose an alarming but chastening thought, that the art which devoured money and human lives, might be doing people harm, instead of good, by slowly undermining their morale, and poisoning their emotions, instead of uplifting and encouraging them? Could it be sane that the law punished physical murderers, while it encouraged moral poisoners at the state's expense?

An honest attempt to answer once more the perplexing question *What is Art?* could no longer be avoided by responsible people, sensitive to what was happening around them. Despite the stream of books that still poured out, a long line of systematic thinkers had reached quite nebulous or lame conclusions. But in the past some teachers, notably the prophet Mahomet and the philosopher Plato, had been more alive to the destructive power which bad art exerts through enslaving the emotions. So they reluctantly concluded that it would do less harm to weak mortals if all art was strictly controlled or forbidden, than if any and every art was tolerated.

The modern world had turned this precept upside down. People had grown insatiably greedy, so anxious not to be deprived of any sensuous or intellectual excitement, that they indiscriminately encouraged art of every kind, however degrading it might be. This slovenly modern license, in Tolstoy's view, was worse than the ancient severity, and inflicted more irreparable damage on human beings.

The state of art in late nineteenth-century Russia and Western Europe revealed to him an ever-widening gulf between the taste of the urban educated and rural uneducated classes of society. The art promoted by the former (with some notable exceptions, like Tchaikovsky's music) was becoming steadily emptier, more meaningless to the vast majority of people, and even to themselves. In growing more perverse, the art of urban people (whether they were aristocrats, *bourgeois* or artisans) had become stereotyped, impoverished in form and trivial in feeling. At the time he wrote, so Tolstoy believed, it was narrowing down to constantly repeated patterns of three basic emotions, none of which were spiritually edifying or constructive—namely personal pride, sexual desire, and weariness of life. Of these three, sensuality, as the easiest and most familiar, common to animals as well as human beings, was coming to the fore in modern works of art, especially in literature, obsessed with physical excitement, from the Renaissance stories of Boccaccio down to the recent novels of Marcel Prévost, whose *Demi-Vierges* (1894) had just become a sensational best-seller.

People of all classes, infected to the core by this educated erotomania, were multiplying rapidly throughout Europe and America. Only in predominantly peasant countries did the majority remain immune from that disease, partly because they were lucky enough to have remained illiterate, but also because they had less leisure to indulge in vice, and still preserved a vigorous traditional folk art, associated with a far older way of life.

While it became blatantly vulgar and cynical in popular forms, a more sophisticated branch of literary art was sinking into a feebly pretentious verbal sport. To illustrate this trend, Tolstoy quoted (with an effective touch of malice) some verses from the celebrated French poets, Béaudelaire, Mallarme, and Verlaine. While his selection is unkind to the rarefied talent of these poets, it provides a salutary warning of what chaotic verbiage could even then masquerade as literature.

The startling fact remained that such anaemic, debauched or idiotic art had won serious attention and renown, instead of the scorn and condemnation which were all that it deserved. Tolstoy regretted that the jaded modern palate was ready to be tickled by any new snobbery in taste. For most practitioners of contemporary art had joined an organized money-making profession, advertised by critics who were paid to keep it going (regardless of its quality), as a vested interest on which they depended for their living.

Tolstoy earned the undying hostility of professional art critics by contending that most of their work was unwanted and misleading, if not spiritually destructive. 'If any work of art incorporates real feeling,' he pointed out, 'whether of a moral or immoral kind, then that feeling will be conveyed to other people. Once it is conveyed to them, they will experience it, and all further explanation becomes superfluous. But if the work fails to infect people emotionally, then no amount of explanation can ever render it infectious. If it were possible to explain by mere words and argument what the artist wanted to achieve, then he himself would have used those very words! But he chose his art because that was the sole medium through which he could communicate what he had experienced.'

Since art critics are rarely art-lovers, they are seldom capable, like more spontaneous people, of being carried away and moved by works of art. When they paid for their educated minds by atrophied emotions, they were bound to promote confusion and poverty of taste among the public who had been persuaded to believe in them, and adopted their coldly analytic attitude. Schools and academies, preoccupied with teaching art, corrupted taste still further. For how could schools instruct classes in the mystery of imaginative feeling without debasing it? The only thing which they could and did teach successfully was the technical means of imitating works previously experienced by real artists.

Such schools bred self-centred artistic cliques, wedded to a set of formulae, jealous of their scholastic privileges, and frightened of being surpassed by more gifted outsiders. They therefore strengthened an organized hypocrisy of art, a closed trade union for commercial gain, akin to that business-like religious hypocrisy produced by seminaries for training priests. In these academies successful pupils were rarely the most talented or sensitive, but calculating careerists rose to the top.

Tolstoy cited Wagner's operas, in particular *The Ring of the Nibelungen*, as examples of *counterfeit* art on the most lavish scale. By combining and bringing into play the whole conventional arsenal of dramatic, musical and technical *effects*, by making a violent assault on all the senses, it had managed to take by storm the German public, and afterwards win world renown. Critics wrote endlessly about it, delighted to have something so complicated to explain, and soon this meretricious bag of tricks was established as the greatest modern masterpiece. Its extravagant renown blinded people more than ever to the quiet modesty of real art. While Tolstoy's hatred of Wagner was derided at the time, he is nearer to the contemporary view, which has long since taken Wagner down from his exalted nineteenth-century pedestal.

If Tolstoy says little about intellectual or abstract forms of art, it is because they cannot qualify as art at all if they convey no feeling, either good or bad, but remain cerebral exercises. For him the *stronger* the infection which it communicates, the more effective any art must be, regardless of its quality. Only that elusive quality contained the distinction between good and evil. He remarked with foreboding that vulgar and trivial entertainment had already usurped the esteem and public fame deserved only by a pure religious art, which people needed most of all to clarify their minds and conquer disintegrating impulses.

Of course Tolstoy never confused 'religious' art with that patronized by Churches. He defined it broadly as an art which enlarges and unites people's emotional life, enabling them to share similar feelings with people throughout the world, who are capable of experiencing them. Therefore its *universal* appeal distinguished it sharply from the sectional lure of patriotic or blatant national art, which encouraged chauvinistic hymns and racial epics, pompous monuments to leading statesmen, victorious generals, etc. While the latter might unite people sectionally, it did so at the expense of training one national or social group to despise and fight its counterparts and rivals. By fostering provincial self-worship and boundless national conceit, it led to international hatred, followed by self-destruction. It pictured war as a glorious adventure, or a noble sacrifice on every national altar.

Tolstoy still revealed a bias in favour of Christianity, for religious art shares the handicap of its patriotic rival, whenever the emotional unity achieved by one religion is confined to its own band of followers. Therefore orthodox Mahometans, Christians or Jews, so long as their art excludes one another, through blind partiality for their own religion, must all maintain a state of holy war against infidel outsiders. Hence the only art, deserving the title of good and universal—without qualification—and more truly religious than any creed, must rise to a sphere beyond racial pride, class prejudice or religious upbringing. If that was thinkable and desirable, it should be possible.

Tolstoy tried to conjure up a mass of isolated people, mentally alien to one another, spiritually asleep, sullen, suspicious, out of harmony, till suddenly a beautiful story, poignant drama or touching song, kindles their hearts with an electric spark, transforms their state of mind, and brings them together in a warm current of sympathy. If such uplifting phenomena can occur, then art could satisfy Tolstoy's otherwise naïve claim for it, as an instrument promoting human progress, able to guide by wisely directed feeling the day-to-day behaviour of unstable multitudes, uniting in a single stream the clearer aspirations of the past with the muddled cravings of the present.

He honestly observed, however, that the spread of *counterfeit* modern art threatened to wield a more devastating power. Trading on human lust, snobbery and vanity, endowed with the cunning of a skilful prostitute, it turned this organ of potential growth into a subtle weapon of destruction. A perverse taste would gradually become ingrained through vicious force of habit. People, persuaded by advertisement to eat stale or tasteless food, would soon prefer it to stimulating healthy fare, and they would surrender to the easy lure of exciting, soulless art as readily as they took to physical drugs, like tobacco, alcohol, and opium.

For counterfeit art provided a wide choice of seductive mental narcotics, which weakened the brain and paralysed the will even more thoroughly than physical intoxicants did. The exploitation of mass literacy for sheer commercial gain, without any criterion of taste, Tolstoy foresaw to be that hideous menace to human sanity and culture, which it has since become.

Sooner or later it would dawn upon the long-suffering public that they were being doped, debauched and swindled by their so-called educators and entertainers. Simple people, whose sphere of art was folk-lore and religious legend, could not possibly respect so-called modern artists, boosted by the press and lionized by society. They could still revere the physical strength and courage of a Hercules, or the spiritual power shown by a self-renouncing Buddha. But when they saw, not a few strong or exemplary human beings, but hundreds of slovenly painters, flashy and pretentious poets or novelists, vulgar music-hall celebrities and actresses, praised to the sky as if they were the priesthood of some new revelation, and paid colossal salaries, simple people began to grow bewildered and then to despise and hate the educated class which could exalt such trivial creatures.

Although he did not live to witness the non-stop blast of cheap mass entertainment, peculiar to the twentieth-century, Tolstoy clearly diagnosed its character in the counterfeit art of his own day, and foresaw the fight to gain control of it, while it spread like a plague throughout the world.

VI

Despite the vast energy that poured into his exacting work, Tolstoy remained a very robust and physical man. But he revealed throughout his life that bodily gratification of his sexual desires degraded and tormented him. Whether he experienced peasant women, gypsies, or Cossack girls, he was haunted by remorse and shame. Marriage and the cares of a growing family, immersion in agriculture and the composition of *War and Peace*, seem to have kept him calmer for a period. But the novel *Anna Karenina* indicated that years of marriage had not yet extinguished either his physical passion or his earlier repulsion for it. As he grew older, the evil destructive powers of sex began to prey upon his mind more insistently than they had done in his youth. He began to believe that the sexual instinct in a civilized human being tended to stifle and kill love rather than to fulfil it, and rarely rose above a self-centred lust, which, when it gained the upper hand, pushed men and women down into an abyss of vice and crime. Here the *Kreutzer Sonata* (1889) illuminated Tolstoy's latest attitude to marital relations, as clearly as his essay *What is Art?* summed up his revised judgement of modern imaginative activity. Both drew far-reaching and drastic conclusions, though based on a lifetime of wide experience and thought.

The *Kreutzer Sonata* gives a lurid and painfully detailed picture of how a sensual though conscience-stricken husband depraves his innocent wife, infects her with the inescapable curse of his own sexual greed, and finally murders her in a fit of jealousy. In a postscript Tolstoy explained in no uncertain terms the message which he intended this novel to convey. The young men of his day, he said, were wrongly brought up to believe that after the age of puberty they should either marry or take prostitutes. Cynical doctors found it easy to convince them that their health would suffer if they did otherwise. Chastity was sometimes talked about by priests, but rarely taken seriously, if not openly despised.

The physically 'experienced' man would later marry a pure girl and demand from her the same gratification to which he had grown accustomed. 'By this means,' Tolstoy pronounced, 'husbands murder their wives morally, by persuading them that the sexual pleasures of apes and Parisians are legitimate and even praiseworthy for civilized human beings.' Consequently a married couple, whom love had once united, could turn into a couple of mortal enemies, cold and hostile egoists, determined to extract the maximum enjoyment from each other, each poisoning the other's life.

Tolstoy concluded that the goal of physical satisfaction, even in a married state, was apt to turn into a vicious self-indulgence, an obstacle to the service of God and other human beings, and he urged that prolonged continence was both desirable, and less injurious to mental and physical health than cultivated lust. He was taken aback by the conclusion forced upon him, rejecting any compromise. But he maintained that chastity must be the aim of any morally enlightened human being, even if it proved beyond his strength. The ideal should be approached, but never realized. For the light shining ahead of a man could lead him safely through the darkness, though he never reached the source of light.

Pursuing his consistent, exasperating, logic, Tolstoy demanded a revised approach to existing relations between men and women, leading towards a firmer moral feeling, which would cease to regard physical union as a healthy or normal pleasure, or the preliminary to a more exalted state of mind, but rather as an animal condition, excusable only as a means of procreating children. Whoever cannot stomach such monastic exhortation, may be consoled to know that Tolstoy spent a dissipated youth, fathered thirteen legitimate children, and only started to preach this unattainable ideal in his austere old age.

His critics naturally objected that no normal man would follow such a rule of conduct, and that if he ever did, the human race might be doomed to vanish from the earth.

Tolstoy forestalled this objection, when he observed that, since chastity remained a mere counsel of perfection, the dread of human self-extinction by that means need worry nobody. In any case, he added, the eventual destruction of mankind, formerly only a widespread religious belief with a mystic sense of divine judgement, is now fully confirmed by men of science, who deduce it from the cooling down of the earth and irrefutable physical data.

A more pressing question alarmed Tolstoy—that the human race would systematically destroy *itself* before it was blotted out by any geological calamity—when it felt so disgusted with its vile behaviour that it pined to commit suicide. Unless it either made, or aimed at, further moral progress, what vigorous emotional incentive could survive to spur it on? If human beings continued to degenerate, till they became incurably contemptible in their own eyes, then nobody could lament their quick extermination, which might be welcomed as a merciful release. *The Kreutzer Sonata* is unique in its sombre and sweeping denunciation of the destructive power of sex in modern life. Sex as an ever-present curse, which can cripple every effort made to evolve in a spiritual sphere, also dominates *The Death of Ivan Il'yich* (1886), *The Devil* (1889) and *Father Sergei* (1890). None of these stories can be dismissed as namby-pamby moral parables, like some of Tolstoy's peasant tales. They are all energetic, sharply designed and tense, but being less sensational than *The Kreutzer Sonata* (which described an actual murder) they attracted scant attention.

In his *Essay about the Sexual Question* (1901) Tolstoy stated bluntly that the worst ugliness of life today springs from the *physical* power exercised by women over men. But since this power of women depends on male sensuality, he found that the root cause of human disorder is man's lust. If men strove harder to free themselves from slavery to lust, they would save their souls from surrender to the spell of vicious women, and emancipate better women in a generous manner. Tolstoy hardly touched on either male or female homosexuality as a reaction to the *impasse* in the battle of the sexes. But he appears to have regarded it without much interest as one of many physical aberrations.

In the same essay Tolstoy stated his attitude to birth-control (curiously similar to that of the Catholic Church, though more outspoken). While in favour of natural birth-control by means of continence, he condemned new contraceptive methods as an evil device for increasing the scope of human lust, while escaping the rigours of childbirth and the cares of bringing up a family. 'It is no use writing about this, or trying to refute it, any more than to refute a man who proves that it is useful and pleasant to copulate with corpses. . . . One must only wonder at the degeneration and blunted feeling that led to such a thing. There are no crimes against morality,' he concluded, 'which people conceal so carefully as those provoked by sexual desire. There is nothing about which people feel so violently or disagree so much. For acts which are to some a horrible crime appear to others a normal

Q

comfort or natural pleasure. However that may be, the fact remains that sexual vices ruin individuals more than any other vice, and thereby stop the whole forward movement of mankind.'

VII

Tolstoy first became widely known abroad in his joint capacity as a popular evangelist and an eccentric aristocrat who cobbled shoes, and ploughed his own fields, dressed in a peasant smock. It was not till 1879 that the first French translation of *War and Peace* appeared in Paris, thanks to Turgenev's disinterested efforts. Even then (though Flaubert recorded his enthusiasm for it) the public hardly read the book, which sold only a few hundred copies. Similarly in Russia, he rose to fame as a social and religious rebel, not as a great literary artist. But people began to bombard him with queries and appeals for help, which he had to answer. Therefore, during his last two decades, Tolstoy found himself a public oracle, constantly obliged to write and speak on vital topical problems.

In many cases he saw further into the essence of practical matters than the statesmen and business-people responsible for dealing with them. His *Letters on Henry George* (1897) and *A Great Iniquity* (1905) urged the Russian Government to adapt the American Henry George's ingenious scheme for taxing land values. That plan appealed to Tolstoy, because it seemed just, simple to enforce and drastic in effect.

It proposed a law to assess the value of all land, agricultural, industrial or urban, according to its profitability. Thereafter, everyone owning land would be obliged to pay to the government the whole yearly rentable value at which it had been assessed. This simple tax would provide the government with so much revenue that it could abolish more complicated taxes, which employed an army of unnecessary officials, and still proved harder to collect. By obliging the majority of large landowners to sell their land, the scheme would convey the following benefits: (1) Agricultural land would pass, without violence, into the possession of men who worked on it. (2) A vast amount of hitherto uncultivated land would become available to landless peasants, who would otherwise be forced to migrate to unhealthy towns. The physical health, moral sanity (dependent on a strong agricultural backbone) and economic balance of the whole nation were thus at stake. Some social reformers have pointed out that if a practicable variant of the Henry George system had been adopted (as it could have been by the all-powerful Russian Government) the peasants would have received the extra land for which they craved, and also learned that private property imposed on them a duty to contribute to public expenditure. They would thus have grown less amenable to reckless promises made by revolutionary parties, and less infuriated by revengeful hatred of landowners who clung to their remaining land. Also the latter, by being forced to sell, might have escaped the direr penalty of being expropriated without any compensation, or murdered, as they were in 1917.

The *Letter to a Hindu* (1908) and *Gandhi Letters* (1910) touch on a matter which afterwards assumed world-wide importance. Only ten years after Tolstoy's death, Gandhi, who described himself as 'a humble follower of that great teacher', started to organize the *'non-co-operation'* movement throughout India. By practising passive resistance to British administrative orders, but without inflicting bloodshed, this movement, under Gandhi's direct control, created the cumulative moral impetus which undermined, and eventually destroyed, the whole fabric of British rule in India.

The amazing authority which Gandhi wielded, through the personal veneration which he inspired in millions of Hindus, is due to the fact that he practised with dogged perseverance the main precepts which Tolstoy could only preach.

But Tolstoy warned his Hindu correspondent that new forms of justification for human misdeeds, termed *scientific*, were taking the place of antiquated and obsolete religious claims. These attempted justifications were as misleading as the old ones, but because they were *new*, their falsity would not be recognized until they had done much harm. Whereas men of old had tortured and murdered each other in the name of *God*, 'those who inflict identical evils among us today' act in the name of *the people*, and use the pretext of public service and scientific progress.

'One might have expected and hoped that in the immense Brahman, Buddhist and Confucian worlds, this new scientific mania would *not* establish itself, and that the Chinese, Japanese, and Hindus, once their eyes had been opened to the colossal religious fraud which supported violence, would then advance directly to a recognition of the law of love, which had been so forcefully expressed by the great Eastern teachers.' Unfortunately the barbarous scientific superstition, replacing the religious one, had been accepted and had secured a stronger hold, even in Asiatic countries. 'If the English managed to enslave the peoples of India, it was because the Indians still recognized brute force as the main principle of social order . . . A single commercial company enslaved a nation of two hundred millions . . . Do not the figures alone explain that it was not the English who enslaved the Indians, but the Indians who willingly enslaved themselves?' (*Letter to a Hindu*, 1908).

In his eighty-second year Tolstoy wrote that if only he were younger, he would have visited China! [1] Towards the end, 'the peaceful laborious Chinese peasants', whom he had never seen, appealed to him more than his Slav compatriots, whose instability he knew. 'Those who can fulfil our mission,' he pronounced, 'are the great and wise Chinese people. Liberty will come from the Eastern peoples after the Western ones have lost it beyond recall.' The *yellow peril*, seen through Tolstoy's eyes, might turn miraculously into a yellow salvation, provided that the Chinese never succumbed to that soul-destroying course which more barbarous Europeans had recently embarked upon.

In a letter written in 1906 he warmly commended the Chinese, 'who have suffered so terribly from the crudely selfish and avaricious cruelty of European countries, but up to the present have replied to all the violence done against them with a display of majestic and wise composure, and have preferred to use patience in the struggle against force'.[2] He even praised China's territorial cession (1898) of Port Arthur to Russia, Kiaouchow

---

[1] D. Bodde, *Tolstoy and China*, p. 29, Princeton, 1950.   [2] ibid., p. 51.

to Germany, and Weihaiwei to England. He understood Kipling's words: 'They let the legions thunder by, with patient proud disdain.' But he expressed concern that his correspondent, a certain Mr. Ku, had written a book suggesting that it was now time for the Chinese to retaliate in kind against encroaching European armies.

'I see from your book that some light-minded people in China, called the Reform Party, believe that this change should be made by doing the same as Europeans have done, i.e. replacing a monarchical government by a republican one, and establishing that same preponderance of armed forces and urban industry as now exists in the West.' If the Chinese are foolish enough to follow that evil example, Tolstoy concluded, 'then they will lose their most precious spiritual asset, their own *Tao*, their traditional way of life'.

Tolstoy distrusted all modern political movements, which tended to enlarge the state apparatus or increase the power of politicians, whether they were called socialist or conservative, progressive or reactionary. He suspected that they all embodied either old theological or new pseudo-scientific superstitions, and sought to enforce by rigid external organization, results which could only fruitfully be worked out by individual wills. He therefore firmly opposed the prevalent belief that an advance towards state socialism would confer startling new benefits on human life.

Tolstoy urged that modern socialism (which relied on the state and a mass of legislation) could never lead human beings into good or creative action, *unless* it both maintained and extended their sense of personal responsibility and moral conscience. But, so far socialist doctrine and practice were working steadily, hand in hand, to undermine and violate those very feelings. Clear personal judgement was on the verge of vanishing, whether in the collective hatred stimulated by class warfare and national pride, or in the surrender of initiative to syndicalist societies, or in a numbed submission to the machinery of bureaucratic government.

Tolstoy blamed the socialist *superstition* for having injected into politics a false religious glamour. It had tried to blend the absurd doctrinaire enlightenment of the late eighteenth-century encyclopaedists with the sweeping historical optimism brought into vogue by mid-nineteenth-century materialists—whereas a self-respecting modern man should only be devoted to non-political aims, remaining on his guard in any political attachment.

In 1901 he told his French visitor, Professor Paul Boyer, how he deplored the way in which people pinned their faith on economic panaceas, like the clumsy attempt to remedy industrial evils by putting them under the uniform control of civil servants. 'The time will come when socialism will show itself to be a savage and monstrous system. I shall not live to see that time, but you may . . . Addressing itself to man's commonest instinct, his stomach, by promising to satisfy all his material desires (a promise which, incidentally, it will never be able to fulfil by the means it offers), it ignores love, thrives on hatred and envy of the rich, and is itself permeated by a morbid thirst for wealth, reminding one of the thirst of fleas hurrying to a pile of vomit . . . If socialism triumphs, the world will become desperately repulsive.' [1]

The growing self-assertion shown by revolutionary parties in Russia after 1905 turned Tolstoy's distrust of them into an open battle. In the previous century he had denounced the conceit or complacency of ruling liberal reformers. But he now found the rising socialists more dangerous than the waning liberals, because they amalgamated and tried to practise two colossal lies, the old liberal lie of unrestricted personal liberty, and the new intellectual lie of scientific rule. He said that the underlying socialist mood reminded him ominously of the old coercive Russian orthodoxy, and that we shall either have to renounce industrial civilization or reintroduce the whip.

Transforming Russia into a Western constitutional state provided no solution, because the so-called democratic state, even in the West, was returning insidiously to the despotic tyranny of earlier monarchical states. And while the subjects of a frankly despotic government could still protest, and cling to

[1] A. Nazarov, *Tolstoy*, p. 295, London, 1930.

their inward freedom, the citizen voters of a democratic state were forced to play a formal part in muzzling their own consciences. 'These free men,' he commented, 'recall the prisoners who imagine that they are enjoying freedom, because they have the right to elect the gaolers entrusted with the administration of their prison.' In Tolstoy's view the mid-nineteenth-century abolition of slavery, while it destroyed an obsolete agricultural bondage, archaic and uneconomic, had substituted a more inescapable form of industrial slavery, and one that held a greater number of people in its grip. In this tightening economic network, binding every man to his national industrial machine, Western constitutional nations differed but slightly from the Russian autocracy.

'In England, France and Germany, the pernicious character of governments is so masked, that people belonging to those nations point to events in Russia, and imagine that what is done in Russia can happen only there. But I regard all governments, not only the Russian government, as intricate institutions, sanctified by tradition and custom, for the purpose of committing by force and with impunity the most revolting crimes. And I think that the efforts of those who wish to improve our social life should be directed towards the liberation of themselves from *national* governments, whose evil, and above all, whose futility, is in our time becoming more and more apparent.' Tolstoy observed without dismay symptoms of the approaching collapse of the Russian Empire. For he hoped that it would be the destructive prelude to a revived moral force, destined to sweep away 'the whole false Christian civilization of Western Europe'. Although he harboured no unfriendly feelings towards individual Jews, it is noteworthy that he opposed political Zionism on identical grounds. To see the horrors overtaking Europe in the progress of the bloodstained modern state, and then to wish to create a new Jewish state, he noted, 'is an abomination and a crime'.

Tolstoy has rightly been charged with short-sightedness and lack of common sense. For he played into the hands of the same revolutionaries, whose anger he tried to calm and check. When the critic, V. Stasov, told him that he was responsible for the outbreak of the 1905 revolution, Tolstoy replied with some misgiving: 'I cannot agree with you in the role which you assign to me in making our revolution. For both the intelligentsia, and the proletariat following it, have no ideals of any kind, nothing but phrases.' He admitted, however, that in his *human weakness*, he had rejoiced that his ideas were spreading widely: 'I say, *in my weakness*, because I cannot decide whether it is now necessary for my thoughts to be spread or promoted. I know only that I was obliged to express them at the time. As for their conscious employment in the service of revolution, bloodshed, and evil—I know without the slightest doubt that this ought *not* to be. Obviously soldiers should not shoot their brothers or other people, but should refuse for God's sake to do this; they should equally refuse to help *any* revolution, i.e. the replacement of one Government by another' (Letter, 1910).

Unlike the original Slavophils, Tolstoy refused to tolerate the state in the guise of a painful but necessary evil, which might gradually be reduced by patient efforts to restrict its scope. In the heat of his denunciation he seemed to believe that adult human beings could calmly manage their own affairs without any state. And even if the removal of governments led to fighting in the streets, he preferred a moderate outbreak of internal anarchy to the precarious armed camps, vibrating with mutual suspicion, into which governments had already herded their dazed citizens as a prelude to more devastating wars.

Tolstoy's paradise of human statelessness stands on a par with his twin ideals of chastity and an active sense of brotherhood, all three equally unrealizable, since they exact a degree of spiritual maturity which few men were ever likely to attain. But for him the unattainability of any goal provided no valid obstacle to action taken in that direction. Therefore people should continue to resist (without inflicting violence) all governments or organized unions, which throve on the abuse of institutional power, and paralysed individual judgement.

In 1910 Tolstoy received an invitation to attend a big Slavonic Congress to be held in Sofia. He refused, but seized the occasion to write a letter explaining why he could never participate in conferences of this kind. 'Union of men—that in the name of which we have come together—is not only the most important affair of human beings—but I see in it both a sense, a goal, and a benefit to our lives. Yet in order that this attempt should do some positive good, it must be understood in its proper meaning . . . All valuable activities of the human soul, as soon as they are carried to extremes, not only cease to be useful, not only fail to bring even a little benefit, but become pernicious, and frustrate the attainment of the object towards which they appear to strive. So it is with religion, once it allows blind fanatical faith, with love, once it allows conflict and dissension, with service to men, once it allows coercion of other men.

'Undoubtedly united people are stronger than the disunited, the family stronger than the individual, a band of robbers stronger than one robber alone, the community stronger than its individual members, a state united by patriotism stronger than nationalities which are broken up. But the point is that the advantage of those who are united, and the inevitable result of this advantage, namely the enslavement or exploitation of the disunited, provokes in the latter the impulse to unite, first in order to resist coercion, but later in order to inflict it.

'It is natural that Slav nationalities, now experiencing the evil effect on themselves of Austrian, German, Russian or Turkish states, strive to oppose this evil, to join together in their own organization; but the latter, if it ever takes shape, will be drawn into similar action . . .

'Whether this union consists of families, bands of robbers, communities of states, nationalities, or even a holy alliance of states, such associations not only fail to help, but more than anything else *obstruct* the true progress of mankind. And therefore—I at least think—we must never encourage such partial unions, but always oppose them. If we recognize as the ultimate object of human life a union which is world-wide and religious, then that very acknowledgement denies all other principles of union.' [1]

<hr>

[1] *Slavonic and East European Review*, p. 246 et seq., vol. 8, 1929.

Apart from bitter economic conflicts between rival states, Tolstoy diagnosed another fierce internal war, which would be waged between modern government officials, drunk with power, and private citizens, still robust enough to stand on their own feet. He admitted, without consoling self-delusion, that so far governments monopolized the overpowering weapons in this civil war. But they were obliged to stupefy their citizens systematically, in order to maintain their co-operation. They therefore administered mental and physical drugs, carefully designed to blunt their moral sense, and weaken their initiative.

Tolstoy pointed to the world-wide increase in the consumption of tobacco, alcohol and opium as symptoms of human deterioration. But he maintained that the fleeting personal pleasure, which these gave to their consumers, masked a more systematic utility as drugs encouraged by the state, and designed to stifle resistance to its sinister demands. He even classified familiar pastimes, such as regular newspaper-reading, indulgence in rapid movement and nervous thrills, as undoubted *mental narcotics*. He clearly saw the beginning of that control of mass emotion by those who pull the strings of public entertainment, but he confined himself to the few examples which he knew.

If a man wants to do something of which he feels ashamed, to take a prostitute, steal or kill, he drinks first in order to pluck up courage. 'It seems to people that a slight stupefaction, a little darkening of the judgement, cannot have any important influence on them. To think in this way is like supposing that it may injure a watch to be struck against a stone, whereas a little dirt introduced inside it can do no harm. In fact, tiny alterations in the domain of consciousness may produce boundless effects on human conduct' (*Why do men stupefy themselves*, 1890).

Tolstoy praised Dostoyevsky as an honest psychologist, when in *Crime and Punishment* he skilfully made his Raskolnikov decide to murder the old moneylender, not when he stood before her axe in hand, but while he was thinking and otherwise unoccupied. Just when he needed clarity of mind, Raskolnikov clouded his judgement by drinking a glass of beer. Tolstoy added that public authorities exploited the same weakness. During a battle officers would order an attack from soldiers who had previously been given alcoholic drink. He asserted, as an eyewitness, that most of the French soldiers who took part in the final assault on the bastions of Sevastopol were roaring drunk. One redeeming feature of this permanent civil war lay in the fact that enterprising individuals invincibly launched new undertakings, without the least help from governments, and often in the teeth of governmental resentment. Tolstoy felt convinced that the age of veneration for national governments and their statesmen, despite the armed power and public hypnosis which they still exerted, was already on the wane, and would soon turn into sceptical ridicule. He claimed, indeed, that the time was fast approaching when to call a man a patriot would be the worst insult you could offer him. For men of awakened conscience would recognize how deplorably obsolete it was to despise or injure foreign countries, and blindly to glorify the exclusive state system in which they happened to have been born and bred.

So long as national governments continued to exist, they would distrust and betray each other, so that no agreement between them to undertake disarmament could ever be feasible or binding. Therefore international conferences on this subject must be either a gross stupidity, a pastime to justify the existence of diplomats, or a deliberate fraud. As for The Hague Conference of 1900, Tolstoy caustically observed, the Russian Government convened it by inviting other governments to discuss disarmament, while it was secretly increasing its own army. In order to keep up appearances, the others felt obliged to accept the Russian offer, with the result that a crowd of delegates, drawing handsome salaries, met in The Hague for several weeks to talk about the establishment of a peace in which not one of them believed. To call for peace and preach it in these circumstances was like urging sobriety in a public house which throve on drunkards.

VIII

Mental drugs must, however, be skilfully administered, and in doses corresponding to the degree and type of stupefaction needed. Far from diminishing the amount of dull, distasteful or destructive work, they could make it more alluring. While some private people take drugs for the sake of blank oblivion, others to find exhilarating spiritual escape, the function of drugs promoted by the state is to direct the mind of every citizen towards the jobs which his government requires.

Hard, persistent daily work is thus exalted as a cure for every ill, an antidote to disillusion, the sole reliable guide to human happiness and satisfaction. But Tolstoy ventured to inquire: have we thereby abdicated our right to consider the sense and purpose of our work, or to value it by its results? The manufacturers of, and dealers in, opium, tobacco, and alcohol, the inventors and makers of many weapons of destruction, military men, etc., they all *work*, yet obviously mankind would be better off, were all these workers to stop working in their negative jobs. Then a vast number of people work very hard to fulfil duties which, so they say, are imposed upon them by religion or scientific progress.

Here too is colossal waste, and useless effort, because 'much of what is called religion is simply the science of the past, and much of what is called science is the religion of today. . . . It is quite likely that theology or philosophy, esteemed as most important sciences by a former generation, may come to be regarded as childish twaddle by a future one. Unless therefore our century forms a complete exception, it needs no great boldness to conclude by analogy that, among the kinds of knowledge absorbing the attention of our many learned men, and which are now called *scientific*, there are some which will be regarded by our descendants in the same way as we now regard the rhetoric of the ancients, or the scholasticism of the Middle Ages' (*Non-Acting*, 1893).

While Tolstoy admitted work to be as much a mental need as nourishment was a physical one, he could not rank it as a sacred duty, or an unqualified virtue, for it could easily become a moral anaesthetic. And work, 'aiming solely at the profit or fame of the worker (which is bad and self-conscious), makes not only men but ants into cruel animals. . . . The most cruel men were always busy.

'We frequently meet people who are so busy that they never have time, either to be generous, or to ask themselves whether their work is not doing more harm than good. They will listen to you attentively, but scornfully reply: "It's all very well for you to argue. You have nothing special to do. But what time have I got for discussions? . . . I have to organize the army; I have to build the Eiffel Tower, to arrange the Chicago Exhibition, to pierce the Isthmus of Panama, to investigate the problems of heredity or telepathy, or to find out how many times this classical author has used such and such words" ' (*Non-Acting*, 1893).

Tolstoy's tirades against the abuses of modern science are so repetitive, that they have led some exasperated readers to dismiss him as an archaic, reactionary fanatic. Yet he was never an enemy of science, for he fought only scientific conceit and learned barbarism. 'Science can study everything in the world,' the scientist proudly proclaims today. 'But really, is not everything a bit too much?' Tolstoy rejoined (*Modern Science*, 1898).

Narrow uncultured scientists pursued science for science's sake, a creed which forced them to analyse exhaustively, but blindly, not what people needed to make life kindlier and brighter, but any novelty that came to hand, however trivial or destructive it might be. Therefore science began to gratify an insatiable curiosity about everything, except the things most worth knowing, and seduced people with a promise of perpetual increase in their physical ease and pleasure, regardless of any damage which these might inflict on character. But Tolstoy exempted *true science* from this sweeping judgement, explaining that it is often persecuted by its contemporaries, 'because it reveals the mistakes made by pseudo-scientists, and points towards new unaccustomed ways of life'. Hence its unpopularity and hard struggle against scientific vested interests, in order to qualify as *scientific*.

The spread of so-called scientific education (whatever else it had achieved) had clearly failed to discipline or harmonize human feelings. While late nineteenth-century liberals talked glibly about the supremacy of 'public opinion', and of education as the spearhead of reform, Tolstoy pointed to the ominous fact that, in countries still devoid of any accepted intellectual standards, public opinion sprang largely from artificial excitement of the crudest mob passions.

Therefore he deplored the cowardice and short-sighted stupidity (disguised as tolerance) which treated theatres, concerts, music-halls, and bookshops as merely money-making purveyors of cheap entertainment, designed to amuse the public when it felt tired or bored, or to divert serious concern by cracking jokes about distressing topics of the day. Neither did he want the state to stupefy its citizens completely, by taking command of all art and entertainment.

It is still a striking modification of Tolstoy's so-called anarchist outlook that, despite his horror of state omnipotence, he decidedly preferred a severe *negative* censorship (which only the state could enforce) to that unbridled debauchery of words and taste which started after the Russian censorship was lifted in 1905. 'I do not agree with complete freedom of the press,' he frankly told his friend the sectarian peasant, S. T. Semyonov, in 1907. 'Admittedly censorship may miss its objective, but too much freedom brings with it a graver evil, for it immediately lifts up such qualities of filth that it soils the whole imagination.' [1]

In the spring of 1905 a deputation of literate young artisans came to visit him in Yasnaya Polyana, and pestered him with leading questions. He noticed that their minds were muddled and inflamed by sensational newspaper stories, by party disputes in the Duma, etc. When they naïvely asked him what else they ought to read—instead of presenting them with some of his own printed tracts—he told them that they needed only to learn how to live better, and that they could discover, even if they read nothing. 'Blessed are those who read no newspapers,' he concluded with a smile. 'Blessed are the illiterate, and those who are not led astray by the intelligentsia.' But he advised them seriously, if they felt a strong desire to study, to pay less attention to what was written at the present time, and to read more older literature, because, he explained, 'that will not corrupt and spoil your minds'.[2]

---

[1] S. T. Semyonov, *Vospominaniya*, p. 96, St. Petersburg, 1912.
[2] op. cit., p. 141.

IX

Tolstoy's last years were darkened and overshadowed by that family conflict, which his biographers have described in detail, and which ended in his flight from home, to find his death in the railway station at Astapovo. But he had several times been on the verge of leaving Yasnaya. Twice before, in 1884 and 1897, he had tried to go, and was not stopped by fear or indecision, but by an overriding sense of duty to his wife, whom he still loved and pitied. He felt that to remain at home imposed on him a greater feat of self-denial than to escape.

In 1892 Tolstoy had transferred all his estates to his wife and nine surviving children, by legal deed. He frequently expressed a fervent wish to live and work among the peasants. Being a man of exceptional physical strength and pertinacity, he might have done this better than most of his disciples, who failed in the attempt. But his wife, apart from resenting his attitude, threatened to commit suicide if he ever left her. Her morbid jealousy and suspicion, her outbursts of hysteria, tormented him. Chertkov called her 'a cruel gaoler, who hates his soul', and said about her, 'Had I such a wife, I would long ago have shot myself or run away to America.' [1]

Prophetically enough, hints at this latent struggle are visible even in the warmly idealized family life of *War and Peace*, when the disillusioned Prince Andrew warns his naïve friend, Pierre, 'Never marry, till you can say to yourself that you have already done all you are capable of doing, until you have ceased to love the woman of your choice, and seen her plainly as she is—Marry when you are old and good for nothing—otherwise all that is fine and noble in you will be lost, wasted on trifles. Tie yourself up to a woman, and like a chained convict, you lose all freedom!'

In his final will, Tolstoy had named his daughter, Alexandra, as his literary heir, but appointed Chertkov as sole editor, in charge of publishing his work. Tolstoy's secrecy about this will, his wife's fears that she and her children might be deprived of their rightful inheritance, preyed upon Countess Tolstoy's mind.

[1] A. Maude, *The Final Struggle*, p. 27, London, 1936.

She made frantic efforts to find the will, and was determined to destroy it, while Chertkov was equally determined to keep it hidden from her. Tolstoy wrote in his private diary (30 July 1910): 'Chertkov has drawn me into strife, and that is very hard and repulsive to me . . . they tear me to pieces.' On the night of 28 October, when he heard his wife ransacking private papers in his study, he received that final jolt which impelled him to carry out his long-cherished intention to leave his home for ever.

N. MIKHAILOVSKY

from a photograph

CHAPTER VII

REPRESENTATIVE *NARODNIKS*

I

FROM the day of its awakening, that scattered handful of well-intentioned Russians, which claimed the proud title of *intelligentsia*, was doomed to suffer as the plaything of current political prejudice and passions. When we try to examine the chequered course of the *narodnik* intellectual movement, to explain its inflated importance, to pin down its much-vaunted anti-bourgeois and partly anti-European character, we find it full of oddly assorted components, in which sincere but disembodied thought, agrarian nostalgia, dislike or envy of the Europeanized nobility, frustrated national ambition, moods of heroic self-abasement, and a thirst for martyrdom, all played distinct and sometimes conflicting parts.[1]

The *men of mixed ranks* first questioned the practical utility of various foreign doctrines which had charmed their aristocratic predecessors for imaginative reasons. Hegel, Schelling, Saint-Simon, Auguste Comte and the Positivists, had failed to provide that master-key to Russian social problems, which Russian radicals so strangely but persistently tried to find in European social teachers, who had rarely given them a passing thought.

In their precarious floating position, poised between the higher classes and the illiterate peasants, these politically-minded *narodniks* saw themselves as the new nerve and brain which could give shape to inarticulate strivings, stirred by the Emancipation Edict of 1861. They conscientiously threw themselves into research about unique features which separated Russian life from Europe. They studied peasant customary law, the commune, the craftguilds (*artels*), soaked themselves in wise proverbs and edifying

---

[1] An exhaustive account of the Russian populist movement in all its ramifications is given in *Il Populismo Russo*, by F. Venturi, Turin, 1952.

folk tales, awoke to the timeless beauty of traditional peasant songs and dances.

But they also passed bitter partisan judgement against good Russian writers, who had firmly refused to work within the blinkers of their narrow utilitarian morale; condemned Tolstoy and Dostoyevsky as 'reactionary' or 'politically indifferent', and despised Pushkin for having been joyously epicurean and therefore 'devoid of social conscience'. Because they lacked self-reliance and stability, the *narodniks* could rarely appreciate individual feats of intelligence and talent. By sentimentalizing the common people *collectively*, they placed themselves lower than a mob to whom they attributed quite imaginary virtues. From the survival of a great but ancient peasant art, they drew absurdly false conclusions about the modern peasant's character.

Harsh critics of a world in which they held no place of honour, vague prophets of another social order which had not yet materialized (and would reject them when it did), their efforts produced none of the results for which they strove. But they completed a major mental transformation, from which their Marxian rivals were the first to reap material benefit. The best *narodnik* writers, like Gleb Uspensky and Karonin, swayed many minds by blending sociological obsessions with a fresh imaginative appeal. But their ideas were far more forcefully stated by Tolstoy, and even earlier by Turgenev.

The novelist, Gleb Uspensky, showed how the peasant withered and declined, the moment he was transplanted from his rural environment, how he drew from the *power of the soil* an almost equal measure of endurance and fatalist passivity. Although he could work like an ox in agricultural labour, nature taught him to accept a cruel capricious force, which might destroy his crops overnight. He was accustomed to harsh government, and distrusted cocksure revolutionaries, who tried to convince him that he could throw off his burdens by revolt. And even when the peasant began to wear better clothes, to read newspapers and books, to shed his darker superstitions, to discover that the earth did not rest on three whales, or those three whales on an elephant, he began to doubt whether this mental development helped him to live better; it disturbed him to be educated beyond the range of his immediate agricultural needs.

II

N. Mikhailovsky (1842–1904), son of an upper-class government official, made the first serious attempt to canalize widespread *narodnik* sympathies into a coherent line of thought, and thence into a programme of reform. From 1868 to 1884 he worked for the influential journal *Fatherland Annals*, and from 1892 till 1904 he edited *Russian Wealth*. He soon became the recognized leader of practical *narodnik* activities, while remaining respectable enough to command the attention of a liberal reading public.[1] But he romanticized the *commune* as fatally as any official Slavophil, by maintaining that the agricultural order peculiar to Russia, not only differed radically from that of bourgeois Europe, but demonstrated moral superiority to it. 'We must avert the *proletarian plague* which now rages in the West, and threatens to infect Russia in the immediate future,' became his motto. Whereas labour pressure in Europe demanded revolutionary measures against owners of industrial property, the labour problem in Russia remained conservative, for it could be solved through the continued handling of such matters by people who already work on them, and by preserving the ancient mode of agricultural property.

In order that the peasants should be guaranteed their *status quo*, Mikhailovsky called for drastic intervention by the state to save the *commune* from the natural disintegration which it was undergoing. This surrender of judgement to archaic impulse was perhaps his worst mistake. Later in the *Journal of the People's Will* he occasionally remarked that communal ownership should cease to be a sacred fetish. But he was astonishingly blind to the fact that the stagnant *commune* blocked one of the improvements which he aimed at, an escape from hopeless poverty. He would

[1] J. Billington, *Mikhailovsky and Russian Populism*, Oxford, 1958, provides the most comprehensive recent study of this subject.

have preferred to starve together with the peasants in their quiet villages, rather than see them drink themselves to death in noisy towns. But he failed to see that agricultural inefficiency itself must drive them to the towns.

Tolstoy was an enterprising farmer, who invested his money in the land, whereas Mikhailovsky with the *idée fixe* of an agrarian politician, totally unversed in scientific agriculture, fell back on the *commune* as the sole local antidote to that obsession with the spread of large-scale industry, which dominated official circles in the late eighteen-seventies and eighties. 'To tell the truth,' he wrote to Lavrov frankly, 'I fear reaction in Russia less than I fear revolution. But to teach people how to handle a revolution, if it comes, in the way they ought to handle it, remains our duty, and a possibility. . . . The fight against the old gods hardly concerns me now, because their song is sung, and their fall is only a question of time. But the new Gods are more dangerous, and in that way worse.' [1]

In his public controversy with Dostoyevsky about the latter's novel *The Devils*, he advised the author to reckon with the latest *devil*, the pursuit of *national* wealth, which had taken possession of the Russian ruling class, coupled with individual beggary and with an over-specialized division of labour, which turned men into disgruntled cogs in a national wealth machine.

In 1874 the Government started to arrest and imprison numerous innocent enthusiasts, who had gone to live and work among the peasants in remote villages. Mikhailovsky's attitude hardened correspondingly, and in the newly-founded illegal journal of his party he began to justify acts of terrorism for personal protection and self-defence against morally indefensible actions by the Government. In 1879 an internal schism over this principle led to the foundation of the extremist group, *The People's Will*, which now justified political assassination, on the same principle as killing poisonous vipers. This had Mikhailovsky's support, but he was strenuously opposed by the more gradualist Marxian, Plekhanov, who founded a dissident group, the so-called *Black Partition*.

[1] Quoted N. Rusanov, *Golos Minuvshavo*, February 1913.

Mikhailovsky now impressed on all his followers that it was time to shed quietist prejudice about the futility of meddling in political affairs. 'You fear to work for a constitutional government in the future, because you believe that will bring with it the hated yoke of the bourgeoisie. But look around you!—that same yoke already lies on Russia under the rule of the august autocratic Emperor. The bourgeoisie, growing up under the shelter of the Tsar's ermine robe, will eventually tear it to pieces, and what will you say then about the judgement pronounced by history? By abstaining from political action, have you held back the bourgeoisie? No, you have helped it, because the more despotic the policeman is, the more easily can the *kulak* plunder.

'Whereas in Europe autocracy hindered the bourgeoisie, to our bourgeoisie it is a strong support. . . . That is Europe's misfortune, but it can be our lesson. We must therefore win our political liberty *before* the commercial class becomes so firmly established, that it will no longer need the autocratic Tsar and his emanations. . . . Tear away that once magnificent but now moth-eaten royal robe, and you will find beneath it a flourishing and active bourgeoisie. It has not yet taken independent political shape, because it still hides in the folds of the Tsar's robe, whence it can more comfortably fulfil its historic mission to pillage other people's personal property and work.' [1]

III

Mikhailovsky could not see his country as a passive victim of alleged historical laws, doomed to go through the operation of the familiar Marxian formula, the slow but relentless ruin of the peasant, the increasing misery of the artisan, the predestined sequence of feudal autocracy, bourgeois and proletarian revolutions. But Marx's later observation of events in Russia, led him also to modify the inflexibility of that logic.

It is striking that during the conflict which split the Russian socialists in the eighteen-eighties, Marx showed far more sympathy with the impetuous agrarian Mikhailovsky than with the

[1] *Vyestnik Narodnoy Voli*, No. 2, October 1879.

cautious tactics of his own follower, Plekhanov. Marx and Engels expressed their admiration of the Executive Committee's letter to Alexander III (approved by Mikhailovsky), and said that it showed the revolutionaries to have among them men with a truly 'statesmanlike cast of mind'.

Mikhailovsky, in his review of the Russian edition of *Das Kapital* (*Fatherland Annals*, No. 4, 1872), had stated his appreciation of Marx's analysis of Western capitalism, but noted its limited applicability to contemporary Russia. 'Marx's book appears at a most opportune moment. . . . Although he acts as a revolutionary ferment in the West, he cannot possibly cause disturbance to the social peace of our country. For the ideas and interests against which he fights are still far too weakly developed among us.'

In the correspondence between them which ensued, Marx protested that his sketch of the genesis and growth of capitalism in the West was being *wrongly* turned into a master-key to open every lock, a historico-philosophical theory which could exhaustively explain the present and future of economic change, to which all nations must submit, in whatever historical circumstances they found themselves.

To judge the Russian case on its own merits, Marx overcame his Russophobia to the extent of learning the Russian language well enough to study contemporary documents and books. He reached the following enigmatic conclusion, which he communicated to Mikhailovsky in a letter: 'If Russia continues to follow that course which she has been following since 1861, she will miss the finest opportunity ever given to any nation to avoid the evils inherent in the capitalist order.' [1] Mikhailovsky seized on this last sentence as an important admission by Marx that Russia was not *bound* to fall under the sway of Western capitalist order, but could make her own *salto mortale* into the alluring realm of socialism, and thereby skip the intermediate purgatory. But there was no evidence that Marx had been infected by *narodnik* sentiment or by fresh doubts about 'the idiocy of village life' (as he contemptuously described it). For in his answer to Mikhailovsky's article of

[1] Y. Gardenin, *Pamyati N. K. Mikhailovskavo*, p. 85, Moscow, 1904.

October 1877 (*Fatherland Annals*), he repeated that it was an absurd prejudice to regard the *commune* either as original, commendable, or specifically Slav, and that the breaking up of backward village communities, in every country which retained them, was a *sine qua non* for their subsequent Europeanization.

Yet Marx was evidently anxious not to damp *narodnik* ardour by too many theoretical cold douches, for in the preface to the second Russian edition of the *Communist Manifesto* (1882) he and Engels made this encouraging concession to lovers of the rural *commune*: 'If the Russian revolution becomes a signal for the outbreak of a workers' revolution in the West, so that these two revolutions can fulfil each other, then the present Russian village *commune* might serve as a starting-point for communist development.'

Undoubtedly Marx felt attracted by the boldness of Mikhailovsky and his followers, even when they went against his systematic judgement. He frankly admired their implacable initiative, and called them sound people, 'simple, efficient and heroic'. That did not prevent Engels from expressing a sceptical opinion in a letter to Plekhanov (February 1895), where he wrote: 'It is impossible to argue with that generation of Russians, which always dwells on the natural communist mission that will distinguish *Holy Russia* from other profane people. In a country like theirs, where modern large-scale industry is propped up by archaic peasant *communes*, where all phases of civilization exist simultaneously, shut off from the outside world by a Chinese Wall erected by despotic power, we cannot be surprised if the most bizarre and fantastic ideas are generated and combined. . . . Indeed, a *narodnik*, once he has given up terrorism, is easily transformed into a Tsarist' (*K. Marx & F. Engels, Sochineniya*, vol. 29, p. 385, Leningrad, 1946).

Though Mikhailovsky broadly agreed with Marx's diagnosis of industrial evils, he did not follow Marx in prescribing how to cure them. He deplored that Russia had grown excessively urbanized and grossly commercial, even under autocratic rule.

Therefore he urged the peasant-loving intelligentsia to act before it was too late, to justify their own existence by moulding their hitherto inert compatriots into intelligent, constructive social rebels.

In April 1878 he wrote anonymously in the illegal *Flying Page* some lines which stimulated the terrorist activity of *The People's Will*. They fed the sentiment which had recently been aroused by the acquittal of Vera Zasulich by a liberal-minded jury, after her attempt to murder General Trepov. 'A Constitution, an Assembly of the Land . . .' Mikhailovsky wrote: 'social affairs must now be handed over to agents of society. If this cannot be done through elected representatives, a secret committee of social security must be formed, and then woe to the madman who stands in the path of history. Decisive moments must bring forth decisive people.' [1]

At the same time he wrote openly in *Fatherland Annals*: 'Evil must be fought by cruel or terroristic methods. . . . The enemy must be treated as an enemy, and that permits the use of force and cunning as our weapons. But the responsible individual must never be allowed to hide behind the group, or renounce his own power of decision by blind surrender to authority.' For that would be as bad as surrendering to the Tsar's autocracy, which they were fighting to destroy. In the second number of the *Journal of the People's Will* (October–November 1879) he warned his colleagues against fighting for a constitution, which might strengthen the state in the exploitation of its subjects. If people meekly handed back their hard-won independence to a new bureaucracy trained in bourgeois habits, then the benefits of the new era would quickly fade away.

As for the intelligentsia, unless they were ready to sacrifice personal security and comfort, if need be, their lives, they would cease to make converts. Hard-pressed people would no longer take them seriously and would start to ridicule them. Partly on this account, and to prove the dedicated sincerity of his colleagues, Mikhailovsky favoured acts of terrorism. For a time these made heroes and martyrs, as he foresaw, but they led later to the extermination of *narodnik* extremists by an exasperated and revengeful government.

[1] N. Mikhailovsky, *Polnoe Sobranie*, vol. x, p. 70, St. Petersburg, 1913.

Mikhailovsky seems to have raised no objection to various attempts made on the life of Alexander II, whether it was to blow up the Imperial train, to dynamite the private dining-room of the Winter Palace, or to hurl bombs into the Emperor's carriage. But throughout that time the Executive Committee of *The People's Will* proclaimed that its campaign of terror was merely a drastic method to bring the Tsar to reason, and compel him to call a Constituent Assembly. Their objectives remained astonishingly moderate and mild, even when they sanctioned murder as a means.

When they finally succeeded in killing Alexander II, the open letter of *The People's Will* to his son, Alexander III, carefully explained that all their subversive acts would stop at once, if the Tsar decided to take the necessary steps. *The People's Will* solemnly undertook in all things to submit to the decisions of an elected popular Assembly, to allow no opposition to any course of action which it sanctioned. For themselves they asked nothing more than an amnesty for political crimes, and the election of a representative assembly under conditions which allowed freedom of the press, of public meetings, and electoral publicity. 'Decide, Your Majesty,' they concluded respectfully; 'two courses lie in front of you; the choice between them depends on you alone. . . . We can only ask fate that your reason and conscience will dictate the sole decision consistent with the welfare of Russia, with your own dignity and obligation to your country.' [1]

But Alexander III, like his tutor Pobyedonostsev, regarded elected popular assemblies as heralds of disaster. Without squeamish qualms about inflicting punishment where he thought it was deserved, he wiped out the organization which had plotted his father's death, and hanged its leaders. Though he thereby destroyed the *narodnik* movement as a political weapon, it remained a school of political education for those who had passed through its active phases. In fact the end of the *narodnik* revolutionary organization signified for many people the beginning of new faiths, not always socialist, derived from it. According to their temperaments, ex-*narodniks* became either sobered sceptical

[1] Y. Gardenin, *Pamyati N. K. Mikhailovskavo*, p. 83, Moscow, 1904.

progressives, like Mikhailovsky himself, or full-blown Marxians, like Plekhanov and many others, or repentant conservatives, like Tikhomirov.

v

Mikhailovsky responded to the extinction of the terrorist campaign by starting to support the constitutional reform movement, whose milder methods, rather than objectives, he had formerly opposed. Historians of this period have not always made it clear that Mikhailovsky could agree with Marx's social diagnosis while rejecting his historical conclusions. While he thought that Marx had done great service by revealing the physical and mental impoverishment which capitalist society could inflict on human beings, he believed that similar evils must emerge in *any* nation-state dominated by industrial organization, whether its management was autocratic or constitutional, government-controlled or private. Marx had himself summed up these negative features and their likely consequences, in a letter to his Russian translator, Danielson, on which Mikhailovsky commented.

'If on the European continent,' Marx wrote, 'the influence of capitalist production, which undermines the human race by over-work, specialized division of labour, by submission to all requirements of machinery . . . will continue, as it has done till now, hand in hand with competition *en grand* on the basis of national armies, governmental debts, heavy taxation, skilled professional warfare—then all those things may at last make it essential to renew Europe by means of the *knout*, and by the forced admixture of European blood with Kalmuck, about which the half-Russian but wholly Muscovite Herzen has prophesied so passionately.' [1]

Mikhailovsky commented on Marx's sally that the latter could afford to be ironical, since Western Europe had gone through the worst horrors of that process, while Russia had still the nightmare of national industrialization in front of her. Let her therefore cease to be deceived by the artificial prosperity of Europe, and start steering her own course, instead of following such a bad

[1] *Pisma K. Marksa k Nikolai-onu*, p. 109, St. Petersburg, 1908.

example. That cautious counsel won him adherents at the time, but Marxians dismissed it scornfully as the product of Mikhailovsky's *subjective view of history*, as an unrealistic surrender to 'archaic reactionaries,' or to millions of petty egoists.

Mikhailovsky stuck to his broad prediction that human beings, trained as tools to increase the sum of national wealth, would sooner or later revolt against mechanical slavery. 'Even if the inevitable pattern of the future were proved by irrefutable logic, which is not the case, we are in no way bound to contribute to that pattern,' Mikhailovsky declared. 'Only for those who do not want to think, everything is thought out in advance, chewed, put in the mouth, and all that remains is for them to swallow! For people who will not stir a finger for themselves, everything can be done by historical necessity' (*Russian Wealth*, January 1894).

Towards the end of the eighteen-nineties, however, Mikhailovsky admitted that the *narodniks* had missed their boat, and foresaw that Marxians would fill the mental vacuum and start to dominate the whole political scene. For the most energetic and politically independent young Russian men and women had either been exiled or fled abroad. The social *mystique*, which formerly attracted people to the peasant, was being transferred to the figure of the urban artisan.

While Mikhailovsky rebuked the lyrically nostalgic *narodniks*, who had indulged in what he later called the *dangerous lie* of idealizing the peasantry, he felt disgusted by the new Marxian fashion of contrasting an allegedly 'idiotic' peasantry with clearheaded purposive factory-hands, who were often a philistine rabble. For he hated conceit in *any* class, and identified classconsciousness with ignorant sectional vanity. This ruined strong and honest minds by making them surrender to murky movements, springing from mass fear and envy, and moulded by the degrading herd instinct of collective mimicry.

In his essay *The Hero and the Crowd* (1882) he had recalled how easily medieval crowds were hypnotized by mass hysteria, but expressed the hope that severe lessons taught by modern history might push the nineteenth-century crowd one stage further along the road to self-command. Yet he saw how premature it was to build any substantial future on vague hopes, and calmly predicted that the advance of contemporary Marxism would soon bury him alive, 'together with that cause which I served', and would lower him into the gilded coffin of 'historical significance', at the same time as the 'new thought' began to build an awe-inspiring temple for itself out of the ruins of his former cause.

VI

Peter Lavrov (1823–1900), a modest artillery officer of noble birth, who taught mathematical science in the Artillery Academy of St. Petersburg, later acquired a fabulous though short-lived fame as a guide, philosopher, and friend to revolutionary Russian youth. His grateful disciples said about him that he lit their way along the straight and narrow path, and saved them from falling over numerous theoretical and practical stumbling-blocks. By nature a kindly teacher, bent on a gradual awakening of young minds, a sworn antagonist of the catastrophic firebrand, Bakunin, he remained careful and eclectic to the marrow of his bones, and none the less advocated an outbreak of agrarian revolution when the time was ripe. His claim in later life to be a Marxian was not recognized by Marx, who caustically remarked that Lavrov had read far too many books to be left with a single clear and firm opinion of his own. Turgenev liked him as a person, but called him a pigeon who tried in vain to be a falcon.

Though Lavrov showed more benevolence than common sense, and more learning than lucidity of mind, he acted with consistency of purpose and moral courage. In 1865 he helped to found a sewing co-operative for poor girls in Petersburg, and became a voluntary worker for a society which published cheap editions of serious books for the newly literate reading public. Personally devoted to the exiled Chernyshevsky, he played a prominent part in raising money through *The Literary Fund* to help him and his family, and he stirred up appeals to the Government for Chernyshevsky's harsh sentence of banishment to be revised.

After Karakozov's attempt to murder Alexander II, Lavrov suffered the familiar fate of intellectuals who had dared to criticize the Government. He was arrested and exiled to a remote provincial town (1866). While living there, he wrote under a pseudonym his *Historical Letters* (1868–9) which suddenly became the gospel of Russian youth in the early eighteen-seventies, and fed that mood of disinterested exaltation which sent thousands of urban students to seek arduous work in primitive villages.

The censorship officials dryly summed up the contents of *Historical Letters* in the following terms: 'They allege religion to be the fruit of mass ignorance and a weapon in the hands of the authorities, insinuate that private property is robbery, and laws a dictatorship of the ruling class. They urge that every progressive person must aim at breaking up the Empire into smaller independent territories.' [1]

That young generation which had so recently been carried away by Pisarev's critical realists, nourished (like Turgenev's Bazarov) on biology and physics, scorning all past authorities, was suddenly fired by unfamiliar ideas of continuity and social progress, above all made to feel the burden of its unpaid debt to hungry over-worked peasants. 'The book lay under our pillows, and at night, while we read it, hot tears of enthusiasm would fall. . . . What a storm in our souls, how shameful appeared all our wretched petty bourgeois plans to arrange a happy personal life! To the devil with enlightened self-interest and critical realism—to the devil with frogs and experimental science!' [2]

It is hard to grasp today how such a spate of abstract platitudes as Lavrov's *Letters* could have aroused this outburst of youthful ardour. Perhaps it was due to the sweet taste of the first forbidden fruit, or to a vivifying breeze of novelty stirring a long-stagnant mental atmosphere. In any case hero-worship had become a Russian habit, although no single hero remained securely on his pedestal for long. The Lavrov cult hardly survived the

[1] P. Lavrov, *Klassiki Revolutsionyi Mysli*, vol. I, p. 46, Moscow, 1934.
[2] N. Rusanov, *Sotsialisti Zapada i Rossii*, p. 227, St. Petersburg, 1908.

eighteen-seventies, and he has never been rehabilitated, as his contemporary, Chernyshevsky, has been.

In 1870 Lavrov escaped and fled to France, where he lived through the siege of Paris by the Prussian armies, and afterwards tried to raise foreign support to save the Paris *Commune* from being overthrown. In 1882 he visited London, where he had lengthy talks with Marx, and started his connexion with the Executive Committee of *The People's Will*. This was the time when revolutionaries seriously discussed plans for the advent of new international groupings, no longer territorial, but based on personal occupation and professional concerns, and due to take enduring shape over the decaying corpses of outdated national governments.

In 1873 he launched in Zurich the journal *Vperyod* (*Forward*) which he continued to edit until 1876. He published numerous brochures, and a book about the lessons which reformers ought to learn from the failure of the Paris Commune. His high opinion of subversive thought in nineteenth-century Europe was matched by an impassioned missionary hatred of the governmental powers that be. He deplored the fall of the civilized French Republic in her submission to the cunning demagogue, Napoleon III. He followed throughout the wishful thought that, as society inwardly matures, the state element in it will narrow down to a bare minimum. Yet he feared apathy and stagnation, even more than premature revolt, as the deadliest enemy threatening any buoyant civilization. Only recurrent threats of enemy invasion, or ravages of internal strife, seemed to be capable of saving human society from relapsing into the *semper idem* of a tedious suburban ant-heap.

The Bakunists fought Lavrov as a dangerous 'gradualist' because, although he disliked the state as much as they did, he refused to admit that it could be made to vanish overnight. Patient educational work to raise the intellectual and moral (even more than the material) level of the people, became his preliminary motto.

Student circles, cultivating hearts of gold and wills of steel, brotherly relations, sincerity and truthfulness, must never let

themselves degenerate into cold-blooded political conspirators.
He warned them that the most dangerous enemy of the *new
order* might prove to be the inherited vices and ingrown bad
habits of its embittered founders, who would infect it. 'I therefore permit myself to believe that the success, and above all the
rapid success, of the present social revolutionary movement in
Russia depends to a high degree on the moral quality of individuals who now promote that enterprise, and that the neglect of
those preliminary moral requirements may ruin the whole social
revolutionary cause.' [1] If Lavrov laboured the obvious, it was
because he thought the obvious had been forgotten or cynically
abandoned.

Thus a handful of strong-minded educated people might
manage to dispel the national and materialist obsessions which
darkened modern life. But after waking up the common people,
without corrupting them, they must be prepared to sacrifice
their own advantages and stand aside. Lavrov demanded from
his followers more idealism than common sense, and Marxians
began to sneer at keen young men and women who left luxurious
homes and secure jobs, in order to inhabit dirty huts in remote
Russian villages, where they could work as carpenters, cobblers
or midwives, until they felt worthier of preaching their gospel
of social regeneration. But these patient martyrs, dear to Lavrov's
heart, were mostly arrested by the Government, and they were
succeeded by hardened terrorists, nurtured on hatred and systematic vengeance.

Lavrov, like Chernyshevsky before him, had at first turned
towards America as a land of hope, exemplifying the anarchist's
ideal of a strong society ensured by a weak government, blessed
with a constitution in which fundamental laws were safeguarded
by the Supreme Court against the caprices of any executive
power. During the American Civil War he wholeheartedly
supported the northerners against the Southern owners of negro
slaves. But afterwards he cooled down considerably, and began
to warn prospective émigrés, who had grown tired of Europe,
not to be deluded by a promised land riddled with cant and

[1] *Narodniki Propagandisti 1873*, p. 102, St. Petersburg, 1908.

humbug. A republican state, he urged, could turn out to be as venal, coercive and chauvinist as a monarchical one. In this way he feared that America might become painfully like Russia. While Lavrov admired the safeguards provided by the American federal system, he criticized it for having retained too many vices of the old unitary state. He finally linked the corruption of American politics after the Civil War with the unquestioned supremacy of *nouveau-riche* industrialists, who held nothing more sacred than the almighty dollar.

In 1882 Lavrov was expelled by the French Government and took refuge in England, where he wrote numerous articles and a preface to Stepniak's celebrated book, *Underground Russia*. After his return to Paris in 1885, he contributed to *Le Socialiste*, published in Geneva, and to *The Banner* in New York. But he was nearly an extinct volcano, a lonely and rather pathetic figure, despite his loyal following of uprooted Russian students, to whom he still preached a dedicated preparation for the next revolutionary crisis, in whose spiritual importance blunter minds than his were ceasing to believe.

VII

Lev Tikhomirov (1852–1923), son of a military doctor, editor of the journal published by *The People's Will*, the leading propagandist of that illegal party, member of the Executive Committee which organized the murder of Alexander II, created a widespread sensation when he abandoned his party in 1881, and still more when he published in 1888 his outspoken brochure of recantation *Why I ceased to be a Revolutionary*.

Tortured by sincere remorse, Tikhomirov felt an inward compulsion to lay bare his motives for following a drastic line, which he now wholeheartedly condemned. Experience had gradually convinced him that, after 1881, revolutionary Russia, in the shape of a serious creative force, was fading out, and that the surviving revolutionary personalities, who had grown 'terribly petty', represented 'no longer a storm, but a mere ripple on the surface of a sea which was already calming down'.[1]

Moved by a strange mixture of ambition for notoriety and self-abasement, he distributed his political confession to a number of important people in Russia and abroad, and he wrote a humble letter to the Minister of the Interior, inquiring in what manner he might suitably appeal to the Tsar for permission to return to Russia. 'What I endured as a conspirator,' he admitted, 'my increasing knowledge of what in fact happened in French political life, my theoretical but wider understanding of socialist affairs —all drove me to conclude that our political ideals, whether liberal, radical or socialist, were a tremendous darkening of the mind, a frightful lie, and a stupid one at that.'[2]

From Alexander III he received both a pardon and a full restoration of his civic rights. After his return to Russia he struggled to feel less like a fish out of water, but soon demonstrated how hard it is for a former professional revolutionary to become re-absorbed as a normal citizen. For, instead of renouncing all political entanglements, he turned into a religious zealot, *plus royaliste que le roi*, seeking to allay his pangs of conscience by self-imposed expiatory work. He submitted to every severe fast and observance prescribed by the Orthodox Church, anointed his toothbrush with holy oil, at breakfast would make the sign of the cross over his egg before he started to eat it, and wrote regular articles for the ultra-nationalist *Moscow News*. He nevertheless complained to Pobyedonostsev that for earnest monarchists like him there remained deplorably limited opportunities to write and influence people as fully as he wished. He struggled hard to swim against the rising democratic tide, but his intense over-abstract style could never have made him a persuasive or popular journalist.

Seeking atonement through the Orthodox Church, he commended for himself the classic stages of spiritual progress laid down by the Church Fathers: 'God's slave in submissive fear, God's hired labourer working for a reward, God's son living for

---

[1] *Vospominaniya L. Tikhomirova*, ed. V. Nevsky, p. xi, Moscow-Leningrad, 1927.   [2] op. cit., p. 282.

S

love of the father', but he confessed: "To tell the truth, the thought of God does nothing but make me unhappy, and I am sick of that unhappiness.' He also remarked with rancour in his diary on the gross self-indulgence of the higher clergy, their failure to inspire respect, and could not forgive the Metropolitan for taking refuge under an umbrella, when it rained during a church procession in Moscow.

Compared with 1881, Russia seemed to him thoroughly alive, 'though not according to our taste. I saw everywhere that people were working energetically, and each following his own mind.' But he regretted that the buoyancy and enterprise, which he noticed on his return, depended too exclusively on the robust figure of Alexander III. 'If only the Tsar could have lived for another ten years', he wrote in 1894, 'he would have created a new epoch for Russia. But now there are no talents left, no leaders, not a single person of whom one might say—here is the centre of co-ordination.' He saw Nicholas II in his father's funeral procession; 'a sympathetic and intelligent face, but he looks absolutely crushed. He looks at nothing and nobody, as if nothing existed around him except his father's coffin.' [1]

Tikhomirov hoped that the published lesson of his life might save other impressionable young people from falling into similar traps. He wrote, he said, for the sake of the distant future, when the blood-curdling events in which he had taken part, having lost their bitter controversial actuality, would be soberly understood. 'I want to remember clearly, to tell posterity exactly what happened, to describe, but not to judge.' Sheer boredom and emptiness of mind had driven him and many fellow-students to seek exhilaration in underground conspiracy. 'We then believed', he said, 'that the world develops through revolutions, as in the law that the earth revolves around the sun.'

He reserved his harshest comments for some revolutionary leaders, who least of all deserved the saintly aureole with which youthful hero-worship had crowned them. He called the Pope of Russian Marxians, Plekhanov, dry, self-centred, devoid of generosity, both irritable and spiteful in his behaviour. Though

[1] op. cit., p. 424.

his father was a landowner ruined by drink, he himself had the cautious temperament of a lawyer and the congested mind of a pedant. He complained that Plekhanov lived comfortably with his Jewish mistress at the expense of revolutionary funds, and yet failed to rise above a typically Bohemian milieu of chronic disorder and dirt.

Although he had been a close friend of the regicide Sofia Perovskaya, he later summed her up as an ambitious despotic woman, content to surround herself with mediocre men, who flattered her self-importance. As for the mild mentor Lavrov, he had sought refuge in idealistic formulae when everything around him lay in ruins. A more vital man would at some stage have asked: 'Is my formula true or viable?' But such a question never entered Lavrov's head. Having formulated a theory, he settled down inside it, and might have lived there for a thousand years. Such a man, who never tried to face the changing facts, lived in a spiritual prison of his own making, and the sham vaunted *stability* of his convictions bore no relation to the real stability of an alert receptive instinct. While the impassioned Tkachev could not endure the ruin of his cause, and went out of his mind, while others drank themselves to death, Lavrov's *cause* had no palpable existence, 'for it neither inspired, attracted nor infuriated anybody'.[1]

He spared a few kind words for the charm, beauty and sincerity of the devoted terrorist Vera Figner, but deplored that her attractive temperament was spoiled by the colossal muddle of her politically poisoned mind. He felt suspicious of many Jews who had profitably attached themselves to good positions in the revolutionary movement. 'Jews are partial to socialism,' he observed, 'and at present they are right from their own standpoint, because it is a doctrine through which Jews may make themselves masters of the world.'

Mutual enmity among its members, and a morbid sense of isolation, seemed to him inevitable results of prolonged conspiratorial activity. 'One begins to be frightened of every personal attachment, and little by little one tries to avoid personal

[1] op. cit., p. 308.

relations altogether.' He lamented that he had dragged his wife into a dark hole from which there was no escape, and had brought into the world children whose future was empty and prejudged. His baby boy could hardly lisp, and some busybody would already ask him jokingly: 'Shura, tell me what you are, an anarchist or a social revolutionary?'

Worst of all, a conspirator by conviction could sink so easily to the level of a spy by trade. Both occupations were burdened with such a long chain of crimes committed in the high-sounding name of public service, that any sudden upheaval of conscience was enough to make a man switch over to an equally drastic change in the kind of service which he undertook. Therefore people ought to be less surprised when a revolutionary turned into an agent of the secret police, or an anti-social atheist became a Christian zealot.

Naturally the publication of *Why I ceased to be a Revolutionary* roused a storm of angry vituperation from his former colleagues, and caused both Plekhanov and Lavrov to publish pamphlets denouncing Tikhomirov and deploring his 'pathological' case. Henceforth he lived in daily fear of vengeance from enemies whose wounded vanity would never forgive what he had said about them. Though not a natural coward, Tikhomirov gave the impression of a haunted man who feared at any moment to be struck down by some secret blow.[1] Yet even his enemies admired him for his firm refusal to denounce or betray a single associate.

He had stipulated, before he returned to Russia, that he should never be cross-examined about his revolutionary past. The Government adhered loyally to this undertaking, and Tikhomirov made sure that no one could accuse him of ever having been a *provocateur*, or a callous careerist who sought advancement over the corpses of his former friends. He wrote with sad disgust about the ex-Narodnik Degaev, who confessed to being a traitor, after the police had promised to spare his life *on condition* that he sought out and *murdered* a fellow-revolutionary.

Though Tikhomirov now cherished no higher ambition than to live quietly, earning enough money to give his family the

[1] V. Maevsky, *Revolyutsioner Monarkhist*, p. 47, Noviy Sad, 1934.

modest security which it had hitherto lacked, he was pushed
into playing an important part in state affairs. Ruthless towards
revolutionaries, as only an ex-revolutionary can be, he said about
students who were found carrying sticks of dynamite, 'Such
people must be torn up by the roots.' Experience had made
him such a connoisseur of underground plots, and he had
served the government so loyally since his 'repentance', that
Stolypin employed him in the Ministry for Internal Affairs, and
later recognized his merits by raising him to the high rank of
State Councillor.

His book *Personal Autocracy as the Principle of State Power*
(1897) brought him still closer to official circles, and endeared
him to Pobyedonostsev, to whom he owed his eventual appointment in 1905 as editor of the *Kolokol*, the first journal to impart
an openly militant policy to Orthodox Church affairs.[1] Glad as
he was to extend his sphere of work, the further Tikhomirov
penetrated behind the scenes in administrative circles, the more
he was amazed and horrified by the crass political ignorance and
folly which still prevailed among high officials, by the apathy
which made them deaf to all his warnings, and by the outbursts
of mystical patriotic buffoonery, supported by Nicholas II and
his bigoted wife.

He honestly asserted that he did his utmost to serve Russia
without currying favour with any factions, either among the
deficient powers that be, or among the dark powers that strove
to be, but he favoured a religious autocracy as indispensable for
Russians, and his last book, *Monarchical Government* (1905), must
have made a sharp impression in left-wing circles, where he was
nicknamed the *Karl Marx of monarchy*. For, soon after the
October Revolution, the Bolsheviks banned the book in all
libraries throughout Russia, and nearly every copy of it was
burned or disappeared from view. He himself was allowed to
live on in unmolested silence, though reduced to poverty and
hardship, until he died in 1923.

[1] op. cit., p. 70.

CHAPTER VIII

THREE RELIGIOUS-MINDED INTELLECTUALS

I

THE turn of the century provoked attempts to reconcile the bewildering disappearance of time-honoured landmarks with the immutable demands of a religious conscience. This chapter deals with three men who devoted their lives to that unprofitable pursuit. They cannot be dismissed as isolated intellectual freaks, for they mark the climax of a peculiar double-edged attitude to history, which in a less agitated age may be recognized as a corner-stone of the later Soviet system. They also had a Russian pedigree.

Chernyshevsky, priest's son turned atheist, tried to sanctify his moral and political demands with the same degree of absolute certainty as then belonged to mathematical truths. But Chaadayev, before him, had protested against futile Western efforts to turn history into a branch of natural science. Piecing together an endless mosaic of tiny facts was a labour that led people nowhere, except into a hopeless muddle. Not the past in its entirety (an irretrievable chaos), but only the *picture* of the past, projected by the present, could clarify the sense of vanished epochs and judge their relevance to present needs. Thus every sincere historian, whether consciously or not, selected facts to illustrate the legend nearest to his heart. It was discouraging to find that splendid civilizations, one after another, have crumbled into dust, leaving no legacy of steady sequence or improvement to their successors. Unless the narrative of human history acquired some moral or religious meaning, it turned into a futile farce. That quest for constructive meaning preoccupied the religious-minded intellectuals.

Fyodorov voiced the misgivings of his contemporaries, who found the new scientific idols more sinister than the old gods whom they had superseded. He believed that people born in

V. SOLOVYOV

from a photograph

easier later epochs were often guilty of historical ingratitude. They should thank God for their good luck in inheriting comforts and treasures, which they owed to their ancestors' great fortitude and skill. Yet they frittered away their strength in trivial quarrels, undermining foundations which they had received intact, instead of building on them. For they invoked the laws of change to renounce solidarity with the work of their ancestors, thereby inviting spiritual chaos.

The composer Mussorgsky, despite the profound historical inspiration of his own operas, protested still more emphatically against surrender to dictates of historical fashion, when he said: 'To bring the past into the present, that is my task. . . . But I would like to get away from history, and indeed from all that daily prose, which stifles me. . . . You know my motto—be bold, steer forward to new shores!' He spoke for artists and writers who, like himself, had started by reflecting the angry inconclusive controversies of his age, passed through them, and then found in imaginative work a moral consolation and support which they could no longer extract from their material environment.[1]

II

N. F. Fyodorov (1828–1903), the illegitimate son of Prince P. I. Gagarin and a peasant serf, taught history and geography in primary schools in seven different Russian towns between 1854 and 1868. Then he joined the staff of the Rumyantsev Museum in Moscow, where he remained for twenty-five years a librarian, amazing his more worldly contemporaries by his refusal to accept higher professional promotion, or any rises in his modest salary.

He lived almost like a medieval hermit, gladly shared with needy friends what little money he acquired, and was equally generous in giving away his original ideas. The journalistic intelligentsia, which chased every new and rapidly fading celebrity, hardly knew him, and he never sought their favour. But Tolstoy and Dostoyevsky both held him in high esteem as a

[1] See V. Serov, *The Mighty Five*, New York, 1948.

saintly and brilliant man, who practised the constant mutual aid which he assiduously preached. His principal written work was called *Philosophy of the General Deed*.[1]

His own love for books and learning did not blind him to the fact that the old respect for books as sources of spiritual enlightenment had degenerated into a glib lip-service, which often concealed contempt or hatred for the serious independent printed word. But he found that many modern authors, preoccupied with advertising their own names, and thereby winning fame and money, had only themselves to blame for this cynical reaction. The reading public had become infected by the venal insincerity underlying much of what was written for them to buy.

As a librarian, however, he had to face one pressing problem, how to deal with the cumbersome ballast of too many contemporary books. He lamented that accumulating heaps of them, because they were not sifted by discerning minds, vanished so quickly into the sea of oblivion. He protested against arbitrary snap decisions taken by provincial librarians, who supposed that they could immediately distinguish books of lasting value from worthless or ephemeral ones. He was one of the first librarians to recommend an *international* system of book-lending, and suggested starting one between France and Russia.

He urged that museums, as much as libraries, should be living universities, not tabulated accumulations of ancient and modern junk. A museum should be like a *temple* erected by the sons to preserve sacred legacies handed down to them by their ancestors. A discriminating museum, saving the *best* of the past from callous desecration, restored it to life, resurrected the essence of history from its dead bones. It bridged the gulf separating us from the spirit of our ancestors, who live again in us, and without whom we should not be alive. He recommended establishing the largest number of small local museums with individual character, rather than a few huge oppressive *tombs* of art.

Fyodorov deplored the lack of originality in Russian thought and was indignant that other strains in Europe had capitulated to the inroads of over-rated German philosophers. He called

[1] See *Russkii Arkhiv*, Nos. 2–12, 1904–6.

Kant a pedant, whose chief preoccupation had been to set up obstacles, to tie everybody hand and foot, a free-thinker making himself a gaoler, a fanatic of narrow-mindedness. In Hegel he saw a philosopher-official, born in a Prussian uniform, whose ancestors had been officials, wearing similar uniforms. Only an official from the cradle could have identified the constitutional Prussian state with *God*. His logic, which ended with the absolute idea, instead of with the absolute deed, made no transition from death to life, but provided the last ritual incantation to satisfy a learned caste, condemned to sterile hair-splitting.

To Nietzsche he granted the merit of spontaneous spiritual revolt, in which, however, one evil tried to expel another, for blind undirected will-power took the place of empty thought. His superman, a victim of drunken philosophic ravings, turned out to be a sub-man, worse than any beast, since he sought his perverse happiness in violence, enjoyment of military glory and lust for power.

Fyodorov urged that all the mental efforts of German philosophers had not managed to save modern society from degenerating into a soulless collection of petty specialists, between whom no inner spiritual link or kinship could survive. The degree of absorption in their speciality measured the degree of their alienation from one another. This mutual hostility and envy, which could not be openly displayed without dislocating society, led to cumulative suppressed anger and cold hypocrisy. In exchange for the heavenly paradise of self-denial, so difficult to win, everybody had been shown the wide-open gates of an effortless earthly paradise, sensual, self-loving, cruel, and inwardly hopeless. We are witnessing the death of all philosophy, Fyodorov said, because no single thought unites us, and because thought and deeds perpetually clash.

The sole remedy for a society, seething with barely concealed mutual hatred, must lie in a revival of that sympathetic understanding felt by good sons towards their fathers. Only through prior respect for our fathers, and still more for remoter ancestors, could we recover that warm inward kinship, which makes brotherhood more vital than an empty word. But to secure *effective* brotherly co-operation in the present a human representative is indispensable, standing firmly in the father's place. He must be a wise and responsible paternal ruler, who never surrenders to public pressure or legal compromise, but obeys only God and his own conscience. Such a ruler helps his subjects by trying to make them like himself in doing their duty, but he never strives to level and standardize individuals, or to replace their natural inequality by the loathsome schema of a theoretical *average man.*

Multiplying laws and institutions reflect the deep distrust which members of modern society feel towards one another. They try to distract attention from a bitter civil war of sectional claims, deprived of underlying personal obligation. But in a merely constitutional or republican society, state power must lose all sacred significance for its citizens. For constitutional monarchs, like republican presidents, sink to the level of paid employees, hired for service under a commercial contract. Such societies, wholly ruled by commerce, change into socialist ones, as soon as the greed of a minority has spread to its numerous subordinates, and when the unspoken ideal of labour becomes the minimum of work, providing the maximum of leisure to indulge in unlimited orgies.

Undue reliance on constitutions depraved society by perpetuating mutual suspicion, legalizing strife, and giving less outlet either for the daring of youth or for the tranquil power of maturity. For legislation had no educative value, unless it induced faith in personal duties outside the law.

Fyodorov observed that the triumph of state socialism threatened science and art with a worse fate than when they served the ambition or personal taste of rich merchants and bankers. For under the rule of factory artisans' committees, beautiful things, and whatever study could not be applied to increasing their own physical well-being, would be condemned to extinction. Spontaneous virtues, generosity and self-sacrifice would wither away. The material greed and false equality, preached by socialists, which enabled them to despise the past, and weakened moral obligations to the future, marked a transition from some *attempted* humanity to an equalization of humans with a herd of well-fed cattle or wild beasts.

If it was too late to change insatiably grasping people, events would force them to recognize that a blind unmastered nature remained the enemy of all. '*Our* worst enemy is the desert waste of Central Asia, drying us up with its scorching whirlwinds of dust and sand.' While science, continuing to analyse the world as stubborn facts, hastened the triumph of decay and death, an intelligent scientific revolt, leading men to fight the ravages of hostile nature, might make a move towards co-operative action among civilized men. Only that use of science could lead people out of a stunted, self-centred adolescence towards maturity.

III

Vladimir Solovyov (1853–1900), son of the eminent Russian historian Sergei Solovyov, acquired soon after he had died, some fleeting international fame, for his singular career as a heretical Christian philosopher, prophetic visionary, and almost saintly eccentric. At a time when confused remnants of religious yearnings had not yet been exploited by professional charlatans, and before the wings of soaring philosophy had been neatly clipped into shape by logical positivists, Solovyov's admirers were bold enough to describe him as at once the most typical and most profound of contemporary Russian thinkers.

But even such limited interest in him quickly dwindled, till it is now almost confined to neo-Christian commentators, who have dwelt on his religious features at the expense of sharper qualities and defects, but have tended to ignore his mental scope and insight, wherever these conflict with their own theological concerns. His intellectual severity also prepared the way for more sensational theosophists and fashionable eclectics, who later grouped themselves round Madame Blavatsky, Gurdjieff, and Uspensky.

Solovyov's undoubtedly religious cast of mind grew steadily more polemical, independent, and sardonic with advancing years. The dim scholastic jargon and pedantry, which mar many of his earlier writings, become redeemed in his maturity by touches of imaginative warmth and enigmatic irony. They reveal a judgement more strongly tinged with a prophetic sense of the shape of things to come, like the flair of an explorer who feels the tang of salty air before the unknown sea comes into sight. Although he behaved throughout his life with unworldly indifference to money, professional ambition, and personal popularity, he never shut himself up in a hermit's cell, but responded to deeper undercurrents of his time. Towards the end, fresh conclusions caused him to reject wholeheartedly all the theological objectives which had been sacred to him in his youth.[1]

Already in early childhood, Solovyov's ardent but unstable temperament led him into passionate attachments to such diverse individuals as coachmen, beggars, and young girls. And at the age of nine he started to see erotic visions, which gave him mystic consolation for his unrequited human loves. Although he read voraciously at school, he was not content to be a bookworm, for he also delighted in military parades and boisterous practical jokes.

At the age of fourteen, he suddenly became an atheist, refused to go to church, and embraced the familiar view that materialism would 'transform human beings and start a new chapter in world history'.[2] Within the next four years, however, he had rejected Darwin and the materialists in disgust and swung over to Spinoza, who helped him to discipline his own chaotic mystical experience. This metaphysical search led him to Kant, who cured him of dogmatic conceit, and thence to Schopenhauer, whose Buddhist strain awoke his oriental nostalgia.

During his student years he felt strongly drawn towards various young women, including two of his cousins, but these relationships failed to withstand the strain of his intense analytic approach to them. After 1872 he became convinced that his vocation was incompatible with marriage, and resigned himself to an ascetic bachelorhood. Plunged once more in study, he wrote a thesis for Moscow University, entitled *The Crisis of Western Philosophy* (1874), where he enlarged on the spiritual

[1] See V. S. Solovyov, *Sobranie Sochineniy*, St. Petersburg, 1911–14.
[2] D. K. Mochulsky, *V. Solovyov*, p. 23, Paris, 1951.

bankruptcy disclosed by recent Western thought, though without indicating whether any fruitful alternative could be derived from Russia. Thence he switched over to the history of more ancient civilizations, and became fascinated by the deeper esoteric appeal of some almost forgotten Eastern religious cults. In 1875 he travelled to London, in order to read rare gnostic literature connected with the cult of the mysterious *Sophia*, long worshipped in different shapes as the female emanation of divine wisdom, occasionally materializing in this earthly world. The full rigours of residence in a cheap Bloomsbury lodging-house hardly seem to have damped his ardour, and he made no comment on such humdrum peculiarities of the English scene.

He spent his days studying in the British Museum, and at night sampled some séances arranged by English spiritualistic circles, of whom, however, he quickly tired, pronouncing them to be cunning swindlers, who traded on the foibles of superstitious cranks. But even his quiet existence in the musty reading-room did not pass without excitement. For one day, poring over his volumes there, the divine Sophia appeared before him in a dazzling vision, and he distinctly heard her voice, commanding him to go to Egypt, there to await the next stage of his enlightenment. Far from treating this experience as a hallucination, Solovyov made no attempt to analyse its origin, but acted on it promptly. He packed his modest bags and booked a passage to Cairo, convinced that he would be vouchsafed a further revelation of divine wisdom somewhere on the banks of the Nile.

He spent four months in Egypt, on the pretext of learning Arabic, and claimed to have seen another vision in which his *eternal friend*, Sophia, appeared in a radiant flash surrounded by a sky-blue haze, and communicated to him a conviction of spiritual unity in the world. His sojourn also brought him more tangible adventures. When he retired to the neighbouring desert to meditate, wearing a top-hat and a black European overcoat, he was attacked by Bedouin Arabs, who had never seen such a costume in their lives. He cut such a sinister figure, with his pale face and cavernous eyes, framed in a mass of curly black hair, that they mistook him for an evil spirit. But they only robbed him of his watch and left him to spend the night in the sand. He was later joined in Egypt by his philosophic friend, Prince D. Tsertelev, a fellow-admirer of Schopenhauer, and a writer of graceful verses about the extinction of the universe.

On his return to Russia in 1874, he started to lecture on philosophy at Moscow University. He made friends with Dostoyevsky, whom he accompanied on a visit to the famous Optina monastery. Dostoyevsky, who was working on *The Brothers Karamazov*, took a fancy to the handsome and eloquent young philosopher, and is said to have drawn on him for the character of his gentle neophyte Alyosha, but also probably for some sardonic twists in Ivan Karamazov's dialectic. On the accession of Alexander III in 1881, Solovyov pleaded firmly in a lecture at Petersburg University that the Emperor's first duty was to pardon his father's murderers, win the hearts of his subjects by setting an unprecedented example of Christian conduct, and thereby establish his moral authority on an unshakeable foundation. For this pronouncement he was cheered by an enthusiastic audience, but the university authorities sent him a formal reprimand and an order to stop lecturing until further notice.

In November of the same year he resigned from his university post. Although the Rector assured him that he was not expected to resign, Solovyov persisted. He thus became a writer relying on his own resources, without any institutional axe to grind, earning eventually through his sharp and outspoken utterances the nickname *enfant terrible* of the Russian intelligentsia.

IV

With a mounting contempt for bourgeois comforts and security, he lived thenceforth the homeless life of a wandering monk without a monastery. His simple room in the Hôtel d'Angleterre in Petersburg was constantly beseiged by a motley crowd of visitors, students, struggling writers with petitions, and religious eccentrics. The moment he had money, he would give it away to the first plausible petitioner. He presented his winter overcoats to any poor visitor without one, and he habitually overtipped the coachmen.

Like a growing number of his compatriots, Solovyov felt dismayed by the spiritual vacuum of current Western philosophy and organized religion. Having sunk into a numb paralysis or irritable anaemia, they no longer inspired their own people, or gave guiding stimulus to primitive outsiders, who formerly admired and looked up to the West. He deplored the indiscriminate stress laid by scientific positivists on a formula loosely called 'survival of the fittest', which seemed to him a cult of savage and vulgar two-legged brutes, deprived of moral judgement, discipline, or imaginative power.

Solovyov dismissed with curt contempt the loud claims of some so-called socialists that they had picked up the fallen banner, and would at last put Christian teaching into administrative practice. He observed that, whereas Christ had appealed to the conscience of good people to help the poor, socialists cunningly tried to make robbery respectable and thereby corrupt the poor, by inciting them to plunder more substantial, if not more deserving, people. Nor could he see any benefit in the new breed of theoretical Nihilists, who raged against the plain necessity of modern banks, trade, monetary capital, and private property.

In any case, he urged, these social institutions acquired importance only when they served as a foundation for building some higher superstructure. Even the formal political unification of all separate countries now professing Christendom (whose practicability he then believed in) would remain an empty and useless shell, unless a heartfelt unification of the perpetually squabbling Christian Churches had preceded it. He therefore began to rack his brains for any conceivable method whereby self-centred sovereign nation-states might be combined, raised to the level of a workable theocracy, and thence start to bridge the ominous gulf which now divided criminal national politics from any honest personal morality. His *La Russie et l'Eglise Universelle* (1889) envisaged a complicated but mutual plan of action worked out between the Pope and the Russian Emperor to organize a new type of Holy Roman Empire, designed to stop the ravages of contemporary international cannibalism. In this curious compact, the Russian ruler would give his full material support to the moral authority of the Roman high priest, and the Orthodox Church would obediently acknowledge the Roman See as its superior.

Like Chaadayev in the reign of Nicholas I, Solovyov deplored the boastful claims advanced by a fabulous 'Holy Russia', that it incorporated an exemplary theocratic state. He admitted that the practical and social-minded Roman Church, despite its worldly defects, had till now done infinitely more than the Orthodox state-church to promote 'the kingdom of God on earth'. He knew that incurable Russian national *mystique* was still leading her towards disaster, and clearly foresaw his country's humiliating defeat by Japan, when he wrote in 1894:

> 'Russia, forget your former glory,
> The double-headed eagle has been crushed,
> And your torn banners handed over
> As playthings to the yellow children . . .
> He who neglects the law of love,
> Must be abased in fear and trembling.
> The Third Rome lies in ashes,
> And a fourth there will never be.'

His essay *Byzantinism and Russia* (1896) explained how the Orthodox Church, poisoned by its inheritance of Byzantine politics ('the East of Xerxes, not the East of Christ'), had lost the last vestige of a right to guide other Christian Churches. Real religion had been killed in Russia, slowly strangled in the red tape of a government department, and thereby ceasing to act as a free creative art. Though Orthodox ritual retained relics of its former purity and beauty, servile state service, hand in hand with compulsory hypocrisy, had long since smothered the soul of the Orthodox Church, and debauched its priests. 'To fear Catholic propaganda means no longer to believe in the inner force of our own Church. But if we have truly ceased to believe in it, why should we continue to defend our Church at all?' he boldly wrote in 1884. In 1896 Solovyov took communion in a Uniate (Graeco-Catholic) Church, though without breaking off his diplomatic relations with Orthodoxy. A bitter but somewhat absurd controversy ensued, as to whether or not he had become a full Catholic convert, and hence a renegade to his native faith.[1]

The answer should be simpler, for he had by then abandoned belief in any and every ecclesiastical authority, and frankly described himself as a religious free-thinker. 'I am as far removed from the cramping narrowness of Rome, as from that of Byzantium, Augsburg or Geneva,'[2] he wrote to V. Rozanov in 1892; and he began to shun all churches as obstacles, which now did more to confuse human beings than to promote in them a fruitful religious state of mind.

When he finally awoke to the practical futility of grandiose theocratic plans to fuse established churches with existing nation-states, the modern survival of the old historic Christian drama, together with the institutions which revolved around it, sank into an irrelevant puppet-show for him. He reached a similar conclusion about the blighting effect of state administration, in bureaucratic national forms. 'We must resolutely separate,' he said, 'the national character of a people from the nationalist policy of its government, by distinguishing the fruits of each. We see the fruits of English national character in Shakespeare, Byron, Berkeley and Newton, of English nationalist policy in world-wide plunder, of German national character in Lessing, Kant and Schelling, of German nationalism in the subjugation of its neighbours by military violence and fraud.' But every national self-idolization would sooner or later find its bitter end in self-destruction. The legend of *Narcissus* ought to edify not only individuals, but whole nations.

About his own country's aspirations he preserved enough detachment to observe: 'Our non-European and anti-European cravings, our artificial *originality*, always were, and still are, nothing but the emptiest pretensions. To break away from them

---

[1] K. Mochulsky, *V. Solovyov*, pp. 217–20, Paris, 1951.
[2] ibid., p. 211.

T

is the first condition of our progress. Better to renounce patriotism than destroy conscience' (*The National Question in Russia*, 1891).

He began to regret that he had wasted so much time and energy in advocating what he now saw to be such sheer delusions as the re-unification of Christian Churches, the reconciliation of Jews with Christians, the elevation of overgrown nation-states to a harmonious theocratic level. No honest person could now believe in such colossal naïvetés, or try to bring them into being. Priests and theologians between them had managed to make organized Christianity either a repulsive fraud, or such a dreary and petty business that it bored men to extinction. He thought it right to warn people that the waning churches would nevertheless make a final bid to recover their authority, and reconquer many human beings who inwardly rebelled against them.

Therefore the latest course of Christian politics, instead of moving gradually, though with strenuous effort, towards a moral goal (as he had formerly believed) began to assume a sinister and catastrophic character. The universal Church, due to embrace mankind from China to Peru (if it ever materialized), would now emerge on earth, not as a blessing, but as a frightful curse. For every *official* union entered into between the Churches of the world, as arranged by their leading representatives, would seek to perpetuate their rule, and at least ninety per cent of the corrupt modern monks and clergy would be readily persuaded to go over to the side of *Anti-Christ*. Only a small, persecuted minority would remain 'unshaken, unseduced, unterrified', and continue to wage its unequal struggle against the passions of the human crowd, on the verge of being totally hypnotized by the prevailing powers of darkness.

Instead of seeing the future, as he used to do, through a rosy optimistic haze of hard-won moral triumph, Solovyov began to reckon with the overwhelming power of evil, no longer as a blank negative obstacle, but as a dynamic undermining force. His *Story of Anti-Christ* (1900) provides at once an admirable confession of his tremendous mental errors, and a parody full of ironic eloquence, revealing the fulfilment of his much-discussed theocratic state, as nothing better than the concealed devilish empire of Anti-Christ, successfully established on this earth.

The story starts after a series of future international and civil wars, when the mangled Western nations, freed at last from the new *Mongol yoke*, had managed to create an effective United States of Europe. An active and persuasive busybody, who called himself 'the coming man', then managed to advertise his merits so persistently that the weary people elected him President of these United States. After a single year of skilful rule, he established a world-wide monarchy in his name, and became universally acclaimed as 'the great peacemaker'. He next triumphantly solved the main social and economic problems of the day, and managed to provide all his subjects with more than enough to eat and drink, without making them unduly discontented.

Having thus settled strident material concerns, he summoned a conference of Christian Churches to Jerusalem, already the capital of an autonomous state, inhabited and ruled by Jews. He built a huge Imperial temple there, dedicated to the approaching unity of all religious cults. The Emperor was a handsome, eloquent, and charming person, and nobody knew that he had secretly sold his soul to the devil, for he went out of his way to please everybody.

He restored the Pope to his throne in Rome, gave orders for a world museum of Christian archaeology to be founded in Constantinople, and attracted Protestants by endowing a world institute for the examination of all scriptural texts. At last in a tensely dramatic speech, he asked that all should recognize his absolute authority in reward for the immense service which he had rendered, alike to Protestant, Catholic, and Orthodox Churches. The majority of Church delegates were persuaded by his winning words, and took their places by his side. The few leaders, who still dared oppose him, were struck down by artificial thunderbolts, released by the evil Cardinal-magician, who was afterwards elected Pope. The remnants of faithful opposition then retired to fast and pray in the desert, where they were joined by Pope Peter and the Elder John, who had meanwhile risen from the dead. Thus the true Churches and their scanty followers finally achieved reunion, not triumphantly and formally in the Imperial temple, but secretly in the desert, shortly before the second coming of Christ.

During the troubled reign of the Anti-Christ Emperor, new unheard-of forms of demonology and mystic lust began to spread among his subjects. When the Jews rebelled against him, he sentenced to death all insubordinate ones, whereupon a civil war ensued between the Emperor and his subject-peoples. His short reign was ended by the end of the world.

Solovyov's *Story of Anti-Christ* was preceded by his *Three Conversations*, written in the same year, and designed to clarify the modern struggle against *evil*, from four distinct standpoints. It takes the form of a Platonic dialogue between a patriotic general, a cynical politician, a naïvely idealistic prince (like Tolstoy) and a Mr. Z (not unlike Solovyov himself). The speeches of the general reveal a traditionally religious man, who nevertheless found the most complete moral satisfaction he had ever known in committing murder, '. . . and not an ordinary little murder, for in the course of one hour I killed over a thousand men'. He still remembered this act of his, not only without remorse, but as 'something great, holy and honourable'. The men he had mown down with his artillery were Bashi-Bazouks who had razed an Armenian village to the ground, tortured and massacred its inhabitants, and roasted babies before their mothers' eyes.

The politician, a mild and moderate liberal, would prefer to overcome evil by ignoring its existence. He talks about peaceful progress and the spread of civilized polite behaviour, assuming that for states, long since consolidated by war, militant expansion had conveniently become obsolete. Mr. Z, whose views have more substantial reference to the future, shows sympathy for the general, but spurns both the liberal politician and the pacifist prince. He is severe in facing facts, calls it sheer idiocy to forgive every wrong and to repay evil deeds by goodness (which a wicked recipient would certainly despise). He told a cautionary tale to warn against sentimental evangelists, and to illustrate how scoundrels are infuriated and made still more vindictive, when they are met by feeble and calculated acts of kindness.

Solovyov had previously ridiculed the ascetic self-denial of the most advertised Tolstoyans (who carried Tolstoy's teaching to absurd extremes) when he wrote during the 1891 famine: 'Our hungry people reached a degree of *simplification* which embarrassed even our best-fed *simplifiers*. While they still pronounce a poverty-stricken life to be a good one, they stop short of accepting the normality of death by slow starvation . . .' (*The People's Misery and Social Help*, 1891).

Mr. Z concluded that people were still free to choose between violent or peaceful methods in resisting the insidious growth of evil throughout the world, but their final choice might depend on a picture of evil's short-lived triumph and ultimate self-destruction. He provides that in the vivid *Story of Anti-Christ*, an imaginary forecast of probabilities drawn from present facts.

Solovyov can hardly be blamed for seeking new threads of sense and sequence amid the chaos of contemporary history. And what he said about the approaching end of the world need not be termed apocalyptic, where it signified the *real end* of European history in its consecutive stages, ancient, medieval and modern. For he believed that the former main road of individual growth and aspiration had been abandoned by Western nation-states. He saw their regimented citizens left to the mercy of commerce and spasmodic emotional waves, unsteadily controlled by bogus progressives or blind conservatives. Instead of the former developing drama of lively creative personalities, a set of political *marionettes* had appeared upon the scene, imitating traditional movements of the past, playing with scientific technique and atavistic passions, but principally manœuvring to expand their own prestige and power at the expense of those they ruled by force and fraud.

Solovyov said that he felt the wings of a dark shadow hovering over the twentieth century, which would usher in an era of convulsive wars and widespread revolutions. God would surely punish all conceited Western nations, including Russia, when their collective crimes and follies reached a climax, and he fore-saw (not without relish) the ominous shape which that punishment might take. While the nations of the West continued to squabble and disintegrate through laziness and greed, Japan and China would learn their lessons and unite against the West. The tables would thus be turned on Europe and America.

'When China, waking up like Japan, begins with the aid of machines to make European goods, when its hitherto inert masses respond to the challenge of Western countries, and intensify the terrifying economic competition from which exhausted Europe is already suffering—in a word, when the artisans of the West see their factories closed down, their work coming to an end, what will happen next?' (*Europe and her Rivals*, 1896). The easy-going Western workmen could no longer organize strikes for higher wages and shorter hours of work, when their tougher and more industrious Eastern competitors had taken their raw materials and captured all their markets.

Not only the Far Eastern races, but the Arabs of Africa and Asia would revolt against economic infiltration from the West (even though it helped them), until Western countries found themselves involved in a bloody struggle against nationalist Islam. Finally, the yellow races, now equal to the West in scientific skill and economic strength, and overwhelming in sheer numbers, would seize their opportunity to start a new pan-Mongolian conquest and overrun the whole of Europe.

To start with, the cleverly imitative Japanese would draw together the hitherto disunited brown and yellow peoples of Eastern Asia, arouse their latent hatred and envy of alien white intruders, i.e. European and American traders, administrators, and missionaries. The political fusion of these races would follow in the wake of their *emotional* unification against Western inter-lopers. Then an amalgamated Japanese-Chinese Empire would mobilize a well-equipped army of four million men in Chinese Turkestan, whence it would invade Russian Central Asia, and advancing through Russia, penetrate to the heart of Europe. Finally in Paris, organizations of workmen, now proud to be 'without a country', would rebel against their government, and the capital of Western culture would joyfully open its gates to conquerors from the Far East.

The new Mongolian yoke, imposed upon humiliated Western countries, would last for half a century at least. At first the influx of hungry Asiatic artisans to work abroad would provoke dismay among their ruined and unemployed Western competitors, but gradually it would lead to organized resistance, and to the creation of secret international societies, designed to obstruct and expel the yellow races.

Only through a desperate struggle to escape from this cruel purgatory of servitude to revengeful Asiatics, would Western nations learn to overcome their national arrogance and cut-throat economic rivalry, and thereby achieve at last a super-national organization.

In his last talk with Prince S. N. Trubetskoy, a few days before his death, Solovyov reverted to his belief that the main line of European history had ended. 'Loaded with a lot of clumsy moral baggage, the Western peoples now start to wage their war against China . . . yet they have no genuine spark of Christianity left inside them, no higher ideals than in the age of the Trojan Wars—but then at least bold young warriors went forth, while now shrunken old men go into battle.' [1]

But while he painted in sombre colours this catastrophic retribution, he observed that there might be worthier nations, and individuals, who could escape from it. And though he repeated that the current clap-trap about expanding material progress for everybody was banal and physically impossible, he remained far from attracted by the rival appeal of a new dark age, in which 'vigorous young barbarians' would conquer and supplant the relatively civilized white races. He doubted whether that vaunted virgin strength existed anywhere, except in Rousseauesque imaginations. The yellow races were not younger, but far older than the white ones, and what about 'the cannibal islanders who ate the explorer Cook'? [2] Or could we soberly believe that black

[1] *Vyestnik Evropy*, vol. 5, p. 412, St. Petersburg, 1900.
[2] *Sobranie Sochineniy*, vol. 10, p. 225, St. Petersburg, 1911-14.

Africans had been designed to revitalize a decrepit Western world?

Solovyov clung to a tangible spiritual legacy of Europe, as the sole force still capable of raising human beings (whether of European ancestry or not) to a higher level, even though it might rely on nothing more spectacular than the helpful efforts of good and gifted people.

In *The Secret of Progress* (1897),[1] he introduced a fairy tale, to illustrate the only kind of progress which he believed to be worth having. A hunter had lost his way in a dark forest. He sank down exhausted on a stone, facing a broad and turbulent river. Gazing into the dark depths, he listened with a heavy heart to a woodpecker tapping on a tree trunk. Then somebody touched him on the shoulder. He saw before him a bent old woman, thin and wan like a withered pod. Her eyes were stern, and tufts of grey hair grew in her cleft chin. Her clothes, which had been made of rich and sumptuous material, now hung on her like rags.

'Listen, my brave lad,' she said. 'There is a place on the other side of the river—a real paradise. Once you reach it, you will forget your troubles. You will never find your way alone, so I will guide you there; it used to be my home. But carry me over to the other side, for I can hardly stand. Though I have got one foot in the grave, how little I want to die.'

The hunter was a good-hearted fellow. Although he did not believe a word of the old woman's talk, and was not tempted by the prospect of carrying her, and wading across the swollen river, he looked at her as she coughed and quivered. 'She must be at least a century old, and have borne a lot of burdens in her time. I must try to help her.'

'Well, grandmother,' he said, 'climb on my back and pull your legs in.' When the old woman clambered on to his shoulders, he felt a leaden weight, as if a coffin with a corpse had fallen on top of him. He could barely walk. 'Well,' he thought, 'it would be a shame to go back on my word.' The moment he stepped into the water, he felt relief, and with every step he

---

[1] *Sobranie Sochineniy*, vol. 9, pp. 84–6.

took the weight grew lighter. He went straight on, without looking back. But when he reached the other side, he turned around. Oh wonder! Instead of the old woman, he now saw clinging to him an indescribable beauty, a fairy-tale princess. She took him to her home, and he never again complained of loneliness.

In order to make doubly sure, Solovyov pointed the moral of this story. Contemporary man, in his hunt for fleeting pleasures, had strayed from the straight and narrow path. Before him flows the dark and stormy current of life, which he must cross, while time, like the woodpecker in the story, mercilessly counts the opportunities which he has missed. Behind him stands the sacred legacy of the past. He must carry this precious burden across the present flood of history; let him see that there is no other way to end his wanderings.

Modern man may no longer believe in fairy tales. But what right had he to inherit the work of ages, when he did nothing to earn these rich rewards by his own efforts? Even if he saw no profit for himself, could he not carry the burden of ancient sanctity out of reverence for her age, pity for her decline, shame for his cold ingratitude? Only if he saved her, could he save himself. That was the secret of further progress, and there could be no other.

V

The paradoxical V. V. Rozanov (1857–1918) appeared to his many contemporary detractors as a reactionary and incoherent babbler of startling verbal riddles or mystic obscenities. But his scanty admirers revered him as a pillar of Orthodox society, a subtle intellectual supporter of a religious conservative culture, of personal integrity and the intimate sanctity of Russian family life. A few later critics, like D. S. Mirsky (who over-praised him) and S. Kotelyansky (who translated his *Fallen Leaves* and *Solitaria*), recognized his mastery of impressionistic language, but on the whole posterity has ignored him. He none the less provides an instructive and *outré* example of ingrained emotional duplicity, leading towards that fluid shiftiness which characterized the dis-integration of Russian thought at the end of the nineteenth century.

Rozanov rendered his most powerful impressions in vivid, precise, but fragmentary and organically unrelated outbursts. Based on isolated emotional facts, he stated them like atomic propositions in the manner later given philosophic sanction by the logician Wittgenstein.[1] Especially when they are bold and clear, these statements clash with one another in a picturesque duality. His scattered thoughts are no less genuine through being contradictory, and they emerge naturally in the form of aphorisms, spontaneous entries in a diary, which makes a private running commentary on burning topics of the day, the rapid decline of culture, the possible preserving value of a modern monarchy, the essence of marriage and family life, notably the mysterious links between the sexual instinct and inward religious faith. 'Such men as Buckle or Spencer, Pisarev or Belinsky, who have said no more words about sex than about the Argentine, are at the same time astonishingly atheistic' (1910). He liked the sexual piety of Judaism, but hated the modern commercial Jew; admired the beauty of ancient religious ritual, but found Christians drab and dreary.

Thus in the same breath he would curse and bless the Jews, appeal to Christ and denounce the blighting effect of Christianity on the joys of earthly life. 'The Church is the only poetic and profound thing left on earth—how mad I was that for eleven years I made every possible effort to destroy it' (1911). His abrupt style and unfamiliar verbal combinations were not cold-bloodedly designed to *épater*, but sincerely to reveal his private thoughts, and to escape from the treacherous clichés of a faded, stale, and bookish jargon. 'I write for a few friends—perhaps for nobody.'

After graduating from Moscow University in 1881, Rozanov spent ten years as a secondary school teacher in the Russian provinces. In 1880 he had married Apollinaria Suslova, the 'emancipated woman' with whom Dostoyevsky travelled to

[1] L. Wittgenstein, *Tractatus Logico-Philosophicus*, with introduction by Bertrand Russell, London, 1922.

Germany in 1865. The marriage was a miserable failure, but his wife refused to grant him a divorce. In 1889 he married again, unofficially but happily, and in 1899, after a brief spell in the civil service, he became a regular contributor to the daily *New Times*, until that conservative journal was suppressed by the Bolsheviks in 1918. He never cared for journalism except as a means of livelihood, less painful to him than schoolmastering, and he republished his better articles in books. 'Newspapers will pass away', he wrote hopefully, 'like the eternal wars of the middle ages. . . . People will begin to regard the reading of newspapers as simply indecent, cowardly' (1910).

Without being a devotee of Dostoyevsky, he felt a more basic spiritual kinship with him than with Tolstoy, and although he never shared Dostoyevsky's haunting sense of guilt, he felt the same simultaneous attraction towards contradictory poles of feeling. He called Dostoyevsky a man devoid of faith, who thirsted for it all the more, and wrote a much-discussed commentary on his *Legend of the Grand Inquisitor* (1889). He produced several original, but diffusely written volumes of sociological essays, including *The Twilight of Enlightenment* (1899), *The Family Problem in Russia* (1903), *The Russian Church* (1906). In 1911 he brought out a penetrating study of Christianity in its more destructive aspects, entitled *The Dark Image*, followed by a sequel, *People of Moonlight*, dealing with male and female homosexuality —a subject hitherto rarely discussed in Russia. He maintained that the artificial mortification of the human senses and stunted emotional life, achieved by puritan moralists, had in fact encouraged sterile homosexual love, perversity and lust. Since the pain of the world was conquering its joy, religion preyed on people's minds, but for the same reason they had started to revolt against gross deceptions practised on them by the Christian Churches. His most mature aphoristic mode of writing emerged finally in *Solitaria* (1912) and *Fallen Leaves* (1913–16).

Rozanov admitted frankly that he had been a most unsatisfactory school-teacher, because he could never follow any organized system. 'A single sympathetic face', he wrote later, 'could drag me into the revolution as it could into the Church, and strictly speaking I always went to people, and after people, but never towards a system' (*Solitaria*, 1912). Because he could not bear the ugliness of the critic Vengerov, who was 'fat and black, like a big-bellied beetle', he wrote against him, although he bore no grudge against his work. The routine drill and discipline, inherent in normal school-teaching, outraged his spontaneity. Hating to be bound to any consistent course of action, he preserved a stubborn will to dream. And it upset him that while he dreamed about a satisfying new philosophy, in which the potential world became more important than the actual one, he had to take the class-register, listen to what his pupils answered about kings, tsars, popes, generals, dates of battles and peace treaties, 'while the director is watching from the door to see how I conduct my lesson' (1912).

Rozanov concluded that the kind of knowledge imparted by Russian schools was mostly irrelevant and useless, that the net result of ramming the Bible and New Testament precepts down children's throats was to turn them into lifelong atheists, and that the enforced study of textbooks, crammed with patriotic history, made its victims begin to despise their country's past, and later to hate its present, until they yearned to throw in their lot with 'the party of action', i.e. the revolutionaries.

In short, the Russian school-system, apart from the 'three R's', had been ruined by the grand illusion of moulding artificial citizens to serve a mighty state. While failing to create those model citizens, it successfully corrupted its pupils' minds and stupefied their feelings. Rozanov held the schools responsible for the growing mass of patient, long-suffering imbeciles, and for 'those bloodless shadows who now frighten us'.

The Russian universities, in Rozanov's view, went one stage further along the downward path. Despite their inflated intellectual pretensions, they had turned into stereotyped diploma factories for state service. Their standard was set by the obtuse civil servants who watched over them, while the mental apathy of herded students was promoted and matched by the smug pedantry of their professors, who secretly believed in nothing. 'It is certainly not the universities that have educated the genuine

Russians', he observed, 'but the good old illiterate nurses' (1912). Thinking as he did, in terms of humanistic rather than of technical education, he urged that careful private reading and reflection on every page of Tolstoy and Dostoyevsky would do infinitely more to develop young people's minds than any amount of school instruction. For this whole educational *impasse* Rozanov blamed state interference, for having clumsily overstepped its proper limits as a regulator, and substituted the observance of endless official rules for the proper exercise of judgement and initiative.

What struck Rozanov most about the boys who faced him from the school bench was a strange emotional blankness, which could not be explained by physical deformity or malnutrition. Though they were healthy animals, they seemed to lack the inmost core, out of which every talent and impulse had to grow, the fire of spiritual energy or mental perseverance. A blank cynical indifference to culture seemed to have captured the younger generation at the end of a century which had been richly creative in several arts as well as in the technical sciences. Was it a natural reaction against a generation of titans that it should be followed by a crowd of stunted dwarfs, too shrunken and animal to be capable of worshipping anything higher than their own petty physical comfort? That modern tragedy could not even be exhilarating, since it lay in an exclusion of any tragic possibility, of voluntary sacrifice or hardship (cf. *The Twilight of Englightenment*, 1899, *passim*).

In his brochure *The Weakened Fetish* (1910) and still more vigorously in his *About the Supposed Sense of our Monarchy* (1912), Rozanov dashed the hopes of those compatriots who urged that the spark smouldering in Russian souls could be revived by a revitalized autocracy. He explained that autocracy, which depends for any success on strength of character, had now become fatally identified with the administrative machine. The formula *l'état c'est moi*, intended to incorporate the full bloom of absolute monarchy, had proved to be its most drastic limitation and the beginning of its downfall. Former kings could be judged as individuals, to the extent that they either fulfilled or abused a sacred trust, but the monarch who became obliterated in the all-devouring state-machine destroyed his personal *raison d'être*. He could be held responsible for a horde of parasitic civil servants, whose activities he was powerless to control. In the end he would become as fiercely hated as the government departments which multiplied and flourished in his name, while whole countries, whose blood they quietly sucked, fell into frustration and decline.

'In a never-ending flood, through summer heat and winter frost, those papers pour and flow . . . formally polite, in rather heavy sentences, yet intelligible to those who make an effort, they circulate throughout the boundless Empire. They flow along, by no means stormily, but relentlessly like the passage of time itself, equally devoid of passion, fear, sympathy, or joy. . . . Russia laments the death of a tsar, and one passage in a circular shows a rouble as worth only sixty copecks—will anyone be reproved? Next, it seems, not only has another reign begun, but the age has been transformed, the monarchy has fallen and been replaced by a republic. . . . Yet the writing on those papers does not even quiver, the dim language grows no clearer, not a single document either slows down or passes more quickly through the vast machine' (*About the Supposed Sense of our Monarchy*, 1912).

Though Rozanov preferred monarchy as a lesser evil, he believed that under any other form of government, the Russian multi-national state, in order to preserve its precarious unity, would still need a bureaucratic clergy and a vast army, supported by a police force, for whose constant maintenance alone the people would continue to be squeezed and crushed. Hence the government could never hold the loyalty of its subjects unless it kept them at a safe distance from the state apparatus, and carefully disguised or concealed the unsavoury truth about it.

He thought that the gap in civilization between Russia and the West had diminished, to the advantage of the former. Even if official Russia had not risen much, Western Europe had fallen lower rapidly. After the horrors committed during the Franco-Prussian War of 1870, Germans no longer shouted so loudly about the Russian monopoly of barbarism and brutality. After the filth which rose to the surface of French government circles during the *Dreyfus* case, the French could no longer talk so glibly about the proverbial corruption of Russian government officials.

If Rozanov believed in any definite step forward, it was simply in the hope of rising slightly after having fallen to the lowest depths. He did not talk naïvely about a renewed flowering of Russian art and culture, because he knew that it could be healthy in its moral stimulus only if state policy did not pervert it. The European phase of Russian culture, which Peter the Great had set in motion, was visibly declining. The vitality and splendour of that two-hundred-years' carnival had petered out, and little remained of it except smouldering torches and ancient tattered masks, which had no charm for sober contemporary people. 'It is in this state of mind, full of repulsion for the period just completed, that our society now stands, evidently on the frontier between two eras of our history, of which one is already ending and the other has not yet begun' (1912).

Meanwhile, after creating so abundantly, modern Europeans had forgotten the value of their work, abandoned what they had striven for, and started to destroy it. Ought Russians to follow the example set by these blinded madmen, help them to burn down their beautiful old homes, and dance triumphantly over the ashes of their former glory? No, Rozanov answered: 'a slave would act thus, but not a friend'. Russians had shown their respect for the old Europe by bringing her priceless treasures to themselves, to enlighten and develop them, in order to become a worthier successor. They could do better than infect themselves with modern European greed and national corruption.

But even though they decisively turned away from what Europe was now doing, they should try to soften the suicidal blows which she was inflicting on herself. The ultimate Russian future lay in a new synthesis of Eastern culture, in which her hitherto mute Asiatic citizens, as well as the monks of Mount Athos and persecuted Old Believers, would play a more decisive part than all her philistines and self-satisfied radicals, recently educated in Paris or Berlin.

Russia had temporarily condemned herself to live under

a mental dictatorship of European 'progressives', Rozanov
lamented: 'and yet this generation has no intrinsic importance
whatsoever. . . . What do we really know today about the people
of the eighteen-twenties? Only what Pushkin told us. . . . Hence
the conclusion—better to live and work as if nobody else existed,
as if you had no contemporaries at all. . . . Perhaps I understand
nothing, but when I meet a man with a progressive public interest,
it is not that I am bored, not that I bear ill-will towards him, but
in his company I feel that I am dying' (1911).

Rozanov thought that Russians had altogether failed to grasp
the warning sense of Gogol's brilliant pictures of moral morons
and monstrosities. Already one hundred years ago Gogol had
pointed to 'dead souls', not in the limbo where they ought to be,
but dominating Russian life. Brushing aside his terrifying types
as either caricatures or extinct monsters, his readers started off
their compensatory pursuit of abstract humanitarianism and their
craze for physical science. But then how quickly all this science
and humane progress had turned into a flood of words and formulae, like Gogol's symbolic *troyka*, rushing madly onwards, but
without a single guiding principle, ready for any trivial and
destructive use, accessible to everybody's whim.

Though Rozanov remained a spiritual conservative, and has
been loosely called a monarchist, he can hardly be classed as a
political reactionary. In his most outspoken statement on the subject, *The Weakened Fetish* (1910), he decisively took leave of
monarchy in its senile stage, and pronounced that even a republic
stood for a higher degree of hope, youth and creative effort.
Then in the throes of the 1905 revolution he saw with alarm
that a new type of political madness was taking hold of people's
minds, a sham economic religion designed to fill the colossal void
of true religious feeling. 'God will want to destroy politics altogether, after it has covered the earth with blood, deceit, and
cruelty. Politics must vanish from the face of the earth,' he
repeated like a prayer (1912).

He none the less accepted and explained the 1917 revolutions
as God's punishment for so much human vice and folly, a retribution which was merited and could not profitably be analysed,

except in moral terms. 'We are dying like clowns . . . because we can respect ourselves no longer, we are committing suicide. Strange fate! All our lives we crossed ourselves and prayed, and then we threw away the Cross—so easily. It is not that the sun has gone out for us, but we have abandoned ourselves . . . The labourer is a Nihilist—"I want to work less and I don't want to fight". And the soldier throws down his rifle, the workman leaves his bench; the land is left to bear fruit on its own. . . . But the revolutionary has hardly worn out his first pair of stolen boots before he sinks into the grave. *God spat, and put out the candle.* . . . We Russians were made for ideas and feelings, for prayer and music, but not to rule over people. Unluckily we ruled one-sixth of the earth's surface, and thereby ruined it, body and soul. . . . Enough talk about our stinking Revolution and our mouldy Empire, rotten to the core; they are worthy of each other. . . . Christ is powerless, silent; the sun is more powerful and beneficent. . . . Man is not dead, for he still groans. If only he would die, then it would be easier for civilization to breathe again' (*The Apocalypse of our Time*, 1917).

In 1918 Rozanov had retired to Sergiyev-Posad, a quiet provincial town dominated by a monastery. It was there that he composed his final words about the meaning of the Russian revolution, which appeared to him all the more apocalyptic, because it coincided with the natural end of his own life, precipitated by cold, hunger, and exhaustion, which afflicted him, but did not cloud his mind.

U

CHAPTER IX

THREE THINKING STATESMEN

I. K. POBYEDONOSTSEV

KONSTANTIN POBYEDONOSTSEV (1827–1907), Professor of Civil Law at Moscow University, Senator, prolific author, tutor of Alexander III, Procurator of the Holy Synod, and a partial model for Dostoyevsky's sinister figure of the Grand Inquisitor, exercised extensive power behind the Russian governmental scenes throughout the reign of Alexander III. He personally advised the Tsar to ignore the appeals made by Tolstoy and V. Solovyov that he should set an example of Christian clemency by sparing the lives of his father's murderers. He drafted the severe manifesto of 9 April 1881, which put an end to any surviving hopes that the parliamentary constitution, promised by Alexander II, might be granted by his successor.

He has been almost unanimously condemned as the man who tried to *freeze* Russia into petrified immobility, who plunged her into that troubled and frustrated slumber, or apathetic gloom, which afflicted active Russian intellectual circles throughout the eighteen-nineties. Even the aristocratic anti-revolutionary K. Leontiev deplored his blighting influence on national life, called him, not a genuine conservative, but a man 'who may manage to stop further decay like a frost, but can never help any living thing to grow'.

Pobyedonostsev promoted the compulsory diffusion of official Orthodoxy (as part of the long-term policy for binding together the rebellious non-Russian nationalities of the centrifugal Empire). And he directed a systematic persecution of all anti-governmental sectarians, who put conscience before their duty to the state. But during the reign of Nicholas II his influence on state affairs steadily declined, with the growing preponderance of urgent economic questions over ancient religious disputes, although he remained in charge of the Holy Synod until 1905.

While it would be far-fetched to suggest that he concealed un-acknowledged merits as a statesman, he was less blankly negative than he seemed, and his thoughtful scepticism about sacrosanct political institutions showed a long-term clairvoyance. The manner in which he has been condemned as the high priest of black reaction, spreading his owl's wings over the Russian Empire, has done too little justice, either to his brilliant analytic mind, or to his excellent intentions. Had he been able to devise some less stultifying method of imposing the mental control and spiritual discipline which he found indispensable for Russian citizens, he might have avoided a multitude of disappointments.

In one of his outspoken letters to Alexander III he urged, as the supreme task facing modern government, the need to *quieten* agitated and unstable minds, to soothe the fever of confused social thought and personal greed, which had run off their natural course and been roused to a pitch of crazy irritation—to stop the pretentious and ignorant chatter about public affairs which pre-occupied too many private people, distracting their minds and energy from their own limited sphere of work.

'That is why,' he concluded, 'I have always held the opinion that it is quite impossible to undertake any basic or beneficial reforms, so long as the present untrammelled and licentious free-dom of the press remains uncurbed.' [1] The vast but irresponsible power, wielded over human minds by modern newspapers, to-gether with the absurdly exaggerated importance recently attached to so-called representative and parliamentary institutions, re-mained Pobyedonostsev's twin *bêtes noires* throughout his life.

At present 'any vagabond babbler or cunning tradesmen', he complained, 'could found a newspaper, and then persuade people to take it seriously as "an organ of public opinion". But in order to increase their sales among the public, these journals were next obliged to raise their voices to a scream. Thus they began to spread throughout newly literate half-educated circles a current of unbalanced cravings, morbid curiosity and a taste for per-nicious personal slander. In Russia', said Pobyedonostsev, 'the popular press has turned into nothing less than an instrument of

[1] *Pis'ma K. Pobyedonostseva*, vol. 3, p. 367, Moscow, 1925.

national dissolution, darkening and exciting people's minds, but never enlightening them at all. It sows the seeds of conflict and discontent among otherwise peaceful and decent people.' [1] While he readily granted that a high degree of intellectual liberty was needed to promote genuine scientific studies, he contended that it was absurd for mere newspapers to make such claims, and criminal for any government to admit them. 'What above all would benefit our press is more impediments and not more liberty.' [2]

Pobyedonostsev opposed with equal fervour the introduction of a democratic parliamentary constitution to the Russian Empire. He saw the modern *parliamentary fetish* plainly, not as a salutary method to curb state power, but as a disguised campaign to replace the unlimited authority of a sovereign (who had some conscience) by the crushing power of a mechanically complicated institution (devoid of either conscience or personality).

He based his hostility on a reasoned disbelief in the benefits so far achieved by representative institutions as they had developed in the West. But he spoke, though with less conviction, about a feasible alternative, the revival of that *miracle, mystery and authority*, which he ascribed to the *potential* Russian Empire (not as it was then) but as it ought to be, and might eventually become. This attitude, if unduly optimistic, was hardly more irrational than other current political beliefs. Though weak in constructive statesmanship, it had the merit of a logical severity which faced unpleasant facts, without being blinded by Utopian economic blueprints.

Moreover, knowing the court bureaucracy at such close quarters, Pobyedonostsev could not be dazzled by its magnificent façade. Far from turning into a chauvinistic Russian, he was dismayed by the feverish growth of modern nationalist movements. He observed acutely that national pride had never acted as such an irritant poison throughout society, as since it had blended with democratic institutions.

Some of his private letters reveal his bottled-up misgivings

---

[1] Speech, 8 March 1881, *Russkiy Arkhiv.*, no. 2, 1907.
[2] K. Pobyedonostsev, *Mémoires Politiques*, p. 106, Paris, 1927.

about the Russian autocracy, better than his more circumspect public pronouncements. 'My heart aches', he wrote to Catherine Tyutchev, 'when I see that crowd of counsellors and high officials, heartless, vulgar, terrible to say, foul people' (March 1881). Earlier in 1877 during the crisis of the Russo-Turkish War, he had written to Catherine Tyutchev a frank estimate of Alexander II in his later years: 'On whom can we now rely?' he asked. 'The Emperor has sunk into a state of fatalistic apathy. But throughout his life he seems to have been instinctively afraid of able men, and avoided their proximity; he preferred to surround himself with nonentities, because he felt more at ease with people of that sort' (Letter, 1877).

In another letter about the incident of March 1887, when a number of young men carrying bombs, were arrested on the Nevsky Prospekt in Petersburg (including A. Ulyanov, Lenin's brother, who was afterwards condemned to death), he called on all responsible Russians to inquire how far the older generation (by giving them such a foolish upbringing) could be held responsible for crimes committed by their children. 'In the whole of Western Europe socialist conspiracies and bomb explosions have become daily facts. From there the evil spreads, no doubt as a punishment for our grievous sins. . . . Let us be under no illusion; there exists a tribe of men, which multiplies among us disturbingly, men without reason and deprived of conscience, degenerate victims of a bogus civilization.

'It is impossible to keep watch on all of them, still more impossible to cure those who have gone out of their minds. But let us examine ourselves and ask whether we also are not to blame. It seems that we should have among us fewer of these subversive young people, if we had not imported a system of education, alien to our traditions, a system which pulls people out of their natural environment, in order to saturate them with cravings, fantasies and absurd demands, and then throws them into the vast arena of life without any discipline, but with a monstrous self-esteem, which expects everything for themselves and gives nothing in return.' [1]

[1] ibid., p. 560, Paris, 1927.

Pobyedonostsev felt equally appalled by the modern transference of religious sanctity to humdrum political innovations, in
particular, to 'the *parliamentary farce*, the supreme political lie
which dominates our age'. If people reposed deep confidence in
their rulers, it could only rest on faith (which need not mean
identity of religion), on a simple conviction that their rulers were
guided by some motive less selfish than that of making a profitable career. But a modern democracy, Pobyedonostsev urged,
expected bribes, and not religion, from its leaders. The latter's
indiscriminate tolerance showed disrespect for the firm beliefs
of better citizens. Democratic rulers had become cunning manip-
ulators of votes. While in theory universal suffrage had given
voters a clearer voice in managing their own affairs, in practice
elected parliaments, in countries which had adopted them, served
conspicuously to gratify the worldly ambition and personal
vanity distinguishing their representatives.

To the parliamentary candidate his constituents represented so
many numbers in a herd of cattle, and he as their temporary
possessor, resembled the rich nomad whose flocks constitute his
whole capital. But the moment he was elected, his constituents
lost importance for him, until the next election campaign arrived,
when he had again to win their favour by lavish flattery and lying
phrases. 'Men conscious of their duty and capable of disinterested
service would not descend to this soliciting of votes and to crying their own praises at election meetings' (*Reflections of a Russian
Statesman*, London, 1898). Honest and able people could with
increasing difficulty be persuaded to become parliamentary candidates. Thus it turned out that while popular election was said to
favour the most intelligent and capable, in fact it promoted the
most impudent, corrupt and conceited types.

The result of this burdensome method of government, instead
of restricting and de-centralizing state authority (which it originally claimed and tried to do) was to replace the nominal absolute
power of the sovereign by a more paralysing absolute bureaucracy. Thinking of Alexander III, rather than of his puny
son, Pobyedonostsev ascribed to the sovereign's person the
saving grace of a rational will, and loyalty to personal belief,

qualities which could never survive in tortuous party strife and intrigue behind the scenes of parliaments. The latter threatened to grow into anonymous monsters, which in the name of everybody's freedom, multiplied a harmful and needless network of laws, hampering every activity which they were expected to promote. And democratic statesmen, instinctively aware how transitory their reign might be, set out to grab the fruits of office, and became afflicted by a thirst for fame and applause, which clouded their judgement of national needs.

Pobyedonostsev, like other Russian conservatives, opposed parliamentary democracy so obstinately, not because he distrusted ordinary people more than their superiors in rank, but because he felt convinced that democracy—taken too seriously—would debauch hitherto decent common people, and would lead to a cynical intellectual tyranny over them, more inescapable and degrading than monarchical autocracy. He regarded the average Slav as congenitally lazy and unreliable, unless spurred by severe leaders, but he always praised middle-class virtues, and admired *self-made* professional men as the best servants of a stable social order. He despised 'typical bureaucrats', and repeatedly advised Alexander III to promote the ablest men to high positions.[1]

If Pobyedonostsev was right in attributing the *past* growth and power of Russia to autocratic rule, his talk about the boundless mutual trust which still bound the Russian people to their Tsar sounded out of date and artificial. Neither Alexander II, isolated and suspicious of everybody, nor his still more secluded son, nor the officials, absorbed in making their own careers, could provide those living creative links between government and society, which Pobyedonostsev envisaged, mistaking a pious wish for an accomplished fact. Those higher ranks would have to undergo a drastic, miraculous regeneration, before they could start to serve a healthy form of social liberty, guided by firm disinterested people. Though Alexander III came nearest to Pobyedonostsev's ideal of a stern fatherly monarch, his range was narrow, and Alexander cannot be absolved from a reluctance to

---

[1] See 'Pobyedonostsev on Government Instruments', by R. F. Byrnes, in *Continuity and Change in Russian and Soviet Thought*, Harvard University Press, 1955.

cope with Russia's agricultural stagnation, although he did much to stimulate her industry. Had his reign not been cut short by unexpected death at the age of fifty, he might, however, with Vitte's help, have forestalled Stolypin's beneficial agricultural measures.

On this vital national issue Pobyedonostsev showed more insight and common sense than he has been given credit for. He complained that while energy and money were poured out in colonizing wild regions of Siberia and Central Asia, the peasants in European Russia were reduced to penury by the stranglehold of primitive communal agriculture. He wrote plainly that the sole remedy was to emancipate the peasant by making him independent of the *mir*, by abolishing the absurd collective responsibility for paying taxes, and by granting to each individual peasant in perpetual freehold the amount of land to which he was entitled. He remarked that this solution, although the only sound one, was obstinately blocked both by so-called liberals ('It would make our pseudo-liberal press yell with rage, since they always defend any institution which approaches socialism')[1] and by national conservatives, who were imbued with muddle-headed Slavophil sentiments about sacrosanct village customs, and frightened that the peasants, once endowed with land, would turn into subsistence small-holders, and refuse to labour on the landlords' fields.

But while he pleaded that the peasant should be released from slavery to the *mir*, he accused of criminal neglect those educated people who ought to have acted as the peasants' moral guardians. 'Everywhere taverns are being opened, and poor people, left to their own devices (since no one takes any responsible thought for looking after them), begin to drink, to shun work, and become the unhappy victims of tapsters and village money-lenders.'[2]

Though the peasant had more substantial cause to grumble, all classes of society, infected by the example set by slanderous publicists and political climbers, had grown chronically discontented with their lot. 'Today every private soldier aspires to the dignity

[1] K. Pobyedonostsev, *Mémoires Politiques*, p. 111, Paris, 1927.
[2] Speech, *Russkiy Arkhiv*, no. 2, 1907.

COUNT S. VITTE

from a photograph

of a general, and seeks to attain it, not by hard work, duty performed, or distinction gained, but by accident or sudden acquisition, incited like a gambler by the lure of gain.'[1] The possessors of swollen and fictitious values, then try to traffic with them on the public market, like brokers advertising worthless shares. Such men, unprepared for responsibility by steady work and disciplined character, push themselves into high positions where they can indulge their lust for power.

Pobyedonostsev favoured personal autocratic rule through a *modern* administrative and legal system,[2] *not* for mystic reasons, but as a human curb on state aggrandisement, and a lesser evil than mob bureaucracy. While he made the Church into a competent civil service, in politics he showed more talent for diagnosis than for undertaking curative treatment. But he consoled himself by observing that the false idols, set up by his contemporaries, would be overthrown by their children or grandchildren. He appealed to history as the sole impartial witness to the fact that the most durable benefits to mankind have come from a minority of gifted and industrious human beings, but never from any superstitious faith in the educative power of institutions.

II. COUNT SERGEI VITTE (1849–1915)

Considering how precariously the welfare of an autocratic state must hinge upon the character of its autocrat, fate provided the Russian Empire during the last two centuries of its existence with a generous sprinkling of vigorous, intelligent and well-intentioned monarchs. Incompetent weaklings or dangerous imbeciles, like Peter III or Paul I, were discreetly murdered by more enterprising relatives, until humanitarian scruples peculiar to the nineteenth century, deprecating such drastic methods, began to prevail, even in court circles. For better or for worse, Peter the Great, Catherine II, and the first two Alexanders, were more

---

[1] K. Pobyedonostsev, *Reflections of a Russian Statesman*, p. 90, London, 1898.
[2] Pobyedonostsev wrote a three-volume *Course on Civil Law*, and was an active member of the government committee which drafted the judicial reforms of 1864.

active in statecraft than the chief ministers who advised them. For they remained responsible rulers who, despite their fair share of personal vices, imprinted constructive sovereign ideas on the abundant raw material provided by their expanding Empire, and bequeathed to it an enduring legacy of adaptable institutions, a sense of large-scale magnificence, and some wholesome respect for science and the arts.

The outstanding Russian statesman of the early nineteenth century, the super civil servant Speransky, hardly approached the stature of a Richelieu or a Talleyrand. Indeed it is doubtful whether Nicholas I, who hated independent minds, or Alexander II, who instinctively shunned his intellectual superiors, would have known how to use a Richelieu, had they ever been endowed with one. But the growing complexity of social organization in the mid-nineteenth century demanded a more thorough understanding of high finance, international trade and modern industrial technique than Alexander II had been able to provide—a situation which his less talented son, Alexander III, promptly recognized and took energetic steps to remedy.

Simple and plain-spoken, but firm, industrious and persevering, astonishingly devoid of vanity, Alexander III had the uncommon sense to recognize his duty by entrusting the economic development of Russia to men far abler and more experienced than himself—and to know that he needed, not only a statesman with vision and driving power, but a technical *entrepreneur*, thoroughly versed in business management on a colossal scale. Alexander gave priority from the start to the material welfare of his country, and he strenuously avoided the intermittent wars which had tortured and impoverished it in previous reigns. Towards the end of his short reign, he discovered in Sergei Vitte a most energetic, versatile, and constructive statesman, and a man who never became either a courtier flattering the monarch, or a demagogue currying favour with the crowd.

From his father, who was of Baltic Dutch origin, and served in the department of state lands in Tiflis, Vitte probably inherited his love of order and hard work. Through his maternal grandmother, a Princess Dolgoruky, he maintained a sense of solidarity with the more enlightened section of the Russian aristocracy. After studying mathematics at the local university, he entered the service of the Odessa railway company as a clerk in the ticket office, earning a humble salary of 200 roubles a month. Gaining wider experience throughout the lower grades, as assistant station master and traffic controller, he quickly earned promotion by his astonishing ability. During the Russo-Turkish War of 1878 he ably organized the complicated movement of armies and military supplies to and from the Balkan battle fronts. At the end of the war he was appointed Director of the South-Western Railway, nominally a private company, like all the main Russian railways, but with the greater part of its capital guaranteed by the state.

In 1891, while escorting a train in which Alexander III was travelling, he received an order to speed it up, but brusquely refused to obey, exclaiming that he had no intention of breaking his Emperor's neck. The abrupt remark was passed on to Alexander, who immediately took a liking to Vitte, and soon afterwards appointed him Director of the Railway Department in the Ministry of Finance. The transfer to state service, though not financially advantageous, promoted him in rank and prestige, for the Emperor conferred on him the title of Actual State Counsellor, which enabled him to jump over the heads of older members of the hierarchy, and thereby earned him bitter enemies among them.

Under Vitte's masterly control, the frequent deficits hitherto incurred by the state railways soon turned into a substantial profit, and he began to buy out inefficient private companies for the benefit of the state. It seems that the private railway kings and concessionaires of the early railway age in Russia did better in the initial boom of large-scale construction than in subsequent routine management. In his memoirs Vitte mentioned three wealthy Jews, Polyakov, Blyuk, and Kronenberg, who had all started as small agents or sub-contractors—also the Baltic German engineer von Meck, who, after making millions, suffered heavy losses through his construction of the Libau railway. Another railway magnate, N. Derviz, having amassed a huge fortune, sold out his enterprises and retired to Italy, where he built himself a palace, maintained a private theatrical company, and lived in the style of art-loving eighteenth-century grandees.

In 1892 Vitte became Minister of Communications, and in the same year Minister of Finance. The Tsar, who had promoted him so rapidly, was repaid not only by the unsparing labours of his protégé, but by a personal devotion, which provides a key to Vitte's consistent outlook on a statesman's duty, and to his otherwise inexplicable loyalty to the unworthy Nicholas II.

Vitte deplored the prevalent opinion accepted by many people, who had never met him, that Alexander was an embittered reactionary, a man of gloomy blunted feelings and mean intelligence. He maintained, on the contrary, that such nobility of mind and purity of character, as the Emperor possessed, could only be bred (though rarely even then) under those hereditary rules which save the most responsible people from selling their souls to the devil, and raise them above the cunning ambition which afflicts ordinary mortals 'on the make'.

Alexander compensated for his mediocre education by an absolute honesty and unswerving sense of duty. When he felt uncertain about any course of action, he remained silent, but his words, once they were spoken, never conflicted with his deeds. As soon as he had given any promise, he could be relied upon like a rock. He never indulged in fine phrases and statements of far-reaching intention, forgotten as soon as they were spoken.

Whatever defects can be imputed to Alexander, he was the only Russian Emperor of the last two centuries whose reign passed without involving his country in a single war. Vitte called that his greatest service, because he had given Russia those thirteen years of peace without making a single dishonourable concession to a foreign power. During that period his solid sense of justice, his strong will and plain good-natured face, began to inspire a blend of puzzled respect and fear in the leaders of other European states. In this unspectacular manner, Alexander, who inherited the throne, after the murder of his father, in singularly unfavourable circumstances, managed in a few years to raise the international prestige of Russia to a new high level, without shedding a drop of Russian or of foreign blood.

The Emperor, who had served in the Russo-Turkish War of 1878, confided his inflexible conviction to Vitte: 'I am glad that I have seen all the horrors linked with war, and after that experience I think that every human being, who has a heart, cannot possibly want war, and that every ruler, to whom God has entrusted the care of a nation, must take all possible steps to avoid the miseries of war, unless he is forced into it by his enemies —in which case the crime, curses and fatal consequences of that war will certainly fall on the heads of those who have provoked it.' [1]

Vitte's brusque energetic manner appealed to Alexander, who was equally direct. When in 1892 Vitte announced that he had decided to marry the wife of a Jewish doctor, Alexander, though a model of domestic probity, and inclined to dislike Jews, promptly ordered the Holy Synod to put through the divorce formalities within three days, and is reported to have remarked: 'As far as I am concerned, Vitte can marry a goat if he likes, so long as he goes ahead with my work.' When at the same time Vitte was told that his wife could never be received at court, he took the ban in good part, as a natural penalty for his social *mésalliance*. The pillars of Petersburg society, though they turned up their noses at his wife, and intrigued against him behind his back, were ready to sit meekly in the upstart Finance Minister's ante-chamber, whenever they needed loans or government support.

When on another occasion Alexander asked him bluntly, 'Do you side with the Jews?' Vitte asked the Tsar's permission to answer him by asking another question: Could the Tsar drown all the Russian Jews in the Black Sea? If he could, then such a solution was understandable. But if he could not, then the only other solution was to give the Jews a fairer chance to live, by gradually abolishing discriminatory laws which now harassed

[1] S. Vitte, *Vospominaniya*, vol. III, p. 371, Berlin, 1923. Vitte's memoirs are not reliable on facts, especially in parts written to justify his own political actions. But they reveal his character and intentions.

their existence. The Tsar made no reply, but he continued to give Vitte his full confidence and support.

Alexander, despite his patriarchal love for peasant Russia, had made up his mind that no country without its own large-scale industry could make *independent* progress in the nineteenth century. He therefore reversed the predominantly low tariff policy of his father (who had none the less raised tariffs on certain imports in 1876) and insisted on a systematic use of protective tariffs for promoting Russian infant industries. That major change of policy was given impetus by Vishnegradsky, Vitte's predecessor at the Ministry of Finance, and energetically promoted by Vitte himself. It provoked a tariff war between Germany and Russia, which severely strained their political relations, until the Trade Treaty of 1894 concluded the dispute to Russia's advantage.

Bismarck, in his initial retaliation, had started to subject Russian exports to higher tariffs than similar products from other countries, including those from the United States, then Russia's chief competitor in the export of agricultural produce. But as soon as Germany enforced this maximum tariff on Russian goods, Alexander promptly approved Vitte's proposal to raise sharply Russian tariffs on German imports. All his more cautious fellow ministers, except the Minister for War, opposed this course, but Vitte stood firm, because he knew that the Tsar would not let him down. In the final settlement with Russia, Germany made substantial concessions, which she had previously refused even to discuss, and Bismarck openly admired Vitte for his economic pertinacity.

As Minister of Finance, Vitte controlled the State Bank, the Bank of the Nobility and the Peasant Bank, and with unswerving business acumen made use of the Tsar's unlimited authority to build up Russian industrial strength. He believed in a modernized civil service, but autocratically controlled, to bring Russia up to date. And he saw no drastic conflict between the state and private enterprise, so long as each worked in the spheres where they proved to be most efficient.

III

He pushed rapidly ahead with the Tsar's favourite major project, the construction of the Trans-Siberian Railway, linking European Russia with Vladivostok and the maritime provinces of the Pacific. He established the government vodka monopoly, with the disparate purpose of raising revenue and keeping the sale of alcohol within limits. By improving state credit, he managed to reduce the rate of interest on state bonds from 5 and 6 per cent to 4 and $3\frac{1}{2}$ per cent. He initiated the bold monetary reform, which stabilized the rouble at two-thirds of its former value, put Russia on the international gold standard, and fixed a strict statutory link between the volumes of paper currency in circulation and the permitted size of the gold reserve. The State Council opposed this radical measure so obstinately that it had to be overridden by Imperial decrees (a sign of Vitte's dependence on the Emperor's support for carrying out unpopular reforms). But it revived foreign confidence in the state economy, and attracted to Russia those investments of foreign capital, which Vitte needed urgently for his big development schemes.

Many stupid people, Vitte complained, attacked and slandered him for encouraging foreigners to invest in Russia. Rabid nationalists opposed the influx of foreign capital on principle, but in practice reconciled themselves to it, as soon as they acquired lucrative directorships in many new companies which were being formed. Vitte told a cautionary tale about one of these *genuine Russians*, a retired colonel, who served the exalted principle of exploiting native Russian wealth by the work of purely Russian hands, and who won a concession (through his influence at court) to develop some gold mines in the Chukotsk peninsula. Within a few months this 'patriot' found the undertaking too arduous, sold the concession to a foreign company, but was glad to pocket a substantial profit for himself.

Defending his policy of attracting foreign enterprise, Vitte repeatedly explained how Russia, despite her untapped resources and abundant man-power, was poorly equipped with native capital and technical ability. But the interest on these loans had largely to be paid for out of grain exports, which weighed on the overburdened peasants. During the first years of his financial dictatorship Vitte became so absorbed in his giant plans for industry and transport that, as he admitted later, he neglected the agricultural basis of Russia's economy.

For a time he made light of the peasantry's drastic impoverishment through falling grain prices in the eighteen-nineties, since it promoted a steady supply of cheap labour, through the exodus of peasants to seek work in towns. Had Vitte studied the peasant situation earlier, he would undoubtedly have hastened the abolition of communal land-tenure, and collective liability for taxation, as anachronisms which crippled productivity.

In 1898 he wrote a long report to Nicholas II, recommending the urgent appointment of a committee, to work out agricultural reforms. Recognizing the heavy work that lay ahead in imposing order upon this long-neglected chaos, he uttered a timely warning: 'Woe to the country which has not nurtured in its population a respect for law and personal property, but on the contrary has admitted so many diverse forms of collective ownership, which, having never been defined by law, are regulated by uncertain custom or by haphazard individual judgement.' But not till 1901 did the Tsar agree to appoint a Royal Commission under Vitte's presidency, to inquire into these matters.

The financial expert Bunge had impressed on Vitte that the medieval commune remained the worst obstacle to peasant welfare, a primitive relic which most nations had got rid of long ago, while Russians had artificially preserved it, because they found more administrative convenience in looking after an inherited herd, than in taking trouble to improve each individual beast. Though the peasant had legally ceased to be a landowner's serf in 1861, he had become a *de facto* serf of the peasant administration. But while the better landowners had formerly helped their serfs by a multitude of personal services, the new salaried landmarshals and officials were coldly bureaucratic in their conduct, and chiefly concerned with holding on to their jobs, or getting promoted.

Vitte noted later—'I then formed a definite opinion, both as to the nature of the malady, and as to how it should be cured. The state could never be strong and healthy so long as its main support, the peasantry, was weak. We are always shouting that the Russian Empire covers one-fifth of the earth's surface, and that we have a population of 140,000,000. But what do we gain by all this, when the greater part of that surface is either barren or half wild?' [1] No human being, he repeated, will work better, unless he can reap the fruits of his own labour. 'But there can be no stimulus to work so long as the industrious are held responsible for the lazy, the sober for the drunken etc.' As a result of Vitte's efforts collective responsibility for payment of taxes was abolished in 1899 in communes where land was held in hereditary tenure, and in 1903 the same relief was introduced for payment of taxes and redemption dues in other communes.

Vitte knew that the peasants were sick of being treated like immature children by a harsh inspectorate. He favoured giving them more voice in deciding their own affairs, and curbing the arbitrary power of land-marshals, who had become official watchdogs. But the Government hesitated to break off its long-standing flirtation with peasant collectivism. Vitte was dismissed in 1903 because he opposed Nicholas II's irresponsible Far Eastern policy. And in 1904 the Tsar abruptly dissolved the Royal Commission on agricultural reform, whose further activity was confined to publishing an exhaustive report in fifty-eight volumes.

Vitte frequently complained about the blend of extravagance and fecklessness which he detected in many landowners. But he knew that they had been hard hit by prolonged agricultural depression, and often struggled to the best of their ability to make both ends meet. He organized loans and subsidies to them through the Noblemen's Bank, and tried to draw the more business-like ones into his new industrial ventures. When they came to him as insolvent debtors, pleading for deferred payments, he was apt to despise them as incompetent farmers. But he considered that, despite their defects, they were better equipped to administer many branches of state service than members of the merchant class, and could still behave as if they believed in

[1] op. cit., vol. I, p. 410.

x

something more important than their personal enrichment and official grandeur.

The moment Vitte had mastered any social problem, he took determined steps to solve it. Although he started to concentrate on the land question rather late in life, he then did everything within his power to break up the decrepit *commune*, whose false glamour had fatally fascinated administrators of the Reform Period. As late as 1905 he proposed that peasants should secure the legal right to leave their *communes* whenever they so desired, but even this project met stiff opposition from the State Council, who used the pretext that it ought to be deferred for consideration by the People's representatives, who were shortly due to meet in the first Government Duma.

The Tsar dismissed Vitte before the Duma met, but it stands to his credit that he initiated and worked out plans for most of the measures subsequently put into practice by Stolypin, and for far-reaching schemes, which were never carried out. Without the big preparatory work done by Vitte's Royal Commission, the land settlement linked with Stolypin's name could never have been accomplished in so short a time.

Vitte repeatedly urged the Committee for the Trans-Siberian Railway to work out a plan for settling thousands of land-hungry peasants in the empty spaces of Siberia. This bold policy, which combined long-term national colonization with a cheering prospect of better livelihood, was judged heretical, well-nigh revolutionary, by many Ministers and State Councillors at the time it was proposed. The root cause for their hostility lay in the fear that it would raise the price of labour on landlords' estates, and instil the already restive peasants with a dangerous craving for mobility.

But Vitte, with characteristic foresight, had persuaded Alexander to appoint his son, the future Nicholas II, to act as Chairman of the Trans-Siberian Committee. Guided in these early days by the financial expert, Bunge, Nicholas showed enough good sense to take Vitte's side, and the government began to promote migration to the more fertile regions traversed by the Trans-Siberian Railway, despite the obstructive tactics of the Ministry of

Internal Affairs to delay the execution of plans approved by other government departments.

Vitte remained sceptical about what he termed 'flabby *Zemstvo* liberalism', and was disinclined to extend the already sufficient powers of local councils, especially in their responsibility for local taxation. His views are clearly stated in the work called *Autocracy and Zemstvo* (1898). Although he favoured municipal self-government to the extent that it promoted the initiative of rising business and professional people, he wanted to guard the latter against meddlesome and cramping interference from official quarters. He also improved the status of artisans by introducing laws to regulate hours and conditions of work in factories, and he initiated a government inspectorate, whose duty included making sure that employers, as well as labourers, fulfilled obligations imposed on them by the new labour laws. But at this point his zeal embarrassed the authorities, and brought him into sharp conflict with secret police agents, whom the Ministry of the Interior already employed as government spies in many factories.

Whereas Vitte approved state arbitration only as a final court of appeal, a last resort to judge serious unresolved conflicts between management and labour, the Ministry of the Interior aimed at maintaining the rigid *status quo* of factory discipline, and relied on espionage and intimidation. Eventually Vitte's more enlightened policy was defeated by the arch police-spy, Plehve, who, after insinuating himself into the good graces of Nicholas II, persuaded him to transfer the whole department of factory inspection to the control of the Ministry of the Interior.

IV

Vitte demonstrated the key position held by a brilliant Finance Minister in a modern state, by wholly subordinating his foreign policy to long-term plans for the orderly economic development of Russia. Since international peace, plus the steady inflow of foreign capital and experts, were indispensable for his industrial programme, he worked patiently for a tolerable *modus vivendi* between the perpetually squabbling Great Powers of Europe—

Russia, France and Germany—aiming at an enduring alliance between all three of them. He believed that as soon as that central pattern took an agreed shape, all other countries would be obliged to fall into line with it. England was then Russia's main competitor in the economic penetration of Asia, but so long as he could negotiate new deals with France and Germany, Vitte had no fear of English hostility. For English policy alone could never prevail against a firm working alliance between three major continental powers.

Both Bismarck and the Emperor William II expressed their admiration and respect for Vitte, despite the stubborn tariff war that he conducted against Germany. In an interview with William II in 1897, Vitte outlined his view of Europe's future in no uncertain terms. He asked William to consider the fascinating opportunities open to a saner Europe, which had decided to *stop* spending piles of money, blood and toil, in order to turn every country into a military camp, terrified of its neighbours. Since this monstrous expenditure on armaments, more than any other factor, both impoverished and demoralized European nations, a prolonged armed peace inflicted almost as much harm on them as open war.

'You should start to think of Europe', he suggested, 'as one united Empire.' (It would have been tactless to talk about *republics* to the German Emperor.) 'Would she not then become infinitely richer, more cultured, and capable of leading the whole world, instead of sinking into decrepitude through incurable mutual enmity and civil war? If the present internal strife went on unchecked, Europe would turn into a sick old woman and lose her present primacy in world affairs.'[1] Then other countries across the sea would grow much stronger, and in a few hundred years the inhabitants of this planet would speak of the greatness of Europe, as we now speak of the vanished glory of Rome, Greece, Carthage, or parts of Asia Minor.

While Vitte was fascinated by his country's economic prospects in developing her untapped Asiatic territory, he remained on guard against the blandishments of adventurers and concession-

[1] op. cit., vol. I, p. 412.

hunters. He maintained that a mighty but relatively immobile China provided the best guarantee that Russia would be undisturbed on her long Eastern frontier. After the Sino-Japanese War of 1895, Japan had demanded from China the cession of the entire Liaotung (Kwantung) Peninsula. Vitte, with the diplomatic support of France and Germany, promptly interceded on behalf of China, persuaded Japan to renounce her territorial demands, and accept in their stead a large monetary indemnity. The Russian Government, dramatically emerging on the international scene to champion the 'territorial inviolability' of the Chinese Empire, rose in world prestige, and gained gratitude and respect, not only from the crumbling Manchu dynasty, but from the already much more influential Chinese professional and merchant classes.

Consistently enough, Vitte induced the leading Chinese statesman, Li Hung-Chang, to visit Russia (1896), ostensibly to take part in the coronation ceremonies of Nicholas II. This visit led to the signature of a most important secret treaty, whereby China agreed that the Russian Trans-Siberian Railway should run through northern Manchuria (where it would be called the Chinese Eastern Railway)—on condition that it maintained the status of a private company, and that Russia made a defensive alliance, obliging her to support China in the event of any further attack upon her by Japan. At the end of eighty years the entire ownership of the Chinese Eastern Railway would pass to China.[1] 'If only we had stuck to this agreement,' Vitte noted later, 'we should have been spared the disgrace of the Japanese war.'

But German intervention in China dislocated Vitte's Far Eastern policy. In 1897, after Chinese had murdered two German missionaries, German forces abruptly seized the port of Kiaouchow. Shortly afterwards the Tsar announced his fateful decision to occupy Port Arthur and the Liaotung Peninsula. Vitte vehemently opposed both German and Russian seizures of Chinese territory, especially the latter, which, he lamented, 'destroyed forever our friendly relations with China'. He even sent a personal telegram to the German Emperor, warning him of the disastrous

[1] B. Romanov, *Rossiya v Manzhchurii*, p. 128, Leningrad, 1928.

consequences bound to follow from this German action. It gave the signal for that scramble between Germany, England, Russia and France in the dismemberment of coastal China, a course which united the Chinese in implacable hatred and suspicion of all 'barbaric' European traders and 'foreign devils'.

Nicholas II refused to allow Vitte to resign in protest; he ordered him to bribe the Chinese local authorities to give up the annexed territory with a good grace—the only time in his life, Vitte ruefully remarked, when he was obliged to resort to bribes in his dealings with Chinese. But on this point Vitte's self-justification disturbed his memory, since payments to the Chinese out of a secret fund began a full year before the Russian seizure of Port Arthur.[1] The Japanese were furious, since Russia now calmly annexed territory which, only two years earlier, Japan, after conquering it, had been induced to hand back to China. Japan nevertheless agreed to recognize Manchuria as outside her zone of influence, if Russia would reciprocate by giving Japan a free hand in Korea. But Nicholas, who cherished a personal rancour against the Japanese, refused to conciliate them by making clear concessions.

Count Muravyov, who had succeeded the more intelligent Count Lobanov-Rostovsky as foreign minister, persuaded the Tsar that Russian acts of brigandage in China were now the surest means of protecting her against the more predatory designs of Germany and England. The War Minister, Kuropatkin, used the Boxer Rebellion (1900) as a pretext to justify Russian military occupation of Manchuria. After the rebellion, Russian troops played a major part in 'pacifying the Chinese'; Cossacks, after tying them together by their pigtails, drowned Chinese by the dozen, and behaved as if they were victors in a conquered country. German and English troops behaved little better. Among the documents seized by their soldiers during the pillage of the Imperial Palace in Peking, was the original secret treaty, signed by Vitte and Li Hung-Chang, which the Dowager Empress had evidently cherished, believing to the last that Russian promises could be more relied upon than those of Western Europeans.

[1] op. cit., p. 50.

Even the blunt War Minister, Kuropatkin, who constantly urged Vitte to build more railways for strategic purposes, began to be seriously perturbed by the Tsar's insane megalomania about the penetration of Asiatic countries. He noted frankly: 'The Tsar thinks about the subjection of Manchuria, the annexation of Korea, a protectorate over Tibet and Persia, the conquest of the Bosphorus and the Dardanelles. . . . These intentions are expressed, not only in His Majesty's remarks, but also in a series of commands, often given without the knowledge of his responsible ministers, e.g. the despatch of Ulanov to Tibet, where he is instructed to work against the English' (*Diary*, 1903).

Unluckily for his country, Nicholas was a ready prey to sly adventurers who flattered him. He entered into the most disreputable national commitments behind the backs of his departmental ministers. Vitte found his work nullified by this royal caprice, most of all in peaceful economic penetration of the Far East. But he himself played with fire, and blindly underestimated military risks inherent in that policy.

V

Though Nicholas showed a dutiful desire to follow in his father's footsteps, these were soon obliterated. For the vanity of this well-educated but characterless young man deflected him from the only course which might have made his reign a constructive continuation of his father's—namely, a sober recognition that, since he was unfit to rule, he must remain a respectable figurehead, leaving the conduct of state affairs in the experienced hands of his father's trusted advisers. Nicholas gave Vitte a free hand at the beginning of his reign, especially in financial policy, but he also lent a ready ear to every flatterer who goaded him into asserting his own feeble will. Thus the patriarchal autocracy of Alexander III soon degenerated into an oligarchy of careerist administrators and rival government departments, who intrigued against each other for favour and for power, while they deprived the state of solid overriding judgement or continuity of purpose.

A Buryat Mongol doctor, called Badmaev, who taught Mongolian in St. Petersburg University, adroitly advertised mysterious medicaments to win him entry into superstitious circles close to the Imperial family. He talked persuasively to them about the approaching collapse of the Manchu dynasty, and urged that it was Russia's national duty to forestall the seizure of Chinese territory and wealth by less worthy European powers, who were plotting to intervene. He claimed that he could organize revolts by Mongols and Tibetans against Manchu sovereignty in China, and would then lead them to seek protection from the revered *White Tsar*.

Ever since his journey to India and Japan as Tsarevich in 1891, the Far East had exercised a morbid fascination over the mind of Nicholas II, in whom Badmaev found a ready listener. Vitte received instructions to hand over large sums of money to start a new Russian trading concern in Mongolia. The subsidized Badmaev thereupon bought hundreds of camels, opened shops in Outer Mongolia, and started to publish a Buryat Mongol newspaper. In 1895 he visited Chita and Peking, and distributed a lavish supply of camels, guns, and cartridges among his primitive compatriots, who were glad to get anything for nothing. Vitte, though he disliked handing over public money to promote bizarre adventures outside his control, nevertheless wrote to the Tsar, saying that he attached great political importance to the commercial links with Lhasa, secured by Badmaev's Buryat emissaries, who could thus help to thwart English designs to dominate Tibet.[1]

After he had signed his agreement to respect the territorial integrity of China, Vitte's conscience made him break off relations with Badmaev, though he pressed on with Russian economic penetration of northern China, so long as it stopped short of conspiracy against the Chinese Government. Unluckily Badmaev heralded a host of shady financial adventurers, who began flocking to the Far East, in search of quick and easy profits. In 1901 an ex-cavalry officer, called Bezobrazov, who spread slander against Vitte, persuaded the Tsar to send him on a mission

[1] V. Semennikov, *Za Kulisami Tsarisma*, p. xxiii, Leningrad, 1925.

to study the exploitation of natural resources in Korea and Man-churia. On the strength of his mandate, Bezobrazov secured a state concession to deal with the timber of the Yalu river valley on the Korean frontier. He sent reports, urging energetic Russian penetration of Korea by means of nominally private trading com-panies, secretly backed by the Russian Government.

Both Vitte and the Minister for War, Kuropatkin, protested against Bezobrazov's mischievous activities. He was not a clever fortune-hunter, but he was deluded by silly dreams of national grandeur. Vitte, in a strenuous effort to be fair, even called him an honest man, though incurably scatter-brained. But the Tsar turned a deaf ear to elementary common sense, and in 1903 brought matters to a head by appointing Admiral Alexeyev, a friend of Bezobrazov, as Regent for Far Eastern Affairs in Port Arthur. Characteristically, Nicholas announced this appointment without informing either his Foreign Minister, or Kuropatkin, who first learned about it from the newspapers.

Vitte observed that, although Japan had been informed officially that Korea remained within its sphere of influence, Russia was unofficially doing her utmost to absorb and dominate Korea. This double-faced activity, being as clear as daylight to the Japanese, roused their anger still further. At the same time, after occupying Manchuria on the pretext of supporting the Peking government against the Boxer rebels, Russia kept military forces there, long after the Chinese Government had been re-established in Peking. Not only China and Japan, but America and England, Vitte confessed, 'all lost confidence in us, condemned our treacher-ous duplicity and demanded our evacuation of Manchuria'. Bezobrazov, and his band of speculators, were strongly supported by Plehve, then Minister of the Interior, whose sinister hold over the Tsar was tightening.

In October 1901, the eminent Japanese statesman, Marquis Ito, travelled to Petersburg for a final attempt to reach some agree-ment which might have prevented war. The essence of his sug-gested compromise was that Japan should receive a free hand in Korea (in fact, instead of in theory) in return for Japan's recognition of Russian rule over the Liaotung Peninsula. But Ito received a cold reception and ambiguous answers. A few months later Japan concluded her treaty of alliance with England. It also suited the cunning German Emperor to push Russia into Asiatic entanglements, and thus strengthen Germany's hold over Western Europe. After meeting Nicholas in 1902 at naval manœuvres in the Baltic Sea, he sent him the provocative parting message: 'The Admiral of the Atlantic Ocean sends his greetings to the Admiral of the Pacific!'

After Ito's departure, Vitte himself made a journey to the Far East, drew the blackest conclusions from what he saw there, and immediately reported to the Tsar that it was imperative to withdraw Russian troops from Manchuria, and conclude a new treaty with Japan. Vitte cannot be suspected of tender feelings for the Japanese, but he was honest enough to deny (what blindly patriotic Russians claimed) that Japan was taking the military initiative, and would have attacked Russia in any case. He put the blame on the folly and duplicity of his own government. He felt sure that if Russia had respected her treaty obligations to China, had refused to back business adventurers, had even accepted the last proposals made by Marquis Ito, there need have been no war.

Since the Tsar had never questioned his immense achievements as Minister of Finance, Vitte owed his dismissal to his outspoken disagreement with the Tsar's Far Eastern policy. He believed that the latter secretly yearned for 'a little victorious war', which would divert attention from internal unrest and gratify his military ambition. Nicholas also bore a personal grudge against the Japanese, ever since he had been wounded by a fanatic when he visited Japan in 1891. In official documents he referred to them as 'monkeys', grotesquely underrated their military strength, and remained deaf to saner warnings. 'Even Japan has its Council of Ministers,' Vitte commented, 'but we have only a council of street vagabonds, like Bezobrazov and his gang.'

VI

When in February 1904 the Japanese made a surprise attack (as they did at Pearl Harbour in 1941) and torpedoed the Russian warships in Port Arthur, Vitte hardly blamed them for being technically the aggressors, through having omitted to declare war formally. He recognized that Russia deserved the attack, by having done everything to provoke it. Only the vain Nicholas believed to the last that the Japanese 'would never dare'. 'The tragic part,' Vitte wrote later, 'is that we were brought to this disaster, not by any invincible force of circumstances, but by sheer stupidity and weakness, by the petty ambitions of a few individuals, to whom Russia really owes her downfall.'

During the shattering defeats on land and sea which Russia suffered from the Japanese, Vitte could only watch in agony the results he had partly foreseen, and struggled to prevent, while the Emperor continued to take part in picnics and sporting events, and to note in his diary how many rooks he had shot. But he failed to note the fact that this was the first time, since the Turkish invasion in the fifteenth century, that an Asiatic country had inflicted military defeat on a European Great Power. Vitte, on the other hand, admitted: 'The Japanese defeated Russia, because they believed in their God much more strongly than we believed in ours.'

When President Roosevelt appealed for an armistice, and offered to settle the conflict by negotiation, Vitte was promptly given the thankless task of trying to secure a favourable peace treaty. Like a petulant child calling in an adult to mend his broken toy, the Emperor informed Vitte that he must never allow a penny to be paid as war indemnity, nor one square foot of Russian territory to be ceded to Japan. Vitte shouldered this heavy moral burden, knowing that if he signed a treaty he would be blamed by the chauvinist war party for making peace prematurely (although Russia had lost every battle to the Japanese), and equally, that if he failed to make a treaty, he would be condemned by the public for prolonging useless bloodshed.

Breaking his journey in Paris, he was hurt by the casual attitude shown to him by the French, as Russia's representative. At that time American public opinion, although it liked neither country, preferred Japan to Russia. America had been slightly alarmed by Japanese aggressiveness in 1895, but when, after forcing Japan to return the Liaotung Peninsula to China, Russia a few years later seized it for herself, American sentiment shifted markedly in favour of Japan. But Vitte never filled any position without transforming it by his creative energy and skill. Now he worked wonders, and turned a hopeless military fiasco into a diplomatic triumph.

During the voyage from Cherbourg to New York, he carefully thought out his plan of action as plenipotentiary of a defeated and nearly bankrupt Empire, and reached the following conclusions: (1) never to betray that Russia really craved for peace, but to give everybody the impression that, if the Tsar had agreed to negotiate, it was solely to meet the desire expressed by all civilized countries to end the war; (2) to behave as befitted the representative of a mighty Empire which had met with a slight misfortune; (3) bearing in mind the political power wielded by the American press, to be constantly attentive and accessible to all its members; (4) in order to win favour with the American public, to behave in what they considered a democratic manner, without pride or aloofness; (5) in view of the influence exercised by Jews in New York (many of them emigrants from Russia), especially on the press, to display a friendly attitude towards them.

Vitte scrupulously adhered to every resolution on this programme throughout his stay in America. He played his difficult part like a superb actor on a colossal stage, perpetually exposed to public scrutiny, and to photographers and journalists, who followed every step he made. He responded punctually to thousands of personal requests for his autograph, and every day he granted long interviews to press correspondents. When his train arrived in Portsmouth, he walked up the crowded platform, thanked the engine driver, and shook hands with him.

Vitte's determined and thoughtful conduct gradually caused the American press and public to swing over from the Japanese to the Russian side. The Asiatic inscrutability, maintained by the Japanese delegates, also worked in Russia's favour.

When Vitte was adamant in refusing Japan's demand to pay a war indemnity, President Roosevelt telegraphed to the Mikado, pointing out that if the Portsmouth negotiations came to nothing,

Japan would no longer find the same sympathy and support in America as before. Having himself initiated the Conference, Roosevelt, like a wise politician, took this final step, to avoid the blow which a breakdown in negotiations might have dealt to his prestige. In the end, Komura, the Japanese delegate, made further concessions to Vitte, only after he had received direct orders from Tokio to do so. When he told Vitte with some asperity: 'You always talk as if you were the victor,' the latter replied adroitly: 'Here are no victors, and therefore no defeated.'

One feature of American life astonished and impressed Vitte profoundly. He noticed that many of the waiters in hotels and restaurants were students of higher educational establishments or universities, who earned money in this manner to pay for their own education. It pleased him that these students were proud of being self-supporting, and in no way self-conscious or apologetic about their menial secondary occupation. On the contrary, they put on their waiters' costume, served expertly at table, and afterwards changed into normal clothes and mixed with the company. Vitte observed with regret that Russian students, however near starvation they might be, would have died of shame to serve as waiters, even in the most exclusive restaurants.

News of the unexpected popularity and sweeping diplomatic success, which Vitte had won in America, gave rise to a new current of envy and intrigue against him in the high circles of St. Petersburg. The rumour was launched that out of personal ambition he had yielded far too much, and gone beyond the Tsar's instructions, that he secretly planned to make himself the first President of a United States of Russia. In fact the only substantial territorial concession made to Japan was the cession of the southern half of Sakhalin island (which Japanese troops had already occupied), and that cession had been sanctioned by the Tsar himself. Vitte remarked that he might have refused to cede it, but that in this one case the Tsar was probably right, as otherwise the Japanese would have broken off discussions.

Only after the Tsar had received congratulatory telegrams from all parts of the world, did he begin to recognize that Russia had won astonishingly favourable peace terms, thanks to Vitte's

skill. Not till then did he condescend to telegraph his own con-
gratulations, and on Vitte's return conferred on him the title
of Count.

Vitte's request for a period of rest was none the less refused.
He returned to Petersburg in a state of nervous and physical
exhaustion, only to find his country paralysed by the convulsions
of the 1905 revolution, and by a total lack of coherent leadership.
The incorrigible Tsar, succumbing to the methodical flattery of
the German Emperor, had just signed with him at Björke an
agreement pledging Russia to fight on Germany's side, if the
latter found herself at war with France. This undertaking flatly
contradicted the existing Russian treaty with France, which
bound her to fight on France's side in the event of war against
Germany. Vitte now understood why the German Emperor had
invited him to stay in Germany on his return from America, and
graciously conferred on him the Order of the Black Eagle. After
a talk with the Foreign Minister, Count Lamsdorf (who had
never been informed about it), they managed to persuade the
Tsar to cancel his infamous new treaty.

Meanwhile Russia drifted like a rudderless ship on a stormy
sea; the government was faced with an empty treasury and a
mutinous army; strikes were spreading, and the Tsar had allowed
General Trepov to become a virtual dictator. As matters went
from bad to worse, the Petersburg press refused to submit to
censorship, and idle factory workers on strike devoted their
time to making angry speeches and marching in procession.
Panic began to spread, and plans were made for the flight of the
Imperial family. Even Nicholas, who hated to take an irrevocable
decision, recognized that he now had either to authorize a downright military dictatorship, or grant a parliamentary constitution. Vitte pointed out to him that he was free to choose the
former, provided he could find someone to undertake it. But
the Tsar finally asked him to draft a plan for constitutional
reform.

Vitte knew that Nicholas, being a weak man, instinctively
relied on physical force (so long as other people could provide it)
and would have preferred a dictatorship, had there been a man

available to impose one. He explained the Tsar's decision to grant a constitution as being prompted by his guilty conscience and frightened desire to make amends. Neither was General Trepov a promising candidate for power, for the crisis had so much alarmed him that he was quite prepared to make concessions. 'Though I am a landowner myself,' he told Vitte, 'I will be very glad to give away half my land, if I am sure that on that condition I shall be able to keep the other half.'[1]

Everyone turned instinctively to Vitte as the one man who could save the country from disaster. But no sooner had he submitted his plan to Nicholas, than the latter called in advisers, and altered Vitte's draft without consulting him. Vitte thereupon sent a brusque message to say that he could never accept responsibility for measures of which he was kept in ignorance, and suggested that the Tsar might do better to form a Ministry from those who had advised him on alterations to his original draft. Knowing that Nicholas distrusted him, and would make him a scapegoat at the first convenient opportunity, he would gladly have been spared the ordeal of becoming the first constitutional Prime Minister of Russia. 'I began to pray to the Almighty,' he wrote, 'that he would lead me out of this maze of cowardice, blindness, treachery, and stupidity.'

But the Tsar still hesitated. Finally the impulsive Grand Duke Nicholas rushed into his presence with a revolver in his hand, and announced that, unless the Tsar promptly signed Vitte's draft, he would commit suicide by putting a bullet through his head. The Tsar in alarm sent for Vitte, and signed the *October Manifesto*, expressing the 'inflexible will' of the monarch to grant his subjects stable foundations for civil liberty, representative government, etc.

Thus Vitte found himself at the head of a new government, but without a free hand, with slender confidence, and chiefly because people closer to the Tsar were frightened of being assassinated if they took office. 'I knew that I was really without power, or with a power perpetually nullified by the cunning, not to say treachery, of Nicholas II.' Vitte later sized up the

[1] I. Vasilevsky, *Graf Vitte*, p. 97, Berlin, 1922.

situation and felt that the prospects for monarchy become forlorn, when among the possible heirs to the throne, not one is capable of leadership. The little Tsarevich suffered from haemophilia, and none of the Grand Dukes had either resolute character or superior intelligence.

'Although by my family traditions and temperament', he wrote, 'I favoured absolute monarchy, my reason tells me, after all that I have lived through and witnessed among those who hold power, that there is no other way out, except a rational limitation, a wall along the high road, to restrict the movements of the autocrat. Evidently this becomes a necessary historical law, in the present stage of creatures inhabiting our planet. Other countries have now passed over to a constitutional form of government, and that transition has not been made without convulsions. Such a state of affairs, even if due to human error, makes it hard for us to maintain a form of government which has been gradually abandoned by all more or less civilized countries, and even by others, who in their general culture stand much lower than Russia . . .

'Measures leading to worse results will be considered good, provided that they go through a representative government, because they thus appear to be willed by everybody, and not by the bureaucracy alone. . . . Probably the universal constitutionalism of today is only a historical phase. After some decades or centuries, human beings will find different forms to correspond to the latest awakening of their consciousness. Maybe there will be born again a yearning for personal aristocratic leadership. But today this feeling no longer exists, for the parliamentary system of government, with all its defects, expresses the present political psychology of peoples, and one cannot get away from that.' [1]

VII

The imperative need to restore public order made Vitte choose P. Durnovo as the best man for the Ministry of the Interior. He believed that leniency in dealing with the revolutionary

[1] S. Vitte, *Vospominaniya*, vol. I, p. 276, Berlin, 1923.

psychosis, which then possessed the public, would merely aggravate bloodshed and chaos. He nevertheless offered ministerial posts to 'progressive' personalities supported by liberal society, like Senator Koni and A. Guchkov, but they refused to be associated with Durnovo. Evidently, Vitte remarked, they feared reprisals in the shape of 'bombs or Brownings'. The sensitive Professor Tagantsev, on being offered the post of Minister of Public Education, put both hands to his head, and ran out of Vitte's study shouting, 'I can't, I can't!'

Durnovo protected from sabotage and malicious injury the brave workmen who chose to remain at their posts, in defiance of those who organized the wave of strikes. He promptly stopped the outbreak of a telephone strike by ordering a military telephone detachment to be held in readiness to take over, and by threatening with immediate dismissal every employee who did not return punctually to work on the following day.

Without Durnovo's masterly handling of tense situations, Vitte might not have managed to pacify the country, but he had to pay the price by sacrificing liberal collaboration, and thereby alienating a large section of the educated public. Later he said that he had made a mistake in appointing Durnovo, even though any lesser man would have become a puppet in the hands of General Trepov's police clique. But Vitte naturally resented that Durnovo had private interviews with the Tsar, who instructed him behind Vitte's back. He wrote frankly: 'I was at one with the Minister for Internal Affairs in recognizing that outbreaks of violence had to be suppressed by force, though I had resolved to use moral persuasion above all else. Violent resistance to our forces had to be suppressed energetically, without sentimental qualms. But the moment order was restored, the laws must again be strictly followed, without indulgence in revenge or licence. I must admit that these precepts are not always observed.' [1]

Vitte authorized equally drastic action to deal with the disaffected army in the Far East. Whole regiments returning along the Trans-Siberian line had mutinied and turned into riotous mobs, looting railway stations on the route. Generals Rennenkamp

[1] op. cit., vol. 2, p. 140.

Y

and Meller were dispatched to Siberia in charge of punitive expeditions. Their method was a simple one, but it produced a magical effect. They first surrounded the troop-trains with picked men, then brought out groups of offending soldiers and flogged them in front of the others. In addition, about 45,000 mutineers were tried on the spot by courts martial and deported to penal settlements in Siberia.

But Vitte's personal unpopularity increased, as much in high quarters as among the opposition groups. With the frank contempt of an impassioned worker for the crowd of idle scandal-mongers who abounded in court circles, he could not avoid making enemies, especially among gold-laced high officials, who held their noses closely to the wind of favour.

His marriage to the divorced wife of a Jewish doctor, his resort to foreign capital and technicians, had made him a welcome target for the so-called Union of the Russian People (commonly known as *Black Hundreds*), who accused him of harbouring 'un-Russian' *cosmopolitan* sympathies. The leaders of this movement, although they were mostly plain swindlers and successful hooligans, busily filling their own pockets under a smoke-screen of patriotic bombast, had won growing sympathy from Nicholas II. 'The pathetic Tsar,' Vitte commented in his diary, 'leaning on this party of political scoundrels, dreamed of restoring the greatness of Russia.'

There remained perhaps more vehemence in resentment against the Jews, than in the stand taken by the Black Hundreds against the influx of foreign capital into Russian industry. The two were connected. Jews were accused of satisfying their private greed with stark commercial ruthlessness. Yet the Government of Nicholas II had a truly criminal record in its own treatment of the Jews. For it both connived at pogroms and secretly organized them, using Jews as scapegoats for public indignation, which would otherwise have been directed against itself. This cynical persecution put even the ablest Jews against the Government, and pushed many otherwise politically neutral ones into the vanguard of the revolutionary movement.

Vitte discovered to his horror that during Plehve's tenure of the Ministry of the Interior, the police department had set up a special printing press for producing bogus proclamations, designed to incite the Russian population to fury against the Jews. Accustomed as he was from his childhood in Tiflis to the lively multi-racial medley of the Caucasus, Vitte deplored cold-blooded racial persecution and the racial arrogance which inflicted it. He saw the shortsightedness of the government's attempt to russify by force the non-Great–Russian national minorities, which (including the Ukrainians) formed a solidly resentful 35 per cent. of the total population of the Russian Empire. He could do little to alleviate restrictions on the Jews. But during his short premiership in 1905, he secured for the Ukrainians the right to print the Bible for the first time in their native tongue, and he persuaded the Tsar to stop the War Minister from recruiting more recalcitrant Finns for compulsory service in the Russian army.

Every responsible person recognized that, without Vitte at the helm, the Russian Government could never command enough confidence abroad to raise a desperately needed foreign loan. One of Vitte's last achievements as a statesman was the negotiation in 1905 of a substantial loan, guaranteed by a group of Paris bankers, despite the sabotage of his opponents, including the Cadet Party, who had sent emissaries to Paris, and tried every means, fair or foul, to block agreement.

In the same year Plehve was murdered by a revolutionary, and a letter from one of his own police-agents, found on his body, gave particulars of a plot against the Tsar's life, in which Vitte was alleged to be implicated. He promptly denounced it as a forgery, designed by his enemies to ruin him. But the old rumour, that he cherished ambitions to supplant the Tsar, began to circulate again. Malicious intrigue finally undermined the morale of Vitte, who confessed: 'I have become wholly disillusioned by those standard-bearers who now hold aloft the banners which I followed all my life, and which I cannot betray until I die, despite all the bitter and shameful feelings which these standard-bearers now arouse in me—most of all their Imperial chief.' [1]

Vitte saw plainly his untenable position, so why prolong the

[1] op. cit., vol. 2, p. 295.

useless agony of holding a premiership deprived of power? He wrote frankly to the Tsar: 'I feel so broken and worn out by the savage campaigns against me, that I can no longer keep that cool presence of mind which is essential for the post of Chairman of the Council of Ministers, especially under the new conditions.' The fickle Tsar accepted his resignation with alacrity, and in April 1906 (six days before the opening of the First Duma) he dismissed both Vitte and Durnovo by decree, and appointed the insignificant Goremykin in Vitte's place.

It was hardly Vitte's fault, but certainly his tragedy, that political idiocy, leading to war and revolution, shattered the new foundations for self-respecting prosperity, which he had tirelessly laboured to construct. While court intrigues insinuated that he was a republican and would-be President at heart, the radicals accused him of sacrificing democratic government to salvage the monarchy, the landowners of ruining them in order to help the peasants, and the peasants of swindling them to save the landlords. Faced with envy and treachery, instead of with grateful support, from the Emperor whose throne he had saved in 1905, unwilling to curry favour with self-centred factions, he could no longer steer the sinking ship of state.

Evidently Vitte had never used his years of financial supremacy to accumulate a private fortune. For in 1912 he informed the Tsar that he would be obliged to accept the private salaried position of Adviser to the Russian Bank of Foreign Trade, unless the government granted him a sum of 200,000 roubles to enable him to continue his meagrely paid service as State Counsellor. The Minister of Finance had the decency and good sense to recommend the grant.[1]

In 1913, during a public enquiry into the disquieting extent (about one-third of the total revenue) to which the Russian national budget depended on the sale of alcoholic liquor, Vitte informed the State Council that his concern, during his own administration of the State monopoly, had always been to protect the people's health, limit their consumption, and never to increase the state revenue by promoting sales of alcohol. The responsible

[1] V. Kokovtsov, *Out of My Past*, pp. 330-2, Stanford, 1935.

ministers were infuriated by Vitte's suggestion that, since his fall from power, the government had flourished on the growth of public drunkenness. It was a sore point, for Tolstoy had also thundered against the vodka monopoly as one of various instruments used by the state to *stupefy* its citizens.

Vitte had constantly overtaxed his strength, and passed his last years in failing health, although he never lost the will to work. When the European War broke out in 1914, he told M. Paléologue, the French Ambassador in Petersburg, that it was sheer international madness, and that if Russia joined in the war, the result would be fatal for her. That 'romantic chimera', as he called it, ridiculous and out of date, Russia's so-called historic role to protect her Slav brethren in the Balkan states, was dragging her once more into misery and disaster.

In 1915, shortly after Vitte's death, the Tsar sent a formal message to his widow, asking her to send him for perusal the interesting memoirs which, he heard, her husband had been writing. The Countess cautiously replied that she regretted her inability to send them to His Majesty, as they were kept abroad. Soon afterwards an official from the Russian Embassy in Paris travelled to Biarritz, where he forcibly entered and ransacked Vitte's villa. But his widow had wisely taken the precaution of depositing all her husband's private papers in a bank at Bayonne, so that the part played by Vitte in his country's recent history could not be wholly falsified by posterity.[1]

VIII

P. STOLYPIN

Peter Stolypin (1862–1911) a man of ardent temperament and clear mental vision, honest, brave, and scrupulously just

[1] No full-scale biography of Vitte has yet been written, and most of the published studies of his work are saturated with political controversy. The following may be profitably consulted: I. Vasilevsky, *Graf Vitte i evo Memuari*, Berlin, 1923; D. Lutokhin, *Graf S. Vitte kak Ministr Finansov*, Petrograd, 1915; V. Korostovets, *Graf Vitte, Der Steuerman*, etc., Berlin, 1929; B. Romanov, *Rossiya v Manchzhurii*, Leningrad, 1928; S. Propper, *Was nicht in die Zeitung kam*, Frankfurt, 1929; T. von Laue, *Count Vitte and the Russian Revolution of* 1905; *American Slavic and East European Review*, February 1958.

according to his lights, but without Vitte's vast range of administrative knowledge, became the last effective statesman of the Russian Empire, when he dominated its political activity from the first State Duma in 1906, until his violent death in 1911.

He believed that hereditary autocratic rule must yield to limited monarchy, provided the latter could be upheld by a strong and alert ministerial executive. For in the case of Nicholas II, far from injuring the enfeebled Russian royal dynasty, there remained no other means of saving it from ignominious collapse. While he recognized that a number of so-called *left-wing* economic measures had become imperative for Russia, he maintained that they could bring the maximum benefit and inspire widespread confidence, not when extracted by threats and mob intimidation from frightened demagogues, but only when they were boldly and skilfully carried out by a responsible independent-minded government.

Acting accordingly, he made a multitude of enemies, both right and left, for he remained straightforward to the point of inflexibility, unable or unwilling to indulge in that shifty game of tactics which prolonged the careers or promoted the popularity of more callous professional politicians. At the same time he did his utmost to collaborate with the newly-constituted State Duma, struggled to divert it from arid ideological disputes or inchoate outbursts of revolt, and to lead it towards a calmer channel of constructive and practicable legislation.

After graduating in the faculty of physics and mathematics at Moscow University, Stolypin had entered the Ministry of Agriculture (1895) where he served two years, then became Marshal of the Nobility at Kovno (1899) where the perpetually wrangling mixed population of Jews, Poles, and Lithuanians, forced him to think hard about how to control and reconcile explosive national minorities within the Russian Empire. In 1901 he became Governor of Saratov, where he handled with quiet determination and patient *savoir-faire* the revolutionary outbreaks of 1905. In 1906 he took Durnovo's place as Minister for Internal Affairs, and later in the same year he succeeded Goremykin as chairman of the Council of Ministers.

Despite the fact that his administrative experience derived from the sphere of provincial government, he managed to shed the more fossilized prejudices of the landowning class, in which he had been born and bred, without losing respect for their occasional redeeming virtues, discriminating judgement and sense of honour. 'The strength of Russia no longer resides in her great landowners,' he pronounced, 'they have outlived their time.' [1] He deplored their lack of economic initiative, and their muddle-headed acquiescence in the stagnant agricultural *status quo*. In 1905, he often refused to send soldiers to subdue the peasants who were setting fire to landowners' houses and pillaging their estates, but went alone, without an escort, to pacify centres of agitation.

Bitter experience, plus practical insight into village organization, made him decide to remove, once and for all, the stranglehold of the *commune*, and simultaneously to raise the productivity of the soil. He provided a fresh incentive by encouraging active yeomen farmers to own the land on which they worked. With a flair for brisk and trenchant summaries of complex programmes, he called his land policy 'a wager, not on the drunken and the weak, but on the competent and strong'.

Throughout his life he took the side of energetic self-reliant individuals in their struggle to break down cramping institutional barriers. He did all he could to protect their efforts from being thwarted, either by the envious communal mob below or by the follies of the clumsy state machine. Yet he struck terror and confusion into the hearts of his right-wing opponents (and even alarmed Lenin as a dangerous rival to the revolutionary party) when he sometimes described his policy as a form of *state socialism*. In fact he most favoured peasant families, who worked their own land, with a minimum of hired labour, and produced a surplus for the market.[2]

Although determined to give a fairer chance to capable peasants, by striking off the chains which bound them to the

---

[1] M. Bok, *Vospominaniya o moem otse*, p. 151, New York, 1953.
[2] See D. W. Treadgold, *The Great Siberian Migration*, Princeton University Press, 1957.

commune, he never claimed that he could make a lazy or a stupid man equal to an industrious or skilful one. He would not subsidize inefficiency, and refused indignantly to maintain a communal usage which enabled the idler members of a family to live as parasites preying on their industrious relatives. 'Is it not clear enough by now,' he said, 'that slavery to the *commune* and the yoke of family ownership constitute a bitter bondage for about ninety million people?' (Speech, December 1906).

He neither pretended nor desired that the provision of better opportunities to rise in the world would eliminate the natural inequality shown by superior ability and property acquired by it. And he refused to erect a single artificial obstacle against the enrichment of enterprising peasants. In any case those who decided to leave the *commune* were more distinguished by energetic character than by their disproportionate wealth.

The word *kulak*, which existed long before Stolypin's day, denoted harsh exploiters of the peasants, as a rule village money-lenders, but did not then cover a separate class of wealthy peasants. The latter exclusive meaning was invented later by the Bolsheviks, to serve their purpose of stimulating class hatred between the more prosperous peasants and the poorer ones, and to gloss over fundamental differences in what each contributed to agriculture.

Of course the *kulak* could be a cunning brute, but he was to some extent a vicious by-product of the decaying *commune*. So long as every energetic peasant was strangled by the ties of communal ownership, he was forced to become a *mir-eater* or a moneylender, in order to extricate himself from that entanglement, and rise to responsible independence. Stolypin in 1907, far from encouraging the survival of the old type of *kulak*, did all he could to sweep away the stagnant environment which had bred him, and made it legal for *every* peasant to leave the *commune*, provided he possessed enough enterprise to set up on his own. State loans and facilities helped him to help himself.

In fact between 1907 and 1914, 2,000,000 peasant families had seceded from their communes and set up as individual proprietors, and by 1917 about 6,200,000 had applied for separation from the *commune*. When at the end of that year, Lenin called on the peasants to 'take the land', they already owned in fact, whether in communal or private tenure, about three-quarters of all the cultivated land in European Russia.[1]

IX

Stolypin quickly recognized that the Government must either give reign to wild revolutionary chaos in the Duma, and remain on the defensive, or seize the initiative and face every storm of hostile criticism with prompt and reasoned action. When he sought closer collaboration between the Duma parties, he received a discouraging response. Though he offered posts in his cabinet to such liberal-minded members as Prince Lvov and V. I. Gurko, and wanted to include one influential Jew, they all preferred to remain in opposition. After Stolypin's firm speeches in the First Duma, the left-wing deputies used to shout, stamp their feet and whistle, with angry and distorted faces. Without retaliating in kind, he concluded that for those who held the reins of power, there could be no worse crime than faint-hearted evasion of responsibility. And he became convinced that, if Ministers were in fact selected from the most numerous party in the Duma (as the *Cadets* demanded), the result would be appalling chaos throughout Russia.[2]

The Second Duma showed itself even more determined than the first to prevent the Government from governing, by keeping up a perpetual buzz of threats, and by making extreme impracticable demands which were bound to be refused. Unable to legislate itself, it turned into a propaganda tribune for promoting unattainable laws. The *Cadet*[3] party, led by the ambitious Professor Milyukov, courted popular support by insisting that landowners' estates should be expropriated and handed over to the peasants, while remaining vague about legal methods to be used. The

---

[1] *The Russian Review*, article by Bertram Wolfe, vol. 6, no. 2, New York, 1947.
[2] B. Pares, *Russia and Reform*, p. 559, London, 1907.
[3] Constitutional democrats.

socialist parties went one better, by promising the peasants the landlords' land without paying one penny of compensation to the latter. Fundamentally Milyukov differed little from the socialists, having like them no other goal than to overthrow the Government by any means, and seize power for his own party. But he knew that he could never do this without leaning on the violent revolutionary parties, 'our friends of the left' as he called them. At the same time, the *Cadets* paraded a show of loyalty to the Tsar, hoping thereby to win the conservative masses to their side.

In the peculiar emotional climate of that time, eloquent left-wing sympathies in politics had become a *sine qua non* for intellectual snobs, and, far from handicapping professional advancement, they tended to promote it, often at the expense of merit. Milyukov did nothing to discourage agitators who spread personal slanders and gross falsehoods to discredit honest members of the government. Lawyers and intellectuals, who flaunted their defiance of the established order, would receive the most influential and lucrative appointments, even if they were professional nonentities compared with their conservative rivals, who were indiscriminately abused as 'hirelings of the Government'. When a Jew was accidentally killed during a riot to free some political prisoners, he was publicly acclaimed a martyr, whereas numerous murders of people, appointed to preserve public order, were openly applauded by the so-called liberal press.

The First Duma had been dominated by the *Cadets*, who tried to overthrow the Government by abuse and ridicule of its representatives. Unfortunately the Prime Minister, Goremykin, who treated the Duma like a formal schoolmaster treats a class of naughty boys, did nothing to raise the government's prestige. Stolypin was then only Minister of the Interior. When the first Duma was dissolved, the Cadets spoiled their chances of being taken seriously as candidates for Ministerial posts, by publishing the notorious *Viborg Manifesto*, calling on all progressive citizens to go on strike against paying any taxes to the government and against serving in the Russian Army. For the Second Duma (convened when he was already Prime Minister) Stolypin had wisely prepared enough feasible legislative projects to keep it busy with constructive issues. He made it clear that he would never allow the Duma to be turned into an ancient Roman circus providing gladiatorial combats to entertain a ribald crowd, and that sensational attacks, intended solely to provoke in the government paralysis of thought and will, would no longer be tolerated by him. 'They shout at us "Hands up!" To these words the Government, calmly conscious of its rights, can only answer "We are not afraid" ' (Speech, March 1907[1]).

Stolypin dealt firmly with the Socialist proposal to nationalize the land without compensation to its owners. He said that such a step, apart from ruining the most cultured class in Russia, could inflict grave injury on the peasants, by weakening their healthy urge to earn the right to more property by harder work. The sturdier self-respecting peasant ought not to be degraded by state charity, and thus deprived of faith in his own powers. Hopelessly backward peasants could stick to the *commune* as a philanthropic institution.

In any case there was not enough cultivable land in European Russia to satisfy the needs of a population which increased by about one and a half million every year. None the less Stolypin allotted a large portion of the Imperial appanage lands for division among the peasants. And he had in mind schemes to colonize Siberia by large-scale emigration, plans which were starting to materialize at the time of his journey to Western Siberia in 1910.

Lenin was seriously perturbed by the boldness and success of Stolypin's agrarian legislation; for he wrote in 1908, that 'if the Stolypin agrarian policy continues for a long enough period, it might force *us* to renounce any agrarian programme at all'.[2] The other left-wing parties in the Duma also did their utmost to thwart Stolypin's projects, whose realization threatened to undermine their own *raison d'être*. But he simultaneously earned the enmity of stubborn landowners, since he had determined to break up the *commune* at any price.

In August 1906, a revolutionary maniac, disguised as a

[1] A. Stolypin, *P. A. Stolypin*, p. 9, Paris, 1927.
[2] *Russian Review*, p. 47, vol. 6, no. 2, 1947.

policeman, entered Stolypin's house while he was receiving petitioners, and hastily threw a bomb, which killed twenty-seven people and wounded many others, including his own fourteen-year-old daughter. He miraculously escaped uninjured, but the Tsar immediately afterwards gave him and his family permanent quarters in the Winter Palace, where they could be better guarded day and night. This ghastly experience, though it failed to deflect Stolypin from his sworn programme of reform by law, disposed him to rely on a strong police force as the surest weapon against the terrorist underground. He remarked that where the sole remaining argument had become a bomb, the only natural answer to it was ruthless punishment. No amount of moral persuasion would turn a man-eating tiger into a lamb. While such an attitude was understandable, there can be little doubt that his recourse to martial law and violent reprisals, but even more, his unhealthy dependence on secret police informers, led to his own undoing.

x

In 1907 Stolypin revealed a plot to murder the Tsar, the Grand Duke Nicholas and himself, and announced that fifty-five members of the Duma were implicated in it.[1] But the Duma refused to allow these deputies to be excluded from its sittings, or even to put them under guard. The government was thereby placed again on the horns of a dilemma. Either it must change the new fundamental laws, established by the *October Manifesto* of 1905, and abolish popular representation altogether—or—by modifying the electoral law, it must secure representatives who would be more amenable, and co-operative with the government. Stolypin chose the latter course. The irresponsible behaviour of the Second Duma had already antagonized so many thinking people throughout the country that its dissolution in 1907 aroused no powerful public indignation.

Elections to the Third Duma conformed to a revised electoral law, which halved the voting rights of landless peasants, and

[1] A Stolypin, *P. A. Stolypin*, p. 10, Paris, 1927.

reduced the representation of non-Russian nationalities. This restriction was, strictly speaking, a violation of the constitution, a tactical *coup d'état*. But it fulfilled Stolypin's aim in producing a Duma which could discuss and enact a far larger body of feasible legislation than either of its predecessors. In fact it improved and enlarged the grant of state credits to the peasants, set up land-experts and agronomists, introduced compulsory insurance (on the German model) of industrial workmen against sickness and accident, and pensions in case of disability. The total cost of all these services was borne by the employer.

True to his policy of de-centralizing responsibility, Stolypin also introduced a bill to create a local *Volost' Zemstvo*, designed to represent peasant interests, and prepare them for self-government, but based on an electoral law which would save the small proprietors from being swamped by the majority of landless and ignorant peasants. Although this bill aroused violent opposition from both left and right, it passed the Duma, and went on to the next legislative body, the State Council. But Stolypin was murdered before the bill was debated there. It became law after the February Revolution (1917), only to be annulled a few months later by the Bolsheviks.[1]

His enemies complained that Stolypin's head had been turned by the exercise of virtually absolute power, and that he showed undue favouritism to his own friends and relatives in making state appointments. He certainly began increasingly to resent damaging criticism, even from the Octobrist party, and he revealed a disturbing sympathy with pan-Slav nationalists. He none the less remained extremely level-headed in handling foreign policy. In 1909, when Austria-Hungary annexed Bosnia and Herzegovina, the governmental patriots clamoured for Russia to resume her time-honoured role of protecting Balkan Slavs, and war seemed imminent. But Stolypin, announcing his policy unequivocally in a public speech, concluded: 'So long as I remain at the helm, I will do everything within my power to avoid leading Russia into war. . . . We cannot cope with any outside enemies until we have destroyed the worst

[1] V. I. Gurko, *Features and Figures of the Past*, p. 722, Stanford, 1939.

internal enemies of Russia, the Social Revolutionaries. Until our whole agrarian reform is carried out, they will not leave one stone unturned in order to undermine our country's strength'.[1] Russia, he urged, needed above all twenty years of peace to enable her to become so healthily transformed, that people would no longer recognize her. The revolutionaries wanted 'great upheavals'; he wanted a 'great Russia'.

In 1909 Stolypin introduced a bill for setting up local government councils in Poland and the nine Western provinces of Russia. It contained provisions to enable the peasants and minor officials to defend their interests against the local landowners (who were often Polish) and the local merchants (who were often Jews). In all these regions, a racially divided population, fostering mutual suspicion and hostility, had hindered the rate of economic progress. In order to protect state interests, certain key posts were reserved for people of Russian origin, and a fixed maximum of places was allocated to Poles, Lithuanians, and Jews. The bill passed the Duma, but the big landlords opposed it bitterly, and the State Council rejected it.

Since his measure had been approved by the more representative of the two assemblies, and blocked by vested interests in the State Council, Stolypin felt on solid enough ground to tender his resignation to the Tsar, and ask for decisive arbitration. He turned it into an issue of the Tsar's confidence in him. He wrote, 'If Your Majesty approves my policy for gradually introducing the people to the work of Government, be good enough to agree to those conditions without which that policy can no longer be carried out. If, however, Your Majesty believes that we have gone too far, and now requires a step backwards, then you should dismiss me and appoint P. Durnovo in my place. There is a third possible line of action, to move neither backwards nor forwards, but remain stationary on the same spot.'[2]

The Tsar agreed unwillingly to Stolypin's terms, confirmed the Statute about the Western provinces by decree (thereby discrediting the State Council), but he seems to have borne a

[1] M. Bok, *Vospominaniya*, p. 299, New York, 1953.
[2] V. Kokovtsov, *Out of My Past*, p. 262, Stanford, 1935.

bitter grudge against Stolypin for having forced his hand, and was planning secretly to replace him as Prime Minister before he was murdered in Kiev. Stolypin had also made an enemy of the Empress by his stand against her favourite, the debauched 'holy man', Rasputin.

XI

After his visit to Western Siberia in 1910, Stolypin went ahead with large-scale emigration schemes, which he extended to Central Asia and Transcaucasia. The Third Duma approved the grant of funds to construct a branch of the Trans-Siberian Railway across the Amur region. Stolypin used grandiose state metaphors to arouse public enthusiasm for pushing forward the industrial development of Siberia with American speed. 'Our eagle', he announced, 'inherited from Byzantium, is double-headed. By cutting off the one head turned towards the East, you cannot turn him into a single-headed eagle. You will merely make him bleed to death' (Speech, March 1908).[1] Siberia was immensely rich in everything, except in human beings. In his detailed report[2] Stolypin pointed to the astonishing fact that during the last three centuries little more than four and a half million Russians (including convicts) had settled permanently in Siberia, and of these a large proportion, one and a half million, had only arrived during the years 1907–1909. The old settlers, descendants of political or criminal exiles, nomad Kirghiz tribes, unruly Cossacks, and peasant refugees from serfdom, still waged an unrelenting struggle against a harsh and rugged nature. Forestry and mining had become securely established in a few regions, yet they had only scratched the surface of Siberia's vast resources. Despite their loneliness and hard life in a severe climate, only about 10 per cent. of those who emigrated had lost courage and returned to European Russia. Though the *virgin lands* challenged human strength, their productivity was not cramped by communal land-tenure.

[1] A. Stolypin, *P. A. Stolypin*, p. 35, Paris, 1927.
[2] P. Stolypin, A. V. Krivoshein, *Die Kolonisation Siberiens*, Berlin, 1912.

The Siberian butter industry, organized after the Danish model through private co-operative societies, had proved one of the most economically successful enterprises fostered by the Government of Alexander III, and tough Siberian hog's bristles for brushes were also bidding fair to become as profitable an export as the more famous furs. Stolypin visualized Siberia, not merely as a land of agricultural settlement, to relieve the pressure of surplus peasant population in European Russia, but as a boundless source of raw materials, new industries and exports for the world market. He drew attention to the need for a corresponding transference of heavy industry to areas of settlement, where towns and railways could be built. He appealed to the pioneer love of adventure to attract factory workers, skilled craftsmen and merchants to wild areas. In all these undertakings, though by less drastic means, he anticipated the policy now pursued by his Soviet successors.

During his troubled years of high office Stolypin gave himself no rest. He suffered from an overstrained heart and knew that he had not long to live. In 1911 he travelled to Kiev, where he took part in the official celebrations inaugurating a memorial to Alexander II. Witnesses observed that he looked worn out while he was attending a gala performance at the theatre, in honour of the Imperial family. During the interval, a man approached the place where he was standing, and shot him at close range with a revolver. The assassin, a young Jewish lawyer called Bagrov, belonged to a revolutionary group, but had mysteriously obtained a ticket for the theatre as an agent of the secret police.

Although the murder of Stolypin appeared to cut short his work, he was already on the verge of natural death, for the autopsy revealed advanced heart disease. Several officials were reprimanded for their negligence in supervising the security measures at Kiev, but worse suspicions were aroused when the Tsar himself intervened to stop more detailed investigation of the case, and Bagrov was hurriedly executed before the tangled skein of evidence leading to his crime could start to be unravelled.

According to Stolypin's daughter, the Tsar visited the hospital after he had died and knelt in prayer before his corpse, while people present heard him repeat several times the word: 'forgive'.[1] Such belated repentant moods were characteristic of Nicholas II, who proved himself incapable of supporting his best and most devoted ministers, and in the end behaved as treacherously towards Stolypin as he had formerly done towards his father's trusted Vitte. Soon after Stolypin's death, all the Tsar's letters to him, and all his private papers, which had any state significance, were sealed, confiscated and removed by a government commission.[2]

[1] M. Bok, *Vospominaniya*, p. 343, New York, 1953.
[2] op. cit., p. 345. It is possible that the Soviet state archives contain unpublished material that might contribute to a full biography of P. Stolypin, which has not yet been written.

CHAPTER X

PETER KROPOTKIN

PRINCE PETER KROPOTKIN (1842–1921) first became widely known to cultured European circles in the guise of an intelligent and versatile Russian nobleman, who abandoned a highly promising professional career for the sake of a quixotic faith, and afterwards cheerfully endured imprisonment, poverty and exile. In all his encounters he radiated a serene and firm benevolence. He brought into the embittered anarchist movement a strain of mellow Victorian respectability and personal warmth, for the first time captivating wide social circles, that had remained impervious or hostile to the sinister spell cast by Bakunin and the grim bomb-throwers whom he inspired.

For Kropotkin's lucid scientific mind made the unattainable earthly paradise sound more plausible, without becoming less attractive. His unworldly almost saintly character, generous conduct, and brave adventurous life, distracted attention from his extreme political naïveté. He created an indelible impression, especially in France and England, on humane scientists, members of the liberal professions, and skilled artisans, many of whom had held themselves aloof from the dirty game of politics, and remained as wholesomely sceptical about the virtues of professional revolutionaries as they were about the merits of professional statesmen.[1] This was the time when pale bearded giants from the wilds of Russia began to cause a flutter in the 'advanced' drawing-rooms of suburban London, when the clear-sighted Somerset Maugham observed how English intellectuals would gather there to gaze with awe upon these daring rebels, who leaned like caryatids against heavy marble mantelpieces, while 'women of letters tremulously put their lips to a glass of vodka'.[2]

Initiated from childhood in patriarchal Russia, Kropotkin shared that normal revulsion felt by sensitive aristocrats of his

[1] Kropotkin partly inspired Oscar Wilde's far-sighted essay, *The Soul of Man under Socialism* (1900).
[2] Somerset Maugham, *Ashenden*, London, 1928.

PRINCE P. KROPOTKIN

from a portrait

time against such customs as forced marriages of serfs, and the removal of young peasants from their villages to serve twenty-five years as conscripts in the Imperial Army. He recalls in his delightful memoirs[1] that he kissed the hands of a family serf, who had been beaten by his father's orders, and how he emphatically exclaimed, 'No, never', when the man muttered, 'You will do the same when you are grown up.' Though he refrained from sentimental hyperbole about the Russian peasant, he admired the quiet efficient manner in which many of them tried to make the best of the half-hearted emancipation terms granted in 1861.

After completing his education at the select School of Pages in St. Petersburg, Kropotkin was appointed to serve in the personal suite of Alexander II, and a brilliant military or court career lay in front of him, had he wished to follow it. But the pompous formalities and wearisome hypocrisy of the court not only disappointed his expectations, but undermined his belief in the *Tsar-Liberator*, whom he found at close quarters to be a haughty, capricious and vindictive man, suspicious of all his advisers, and not sincerely attached to a single person. When the Tsar delivered a speech to a number of newly-appointed Russian officers, and warned them about the punishment which would overtake them at the first sign of disloyalty to the throne, Kropotkin noted his peevish angry look, and remembered with a shudder how in childhood he had seen the same expression on the faces of landlords, when they threatened their serfs 'to skin them under the rods'.

In 1862, much to the anger and amazement of his ambitious relatives, he applied for a commission in the humble Amur Cossack cavalry regiment, and departed with it to serve in Eastern Siberia. He wrote to his brother Alexander that the life of a Guards officer in Petersburg depressed him, that he felt drawn by the hardships and novelty of service in the Amur region, which also promised 'wild grapes, tigers, and a southern climate.'[2] During his five years' military service in Siberia, he lost what little faith in state discipline he had retained, observed

[1] P. Kropotkin, *Memoirs of a Revolutionist*, London, 1899.
[2] P. Kropotkin, *Perepiska*, p. 257, Moscow-Leningrad, 1932.

the more instructive habits of higher animals in the wild country of Transbaikalia, studied geological phenomena, and made some scientifically important discoveries about the structural lines of the main Asiatic mountain ranges.

Charles Darwin's *Origin of Species*, and man's alleged descent from monkeys, was then the talk of intellectual Europe. Kropotkin's observations led him to believe that Darwin's view of evolution had been distorted by his followers, and that the savage jungle laws of sociological Darwinism could be convincingly refuted by the fact of *mutual aid*, practised among higher animals, even carnivorous ones. During his travels in Eastern Siberia and Manchuria, despite the severe struggle for survival, he failed to find, he said, although he was eagerly looking for it, that ruthless internecine strife among animals *of the same species*, claimed by Darwinists to dominate organic life, and to be the chief factor promoting higher evolution in any species. He remarked that when animals are forced to fight perpetually against food shortage, they often emerged from the ordeal so much impoverished in vigour and health, that no progressive development of their species could follow from such periods of debilitating struggle.

It was equally vain to evoke mystical motives as the sole means of conquering mutual enmity. It could not be love, or altruistic brotherly emotion, which induced a herd of horses to form a ring, in order to defend themselves against an attack by wolves. Was it not a simpler instinct of self-preservation, reinforced by awareness of their mutual interdependence? How disconcerting that the behaviour of wild horses should reveal basic rational instincts which had grown weak in civilized human beings—though indispensable for survival and advance in every species.

'If we study animals, not in the artificial isolation of laboratories, but in forest and steppe, and ask, who are in fact the fittest, those continually at war with one another, or those who support one another, we find that animals who acquire habits of mutual aid are undoubtedly much fitter' (*Mutual Aid*, 1902). Moreover the *survivors* (whether animal or human) of famines, epidemics and wars, were never the strongest, healthiest or most intelligent specimens of their kind.

Kropotkin concluded that nature, even when a stronger species constantly preyed upon a weaker one, maintained a guiding emotional unity among members of the *same* species, and therefore failed to confirm that neutral *a-morality* attributed to it by Darwinists. It provided sceptics with edifying examples of wise conduct uncontaminated by religious superstition. Human beings could profitably learn lessons in behaviour from the higher animals.

During his Siberian service, Kropotkin also studied the causes and possible cures, of the chronic economic insecurity which afflicted the Ussuri Cossacks, whose crops were decimated every year by torrential rains or by millions of migrating birds. He sent in a report, of which the Government formally accepted the main recommendations as both desirable and practicable. But action to implement them became irretrievably lost in a tangle of red tape. He described the efforts of a sturdy local municipality, which raised money to build its own watch-tower, but had to send its estimate for approval to St. Petersburg. When the project at last came back approved, two years had passed, and prices for materials and labour had meanwhile risen. So the long-suffering local people had to send a second estimate, and wait again. An accumulation of such incidents convinced Kropotkin that it was futile to try to help the masses of the people by relying on central administrative machinery.

In 1870 Kropotkin's sense of frustration reached breaking-point, and he resigned from the army. In the following year he was offered the congenial and secure post of Secretary to the Royal Geographical Society in Petersburg, but refused to accept it. His motives would seem odd today, when easier material circumstances for everybody have rendered that sort of social indignation out of date, but he explained his act of sacrifice with characteristic simplicity: 'What right had I to those higher joys, when all around me was misery and the struggle for a mouldy piece of bread?'[1] Later he was said to have declined the Chair of

[1] *Memoirs of a Revolutionist*, vol. II, p. 20, London, 1899.

Geography, unofficially offered to him by Cambridge University, because cessation of his anarchist activities was made a condition of acceptance.

In 1871 Kropotkin travelled to Switzerland, where he spent a week living among the watchmakers of the Jura Federation, whom he found to be devoted, modest and industrious people. Their voluntary abstention from alcohol and tobacco impressed him greatly, and personal contact with their friendly craft-guild associations opened his eyes on a better world of real social co-operation, 'totally unknown to the learned makers of social theories'. Here was a shining example of hard-working, disciplined and happy 'anarchy'. He noted with satisfaction that although the Jura artisans revered Bakunin, they had not been infected by his destructive mania, but admired him chiefly as a morally stimulating personality.

On his return to Russia, Kropotkin joined the Tchaikovsky circle of adult self-education, which had recently been formed to improve on the methods of the gangster Nechaev, with whom more respectable revolutionaries now felt ashamed to be associated. The circle prided itself on a total lack of statutes, speech-making, chairmen, and similar European formalities, 'repugnant to the spontaneous Russian mind'. But it counter-balanced this outward looseness by exacting a severe entrance examination to qualify for membership of the circle, which also discussed and judged with candour the character and personal capacities of every candidate who sought admittance. The Tchaikovsky circle tried to infiltrate among the terrorists, to mellow and enlarge their outlook, and managed to dissuade one dedicated young man from carrying out his self-imposed mission to murder Alexander II.

Meanwhile Kropotkin's expeditions to the poorer quarters of Petersburg, disguised in labourer's clothes, began to excite the suspicions of the police, who hired some spies to watch and trap him. In 1874 he was arrested and imprisoned. In the following year he worked out a skilful plan to outwit his jailers, made a dramatic escape and fled to Sweden, whence he took ship to England. Penniless and almost friendless, he promptly started to earn his living by writing articles, chiefly on practical aspects of the anarchist movement, but also on geography and intensive agriculture.

In 1882 Kropotkin left London for France, but in the following year the French police arrested him at Lyons. His trial for sedition there roused some French journalists to write in his defence, and this publicity made numerous fresh converts to the anarchist cause. Incarcerated for three years in the comfortable up-to-date cellular prison of Clairveaux, he none the less pronounced reformed prisons to be basically as bad as the dirty old lock-ups, if only because 'in prisons, as in monasteries, everything is done to break a person's will' (*Prisons and their Moral Influence on Prisoners*, 1887). If man had grown to be the cruellest animal on earth, that was the fault of kings, priests and judges, whose conduct had made him so. Even the best men were perverted by the exercise of power over other men. State criminals in office, wielding power, created many of the private criminals who filled the prisons. It was therefore pointless to turn prisons into more comfortable and hygienic *universities of crime*, when they ought to be swept away, together with the state that made them.

Though he sometimes agreed with his contemporary, Tolstoy, he differed from him in reluctantly advocating that the state apparatus should be overthrown by violence. But he imagined that the turmoil would be brisk and brief, that voluntary professional societies would spring up overnight, and calmly fill the organizational vacuum. He refused to contemplate the probability that single groups might clash in rivalry, or that their members, in the heat of revolution, might become far less amiable and sweetly reasonable than he was himself. Instinctively benevolent people would somehow guarantee a constantly sprouting growth of voluntary groups, bound together by an amicable embrace. Kropotkin preserved a childlike faith in bonds of fellowship uniting men of diverse nationalities and professions, in defiance of state boundaries or national governments.

To the end of his days he used the word *Nechaevism* as a sharp rebuke. And he never faced the fact that an anarchist-communist

society, of the kind he sketched, enjoying free meals, free education, and allocated living quarters, would be bound to rely on
the same coercive state, which he detested, and one equipped
with quite omnipotent ministries of Food, Education, and
Housing.

In his *Appeal to the Young* (1880) Kropotkin shifted his
ground, and pointed to the prevalent danger of turning scientific
research into a fetish. What a terrible mistake, he urged, to
encourage exact studies as useless as counting pebbles on a beach.
Better to confirm and spread the few helpful truths acquired
already, and practise them in life. He appears to have been responsible for the definition of anarchism given in the *Encyclopae-
dia Britannica* (11th edition, 1905) as 'the name given to a
principle or theory, under which society is conceived without
government, harmony in such a society being secured, not by
submission to law or by obedience to any authority, but by
free agreements concluded between various groups, territorial,
professional etc.' He constantly soothed agitated citizens
who dreaded the approach of chaos, by enlarging on the
friendly decorous Parish Council shape, which anarchy could
assume.

Like Proudhon, Kropotkin could not even approve the
violent expropriation of property-owners. At a London Congress
in 1904 he pronounced that such action would demoralize
revolutionaries, and weaken their own incentive to hard work.
'We do not need the bourgeois' money, neither what he has saved,
nor what he has stolen.' In his *Anarchism in Modern Science*
(1912), Kropotkin contended that the dialectical method, permeating Hegel and Marx, now seemed stale and out of date, compared with applied voluntary anarchism, which in its trial and
error came nearer to the inductive experimental method used by
modern scientists. The state socialists continued obstinately to
think in terms of Adam Smith, that iron economic laws, even if
they ruined personal happiness, ruled the growth of society with
fatal inexorability. They could not liberate the flow of history
from that cramping nation-state interpretation, first given to it by
nineteenth-century historians under the spell of Hegel. But they

could no longer justify their claim to be 'scientific' socialists, for anarchists had proved themselves more scientific.

For the anarchist movement, basing itself on data derived from *observing* human beings, found scientific evidence for siding with the individual in his struggle for survival against the overgrown state, and with small professional groups who refused to be strangled by the octopus of bureaucratic combines. Of course the steady growth of state authority in the late nineteenth century was an undeniable fact, but the multiplication of voluntary societies, often cutting across state boundaries, was equally phenomenal, and more encouraging to Kropotkin.

Stirred by his innocent nostalgia for a medieval craft-guild, Kropotkin saw the nineteenth-century nation-state as a stultifying superstructure, which had started to reach its present preponderance as recently as the sixteenth and seventeenth centuries, and had long since outgrown its usefulness. He persuaded himself that numerous functional societies would inherit and transform its few surviving useful functions, after the unitary state had mercifully vanished into limbo. Unfortunately, this tendency was hardly characteristic of the age he lived in, and still less of the present time, when states (far from abdicating to them) are constantly swallowing up voluntary organizations, and the work which they initiated, including whole industries, health services, and trade unions.

Kropotkin's medieval yearnings stopped short of the rustic extreme sometimes urged by Tolstoy and his Indian disciple, Gandhi. On the contrary, he predicted without undue alarm, that all countries in the world would sooner or later follow the industrial example of the West. As a scientific anarchist, he also envisaged a highly desirable obliteration of the old hard and fast distinction between the village and the town. Its benefits would emerge in a new race of industrial artisans who, after finishing their few light hours of factory labour, would rush joyfully to till their fields or gardens with the most up-to-date implements. Kropotkin's enthusiasm for agricultural allotments involved no bias against urban industry. 'Ever since I began to visit factories,' he recalled, 'I took a liking to strong and perfect machinery.

z*

Seeing how a gigantic paw grasps a log floating on the Neva, pulls it ashore, and puts it under the saws, which cut it into boards, or how a huge red-hot iron bar is transformed into a rail after passing between two cylinders, I understood the poetry of machines!' [1]

He had enough common sense to recognize that a rapidly growing world population would starve, unless it raised more food from the same area. But he assumed that machines would provide such abundant leisure that most men, instead of idling, would gladly undertake agricultural work as well as mastering an industrial technique. Work on the land would also restore their physical health and mental balance, threatened by noisy hammers and pistons which might otherwise get inside their brains and drive them mad. Why should men submit to becoming distracted slaves of their own iron slaves? Here Kropotkin complained that adherence to Adam Smith's dogma about *division of labour* had set up a perilous economic fetish, and established in the industrial West occupational castes almost as rigid as the caste system of ancient India.

In the long run, neither individuals nor nations would meekly accept permanent functional specializations, if these conflicted with the natural growth of their capacities. Did it, for instance, serve the long-term interest of Hungary or Russia to tie themselves for ever to producing enough surplus corn to feed the European manufacturing countries? Sooner or later all agricultural nations would become industrialized, challenge commercial monopolies established by their predecessors, and compete with them in the world market. But the new ones would reap the immense advantage of starting off at the fully-equipped stage, which older manufacturing nations had only reached after decades of experiment and groping.

Kropotkin observed that while the number of workmen employed in Russian factories in 1881 had doubled within the last twenty years, their production per head, thanks to machinery, had more than trebled in the leading industries. Other figures, telling the same tale of expanding home industries, pointed

[1] P. Kropotkin, *Memoirs of a Revolutionist*, p. 100, London, 1906.

already to the probability that Russia, like America, would soon manufacture almost everything she needed for her own consumption, and yet remain a self-supporting agricultural country.

Kropotkin was in fact referring to a time-honoured Russian custom, when he urged that cultivators of the soil ought to take up industrial employment during the long winter months. Agriculture, for a shorter period, needed a regular influx of town-dwellers to help gather in the crops. Manual workers need not be categorically separated from brain workers. Even a dense industrial population could feed itself with nourishing fresh produce, provided its members did enough land work to raise high yields from a limited acreage. England's dependence on stale imported food struck him as a most unhealthy symptom.

He cited with admiration the small-holders and market-gardeners of Belgium, who worked like horses, but with scientific sense, and were ready to turn their hands to many different jobs. Denmark gave him another encouraging example. This small country, with a poor soil, after being forced to cede two provinces to Germany, had started intensive dairy and meat farming on a co-operative basis, and rapidly achieved prosperity, without either oppression or pampering subsidies from the state. Danish specialists and methods, introduced to Siberia in the last decades of the nineteenth century, had created the Siberian butter industry.

The 1905 Revolution in Russia raised Kropotkin's hopes, only to dash them to the ground. But he warmly welcomed the world war of 1914, believing that it would destroy, once and for all, the overgrown and obsolete military nation-states which had blundered into it. He nevertheless held the rulers of Germany responsible for the war, since their prolonged aggressive threats had forced other European countries to arm themselves. Curiously enough, the anarchist student who murdered the Archduke Ferdinand at Serajevo, confessed that the writings of Bakunin and Kropotkin had influenced his action. The February Revolution (1917) rejoiced Kropotkin's heart. 'The old authorities swept away, the prisons opened, the Finnish constitution restored, the Red Flag floating over the Peter and Paul Fortress, and all that achieved with comparatively little bloodshed.' [1] Yet he was far from adopting a pacifist attitude, and urged that the duty of every patriotic Russian was to go on fighting Germany till the bitter end.

In 1917 Kropotkin left Brighton for Russia. Sixty thousand people gathered to give him a rousing welcome on his arrival in Petrograd. Kerensky received him with honour, and offered him a ministerial post, which he refused. But he persistently addressed soldiers' meetings, designed to counteract growing Bolshevik propaganda against prolongation of the war. Later he bitterly denounced ,the Bolshevik *coup d'état*, called the followers of Lenin 'Aliens, enemies of Russia, robbers and gangsters', who had 'buried the Revolution', which had hitherto followed such a hopeful anti-state pattern. He lamented that, instead of putting Russia on the path leading towards voluntary federation, the so-called Communists (who never practised communism) would finish by making people hate their very name.

Lenin wisely left Kropotkin unmolested, while many lesser anarchists (too obscure to be revered as public martyrs) were being arrested and deported without trial. Nevertheless he was forced to leave the capital for Dmitrov, a village thirty miles from Moscow, where a modest wooden bungalow with a small garden was assigned to him. He wrote from there an open letter to his friend, the Danish writer, Georg Brandes, denouncing the armed intervention of the allies in the Civil War against the Bolsheviks. He foretold that this gross psychological blunder would achieve the reverse of what it aimed at, by uniting the entire Russian people under a new dictatorship, bitterly hostile to the West. His letter was widely published in the European press, and aroused strong public feeling against the governments which had started the war of intervention.

In another open letter he appealed to artisans of the civilized world abroad, and their friends in other classes, to bring the utmost pressure to bear against their own governments for stopping armed intervention in the Russian Civil War. He

[1] G. Woodcock and I. Avakumovich, *The Anarchist Prince*, p. 388, London, 1950.

admitted that Workers' and Peasants' Soviets in Russia had lost all independent sense, through being mobilized by a state, which, whatever its good intentions, swallowed every living organization that it embraced. The ponderous bureaucratic apparatus, momentarily swept away by Revolution, was creeping back to power with a vengeance. 'When a government undertakes to supply every citizen with a lamp, and even with the matches to light it, such a government becomes a curse . . . like the French civil service, which needs the aid of forty officials to sell a tree blown down by a storm on the national high road. . . . What we are now observing in Russia is what you, workers of the West, ought to avoid at any price, if you value the success of genuine social reconstruction.' [1]

Reduced to silent inactivity while the Civil War was raging throughout Russia, Kropotkin's failing health barely allowed him to cultivate his tiny plot of land. With rather pathetic diffidence, he started to write his last unfinished work on ethics (published in 1922). He explained that honest ethical thought was still a dire necessity and should not be laughed at as an idle intellectual pastime in a time of stress. For recent historical disasters had proved that human beings remained unmitigated sophists, ready to juggle with the noblest theory, to make it justify their criminal deeds. Human conduct could not begin to be moral, until it became untainted either by state authority or church religion. If men could only be restrained from crime and folly by threats of the whip in this life or of hell-fire in the life to come, then they had no right to be called moral beings at all, and would ruin the brighter future which they arrogantly prophesied for themselves.

He tried to make the present crisis less bewildering by drawing parallels from history. Men of old had sought salvation in religion only because life drove them to despair. Both Buddhism and Christianity (the two most ethical religions) started among people already in the throes of social dissolution, weary of wars and government extortions, disgusted by the depraved futility of their rulers. Both these religions grew stagnant, through being

---

[1] G. Maksimov, *Kropotkin i evo Ucheniye*, p. 289, Chicago, 1931.

paralysed by their own institutions, and Christianity dealt itself a death-blow (from which it never recovered) when it allowed itself to be made the religion of the state. Christianity showed most moral sense and power in its early stages, when it protested both in word and deed, against the degrading rule of Roman patricians, and their worship of gross physical pleasures, expensively decorated with an elegant exterior.

Kropotkin noted with regret how little the study of history had so far done to increase insight into human character and conduct. 'To understand character,' he remarked, 'it is unimportant to know what a man did, but all the more important to know what he intended when he did it.' The same thought applied to understanding nations. The history of their proverbs, legends, and fairy tales told deeper truths about their inmost nature than any naked chronicle of their battles, laws and administrative system, which aroused much unprofitable controversy, and rubbed salt into old half-healed wounds of international hatred.

He still pinned his faith on syndicalist and co-operative societies, believing that, as they matured, they would renounce the lust for power, and cease to blackmail or intimidate their more enterprising members. Thus in the course of fifty years they might set in motion a flexible, spontaneous society, rescued from the individual frustration and moral ugliness inherent in every self-centred nation-state. He failed to reckon with a possible alternative that his pet trade unions, lured into expanding size under ambitious leaders, could become as sterile and coercive as the state machine, from which they had originally struggled to escape. Thinking always of the unspoiled watchmakers' guilds he had first admired in Switzerland, he never foresaw that skilled artisans might also become victims of political fraud.

Of course the anarchist's goal approached the sphere of legend. For Kropotkin that was no objection to it, but rather a guiding star, if not a spur to action. He saw this goal steadily, as an exacting counsel of perfection, though in a rosy ideal light, which remained invisible to less imaginative Russian reformers, who saw too plainly its practical unattainability and its disturbing lunatic fringe.

Kropotkin remained a modern scientist in love with ancient fairy tales. His calm benevolence is utterly remote from the homicidal mania depicted by the author, Ropshin, who in his topical apocalyptic story, *The Pale Horse* (1909), unveiled the motives driving his irritable anarchist, George, to commit murder, in a final effort to rouse his blunted nerves—a whining little rebel without an aim, unredeemed either by a fanatic's faith or by a martyr's fortitude.

If Ropshin's type of hooligan degenerate prevailed over Kropotkin's self-disciplined ideal, the human race would hurry towards merited disaster, blinded by clouds of mutual hatred, which no amount of factual science could dispel. But Kropotkin retained the dauntless optimism of an old man, who had faced and survived the worst ordeals. In one of his last letters (May 1920) he repeated: 'I believe firmly in the future.' And in his message to Western workers (handed to the English Labour Party delegation, which visited him in June 1920) he concluded: 'Imperial Russia is dead, and will never be revived. The future of its various constituent parts will be directed towards a large federation of independent units. . . . It would suit the interests of all Western nations that they should recognize the right of each portion of the former Empire to govern itself. . . . I believe that Western Europe will also move in the same direction.' [1]

[1] C. Berneri, *Peter Kropotkin*, p. 14, London, 1943.

INDEX